PREPARE!

An Ecumenical
Music and Worship Planner

2022–2023, NRSV Edition

David L. Bone
and
Mary Scifres

Abingdon Press
Nashville

PREPARE! AN ECUMENICAL MUSIC AND WORSHIP PLANNER 2022–2023

Copyright © 2022 by David L. Bone and Mary Scifres

ISBN 978-1-7910-1566-4

22 23 24 25 26 27 28 29 30 31—10 9 8 7 6 5 4 3 2 1

MANUFACTURED IN CHINA

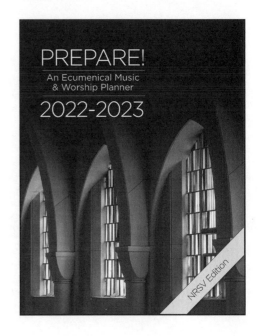

Using *Prepare!*

How We Organize the Resource Lists

Prepare! is designed to give you as many ideas as possible about a given worship service. Use it along with a worship plan notebook that you create, a copy of your church's hymnal, and other supplements you use such as *The Faith We Sing or Worship & Song*. Features of *Prepare!* include:

- The lectionary verses found on left-hand pages of *Prepare!* come from the New Revised Standard Version of the Bible. Where available, we have added psalter numbers from standard hymnals, which are noted in the Resource Key on p. 7. *Prepare!* is also available with lectionary texts from the Common English Bible (ISBN: 9781791011987).
- **NEW HYMNALS LISTED! Two hymnals were added to the resource list last year** (p. 7). *Celebrating Grace Hymnal*, along with *Santo, Santo, Santo*, a truly bilingual hymnal. This hymnal will be especially useful to those serving in Spanish-speaking and bilingual contexts.
- **NEW LAST YEAR!** The **Contemporary and Modern Suggestions** now include the CCLI number from https://songselect.ccli.com. These numbers are used universally by musicians working in these worship styles.
- **AGAIN THIS YEAR! Themes** for the day are listed in the Other Suggestions and found in the **Theme Index** on p. 136. These tools will help with thematic planning when a community is following a thematic/sermon series rather than the Lectionary.
- **ALSO THIS YEAR!** Most **Anthem** suggestions include a link to the publisher's online version of the anthem, which often includes recordings. Simply enter the http://bit.ly/… link in your browser to reach the appropriate page.
- Each week **Primary Hymns and Songs for the Day** are suggested first. These suggestions include various helps for singing the hymns. These hymns and songs have the closest relationship to the scriptures and are widely known. The lengthier lists of **Additional Hymn Suggestions** and **Additional Contemporary and Modern Suggestions** will add variety to your musical selections.
- The musical suggestions are chosen to suggest a wide variety of styles.
- Each item is referenced to scripture and/or occasion.
- **Opening (O)** and **Closing (C)** hymns are suggested for each worship service.
- At least one **Communion (Comm.)** hymn is recommended for the first Sunday of each month and liturgical season. When appropriate, Communion hymns related to the scriptures are noted on other days as well.
- **Additional Contemporary and Modern Suggestions** include not only praise choruses but also global and ethnic music, folk music, and meditative music from traditions such as Taizé. Please note that contemporary songs may also be listed under **Additional Hymn Suggestions**, **Vocal Solos**, or **Other Suggestions**.
- **One word of advice:** Be sure to consult all the music suggestions regardless of the type of service you are planning. In the changing world of worship, no one style defines a song or a worship service. Many items appropriate for contemporary and emergent styles are listed under the **Ad-**ditional Hymn Suggestions, and many resources for traditional and blended services can be found in the **Additional Contemporary and Modern Suggestions** list. **Vocal Solos**, **Anthems**, and **Other Suggestions** may be appropriate for congregational use as well. Don't let the "category" here deter you from using any item that will enhance your worship service. Planners should consult all lists when choosing congregational music.
- **Vocal Solos** and **Anthems** provide ideas for vocal music "performance" offerings, and may also inspire ideas for additional congregational selections.
- The recommended **Vocal Solos** are taken from a group of ten collections that range from contemporary settings of hymn texts and praise choruses to spirituals to well-known classics (see p. 7). Augment these suggestions from your own library.
- The **Anthem** suggestions include new works as well as generally known works that are already in many church choral libraries. Your study of the scripture and hymn texts will lead you to anthems in your church library that are appropriate.
- **Other Suggestions** also include words for worship, suggestions for choral introits and sung benedictions, and ideas for musical responses related to the spoken liturgy.
- Suggestions for **Visuals** are offered for each service. See the article "Visuals in Worship" (p. 4) for discussion on these suggestions. Visual ideas are found in **Other Suggestions**. They have been compiled by Ashley M. Calhoun and supplemented by our authors. Ashley is known for his inventive use of "found" items in creating visual worship settings. Worship committees, visual artists, dancers, and altar guilds can use these ideas to create their own unique worship centers, altarpieces, banners, and dance images. Screen visual artists can use these themes to select appropriate background and theme screens for worship.
- A two-year, at-a-glance **2022–2023 Calendar** follows the **Worship Planning Sheets** (see p. 144). It includes a note on the lectionary years covered in this edition of *Prepare!*
- *Prepare!* uses the *Revised Common Lectionary*. From the Second Sunday after Pentecost to Christ the King Sunday, the lectionary includes two patterns of readings. One pattern includes semi-continuous readings from the Hebrew Scriptures, Epistles, and Gospels. These readings are not necessarily related but allow for a sequential experience of the biblical narrative. **This is the pattern used to determine the scripture texts included in *Prepare!*** It is the pattern followed by most users of the hymnals referenced. In the second pattern, the Hebrew scripture is chosen to relate to the Gospel passage. This pattern is used primarily in traditions where Communion is celebrated at every service of worship. These **Alternate Lections** may be found in *The Revised Common Lectionary* (Abingdon Press, 1992) or online at http://lectionary.library.vanderbilt.edu/. Worship planners may certainly choose to follow the pattern that best serves the needs and traditions of your church. Neither pattern is necessarily better than the other; they are simply different ways of offering scripture in the worship setting over a three-year cycle in the church.

Planning Worship with These Resources

When planning any worship service, it is always best to start with the Scripture and let it guide your thoughts and plans. If your church is not using the *Revised Common Lectionary* but you do know what the scripture text will be for a service, look up that text in the **Scripture Index** on page 137 or consult the **Theme Index** on page 136.

As you read and study the Scripture passages, read all of the suggested hymn texts. The hymns may remind you of anthems, solos, or keyboard selections. It is wise to mark your hymnal with the dates individual hymns are sung to avoid singing some too frequently. The **Hymn Resources** (see p. 7) can enhance congregational singing but should be used sparingly.

Use a three-ring binder to organize your plans. For each service of worship, include a copy of one of the **Worship Planning Sheets** found on pages 141–43 (or design your own!) along with blank paper for listing further ideas. Do not simply "fill in the blanks" for each service, but use the Planning Sheet to guide your work.

Use the suggestions in *Prepare!* along with your own page of ideas to begin making decisions about worship. Will the choir sing a "Call to Worship"? Can a hymn verse serve as a prayer response? Can a particular anthem or vocal solo give direction to the sermon? What prayers will be used?

Once your decisions are made, complete the **Worship Planning Sheet**. Make a separate list of tasks related to that service. Planning worship is an awesome responsibility that can be accomplished with an organized effort along with spiritual guidance.

VISUALS IN WORSHIP
Ashley M. Calhoun

The suggestions for visuals in this planner are meant to help worship leaders use objects and images to increase the impact of the gospel on a people who are increasingly visually oriented. These suggestions can be incorporated into many visual elements: hanging and processional banners, worship settings (whether on the altar or in the chancel or narthex), worship folder covers, and bulletin boards. The ideas can also be used to suggest ways to use classical and contemporary works of art, sculpture, needlework, and photography in worship services.

With more churches incorporating screens and video walls into their worship spaces, there is tremendous potential for the use of still or moving imagery. Also, interpretive movement and drama can be very strong in visual impact.

The visual suggestions in this *Planner* have several characteristics:

- The suggestions are not meant to give detailed plans but to spark your imagination and creativity.
- Some are drawn literally from the lessons; others are thematic.
- The suggestions are organized by reference to the lectionary passages:

O	Old Testament or Easter season, Acts reading
P	Psalm reading or Canticle
E	Epistle or New Testament reading
G	Gospel reading

- Chapter and verse numbers are sometimes given to indicate actual phrases in the scripture passage that can serve as visual elements.
- Themes such as forgiveness, love, or rejoicing are offered to encourage creative use of video and photographic images of people engaged in demonstrating those themes.

So much about worship is visual and intended to strengthen the proclamation of the gospel. The worship space is filled with visual elements that send a message. The church year is a treasure trove of color, texture, symbolism, and visual imagery. Special Sundays and special days in the cultural and denominational calendars also offer opportunities for visual expression. Evaluate the visual aspects of your worship services and find ways to enhance the worship experience with thoughtful, intentional use of visual elements and images.

CAN THE LECTIONARY STILL LIBERATE?

Reasons to Keep Using the *Revised Common Lectionary* in Worship Planning

Mary Scifres

The question arises for worship leaders and ordained ministers, "How does one prepare worship services that allow the flexibility necessary for the work of the Holy Spirit while also ordering the life of prayer and meditation to encourage disciplined growth?" Even in a world enamored with theme-based planning, new lectionaries like *Seasons of Creation* and the *Narrative Lectionary*, the *Revised Common Lectionary* can be one of the best liberators for organizing and designing creative, meaningful worship. Although my writing partner David Bone and I use many resources in our creative planning and respect the diversity of resources available, we still see the lectionary as a helpful tool on which to base inspired worship planning to encourage growth in the life of the church. Even theme-based worship is easily created from lectionary-based worship, as you can see from our addition of **Theme Ideas** to our weekly **Other Suggestions** in this volume.

Attempting to coordinate the message of the musical selections, the visual images, the words of worship with the message of the pulpit is a time-consuming and important task for church staff and worship leaders. Time and again, we hear from worship leaders who discover that lectionary use frees them for creative design time that otherwise would need to be spent in coordination meetings and individualized research. Church musicians, artists, laypersons, worship coordinators, and pastors give many hours each week to plan worship services that proclaim the Word, strengthen and challenge the community, and deepen the participants' faith. Ordained and diaconal ministers face the challenge of writing and choosing texts, prayers, and sermons for worship each week; musicians select, plan, and rehearse a variety of vocal and instrumental music to enhance and facilitate the worship experience of the churches they serve; and church artists and lay worship leaders pursue means of leading worship, preparing the sanctuary for worship, designing additional creative elements, and devising other aspects of the worshiping experience.

The preacher can ease this task significantly by utilizing the *Revised Common Lectionary* and communicating on a regular basis with other church worship leaders regarding worship service needs. A church can find both freedom and unity when the pastoral leadership uses this lectionary as the basis for planning worship and its individual aspects (sermon, hymns, anthems, prayers) without exalting it to a level of sole importance. First, lectionary use prevents the abusive appeal to a limited number of scriptures and topics, toward which some preachers are tempted. Regarding the concern for local needs, the lectionary can provide a means for integrating such needs into the worship service by relating scriptural messages to the current needs and situation of the community. While interpreting the lections for worship, both planners and preachers can find ways of exploring the historical meanings of the texts and bringing such historical understandings into the present.

Second, the pedagogical advantage of using the lectionary to acquaint Christians with the broad tradition of which we are a part can deepen worship and learning experiences of the community of faith. As pastors in the twenty-first century face growing concern regarding the types of "burn out" that result from remaining static in a setting that has become routine instead of a challenge, following the lectionary cycle can open up opportunities for growth and support in a number of ways. Being forced to grapple with difficult texts in addition to familiar passages enlivens the mind and encourages the preacher to look to new exegetical resources and homiletic aids. Support can also come from an ecumenical community of pastors in one's city or county who are studying the same text during the cycle. Study groups within the local church can wrestle with the lectionary scriptures, growing their biblical and theological knowledge in the process.

Likewise, church musicians who wade through piles of contemporary and classical music every season to choose the anthems, organ selections, hymns, responsive psalms, and other musical contributions to the worship service can find a common guide to that selection when the lectionary is used. In the local church, the musician finds the opportunity to be a minister of music and Word when the lections provide the core of the worship service. In a time when the shortage of church musicians affects many churches, a church musician may be able to serve several churches and utilize the same musical selections in each setting. If a church musician, called to full-time ministry of music, can be employed by two or three local congregations who agree to use the same anthems and hymns each week and to schedule worship services at different times, both musician and congregation can benefit from this new approach to music ministry that supports full-time service and receives music of high quality. The possibilities for providing equitable salaries for ministers of music as well as nurturing several local church communities through Spirit-filled, well-performed music are enhanced when the unifying elements of ecumenical cooperation and common lections are available.

In terms of teaching, the lectionary can provide a helpful method of coordinating the community worship experience of Sunday morning with all of the other events—church school, weekly Bible study groups, prayer and devotional groups, music rehearsals, singing and praise gatherings, and other small groups—in the life of the church. Small groups, which sometimes seem to go off in their own directions, away from the Sunday morning community, would more easily feel a part of the fold with the integrative element of the lectionary. And the educational system of the church, which so often leaves teachers and students feeling excluded and separated from the worshiping body, can find inclusion in the integrative element of the lectionary. Children sit through sermons and find meaning in mysterious hymns much more easily when the basic scriptural text has been heard and discussed in church school prior to worship or explored in church school after worship!

Overall, lectionary use can provide an integrative and unifying element to the entire life of the church, when used in its various dimensions through curriculum, worship resources, music selections, and local cooperative church events. Where proclamation of the Word is central, that Word can and should be the integrative element of a holistic worship service. In churches that seek to reach people with a message that is unified thematically, lectionary use provides a scriptural base that all planners know well in advance and can utilize when choosing and developing the themes or topics for the Sundays of any given season. When the lectionary is used in this way, choirs or music teams have adequate time to rehearse appropriate music, liturgists or worship facilitators have sufficient time to write or find liturgy and prayers for the service, and other church artists (actors, dancers, composers, visual artists, banner makers, arts guilds, and screen programmers) may plan and prepare their contributions to the service and the season.

Frequent lectionary use need not limit other options during the year. When preaching pastors are called to address a pressing congregational or community issue, lectionary scriptures can provide a starting point to keep the conversation biblically based in worship. When the Spirit calls a preacher or worship team to focus in a different direction, taking a short or even seasonal break from lectionary use is another option. When a sermon series or a church theme pulls worship designers toward different scriptures, the vast indices in lectionary resources can help you reference scriptures even when used on non-lectionary schedules. Even as a preacher who is led by the Spirit, I find myself returning to the *Revised Common Lectionary* to ease the burden on my staff and create a cohesive conversation as we plan not only worship but also the focused life and ministry of the churches we serve.

With this book, we invite your congregation and its worship leaders to begin the process of integrating your various aspects of worship planning by means of the *Revised Common Lectionary*. As thematic ideas begin to emerge in each week's worship service and as the various scriptures provide diverse bases for worship planning, we hope that you will find worship becoming an increasingly growth-filled and exciting aspect of your congregation's life.

Enjoy a free ebook of communion resources, "Is It Communion Sunday Already?!" at this link:
www.maryscifres.simplero.com/communionbook

For additional creative worship, music, and sermon planning ideas, visit:
www.maryscifresministries.com

RESOURCE KEY

AH   *The Africana Hymnal*. Nashville: Abingdon Press, 2015. ISBN #9781426776441.

C   *Chalice Hymnal*. St. Louis: Chalice Press, 1996. ISBN: 9780827280359.

CG   *Celebrating Grace Hymnal*. Macon: Celebrating Grace, 2010. ISBN: 9781936151103.

E   *The Hymnal 1982*. New York: The Church Hymnal Corporation, 1985. ISBN: 9780898691214.

EL   *Evangelical Lutheran Worship*. Minneapolis: Augsburg Fortress, 2006. ISBN: 9780806656182.

G   *Glory to God: The Presbyterian Hymnal*. Louisville: Presbyterian Publishing Corporation, 2013. ISBN: 9780664238971.

N   *The New Century Hymnal*. Cleveland, OH: The Pilgrim Press, 1995. ISBN: 9780829810509.

P   *The Presbyterian Hymnal*. Louisville: Westminster/ John Knox Press, 1990. ISBN: 9780664100971.

S   *The Faith We Sing*. Nashville: Abingdon Press, 2000. ISBN: 9780687090549 (Pew edition).

SA   *The Song Book of the Salvation Army*. London: The Salvation Army, 2015. ISBN: 9780854129447.

SH   *Santo, Santo, Santo*. Chicago: GIA Publications, Inc., 2019. ISBN: 9781622773961.

UM   *The United Methodist Hymnal. Nashville:* The United Methodist Publishing House, 1989. ISBN: 9780687431328.

VU   *Voice United*. Etobicoke, Ontario, Canada: The United Church Publishing House, 1996. ISBN: 9781551340173.

WS   *Worship & Song*. Nashville: Abingdon Press, 2011. Accompaniment, singer, guitar, and planning editions available. ISBN: 9781426709937 (Pew edition).

WSL   *Worship & Song Leader's Edition*. Nashville: Abingdon Press, 2011. ISBN: 9781426709944 (Leader's edition). NOTE: These resources WSL1–WSL222 refer to the written words for worship (prayers, litanies, benedictions) available in worship resource editions of *Worship & Song*.

HYMN RESOURCES

S-1   Smith, Gary Alan, ed. *The United Methodist Hymnal: Music Supplement*. Nashville: Abingdon Press, 1991. ISBN: 9780687431472.

S-2   Bennett, Robert C., ed. *The United Methodist Hymnal: Music Supplement II*. Nashville: Abingdon Press, 1993. ISBN: 9780687430130.

H-3   Hopson, Hal H. *The Creative Church Musician Series*. Carol Stream, IL: Hope Publishing Co.
Hbl Vol. 1. *The Creative Use of Handbells in Worship. 1997.* Hope Publishing #1956.
Chr Vol. 2. *The Creative Use of Choirs in Worship. 1999.* Hope Publishing #8013.
Desc *The Creative Use of Descants in Worship. 1999.* Hope Publishing #8018.
Org *The Creative Use of the Organ in Worship. 1997.* Hope Publishing #8070.

CONTEMPORARY RESOURCES

The Contemporary and Modern Suggestions now include the CCLI number from https://songselect.ccli.com. These numbers are used universally by musicians working in these worship styles.
See also Vocal Solo suggestions from V-3 and V-5 volumes.

VOCAL SUGGESTION RESOURCES

V-1   Pote, Allen. *A Song of Joy*. Carol Stream, IL: Hope Publishing, 2003. Cokesbury Ord. #505068.

V-2   Handel, George Frederick. *Messiah*. Various editions available.

V-3   Hayes, Mark. *The Mark Hayes Vocal Solo Collection*
V-3 (1) *Ten Spirituals for Solo Voice*. Van Nuys, CA: Alfred Music Publishing, 2007. ISBN: 9780882848808.
V-3 (2) *Seven Praise and Worship Songs for Solo Voice*. Van Nuys, CA: Alfred Music Publishing, 2010. ISBN: 9780739037249.
V-3 (3) *Ten Hymns and Gospel Songs for Solo Voice*. ISBN: 9780739006979.

V-4   Scott, K. Lee. *Sing a Song of Joy*. Minneapolis, MN: Augsburg Fortress, 1989. ISBN: 9780800647889, (*Medium High Voice*) ISBN: 9780800647889, (*Medium Low Voice*) ISBN: 9780800652821.

V-5   Various Editors. *With All My Heart: Contemporary Vocal Solos*. Minneapolis, MN: Augsburg Fortress, 2004.
V-5 (1) *Volume 1: Autumn and Winter*. ISBN: 9780800676841.
V-5 (2) *Volume 2: Spring and Summer*. ISBN: 9780800676858.
V-5 (3) *Volume 3: Baptisms, Weddings, Funerals*. ISBN: 9780800679460.

V-6   Walters, Richard, Arr. *Hymn Classics: Concert Arrangements of Traditional Hymns for Voice and Piano*. Milwaukee, WI: Hal Leonard Publishing, 1993. ISBN: 9780793560080. *High Voice*. Cokesbury Ord. #811290. *Low Voice*. Cokesbury Ord. #811233.

V-7   Johnson, Hall, Arr. *Thirty (30) Spirituals*. New York: G. Schirmer, Inc., 1949. ISBN: 9780793548033.

V-8   Wilson, John F., Don Doig, and Jack Schrader, eds. *Everything for the Church Soloist*. Carol Stream, IL: Hope Publishing Company, 1980. Cokesbury Ord. #810103.

V-9   Scott, K. Lee. *Rejoice Now My Spirit: Vocal Solos for the Church Year*. Minneapolis, MN: Augsburg Fortress, 1992. ISBN: 9780800651084.

V-10   Hayes, Mark et al. *From the Manger to the Cross— Seasonal Solos for Medium Voice*. Dayton, OH: The Lorenz Corporation, 2006. Cokesbury Ord. #526369.

Jeremiah 18:1-11

¹The word that came to Jeremiah from the LORD: ²"Come, go down to the potter's house, and there I will let you hear my words." ³So I went down to the potter's house, and there he was working at his wheel. ⁴The vessel he was making of clay was spoiled in the potter's hand, and he reworked it into another vessel, as seemed good to him.

⁵Then the word of the LORD came to me: ⁶Can I not do with you, O house of Israel, just as this potter has done? says the LORD. Just like the clay in the potter's hand, so are you in my hand, O house of Israel. ⁷At one moment I may declare concerning a nation or a kingdom, that I will pluck up and break down and destroy it, ⁸but if that nation, concerning which I have spoken, turns from its evil, I will change my mind about the disaster that I intended to bring on it. ⁹And at another moment I may declare concerning a nation or a kingdom that I will build and plant it, ¹⁰but if it does evil in my sight, not listening to my voice, then I will change my mind about the good that I had intended to do to it. ¹¹Now, therefore, say to the people of Judah and the inhabitants of Jerusalem: Thus says the LORD: Look, I am a potter shaping evil against you and devising a plan against you. Turn now, all of you from your evil way, and amend your ways and your doings.

Psalm 139:1-6, 13-18 (G28/29, N715, P248, UM854)

¹O LORD, you have searched me and known me.
²You know when I sit down and when I rise up;
  you discern my thoughts from far away.
³You search out my path and my lying down,
  and are acquainted with all my ways.
⁴Even before a word is on my tongue,
  O LORD, you know it completely.
⁵You hem me in, behind and before,
  and lay your hand upon me.
⁶Such knowledge is too wonderful for me;
  it is so high that I cannot attain it.
. . . .
¹³For it was you who formed my inward parts;
  you knit me together in my mother's womb.
¹⁴I praise you, for I am fearfully and wonderfully made.
  Wonderful are your works;
that I know very well.
¹⁵ My frame was not hidden from you,
when I was being made in secret,
  intricately woven in the depths of the earth.
¹⁶Your eyes beheld my unformed substance.
In your book were written
  all the days that were formed for me,
  when none of them as yet existed.
¹⁷How weighty to me are your thoughts, O God!
  How vast is the sum of them!
¹⁸I try to count them—they are more than the sand;
  I come to the end—I am still with you.

Philemon 1-21

¹Paul, a prisoner of Christ Jesus, and Timothy our brother,
To Philemon our dear friend and co-worker, ²to Apphia our sister, to Archippus our fellow soldier, and to the church in your house: ³Grace to you and peace from God our Father and the Lord Jesus Christ.

⁴When I remember you in my prayers, I always thank my God ⁵because I hear of your love for all the saints and your faith toward the Lord Jesus. ⁶I pray that the sharing of your faith may become effective when you perceive all the good that we may do for Christ. ⁷I have indeed received much joy and encouragement from your love, because the hearts of the saints have been refreshed through you, my brother.

⁸For this reason, though I am bold enough in Christ to command you to do your duty, ⁹yet I would rather appeal to you on the basis of love— and I, Paul, do this as an old man, and now also as a prisoner of Christ Jesus. ¹⁰I am appealing to you for my child, Onesimus, whose father I have become during my imprisonment. ¹¹Formerly he was useless to you, but now he is indeed useful both to you and to me. ¹²I am sending him, that is, my own heart, back to you. ¹³I wanted to keep him with me, so that he might be of service to me in your place during my imprisonment for the gospel; ¹⁴but I preferred to do nothing without your consent, in order that your good deed might be voluntary and not something forced. ¹⁵Perhaps this is the reason he was separated from you for a while, so that you might have him back forever, ¹⁶no longer as a slave but more than a slave, a beloved brother—especially to me but how much more to you, both in the flesh and in the Lord.

¹⁷So if you consider me your partner, welcome him as you would welcome me. ¹⁸If he has wronged you in any way, or owes you anything, charge that to my account. ¹⁹I, Paul, am writing this with my own hand: I will repay it. I say nothing about your owing me even your own self. ²⁰Yes, brother, let me have this benefit from you in the Lord! Refresh my heart in Christ. ²¹Confident of your obedience, I am writing to you, knowing that you will do even more than I say.

Luke 14:25-33

²⁵Now large crowds were traveling with him; and he turned and said to them, ²⁶"Whoever comes to me and does not hate father and mother, wife and children, brothers and sisters, yes, and even life itself, cannot be my disciple. ²⁷Whoever does not carry the cross and follow me cannot be my disciple. ²⁸For which of you, intending to build a tower, does not first sit down and estimate the cost, to see whether he has enough to complete it? ²⁹Otherwise, when he has laid a foundation and is not able to finish, all who see it will begin to ridicule him, ³⁰saying, 'This fellow began to build and was not able to finish.' ³¹Or what king, going out to wage war against another king, will not sit down first and consider whether he is able with ten thousand to oppose the one who comes against him with twenty thousand? ³²If he cannot, then, while the other is still far away, he sends a delegation and asks for the terms of peace. ³³So therefore, none of you can become my disciple if you do not give up all your possessions."

Primary Hymns and Songs for the Day
"Take Up Thy Cross" (Luke) (O)
  E675, EL667, G718, N204, P393, SH605, UM415, VU561
    H-3   Chr-178, 180; Org-44
    S-1   #141-143 Various treatments
"Change My Heart, O God" 1565 (Jer)
  EL801, G695, S2152, SA409, SH507
"I Was There to Hear Your Borning Cry" (Pss, Baptism)
  C75, EL732, G488, N351, S2051, VU644
"Help Us Accept Each Other" (Phlm)
  C487, G754, N388, P358, UM560
"In the Cross of Christ I Glory" (Phlm, Luke)
  C207, CG183, E441, EL324, G213, N193, P84, SA174, UM295
    H-3   Hbl-72; Chr-113; Desc-89; Org-119
    S-1   #276-277. Harmonization with descant
"When I Survey the Wondrous Cross" (Phlm, Luke)
  C195, CG186, EL803, G223, N224, P101, SH163/164, UM298
    H-3   Hbl-6, 102; Chr-213; Desc-49; Org-49
    S-1   #155. Descant
"When I Survey the Wondrous Cross" (Phlm, Luke)
  E474, G224, P100, SA208, UM299 (PD), VU149 (Fr.)
    H-3   Hbl-47; Chr-214; Desc-90; Org-127
    S-1   #288. Transposition to E-flat major
"I Have Decided to Follow Jesus" (Luke)
  C344, CG497, S2129, SH610
"Have Thine Own Way, Lord" (Jer, Luke) (C)
  C588, CG493, SA705, SH626, UM382 (PD)
    S-2   #2. Instrumental descant

Additional Hymn Suggestions
"O God, as with a Potter's Hand" (Jer)
  N550
"Spirit of the Living God" 23488 (Jer)
  C259, CG233, G288, N283, P322, SA312/313, SH555,
  UM393, VU376
"My Lord, What a Morning" (Jer)
  C708, EL438 (PD), G352, P449, SH356, UM719, VU708
"God the Sculptor of the Mountains" (Jer, Pss)
  EL736, G5, S2060
"Señor, tú ves mi corazón" ("Lord, See My Heart") (Pss)
  SH56
"The Lord of Life, a Vine Is He" (Pss, Luke)
  CG292, WS3155
"In Christ There Is No East or West" (Phlm)
  C687, CG273, E529, EL650 (PD), G317/318, N394/395,
  P439/440, SA1006, SH226, UM548, VU606
"Since Jesus Came into My Heart" (Phlm)
  CG614, S2140, SA907
"Called as Partners in Christ's Service" (Phlm)
  C453, G761, N495, P343
"A Place at the Table" (Phlm, Comm.)
  G769, WS3149
"Where He Leads Me" (Luke)
  C346, SA693, UM338 (PD)
"More Love to Thee, O Christ" (Luke)
  See especially stanza 2.
  C527, CG365, G828, N456, P359, UM453 (PD)
"And Are We Yet Alive" (Luke)
  SA240, UM553 (PD)
"This Little Light of Mine" (Luke)
  N525, SH257, UM585 (See also AH4150, EL677, N524)
"For the Bread Which You Have Broken" (Luke, Comm.)
  C411, E340/E341, EL494, G516, P508/P509, UM614/
  UM615, VU470
"Swiftly Pass the Clouds of Glory" (Luke)
  G190, P73, S2102
"Living for Jesus" (Luke)
  C610, S2149

Additional Contemporary and Modern Suggestions
"Praise You" 863806 (Jer, Stewardship)
  S2003
"Water, River, Spirit, Grace" (Jer, Baptism)
  C366, N169, S2253
"Jesus, Lover of My Soul" 1198817 (Jer)
"The Potter's Hand" 2449771 (Jer, Pss, Stewardship)
"Oh, I Know the Lord's Laid His Hands on Me" (Pss)
  S2139
"How Great Is Our God" 4348399 (Pss)
  CG322, SH458, WS3003
"Freedom in the Spirit" 7127886 (Pss)
"He Knows My Name" 2151368 (Pss)
"In the Secret" 1810119 (Pss)
"These Hands" 3251827 (Pss, Stewardship)
"Cry of My Heart" 844980 (Luke)
  S2165
"We Will Follow" (*"Somlandela"*) (Luke)
  WS3160
"Let It Be Said of Us" 1855882 (Luke)
"Every Move I Make" 1595726 (Luke)
"Everyday" 2798154 (Luke)
"One Way" 4222082 (Luke)
"Take Up Our Cross" 5358955 (Luke)

Vocal Solos
"Have Thine Own Way, Lord!" (Jer)
  V-8   p. 191
"Here I Am" (Jer, Luke)
  V-1   p. 19
"Borning Cry" (Pss, Baptism)
  V-5 (1)   p. 10
"Christ Living Within You" (Luke)
  V-8   p. 177
"Lead Me to Calvary" (Luke)
  V-8   p. 226

Anthems
"God's God the Whole World" (Pss)
Mark Miller; MorningStar MSM-50-9861
SATB *divisi, a cappella* (https://bit.ly/50-9861)

"Give Me Jesus with Jesus Paid It All" (Luke)
Arr. Hojun Lee; Shawnee Press 35029305
SATB, piano (https://bit.ly/35029305)

Other Suggestions
Visuals:
  O   Potter's wheel/clay, hands/clay, building, planting
  P   Sitting/standing, open mouth, hand on shoulder
  E   Letter, old man writing. manacles, heart
  G   Carrying crosses, tower, calculator, document, dove
Opening Prayer: N826 (Jer) or C771 (Pss)
Prayer: C262. You Are the Work of God (Jer)
Create a choral medley or praise band song set, using the traditional
  "How Great Thou Art" and the new "How Great You Are."
Blessing: WSL158. "Here in this sanctuary" (Phlm, Luke)
Sung Benediction: "Let the Peace of God Reign" 1839987 (Phlm)
Alternate Lessons: Deut 30:15-20, Ps 1(See page 4)
Theme Ideas: Cross, Discipleship / Following God, Inclusion,
  Sin and Forgiveness, Welcome

Jeremiah 4:11-12, 22-28
[11]At that time it will be said to this people and to Jerusalem: A hot wind comes from me out of the bare heights in the desert toward my poor people, not to winnow or cleanse—[12]a wind too strong for that. Now it is I who speak in judgment against them.

. . . .

[22]"For my people are foolish,
 they do not know me;
they are stupid children,
 they have no understanding.
They are skilled in doing evil,
 but do not know how to do good."
[23]I looked on the earth, and lo, it was waste and void;
 and to the heavens, and they had no light.
[24]I looked on the mountains, and lo, they were quaking,
 and all the hills moved to and fro.
[25]I looked, and lo, there was no one at all,
 and all the birds of the air had fled.
[26]I looked, and lo, the fruitful land was a desert,
 and all its cities were laid in ruins
 before the LORD, before his fierce anger.
[27]For thus says the LORD: The whole land shall be a desolation; yet I will not make a full end.
[28]Because of this the earth shall mourn,
 and the heavens above grow black;
for I have spoken, I have purposed;
 I have not relented nor will I turn back.

Psalm 14 (G335, N626, SH26, UM746)
[1]Fools say in their hearts, "There is no God."
 They are corrupt, they do abominable deeds;
 there is no one who does good.
[2]The LORD looks down from heaven on humankind
 to see if there are any who are wise,
 who seek after God.
[3]They have all gone astray, they are all alike perverse;
 there is no one who does good,
 no, not one.
[4]Have they no knowledge, all the evildoers
 who eat up my people as they eat bread,
 and do not call upon the LORD?
[5]There they shall be in great terror,
 for God is with the company of the righteous.
[6]You would confound the plans of the poor,
 but the LORD is their refuge.
[7]O that deliverance for Israel would come from Zion!
 When the LORD restores the fortunes of his people,
 Jacob will rejoice; Israel will be glad.

1 Timothy 1:12-17
[12]I am grateful to Christ Jesus our Lord, who has strengthened me, because he judged me faithful and appointed me to his service, [13]even though I was formerly a blasphemer, a persecutor, and a man of violence. But I received mercy because I had acted ignorantly in unbelief, [14]and the grace of our Lord overflowed for me with the faith and love that are in Christ Jesus. [15]The saying is sure and worthy of full acceptance, that Christ Jesus came into the world to save sinners—of whom I am the foremost. [16]But for that very reason I received mercy, so that in me, as the foremost, Jesus Christ might display the utmost patience, making me an example to those who would come to believe in him for eternal life. [17]To the King of the ages, immortal, invisible, the only God, be honor and glory forever and ever. Amen.

Luke 15:1-10
[1]Now all the tax collectors and sinners were coming near to listen to him. [2]And the Pharisees and the scribes were grumbling and saying, "This fellow welcomes sinners and eats with them." [3]So he told them this parable: [4]"Which one of you, having a hundred sheep and losing one of them, does not leave the ninety-nine in the wilderness and go after the one that is lost until he finds it? [5]When he has found it, he lays it on his shoulders and rejoices. [6]And when he comes home, he calls together his friends and neighbors, saying to them, 'Rejoice with me, for I have found my sheep that was lost.' [7]Just so, I tell you, there will be more joy in heaven over one sinner who repents than over ninety-nine righteous persons who need no repentance. [8]"Or what woman having ten silver coins, if she loses one of them, does not light a lamp, sweep the house, and search carefully until she finds it? [9]When she has found it, she calls together her friends and neighbors, saying, 'Rejoice with me, for I have found the coin that I had lost.' [10]Just so, I tell you, there is joy in the presence of the angels of God over one sinner who repents."

Primary Hymns and Songs for the Day

"Immortal, Invisible, God Only Wise" (1 Tim) (O)
C66, CG58, E423, EL834, G12, N1, P263, SA37, UM103 (PD), VU264
- H-3 Hbl-15, 71; Chr-65; Desc-93; Org-135
- S-1 #300. Harm.

"O for a Closer Walk with God" (Jer)
CG679, E684, G739, N450, P396, SA612

"My Lord, What a Morning" (Jer, Pss, Luke)
C708, EL438 (PD), G352, P449, SH356, UM719, VU708

"Praise, My Soul, the King of Heaven" (1 Tim)
C23, CG337, E410, EL864/865, G619/620, P478/479, SA55, SH418, UM66 (PD), VU240
- H-3 Hbl-88; Chr-162; Desc-67; Org-75
- S-1 #205. Harmonization
       #206. Descant

"Grace Alone" 2335524 (1 Tim)
CG43, S2162, SA699

"We Fall Down" 2437367 (1 Tim)
G368, WS3187

"Amazing Grace" (1 Tim, Luke)
AH4091, C546, CG587, E671, EL779, G649, N547/548, P280, SA453, SH523, UM378 (PD), VU266 (Fr.)
- H-3 Hbl-14, 46; Chr-27; Desc-14; Org-4
- S-2 #5-7. Various treatments
- V-8 p. 56. Vocal Solo

"To God Be the Glory" (1 Tim) (C)
C72, CG349, G634, P485, SA279, SH545, UM98 (PD)

Additional Hymn Suggestions

"Steal Away to Jesus" (Jer, Pss, Luke)
C644, G358, N599, UM704

"Alas! And Did My Savior Bleed" (1 Tim)
AH4067, C204, CG182/595, EL337, G212, N199/200, P78, SA159, UM294/359, SH172/173

"I Stand Amazed in the Presence" (1 Tim)
CG576, SA466, SH537, UM371 (PD)

"There Are Some Things I May Not Know" (1 Tim)
N405, S2147

"Come, Thou Fount of Every Blessing" (1 Tim, Luke)
AH4086, C16, CG295/559, E686, EL807, G475, N459, P356, SA830, SH394, UM400 (PD), VU559

"Just as I Am, Without One Plea" (Luke)
C339, CG500, E693, EL592, G442, N207, P370, SA503, SH500, UM357 (PD), VU508

"Savior, Like a Shepherd Lead Us" (Luke)
C558, CG405, E708, EL789, G187, N252, P387, SH538, UM381 (PD)

"Come, We That Love the Lord" (Luke)
CG549, E392, N379, SA831, UM732, VU715

"Marching to Zion" (Luke)
C707, CG550, EL625, N382, SA831, UM733, VU714

"A Woman and a Coin" (Luke)
C74, G173, VU360

"Bring Many Names" (Luke)
C10, G760, N11, S2047, VU268

"Just a Closer Walk with Thee" (Luke)
C557, EL697, G835, S2158, SH584

"Lord of All Hopefulness" (Luke)
CG678, E482, EL765, G683, S2197, SA772, SH464

"Love Lifted Me" (Luke)
CG618, SA853, WS3101

Additional Contemporary and Modern Suggestions

"The Steadfast Love of the Lord" 21590 (Jer, Luke)
"Mighty to Save" 4591782 (Jer, Luke, Pss)
WS3038
"Holy Spirit, Come to Us" (*"Veni Sancte Spiritus"*) (Pss)
EL406, G281, S2118
"My Tribute" 11218 (1 Tim)
AH4080, C39, CG574, N14, SH434, UM99; V-8 p. 5 Solo

"God Is Good All the Time" 1729073 (1 Tim)
"Shout to the North" 1562261 (1 Tim)
G319, SA1009, WS3042
"Amazing Grace" ("My Chains Are Gone") 4768151 (1 Tim)
WS3104
"There Is Joy in the Lord" 1184209 (1 Tim)
"Forevermore" 5466830 (1 Tim)
"One Way" 4222082 (1 Tim)
"Sing Alleluia to the Lord" (1 Tim, Comm.)
C32, S2258, SH685
"Here Is Bread, Here Is Wine" 983717 (1 Tim, Comm.)
EL483, S2266
"God Is So Good" 4956994 (1 Tim, Luke)
G658, S2056, SH461
"Grace Like Rain" 3689877 (1 Tim, Luke)
"That's Why We Praise Him" 2668576 (Luke)
"You Are My All in All" 825356 (Luke)
CG571, G519, SH335, WS3040
"You Are My King" ("Amazing Love") 2456623 (Luke)
SH539, WS3102
"Take, O Take Me as I Am" 4562041 (Luke)
EL814, G698, SH620, WS3119
"Here at the Cross" 7046292 (Luke)
"I Come to the Cross" 1965249 (Luke)
"When It's All Been Said and Done" 2788353 (Luke)

Vocal Solos

"My Lord, What a Morning" (Jer)
- V-3 (1) p. 39
- V-7   p. 68

"Redeeming Grace" (1 Tim)
- V-4   p. 47

"Strength to My Soul" (1 Tim, Luke)
- V-8   p. 352

"God, Our Ever Faithful Shepherd" (Luke)
- V-4   p. 15

Anthems

"Choral Reflection on Amazing Grace" (1 Tim, Luke)
Arr. Roger Ames; GIA Publications G-5926
SSATBB, piano (https://bit.ly/G-5926)

"Song of Grace" (1 Tim, Luke)
Arr. Phillip Keveren; Jubilate Music 46904
SATB, keyboard, opt. flute (https://bit.ly/Jubilate-46904)

Other Suggestions

Visuals:
- O Desert, wind, mountains, earthquake, birds, ruins, mourning, darkness
- P Stray sheep, eating bread, Ps 14:6, poor, joy
- E Christ, 1 Tim 1:15, Paul, glory, crown
- G One sheep, Jesus carrying lost sheep, ten coins, lamp, broom, woman rejoicing, one coin

If your congregation is remembering the anniversary of 9/11 today, you may want to intertwine the broken world theme of Jeremiah 4 with the theme of God's commitment to the lost in Luke 15.

Introit: C583, CG403, EL768, G740, S2214, SH582. "Lead Me, Guide Me" (Luke)

Opening Prayer: N830 (2 Tim) and Confession: N838 (Pss)

Alternate Lessons: Exod 32:7-14, Ps. 51:1-10 (See page 4)

Theme Ideas: God: Shepherd, Grace, Redemption / Salvation, Sin and Forgiveness

Jeremiah 8:18–9:1

¹⁸My joy is gone, grief is upon me,
  my heart is sick.
¹⁹Hark, the cry of my poor people
  from far and wide in the land:
"Is the LORD not in Zion?
  Is her King not in her?"
  ("Why have they provoked me to anger with their images,
  with their foreign idols?")
²⁰"The harvest is past, the summer is ended,
  and we are not saved."
²¹For the hurt of my poor people I am hurt,
  I mourn, and dismay has taken hold of me.
²²Is there no balm in Gilead?
  Is there no physician there?
Why then has the health of my poor people
  not been restored?
9 O that my head were a spring of water,
  and my eyes a fountain of tears,
so that I might weep day and night
  for the slain of my poor people!

Psalm 79:1-9 (G430, N671)

¹O God, the nations have come into your inheritance;
  they have defiled your holy temple;
  they have laid Jerusalem in ruins.
²They have given the bodies of your servants
  to the birds of the air for food,
  the flesh of your faithful to the wild animals of the earth.
³They have poured out their blood like water
  all around Jerusalem,
  and there was no one to bury them.
⁴We have become a taunt to our neighbors,
  mocked and derided by those around us.
⁵How long, O LORD? Will you be angry forever?
  Will your jealous wrath burn like fire?
⁶Pour out your anger on the nations
  that do not know you,
and on the kingdoms
  that do not call on your name.
⁷For they have devoured Jacob
  and laid waste his habitation.
⁸Do not remember against us the iniquities of our ancestors;
  let your compassion come speedily to meet us,
  for we are brought very low.
⁹Help us, O God of our salvation,
  for the glory of your name;
deliver us, and forgive our sins,
  for your name's sake.

1 Timothy 2:1-7

¹First of all, then, I urge that supplications, prayers, intercessions, and thanksgivings be made for everyone, ²for kings and all who are in high positions, so that we may lead a quiet and peaceable life in all godliness and dignity. ³This is right and is acceptable in the sight of God our Savior, ⁴who desires everyone to be saved and to come to the knowledge of the truth. ⁵For
  there is one God;
    there is also one mediator between God and humankind,
    Christ Jesus, himself human,
⁶   who gave himself a ransom for all
—this was attested at the right time. ⁷For this I was appointed a herald and an apostle (I am telling the truth, I am not lying), a teacher of the Gentiles in faith and truth.

Luke 16:1-13

¹Then Jesus said to the disciples, "There was a rich man who had a manager, and charges were brought to him that this man was squandering his property. ²So he summoned him and said to him, 'What is this that I hear about you? Give me an accounting of your management, because you cannot be my manager any longer.' ³Then the manager said to himself, 'What will I do, now that my master is taking the position away from me? I am not strong enough to dig, and I am ashamed to beg. ⁴I have decided what to do so that, when I am dismissed as manager, people may welcome me into their homes.' ⁵So, summoning his master's debtors one by one, he asked the first, 'How much do you owe my master?' ⁶He answered, 'A hundred jugs of olive oil.' He said to him, 'Take your bill, sit down quickly, and make it fifty.' ⁷Then he asked another, 'And how much do you owe?' He replied, 'A hundred containers of wheat.' He said to him, 'Take your bill and make it eighty.' ⁸And his master commended the dishonest manager because he had acted shrewdly; for the children of this age are more shrewd in dealing with their own generation than are the children of light. ⁹And I tell you, make friends for yourselves by means of dishonest wealth so that when it is gone, they may welcome you into the eternal homes. ¹⁰"Whoever is faithful in a very little is faithful also in much; and whoever is dishonest in a very little is dishonest also in much. ¹¹If then you have not been faithful with the dishonest wealth, who will entrust to you the true riches? ¹²And if you have not been faithful with what belongs to another, who will give you what is your own? ¹³No slave can serve two masters; for a slave will either hate the one and love the other, or be devoted to the one and despise the other. You cannot serve God and wealth."

Primary Hymns and Songs for the Day

"O Master, Let Me Walk with Thee" (Jer) (O)
  C602, CG660, E659/E660, EL818, G738, N503, P357, SA667,
  SH612, UM430 (PD), VU560
    H-3   Hbl-81; Chr-147; Desc-74; Org-87
    S-2   #118. Descant
"There Is a Balm in Gilead" (Jer)
  AH4110, C501, CG74, E676, EL614 (PD), G792, N553, P394,
  SH340, UM375, VU612
    S-2   #21. Desc.
"How Long, O Lord" (Pss)
  G777, S2209
"Come Now, O Prince of Peace" ("O-So-So") (1 Tim)
  EL247, G103, S2232, SH235
"More Precious than Silver" 11335 (Luke)
  S2065
"Take, O Take Me as I Am" 4562041 (Luke)
  EL814, G698, SH620, WS3119
"We Give Thee but Thine Own" (Luke)
  C382, EL686, G708, N785, P428, SH643, VU543
"Forth in Thy Name, O Lord" (Luke) (C)
  SA642, UM438 (PD), VU416
    H-3   Hbl-29, 57, 58; Chr-117; Desc-31; Org-31
    S-1   #100-103. Various treatments.

Additional Hymn Suggestions

"O God Who Shaped Creation" (Jer)
  UM443, VU276
"Jesus, Lover of My Soul" (Jer)
  C542, CG406, E699, G440, N546, P303, SA257, SH542/543,
  UM479, VU669
"O Love That Wilt Not Let Me Go" (Jer)
  C540, CG631, G833, N485, P384, SA616, SH314, UM480,
  VU658
"Lord of All Hopefulness" (Jer)
  CG678, E482, EL765, G683, S2197, SA772, SH464
"O for a Closer Walk with God" (Jer, Pss)
  CG679, E684, G739, N450, P396, SA612
"Why Stand So Far Away, My God" (Jer, Pss)
  C671, G786, S2180
"Forgive Our Sins as We Forgive" (Jer, Pss)
  CG694 E674, EL605, G444, P347, SH504, UM390, VU364
"I Love the Lord" 1168957 (Jer, Pss, Luke)
  CG613, G799, P362, N511, SH343, VU617, WS3142
"For the Healing of the Nations" (Jer, 1 Tim)
  C668, CG698, G346, N576, SA1000, UM428, VU678
"What Does the Lord Require of You" 456859 (Jer, Luke)
  C661, CG690, G70, S2174, VU701
"Purify My Heart" 1314323 (Jer, Luke)
"All Who Love and Serve Your City" (Pss, Luke)
  C670, CG674, E570/E571, EL724, G351, P413, UM433
"This Is My Song" (1 Tim)
  C722, CG697, EL887, G340, N591, UM437
"To God Be the Glory" (1 Tim)
  C72, CG349, G634, P485, SA279, SH545, UM98 (PD)
"Take My Life, and Let It Be" (1 Tim)
  C609, CG490, E707, EL583/EL685, G697, P391, N448,
  SA623, SH627/628, UM399 (PD), VU506
"Make Me a Channel of Your Peace" (1 Tim)
  G753, S2171, SA608, SH616 VU684
"Make Me a Channel of Your Peace" 6399315 (1 Tim)
"Baptized in Water" (1 Tim, Baptism)
  CG449, E294, EL456, G482, P492, S2248, SH666
Jesús Es Mi Rey Soberano ("O Jesus, My King and My Sovereign")
  (Luke)
  C109, P157, SH211, UM180
"I Want to Walk as a Child of the Light" (Luke)
  CG96, E490, EL815, G377, SH352, UM206

"Jesus Calls Us" (Luke)
  C337, CG486, E549/550/551, EL696, G720, N171/172,
  SA653, SH604, UM398, VU562
"What Does the Lord Require" (Luke)
  C659, E605, P405, UM441
"More Love to Thee, O Christ" (Luke)
  C527, CG365, G828, N456, P359, UM453 (PD)
"I'm Gonna Live So God Can Use Me" (Luke)
  C614, G700, P369, S2153, SH632, VU575
"Somebody's Knockin' at Your Door" (Luke)
  G728, P382, SH597, WS3095

Additional Contemporary and Modern Suggestions

"Hear Us from Heaven" 4455392 (Jer, Pss)
"Jesus Messiah" 5183443 (1 Tim)
"Jesus, Name above All Names" 21291 (1 Tim)
  S2071, SA82
"Praise You" 863806 (Luke, Praise)
  S2003
"Make Me a Servant" 33131 (Luke)
  CG651, S2176
"Seek Ye First" 1352 (Luke)
  C354, CG436, E711, G175, P333, SA675, SH126, UM405,
  VU356
"Knowing You" 1045238 (Luke)
"Take This Life" 2563365 (Luke, Stewardship)
"These Hands" 3251827 (Luke, Stewardship)
"Be Glorified" 2732646 (2 Thess)
"Lord, Be Glorified" 26368 (Luke, Stewardship)
  EL744, G468, S2150, SA593, SH420

Vocal Solos

"There Is a Balm in Gilead" (Jer)
  V-3 (1)   p. 29
  V-7   p. 44
"Seek First" (Luke)
  V-8   p. 145
"Take My Life" (Luke, Stewardship)
  V-8   p. 262
"Here I Am" (Luke, Stewardship)
  V-1   p. 19

Anthems

"Balm in Gilead" (Jer)
Arr. M. Roger Holland II; MorningStar MSM-50-3903
SATB, piano, solo (https://bit.ly/50-3903)

"Refuge" (Jer, Pss, 1 Tim)
Keith Christopher; Hope C5893
SATB, piano (https://bit.ly/Hope-C5893)

Other Suggestions

Visuals:
  O   Grief, heart, reaching, harvest, poor, heal, spring
  P   Ruins, blood, fire, Ps. 79:9
  E   Praying hands, judge, hand of God, Christ, cross
  G   Ledger, shovel, ten cup, 100/50, oil, wheat, 100/80,
           darkness/light, symbols of wealth
A stewardship focus relates well to today's Luke reading.
Opening Prayer: UM677. Listen, Lord (Jer, Pss)
Prayer: N851. Guidance (Jer)
Prayer: N854 or N863 (Pss)
Prayer: WSL205. "Loving God, we spend so much time" (Luke)
Response: UM588. "All Things Come of Thee" (Luke)
For more resources, see The Abingdon Worship Annual 2022.
Alternate Lessons: Amos 8:4-7, Ps. 113 (See page 4)
Theme Ideas: Faithfulness, Grief, Lament, Prayer, Stewardship

Jeremiah 32:1-3a, 6-15

[1]The word that came to Jeremiah from the LORD in the tenth year of King Zedekiah of Judah, which was the eighteenth year of Nebuchadrezzar. [2]At that time the army of the king of Babylon was besieging Jerusalem, and the prophet Jeremiah was confined in the court of the guard that was in the palace of the king of Judah, [3a]where King Zedekiah of Judah had confined him. . . .

[6]Jeremiah said, The word of the LORD came to me: [7]Hanamel son of your uncle Shallum is going to come to you and say, "Buy my field that is at Anathoth, for the right of redemption by purchase is yours." [8]Then my cousin Hanamel came to me in the court of the guard, in accordance with the word of the LORD, and said to me, "Buy my field that is at Anathoth in the land of Benjamin, for the right of possession and redemption is yours; buy it for yourself." Then I knew that this was the word of the LORD. [9]And I bought the field at Anathoth from my cousin Hanamel, and weighed out the money to him, seventeen shekels of silver. [10]I signed the deed, sealed it, got witnesses, and weighed the money on scales. [11]Then I took the sealed deed of purchase, containing the terms and conditions, and the open copy; [12]and I gave the deed of purchase to Baruch son of Neriah son of Mahseiah, in the presence of my cousin Hanamel, in the presence of the witnesses who signed the deed of purchase, and in the presence of all the Judeans who were sitting in the court of the guard. [13]In their presence I charged Baruch, saying, [14]Thus says the LORD of hosts, the God of Israel: Take these deeds, both this sealed deed of purchase and this open deed, and put them in an earthenware jar, in order that they may last for a long time. [15]For thus says the LORD of hosts, the God of Israel: Houses and fields and vineyards shall again be bought in this land.

Psalm 91:1-6, 14-16 (G43/168, N681, P212, UM810)

[1]You who live in the shelter of the Most High,
    who abide in the shadow of the Almighty,
[2]will say to the LORD, "My refuge and my fortress;
    my God, in whom I trust."
[3]For he will deliver you from the snare of the fowler
    and from the deadly pestilence;
[4]he will cover you with his pinions,
    and under his wings you will find refuge;
    his faithfulness is a shield and buckler.
[5]You will not fear the terror of the night,
    or the arrow that flies by day,
[6]or the pestilence that stalks in darkness,
    or the destruction that wastes at noonday.
. . . .
[14]Those who love me, I will deliver;
    I will protect those who know my name.
[15]When they call to me, I will answer them;
    I will be with them in trouble,
    I will rescue them and honor them.
[16]With long life I will satisfy them,
    and show them my salvation.

1 Timothy 6:6-19

[6]Of course, there is great gain in godliness combined with contentment; [7]for we brought nothing into the world, so that we can take nothing out of it; [8]but if we have food and clothing, we will be content with these. [9]But those who want to be rich fall into temptation and are trapped by many senseless and harmful desires that plunge people into ruin and destruction. [10]For the love of money is a root of all kinds of evil, and in their eagerness to be rich some have wandered away from the faith and pierced themselves with many pains.

[11]But as for you, man of God, shun all this; pursue righteousness, godliness, faith, love, endurance, gentleness. [12]Fight the good fight of the faith; take hold of the eternal life, to which you were called and for which you made the good confession in the presence of many witnesses. [13]In the presence of God, who gives life to all things, and of Christ Jesus, who in his testimony before Pontius Pilate made the good confession, I charge you [14]to keep the commandment without spot or blame until the manifestation of our Lord Jesus Christ, [15]which he will bring about at the right time—he who is the blessed and only Sovereign, the King of kings and Lord of lords. [16]It is he alone who has immortality and dwells in unapproachable light, whom no one has ever seen or can see; to him be honor and eternal dominion. Amen.

[17]As for those who in the present age are rich, command them not to be haughty, or to set their hopes on the uncertainty of riches, but rather on God who richly provides us with everything for our enjoyment. [18]They are to do good, to be rich in good works, generous, and ready to share, [19]thus storing up for themselves the treasure of a good foundation for the future, so that they may take hold of the life that really is life.

Luke 16:19-31

[19]"There was a rich man who was dressed in purple and fine linen and who feasted sumptuously every day. [20]And at his gate lay a poor man named Lazarus, covered with sores, [21]who longed to satisfy his hunger with what fell from the rich man's table; even the dogs would come and lick his sores. [22]The poor man died and was carried away by the angels to be with Abraham. The rich man also died and was buried. [23]In Hades, where he was being tormented, he looked up and saw Abraham far away with Lazarus by his side. [24]He called out, 'Father Abraham, have mercy on me, and send Lazarus to dip the tip of his finger in water and cool my tongue; for I am in agony in these flames.' [25]But Abraham said, 'Child, remember that during your lifetime you received your good things, and Lazarus in like manner evil things; but now he is comforted here, and you are in agony. [26]Besides all this, between you and us a great chasm has been fixed, so that those who might want to pass from here to you cannot do so, and no one can cross from there to us.' [27]He said, 'Then, father, I beg you to send him to my father's house—[28]for I have five brothers—that he may warn them, so that they will not also come into this place of torment.' [29]Abraham replied, 'They have Moses and the prophets; they should listen to them.' [30]He said, 'No, father Abraham; but if someone goes to them from the dead, they will repent.' [31]He said to him, 'If they do not listen to Moses and the prophets, neither will they be convinced even if someone rises from the dead.'"

Primary Hymns and Songs for the Day

"Ye Servants of God" (1 Tim) (O)
 C110, CG420, E535, EL825 (PD), G299, N305, P477, SA97,
 UM181 (PD), VU342
   H-3   Hbl-90, 105; Chr-221; Desc-49; Org-51
   S-2   #71-74. Introduction and harmonizations
"On Eagle's Wings" (Pss)
 C77, CG51, EL787, G43, N775, SH318, UM143, VU807/808,
   S-2   #143. Stanzas for soloist
"God Will Take Care of You" (Pss, 1 Tim)
 N460, SA5, SH289, UM130 (PD)
"Give Thanks" 20285 (Luke)
 C528, CG373, G647, S2036, SA364, SH489
"A Charge to Keep I Have" (1 Tim) (C)
 AH4117, CG623, SA946, SH634, UM413 (PD)
   S-1   #46. Choral Harm.

Additional Hymn Suggestions

"Hope of the World" (Jer)
 C538, E472, G734, N46, P360, UM178, VU215
"Let All Things Now Living" (Jer)
 C717, CG379, EL881, G37, P554, S2008, SH23, VU242
"Eternal Father, Strong to Save" (Jer)
 C85, CG14, E608, EL756, G8, P562 (PD), S2191, SA11,
 VU659
"What Does the Lord Require of You" 456859 (Jer, Luke)
 C661, CG690, G70, S2174, VU701
"Rejoice, Ye Pure in Heart" (Phil)
 C15, CG312, E556/557, EL873/874, G804, N55/71,
 P145/146, UM160/161
"Take My Life, and Let It Be" (1 Tim)
 C609, CG490, E707, EL583/EL685, G697, P391, N448,
 SA623, SH627/628, UM399 (PD), VU506
"Stand Up, Stand Up for Jesus" (1 Tim)
 C613, CG639, E561, SA982, UM514 (PD)
"He Is King of Kings" (1 Tim)
 G273, P153
"We Give Thee but Thine Own" (1 Tim)
 C382, EL686, G708, N785, P428, SH643, VU543
"Fight the Good Fight" (1 Tim)
 E552, G846, P307 (PD), SA952, VU674
"Fairest Lord Jesus" (1 Tim, Luke)
 C97, CG159, E383, EL838, G630, N44, P306, SA77, SH7,
 UM189 (PD), VU341
"I Sing a Song of the Saints of God" (1 Tim, Luke)
 E293, G730, N295, P364, UM712 (PD)
"Where Cross the Crowded Ways of Life" (Luke)
 C665, CG657, E609, EL719, G343, N543, P408, UM427 (PD),
 VU681
"*Cuando el Pobre*" ("When the Poor Ones") (Luke)
 C662, EL725, G762, P407, SH240, UM434, VU702
"What Does the Lord Require" (Luke)
 C659, E605, P405, UM441
"The Church of Christ, in Every Age" (Luke)
 C475, EL729, G320, N306, P421, UM589, VU601
"God Be with You till We Meet Again" (Luke)
 C434, CG523, EL536, G541/542, N81, P540, SA1027,
 UM672/673, VU422/423

Additional Contemporary and Modern Suggestions

"I Have a Hope" 5087587 (Jer)
"Song of Hope" ("Heaven Come Down") 5111477
"You Are My Hiding Place" 21442 (Pss)
 C554, S2055, SH46
"Nothing Can Trouble" (*Nada Te Turbe*) (Pss)
 CG73, G820, N772, S2054, SH292, VU290

"I've Got Peace Like a River" (Pss)
 C530, G623, N478, P368, S2145, SH276, VU577
"Everlasting God" 4556538 (Pss)
 WS3021
"Still" 3940963 (Pss)
 WS3134
"This Is My Story" 7046375 (Pss)
"Who Can Satisfy My Soul Like You?" 208492 (Pss)
"I Stand Amazed" 769450 (Pss)
"All Things Are Possible" 2245140 (Pss)
"Eagle's Wings" 2478168 (Pss)
"Came to My Rescue" 4705190 (Pss)
"Crown Him King of Kings" 206009 (1 Tim)
"When It's All Been Said and Done" 2788353 (1 Tim)
"All Hail King Jesus" 12877 (1 Tim)
 S2069
"King of Kings" 23952 (1 Tim)
 S2075, VU167
"We Will Glorify the King of Kings" 19038 (1 Tim)
 CG360, S2087
"He Who Began a Good Work in You" 15238 (1 Tim)
 S2163
"Majesty" 1527 (1 Tim)
 CG346, SA382, SH212, UM176
"Worthy, You Are Worthy" 17384 (1 Tim)
"Worthy" 2646749 (1 Tim)
"Forevermore" 5466830 (1 Tim)
"I Will Boast" 4662350 (1 Tim, Luke)
"You Are My All in All" 825356 (1 Tim, Luke)
 CG571, G519, SH335, WS3040
"Jesus, Remember Me" (Luke)
 C569, CG393, EL616, G227, P599, SH175, UM488, VU148
"Today" 5775617 (Luke)

Vocal Solos

"On Eagle's Wings" (Pss)
 V-3 (2)   p. 2
"Jesus Is Lord of All" (1 Tim)
 V-8   p. 254
"Sinner-Man So Hard to Believe" (Luke)
 V-7   p. 48

Anthems

"Lord, I Stretch My Hands to You" (Pss)
Jay Althouse; Hope C5277 (other voicings available)
2-part mixed or treble, piano (https://bit.ly/Hope-C5277)

"Rock-A My Soul" (Luke)
Arr. Stacey V. Gibbs; Walton Music WJMS1166
SATB *divisi, a cappella* (https://bit.ly/WJMS1166)

Other Suggestions

Visuals:
   O   War, field, scales, earthen jar, house
   P   Shadow, refuge, fort, eagle, snare, shield/arrow
   E   Newborn, coffin, money, 1 Tim. 6:11b, Jesus/Pilot,
       cross/ crown, generosity, treasure
   G   Purple robe/linen, feast, sores, dogs, five men, angels,
       flames, water, Bible open to Exodus
Stewardship emphasis relates to New Testament lessons today.
Call to Prayer: EL406, G281, S2118. "Holy Spirit, Come to Us"
 (Pss)
Prayer: N863. Justice (Jer, Luke)
Communion Prayer: C774 (Luke)
Alternate Lessons: Amos 6:1a, 4-7, Ps 146 (See page 4)
Theme Ideas: God: Providence / God our Help, Hope,
 Stewardship

Lamentations 1:1-6

[1]How lonely sits the city
　　that once was full of people!
How like a widow she has become,
　　she that was great among the nations!
She that was a princess among the provinces
　　has become a vassal.
[2]She weeps bitterly in the night,
　　with tears on her cheeks;
among all her lovers
　　she has no one to comfort her;
all her friends have dealt treacherously with her,
　　they have become her enemies.
[3]Judah has gone into exile with suffering
　　and hard servitude;
she lives now among the nations,
　　and finds no resting place;
her pursuers have all overtaken her
　　in the midst of her distress.
[4]The roads to Zion mourn,
　　for no one comes to the festivals;
all her gates are desolate,
　　her priests groan;
her young girls grieve,
　　and her lot is bitter.
[5]Her foes have become the masters,
　　her enemies prosper,
because the LORD has made her suffer
　　for the multitude of her transgressions;
her children have gone away,
　　captives before the foe.
[6]From daughter Zion has departed
　　all her majesty.
Her princes have become like stags
　　that find no pasture;
they fled without strength
　　before the pursuer.

Psalm 137 (G72/784, N713, P246, UM852)

[1]By the rivers of Babylon—
　　there we sat down and there we wept
　　when we remembered Zion.
[2]On the willows there
　　we hung up our harps.
[3]For there our captors
　　asked us for songs,
and our tormentors asked for mirth, saying,
　　"Sing us one of the songs of Zion!"
[4]How could we sing the Lord's song
　　in a foreign land?
[5]If I forget you, O Jerusalem,
　　let my right hand wither!
[6]Let my tongue cling to the roof of my mouth,
　　if I do not remember you,
if I do not set Jerusalem
　　above my highest joy.
[7]Remember, O LORD, against the Edomites
　　the day of Jerusalem's fall,
how they said, "Tear it down! Tear it down!
　　Down to its foundations!"
[8]O daughter Babylon, you devastator!
　　Happy shall they be who pay you back
　　what you have done to us!
[9]Happy shall they be who take your little ones
　　and dash them against the rock!

2 Timothy 1:1-14

[1]Paul, an apostle of Christ Jesus by the will of God, for the sake of the promise of life that is in Christ Jesus, [2]To Timothy, my beloved child: Grace, mercy, and peace from God the Father and Christ Jesus our Lord.

[3]I am grateful to God—whom I worship with a clear conscience, as my ancestors did—when I remember you constantly in my prayers night and day. [4]Recalling your tears, I long to see you so that I may be filled with joy. [5]I am reminded of your sincere faith, a faith that lived first in your grandmother Lois and your mother Eunice and now, I am sure, lives in you. [6]For this reason I remind you to rekindle the gift of God that is within you through the laying on of my hands; [7]for God did not give us a spirit of cowardice, but rather a spirit of power and of love and of self discipline. [8]Do not be ashamed, then, of the testimony about our Lord or of me his prisoner, but join with me in suffering for the gospel, relying on the power of God, [9]who saved us and called us with a holy calling, not according to our works but according to his own purpose and grace. This grace was given to us in Christ Jesus before the ages began, [10]but it has now been revealed through the appearing of our Savior Christ Jesus, who abolished death and brought life and immortality to light through the gospel. [11]For this gospel I was appointed a herald and an apostle and a teacher, [12]and for this reason I suffer as I do. But I am not ashamed, for I know the one in whom I have put my trust, and I am sure that he is able to guard until that day what I have entrusted to him. [13]Hold to the standard of sound teaching that you have heard from me, in the faith and love that are in Christ Jesus. [14]Guard the good treasure entrusted to you, with the help of the Holy Spirit living in us.

Luke 17:5-10

[5]The apostles said to the Lord, "Increase our faith!" [6]The Lord replied, "If you had faith the size of a mustard seed, you could say to this mulberry tree, 'Be uprooted and planted in the sea,' and it would obey you. [7]"Who among you would say to your slave who has just come in from plowing or tending sheep in the field, 'Come here at once and take your place at the table'? [8]Would you not rather say to him, 'Prepare supper for me, put on your apron and serve me while I eat and drink; later you may eat and drink'? [9]Do you thank the slave for doing what was commanded? [10]So you also, when you have done all that you were ordered to do, say, 'We are worthless slaves; we have done only what we ought to have done!'"

Primary Hymns and Songs for the Day
"Standing on the Promises" (2 Tim) (O)
    AH4057, C552, CG625, G838, SA522, SH45, UM374 (PD)
        H-3   Chr-177; Org-117
"By the Babylonian Rivers" (Pss)
    G72, P246, S2217, VU859
"By the Waters of Babylon" (Pss)
    G784, P245, VU858b
"I Know Whom I Have Believed" (2 Tim)
    CG588, SA843, SH529, UM714 (PD)
"I Bind unto Myself Today" (2 Tim)
    E370, EL450 (PD), G6, VU317
"One Bread, One Body" (World Comm.) (C)
    C393, EL496, G530, SH678, UM620, VU467
        H-3   Chr-156
"Forth in Thy Name, O Lord" (1 Tim, Luke) (C)
    SA642, UM438 (PD), VU416
        H-3   Hbl-29, 57, 58; Chr-117; Desc-31; Org-31
        S-1   #100-103. Various treatments.

Additional Hymn Suggestions
"It's Me, It's Me, O Lord" (Lam)
    C579, N519, UM352
"My Song Is Love Unknown" (Lam, 2 Cor)
    E458, EL343, G209, N222, P76, S2083, SA149, VU143
"When God Restored Our Common Life" (Pss)
    G74, S2182
"In the Midst of New Dimensions" (Lam, Pss, World Comm.)
    G315, N391, S2238
"I Love Thy Kingdom, Lord" (Pss, 2 Tim)
    C274, CG262, E524, G310, N312, P441, UM540
"Take My Life, and Let It Be" (2 Tim)
    C609, CG490, E707, EL583/EL685, G697, P391
"Holy Spirit, Truth Divine" (2 Tim)
    C241, EL398, N63, P321, SA285, UM465, VU368
"God of Grace and God of Glory" (2 Tim)
    C464, CG285, E594/595, EL705, G307, N436, P420, SA814,
    SH250, UM577, VU686
"I Come with Joy" (2 Tim, World Comm.)
    C420, CG456, E304, EL482, G515, N349, P507, SH682,
    UM617, VU477
"Draw Us in the Spirit's Tether" (2 Tim, Comm.)
    C392, EL470, G529, N337, P504, UM632, VU479
"In the Singing" (2 Tim, Comm.)
    EL466, G533, S2255
"Take, O Take Me as I Am" 4562041 (2 Tim)
    EL814, G698, SH620, WS3119
"Give Me Jesus" (2 Tim)
    CG546, EL770, N409, SH306, WS3140
"My Faith Looks Up to Thee" (2 Tim, Luke)
    C576, CG407, E691, EL759, G829, P383, SA726, UM452,
    VU663
"By Gracious Powers" (2 Tim, Luke)
    E695/696, EL626, G818, N413, P342, UM517
"All Who Love and Serve Your City" (Luke)
    C670, CG674, E570/E571, EL724, G351, P413, UM433
"We Walk by Faith" (Luke)
    CG634, E209, EL635, G817, N256, P399, S2196, SH660
"Lord, When I Came into This Life" (Luke)
    N354, G691, P522
"If You Only Had Faith" ("Si tuvieras fe") (Luke)
    G176, SH132
"Bread of the World" (World Comm.)
    C387, E301, G499, N346, P502, UM624, VU461
"Una Espiga" ("Sheaves of Summer") (World Comm.)
    C396, G532, N338, UM637
"A Place at the Table" (World Comm.)
    G769, WS3149

Additional Contemporary and Modern Suggestions
"I Have a Hope" 5087587 (Lam, Pss)
"Someone Asked the Question" 1640279 (Pss)
    N523, S2144
"Come and Fill Our Hearts" ("Confitemini Domino") (Pss)
    EL538, G466, S2157
"Come to the Table of Grace" 7034746 (Pss, 2 Tim, Comm.)
    G507, WS3168
"He Who Began a Good Work in You" 15238 (2 Tim)
    S2163
"Cry of My Heart" 844980 (2 Tim)
    S2165
"He Is Able" 115420 (2 Tim)
"These Hands" 3251827 (2 Tim)
"Grace Like Rain" 3689877 (2 Tim)
"Sing Alleluia to the Lord" (2 Tim, Comm.)
    C32, S2258, SH685
"Make Us One" 695737 (World Comm.)
    AH4142, S2224
"Bind Us Together" 1228 (World Comm.)
    S2226

Vocal Solos
"Patiently Have I Waited for the Lord" (2 Tim)
    V-4   p. 24
"Here I Am" (2 Tim, Luke)
    V-1   p. 19
"One Bread, One Body" (World Comm.)
    V-3 (2)   p. 40
"The Body of the Lord" (World Comm.)
    V-8   p. 344

Anthems
"I Come with Joy" (2 Tim, World Comm.)
Peter Niedmann; MorningStar MSM-50-6088
SATB *a cappella* (https://bit.ly/50-6088)

"We Are One in the Lord" (World Comm.)
Joseph M. Martin; Hope C6187
SATB, piano, opt. flute (https://bit.ly/Hope-C6187)

Other Suggestions
Visuals: Flags, nationalities, breads
    O   Empty city, widow, tiara/chains, weeping, stag
    P   River, sitting/weeping, harp on willow
    E   Letter, praying hands, tears/joy, women, flame, risen
            Christ, trumpet, treasure, Spirit
    G   Mustard/mulberry trees, sea, plow, sheep, table/meal,
            chain/manacles
Opening Prayer: N830 (2 Tim)
Reading: C412. The Miracle of Communion (World Comm.)
Prayer: N848 (World Comm.)
Opening Prayer: WSL67. "Jesus Christ, Lord" (World Comm.)
Prayer: WSL151. "O God, we are so grateful" (2 Tim)
Call to Communion: UM621. "Be Present at Our Table, Lord"
    (World Comm.)
Communion Prayers: C774 (World Comm.)
World Communion Prayers: UM412, UM556, UM564, WSL151
Communion Response: N786 or N787 (World Comm.)
Blessing: WSL40. "May the Spirit of God" (2 Tim)
Blessing: N875 (2 Tim)
Sung Benediction: "Let the Peace of God Reign" 1839987 (2
    Tim)
Alternate Lessons: Hab 1:1-4, 2:1-4, Ps 37:1-9 (See page 4)
Theme Ideas: Call of God, Communion, Faith, Faithfulness,
    Grief, Lament

Jeremiah 29:1, 4-7

¹These are the words of the letter that the prophet Jeremiah sent from Jerusalem to the remaining elders among the exiles, and to the priests, the prophets, and all the people, whom Nebuchadnezzar had taken into exile from Jerusalem to Babylon. . . . ⁴Thus says the LORD of hosts, the God of Israel, to all the exiles whom I have sent into exile from Jerusalem to Babylon: ⁵Build houses and live in them; plant gardens and eat what they produce. ⁶Take wives and have sons and daughters; take wives for your sons, and give your daughters in marriage, that they may bear sons and daughters; multiply there, and do not decrease. ⁷But seek the welfare of the city where I have sent you into exile, and pray to the LORD on its behalf, for in its welfare you will find your welfare.

Psalm 66:1-12 (G54, N662)

¹Make a joyful noise to God, all the earth;
²   sing the glory of his name;
    give to him glorious praise.
³Say to God, "How awesome are your deeds!
    Because of your great power, your enemies cringe before you.
⁴All the earth worships you;
    they sing praises to you,
    sing praises to your name."   *[Selah]*
⁵Come and see what God has done:
    he is awesome in his deeds among mortals.
⁶He turned the sea into dry land;
    they passed through the river on foot.
There we rejoiced in him,
⁷   who rules by his might forever,
whose eyes keep watch on the nations—
    let the rebellious not exalt themselves.   *[Selah]*
⁸Bless our God, O peoples,
    let the sound of his praise be heard,
⁹who has kept us among the living,
    and has not let our feet slip.
¹⁰For you, O God, have tested us;
    you have tried us as silver is tried.
¹¹You brought us into the net;
    you laid burdens on our backs;
¹²you let people ride over our heads;
    we went through fire and through water;
yet you have brought us out to a spacious place.

2 Timothy 2:8-15

⁸Remember Jesus Christ, raised from the dead, a descendant of David—that is my gospel, ⁹for which I suffer hardship, even to the point of being chained like a criminal. But the word of God is not chained. ¹⁰Therefore I endure everything for the sake of the elect, so that they may also obtain the salvation that is in Christ Jesus, with eternal glory. ¹¹The saying is sure:
If we have died with him, we will also live with him;
¹²   if we endure, we will also reign with him;
    if we deny him, he will also deny us;
¹³   if we are faithless, he remains faithful—
    for he cannot deny himself.
¹⁴Remind them of this, and warn them before God that they are to avoid wrangling over words, which does no good but only ruins those who are listening. ¹⁵Do your best to present yourself to God as one approved by him, a worker who has no need to be ashamed, rightly explaining the word of truth.

Luke 17:11-19

¹¹On the way to Jerusalem Jesus was going through the region between Samaria and Galilee. ¹²As he entered a village, ten lepers approached him. Keeping their distance, ¹³they called out, saying, "Jesus, Master, have mercy on us!" ¹⁴When he saw them, he said to them, "Go and show yourselves to the priests." And as they went, they were made clean. ¹⁵Then one of them, when he saw that he was healed, turned back, praising God with a loud voice. ¹⁶He prostrated himself at Jesus' feet and thanked him. And he was a Samaritan. ¹⁷Then Jesus asked, "Were not ten made clean? But the other nine, where are they? ¹⁸Was none of them found to return and give praise to God except this foreigner?" ¹⁹Then he said to him, "Get up and go on your way; your faith has made you well."

Primary Hymns and Songs for the Day

"I'll Praise My Maker While I've Breath" (Luke, Pss) (O)
    C20, CG336, E429 (PD), G806, P253, UM60, VU867
        H-3   Chr-109; Org-105
        S-2   #141. Harm.
"O Christ, the Healer" (Luke)
    C503. EL610, G793, N175, P380, UM265
"Give Thanks" 20285 (Luke)
    C528, CG373, G647, S2036, SA364, SH489
"O For a Thousand Tongues to Sing" (Luke) (C)
    C5, CG332, E493, EL886, G610, N42, P466, SA89, SH439,
    UM57 (PD), VU326 (See also WS3001)
        H-3   Hbl-79; Chr-142; Desc-17; Org-12
        S-1   #33-38. Various Treatments
"All Who Love and Serve Your City" (Jer) (C)
    C670, CG674, E570/E571, EL724, G351, P413, UM433
        H-3   Chr-26, 65; Org-19
        S-1   #62. Desc.

Additional Hymn Suggestions

"Great Is Thy Faithfulness" (Jer, Pss, Luke) (O)
    AH4011, C86, CG48, EL733, G39, N423, P276, SA26, SH48,
    UM140, VU288
"Lift Every Voice and Sing" (Jer, Pss)
    AH4055, C631, CG638, E599, EL841, G339, N593, P563,
    SH36, UM519
"Heleluyan" (Pss)
    EL171, G642, P595, UM78
"Joyful, Joyful, We Adore Thee" (Pss, 2 Tim)
    C2, CG310, E376, EL836, G611, N4, P464, SA39, SH390,
    UM89 (PD), VU232
"Praise, My Soul, the King of Heaven" (Pss, Luke)
    C23, CG337, E410, EL864/865, G619/620, P478/479, SA55,
    SH418, UM66 (PD), VU240
"All People That on Earth Do Dwell" (Pss, Luke)
    C18, CG331, E377/378, EL883, G385, N7, P220, SA350,
    SH416, UM75 (PD), VU822 (Fr.)
"Jesus Shall Reign" (Pss, Luke)
    C95, CG158, E544, EL434, G265, N300, P423, SA258, SH209,
    UM157 (PD), VU330
"Jesus, the Very Thought of Thee" (2 Tim)
    C102, CG386, E642, EL754, G629, N507, P310, SA85, UM175
    (PD)
Pues Si Vivimos ("When We Are Living") (2 Tim)
    C536, CG265, EL639, G822, N499, P400, SH299, UM356,
    VU581
"O Jesus, I Have Promised" (2 Tim)
    C612, E655, EL810, G724/725, N493, P388/389, SA613,
    SH623, UM396 (PD), VU120
"Take Up Thy Cross" (2 Tim)
    E675, EL667, G718, N204, P393, SH605, UM415, VU561
"Jesus, Priceless Treasure" (2 Tim)
    E701, EL775, G830, N480 P365, UM532 (PD), VU667 and
    VU668 (Fr.)
"How Clear Is Our Vocation, Lord" (2 Tim)
    EL580, G432, P419, VU504
"God, Whose Giving Knows No Ending" (2 Tim)
    C606, CG671, G716, N565, P422
"God of the Sparrow, God of the Whale" (Luke)
    C70, EL740, G22, N32, P272, UM122, VU229
"Lord of the Dance" 78529 (Luke)
    G157, P302, SA141, UM261, VU352
"Heal Me, Hands of Jesus" (Luke)
    C504, CG541, UM262, VU621
"We Cannot Measure How You Heal" (Luke)
    CG540, G797, SH341, VU613, WS3139
"Ten Lepers Facing Constant Scorn" (Luke)
    G179
"Live Into Hope" (Luke)
    G772, P332, VU699

Additional Contemporary and Modern Suggestions

"Song of Hope" (*"Canto de Esperanza"*) 5193990 (Jer)
    G765, P432, S2186, SH721, VU424
"Your Grace Is Enough" 4477026 (Jer, Pss, Luke)
    WS3106
"My Tribute" 11218 (Pss)
    AH4080, C39, CG574, N14, SH434, UM99; V-8 p. 5. Vocal
    Solo
"Awesome God" 41099 (Pss)
    G616, S2040
"Awesome Power" 159338 (Pss)
"Come Just As You Are" 1189479 (Pss)
"Refiner's Fire" 426298 (Pss)
"All Hail King Jesus" 12877 (2 Tim)
    S2069
"I Am Crucified with Christ" 2652874 (2 Tim)
"Through It All" 18211 (2 Tim, Luke)
    C555, UM507
"Thank You, Lord" 865000 (Luke)
    AH4081, C531, SH496, UM84
"Oh Lord, You're Beautiful" 14514 (Luke)
    S2064
"I'm So Glad Jesus Lifted Me" (Luke)
    C529, EL860 (PD), N474, S2151
"People Need the Lord" 18084 (Luke)
    S2244, SA418
"I Thank You, Jesus" (Luke)
    AH4079, C116, N41, WS3037
"Grateful" 7023348 (Luke)
"You Hear" 6005063 (Luke)

Vocal Solos

"Bright and Beautiful" (Pss, Luke)
    V-3 (3)   p. 10
"Now Thank We All Our God" (Luke)
    V-6   p. 8
"I Just Came to Praise the Lord" (Luke)
    V-8   p. 294

Anthems

"Praise God with Song" (Pss, 2 Tim, Luke)
Schutz/arr. Cherwien; MorningStar MSM-50-7082
SATB *a cappella* (https://bit.ly/50-7082)

"If I Forget, Yet God Remembers" (Luke)
Daniel Pederson; Augsburg 0-8006-7805-2
SATB *a cappella* (https://bit.ly/7805-2)

Other Suggestions

Visuals:
    O   Letter, houses, garden, marriage, prayer/chain
    P   Praise, nations, awe, sea/desert, river, feet, refining,
          net, full backpack, fire/water, open space
    E   Christus Rex, chain, open manacles, cross
    G   Lepers, one prostrate, feet, praise, walking
Introit: WS3047, st. 3. "God Almighty, We Are Waiting" (Jer)
Response: C299, EL152, G576, S2275, S2277, WS3133. "Lord,
    Have Mercy" (Luke)
Prayer: C549. Thoughtful Silence (2 Tim)
Prayer of Thanksgiving: N859. Thankfulness and Hope (Luke)
Alternate Lessons: 2 Kgs 5:1-3, 7-15c; Ps 111
Theme Ideas: Faithfulness, Healing, Joy, Peace, Praise,
    Thanksgiving / Gratitude

Jeremiah 31:27-34

[27]The days are surely coming, says the LORD, when I will sow the house of Israel and the house of Judah with the seed of humans and the seed of animals. [28]And just as I have watched over them to pluck up and break down, to overthrow, destroy, and bring evil, so I will watch over them to build and to plant, says the LORD. [29]In those days they shall no longer say:

"The parents have eaten sour grapes,
    and the children's teeth are set on edge."

[30]But all shall die for their own sins; the teeth of everyone who eats sour grapes shall be set on edge.

[31]The days are surely coming, says the LORD, when I will make a new covenant with the house of Israel and the house of Judah. [32]It will not be like the covenant that I made with their ancestors when I took them by the hand to bring them out of the land of Egypt—a covenant that they broke, though I was their husband, says the LORD. [33]But this is the covenant that I will make with the house of Israel after those days, says the LORD: I will put my law within them, and I will write it on their hearts; and I will be their God, and they shall be my people. [34]No longer shall they teach one another, or say to each other, "Know the LORD," for they shall all know me, from the least of them to the greatest, says the LORD; for I will forgive their iniquity, and remember their sin no more.

Psalm 119:97-104 (G64, N701, UM840)

[97]Oh, how I love your law!
    It is my meditation all day long.
[98]Your commandment makes me wiser than my enemies,
    for it is always with me.
[99]I have more understanding than all my teachers,
    for your decrees are my meditation.
[100]I understand more than the aged,
    for I keep your precepts.
[101]I hold back my feet from every evil way,
    in order to keep your word.
[102]I do not turn away from your ordinances,
    for you have taught me.
[103]How sweet are your words to my taste,
    sweeter than honey to my mouth!
[104]Through your precepts I get understanding;
    therefore I hate every false way.

2 Timothy 3:14–4:5

[14]But as for you, continue in what you have learned and firmly believed, knowing from whom you learned it, [15]and how from childhood you have known the sacred writings that are able to instruct you for salvation through faith in Christ Jesus. [16]All scripture is inspired by God and is useful for teaching, for reproof, for correction, and for training in righteousness, [17]so that everyone who belongs to God may be proficient, equipped for every good work.

4 In the presence of God and of Christ Jesus, who is to judge the living and the dead, and in view of his appearing and his kingdom, I solemnly urge you: [2]proclaim the message; be persistent whether the time is favorable or unfavorable; convince, rebuke, and encourage, with the utmost patience in teaching. [3]For the time is coming when people will not put up with sound doctrine, but having itching ears, they will accumulate for themselves teachers to suit their own desires, [4]and will turn away from listening to the truth and wander away to myths. [5]As for you, always be sober, endure suffering, do the work of an evangelist, carry out your ministry fully.

Luke 18:1-8

[1]Then Jesus told them a parable about their need to pray always and not to lose heart. [2]He said, "In a certain city there was a judge who neither feared God nor had respect for people. [3]In that city there was a widow who kept coming to him and saying, 'Grant me justice against my opponent.' [4]For a while he refused; but later he said to himself, 'Though I have no fear of God and no respect for anyone, [5]yet because this widow keeps bothering me, I will grant her justice, so that she may not wear me out by continually coming.'" [6]And the Lord said, "Listen to what the unjust judge says. [7]And will not God grant justice to his chosen ones who cry to him day and night? Will he delay long in helping them? [8]I tell you, he will quickly grant justice to them. And yet, when the Son of Man comes, will he find faith on earth?"

Primary Hymns and Songs for the Day

"Love Divine, All Loves Excelling" (Jer) (O)
  C517, CG281, E657, EL631, G366, N43, P376, SA262,
  SH353/354, UM384 (PD), VU333
      H-3   Chr-134; Desc-18; Org-13
      S-1   #41-42. Desc. and harm.
"Here I Am, Lord" (Jer)
  C452, CG482, EL574, G69, P525, SA1002, SH608, UM593,
  VU509
      H-3   Chr-97; Org-54
"Change My Heart, O God" 1565 (Jer)
  EL801, G695, S2152, SA409, SH507
"Spirit of God, Descend upon My Heart" (Jer, Luke)
  C265, CG243, EL800, G688, N290, P326, SA290, SH277,
  UM500 (PD), VU378
"Thy Word Is a Lamp" (Pss, 2 Tim)
  C326, CG38, G458, UM601
"It's Me, It's Me, O Lord" (Luke)
  C579, N519, UM352
      H-3   Chr-177
"Seek Ye First" 1352 (Luke)
  C354, CG436, E711, G175, P333, SA675, SH126, UM405,
  VU356
"Lord, Listen to Your Children Praying" 22829 (Luke)
  C305, CG389, G469, S2193, SH577, VU400
"Lord, Speak to Me" (2 Tim, Luke) (C)
  CG503, EL676, G722, N531, P426, SA773, SH557, UM463,
  VU589

Additional Hymn Suggestions

"This Is a Day of New Beginnings" (Jer)
  C518, N417, UM383
"O Love That Wilt Not Let Me Go" (Jer)
  C540, CG631, G833, N485, P384, SA616, SH314, UM480,
  VU658
Sois la Semilla ("You Are the Seed") (Jer)
  C478, N528, UM583
"O Day of Peace That Dimly Shines" (Jer)
  C711, E597, EL711, G373, P450, UM729, VU682
"God the Sculptor of the Mountains" (Jer)
  EL736, G5, S2060
"Wonder of Wonders" (Jer, Baptism)
  C378, G489, N328, P499, S2247
"Holy Spirit, Truth Divine" (Jer, 2 Tim, Luke)
  C241, EL398, N63, P321, SA285, UM465, VU368
"Blessed Jesus, at Thy Word" (Jer, Pss, 2 Tim)
  E440, EL520, G395, N74, P454, UM596 (PD), VU500
"Wonderful Words of Life" (Pss, 2 Tim)
  C323, CG163, N319, SA434, SH549, UM600 (PD)
"O Master, Let Me Walk with Thee" (Pss, 2 Tim)
  C602, CG660, E659/E660, EL818, G738, N503, P357, SA667,
  SH612, UM430 (PD), VU560
"O Word of God Incarnate" (Pss, 2 Tim)
  C322, E632, EL514, G459, N315, P327, UM598 (PD), VU499
"Immortal, Invisible, God Only Wise" (2 Tim)
  C66, CG58, E423, EL834, G12, N1, P263, SA37, UM103 (PD),
  VU264
"Lord, You Give the Great Commission" (2 Tim) (C)
  C459, CG651, S2176, EL579, G298, P429, UM584, VU512
"Praise the Source of Faith and Learning" (2 Tim)
  N411, S2004
"Deep in the Shadows of the Past" (2 Tim)
  G50, N320, P330, S2246
"Lord of All Good" (2 Tim)
  G711, P375, VU539
"Break Thou the Bread of Life" (2 Tim, Comm.)
  C321, CG35, EL515, G460, N321, P329, SA802, SH552,
  UM599 (PD), VU501

"Be Thou My Vision" (Luke)
  C595, CG71, E488, EL793, G450, N451, P339, SA573, SH640,
  UM451, VU642
"I Will Trust in the Lord" (Luke)
  N416, UM464
"What a Friend We Have in Jesus" (Luke)
  C585, CG409, EL742, G465, N506, P403, SA795, SH585/586,
  UM526 (PD), VU661
"The Lord's Prayer" (Luke)
  C307-C310, G464, P589, S2278, SH595, UM271, WS3068-
  WS3071
"Hear My Prayer, O God" (Luke)
  G782, WS3131
"Give Me Jesus" (Luke)
  CG546, EL770, N409, SH306, WS3140

Additional Contemporary and Modern Suggestions

"Refresh My Heart" 917518 (Jer)
"The Potter's Hand" 2449771 (Jer)
"You Have Saved Us" 5548514 (Jer)
"Knowing You" 1045238 (Pss)
"Holy and Anointed One" 164361 (Pss)
"Breathe" 1874117 (Pss)
  WS3112
"Show Me Your Ways" 1675024 (Pss)
"Ancient Words" 2986399 (Pss)
"More Precious than Silver" 11335 (Pss)
  S2065
"As the Deer" 1431 (Pss)
  CG49, G626/778, S2025, SA571, VU766
"To Know You More" 1767420 (Pss)
  S2161
"Cry of My Heart" 844980 (Pss)
  S2165
"He Who Began a Good Work in You" 15238 (2 Tim)
  S2163
"Lord, Listen to Your Children" (Luke)
  EL752, S2207

Vocal Solos

"God Will Make a Way" (with "He Leadeth Me") (Jer)
  V-3 (2)   p. 9
"Lord, Listen to Your Children" (Luke)
  V-8   p. 168

Anthems

"Love Divine" (Jer)
Howard Goodall; MorningStar MSM-56-0011
SATB *divisi*, keyboard, opt. strings (https://bit.ly/56-0011)

"Thy Word Is Like a Garden, Lord" (Pss, 2 Tim)
Dan Forrest; Hal Leonard HL-08745683
SATB, piano (https://bit.ly/HL-745683)

Other Suggestions

Visuals:
  O   Sowing seeds, destruction, build/plant, torn
        document, Jer 31:33b, heart, all ages, eraser
  P   Bible, meditation, feet, Ps. 119:103, honey
  E   Child, Bible, Christ, teacher, 2 Tim. 3:16, tools, gavel
  G   Prayer, gavel, scales of justice, woman pleading
Introit: WS3047, st. 3. "God Almighty, We Are Waiting" (Jer)
Prayer Response: CG399, EL751, G471, S2200, SH311/517. "O
  Lord, Hear My Prayer" (Luke)
Alternate Lessons: Gen 32:22-31, Ps 121
Theme Ideas: Covenant, God: Wisdom, God: Word of God,
  Hope, Love, Prayer

Joel 2:23-32

²³O children of Zion, be glad
  and rejoice in the LORD your God;
for he has given the early rain for your vindication,
  he has poured down for you abundant rain,
  the early and the later rain, as before.
²⁴The threshing floors shall be full of grain,
  the vats shall overflow with wine and oil.
²⁵I will repay you for the years
  that the swarming locust has eaten,
the hopper, the destroyer, and the cutter,
  my great army, which I sent against you.
²⁶You shall eat in plenty and be satisfied,
  and praise the name of the LORD your God,
  who has dealt wondrously with you.
And my people shall never again be put to shame.
²⁷You shall know that I am in the midst of Israel,
  and that I, the LORD, am your God and there is no other.
And my people shall never again
  be put to shame.
²⁸ Then afterward
  I will pour out my spirit on all flesh;
your sons and your daughters shall prophesy,
  your old men shall dream dreams,
  and your young men shall see visions.
²⁹Even on the male and female slaves,
  in those days, I will pour out my spirit.
³⁰I will show portents in the heavens and on the earth, blood and fire and columns of smoke. ³¹The sun shall be turned to darkness, and the moon to blood, before the great and terrible day of the LORD comes. ³²Then everyone who calls on the name of the LORD shall be saved; for in Mount Zion and in Jerusalem there shall be those who escape, as the LORD has said, and among the survivors shall be those whom the LORD calls.

Psalm 65 (G38, N661, P200/201, SH492, UM789)

¹Praise is due to you,
  O God, in Zion;
and to you shall vows be performed,
² O you who answer prayer!
To you all flesh shall come.
³When deeds of iniquity overwhelm us,
  you forgive our transgressions.
⁴Happy are those whom you choose and bring near
  to live in your courts.
We shall be satisfied with the goodness of your house,
  your holy temple.
⁵By awesome deeds you answer us with deliverance,
  O God of our salvation;
you are the hope of all the ends of the earth
  and of the farthest seas.
⁶By your strength you established the mountains;
  you are girded with might.
⁷You silence the roaring of the seas,
  the roaring of their waves,
  the tumult of the peoples.
⁸Those who live at earth's farthest bounds
  are awed by your signs;
you make the gateways of the morning
  and the evening shout for joy.
⁹You visit the earth and water it,
  you greatly enrich it;
the river of God is full of water;
  you provide the people with grain,
  for so you have prepared it.
¹⁰You water its furrows abundantly,
  settling its ridges,
softening it with showers,
  and blessing its growth.
¹¹You crown the year with your bounty;
  your wagon tracks overflow with richness.
¹²The pastures of the wilderness overflow,
  the hills gird themselves with joy,
¹³the meadows clothe themselves with flocks,
  the valleys deck themselves with grain,
  they shout and sing together for joy.

2 Timothy 4:6-8, 16-18

⁶As for me, I am already being poured out as a libation, and the time of my departure has come. ⁷I have fought the good fight, I have finished the race, I have kept the faith. ⁸From now on there is reserved for me the crown of righteousness, which the Lord, the righteous judge, will give me on that day, and not only to me but also to all who have longed for his appearing. . . .

¹⁶At my first defense no one came to my support, but all deserted me. May it not be counted against them! ¹⁷But the Lord stood by me and gave me strength, so that through me the message might be fully proclaimed and all the Gentiles might hear it. So I was rescued from the lion's mouth. ¹⁸The Lord will rescue me from every evil attack and save me for his heavenly kingdom. To him be the glory forever and ever.

Luke 18:9-14

⁹He also told this parable to some who trusted in themselves that they were righteous and regarded others with contempt: ¹⁰"Two men went up to the temple to pray, one a Pharisee and the other a tax collector. ¹¹The Pharisee, standing by himself, was praying thus, 'God, I thank you that I am not like other people: thieves, rogues, adulterers, or even like this tax collector. ¹²I fast twice a week; I give a tenth of all my income.' ¹³But the tax collector, standing far off, would not even look up to heaven, but was beating his breast and saying, 'God, be merciful to me, a sinner!' ¹⁴I tell you, this man went down to his home justified rather than the other; for all who exalt themselves will be humbled, but all who humble themselves will be exalted."

Primary Hymns and Songs for the Day
"I Sing the Almighty Power of God" (Joel, Pss) (O)
    C64, G32, N12, P288 (PD), SA36
        H-3   Hbl-16, 22, 68; Chr-101; Desc-37
        S-1   #115. Harmonization
    CG19, E398, UM152 (PD)
        H-3   Hbl-44; Chr-21; Desc-40; Org-40
        S-1   #131-132. Introduction and descant
    VU231 (PD)
"The Trees of the Field" 20546 (Pss)
    G80, S2279, VU884
"Guide My Feet" (2 Tim) (O)
    CG637, G741, N497, P354, S2208, SH54
        H-3   Hbl-66; Chr-89
"We've Come This Far by Faith" (2 Tim)
    AH4042, C533, EL633, G656, SH58
"Just As I Am, Without One Plea" (1 Tim, Luke)
    C339, CG500, E693, EL592, G442, N207, P370, SA503,
    SH500, UM357 (PD), VU508
        H-3   Chr-120; Org-186
"Lord, I Want to Be a Christian" (Luke) (C)
    C589, CG507, G729, N454, P372 (PD), SH621, UM402
        H-3   Chr-130

Additional Hymn Suggestions
"Be Thou My Vision" (Joel)
    C595, CG71, E488, EL793, G450, N451, P339, SA573, SH640,
    UM451, VU642
"Spirit of God, Descend upon My Heart" (Joel)
    C265, CG243, EL800, G688, N290, P326, SA290, SH277,
    UM500 (PD), VU378
"Wind Who Makes All Winds That Blow" (Joel)
    C236, CG226, N271, P131, UM538, VU196
"O Breath of Life" (Joel)
    C250, SA818, UM543, VU202, WS3146
"Come, Holy Ghost, Our Souls Inspire" (Joel)
    E503/504, N268, G278, P125, UM651, VU201
"O Day of Peace That Dimly Shines" (Joel)
    C711, E597, EL711, G373, P450, UM729, VU682
"Spirit, Spirit of Gentleness" (Joel)
    C249, EL396, G291, N286, P319, S2120, VU375 (Fr.)
"Deep in the Shadows of the Past" (Joel)
    G50, N320, P330, S2246
"How Great Thou Art" (Pss, Luke)
    AH4015, C33, CG323, EL856, G625, N35, P467, SA49, SH14,
    UM77, VU238 (Fr.)
"Fight the Good Fight" (2 Tim)
    E552, G846, P307 (PD), SA952, VU674
"He Leadeth Me" (2 Tim)
    C545, CG68, SA645, SH304, UM128 (PD), VU657
"Leaning on the Everlasting Arms" (2 Tim)
    C560, CG640, EL774, G837, N471, SA906, UM133
"Jesus, Lover of My Soul" (2 Tim, Luke)
    C542, CG406, E699, G440, N546, P303, SA257, SH542/543,
    UM479, VU669
"Before I Take the Body of My Lord" (Luke, Comm.)
    C391, G428, VU462
"There's a Wideness in God's Mercy" (Luke)
    C73, CG41, E470, EL587/88G435, N23, P298, SH526,
    UM121, VU271
"Pass Me Not, O Gentle Savior" (Luke)
    AH4107, N551, SA782, UM351 (PD), VU665
"Have Thine Own Way, Lord" (Luke)
    C588, CG493, SA705, SH626, UM382 (PD)
"I Am Thine, O Lord" (Luke)
    AH4087, C601, CG504, N455, SA586, UM419 (PD)
"Forgive Us, Lord" ("Perdón, Señor") 3409466 (Luke)
    G431, S2134, SH505
"Gather Us In" (Luke)
    C284, EL532, G401, S2236, SH393

Additional Contemporary and Modern Suggestions
"The Power of Your Love" 917491 (Joel)
"Open the Eyes of My Heart" 2298355 (Joel)
    G452, SA270, SH378, WS3008
"I Will Call upon the Lord" 11263 (Joel)
    G621, S2002
"Open Our Eyes, Lord" 1572 (Joel)
    CG392, S2086, SA386, SH562
"Shout to the Lord" 1406918 (Pss)
    CG348, EL821, S2074, SA264, SH426
"Awesome God" 41099 (Pss)
    G616, S2040
"How Great Is Our God" 4348399 (Pss)
    CG322, SH458, WS3003
"He Who Began a Good Work in You" 15238 (2 Tim)
"You Are My All in All" 825356 (2 Tim)
    CG571, G519, SH335, WS3040
"Shout to the North" 1562261 (2 Tim)
    G319, SA1009, WS3042
"I Will Never Be (the Same Again)" 1874911 (2 Tim, Luke)
"Came to My Rescue" 4705190 (2 Tim, Luke)
"Grace Alone" 2335524 (2 Tim, Luke)
    CG43, S2162, SA699.
"Something Beautiful" 18060 (Luke)
"I'm So Glad Jesus Lifted Me" (Luke)
    C529, EL860 (PD), N474, S2151
"Hungry" ("Falling on My Knees") 2650364 (Luke)
"Take, O Take Me as I Am" 4562041 (Luke)
    EL814, G698, SH620, WS3119

Vocal Solos
"Spirit of God" (Joel)
    V-8   p. 170
"Stan'in' In De Need of Prayer" (Luke)
    V-7   p. 40

Anthems
"Maya's Prayer for Peace" (Joel)
Tom Trenney; MorningStar MSM-50-6087
SATB, piano (https://bit.ly/50-6087)

"O, My God, Bestow Thy Tender Mercy" (Luke)
Pergolesi/Hopson; Carl Fischer CM7974
2-part mixed, keyboard (https://bit.ly/CM-7974)

Other Suggestions
Visuals:
    O   Rain, thresh/grain, wine/oil, locusts, plenty, people, manacles, blood/fire/smoke, eclipse, red moon
    P   Praise, worship, sea/mountain, storm/calm, sunrise/sunset, rain, river, harvest/wagon tracks, hills, flocks
    E   Spilled wine, boxing gloves, open Bible, scales
    G   Two men (proud/humble), hands (raised/beating chest), Luke 18:14b
Introit: WS3046. "Come, O Redeemer, Come" (Luke)
Call to Confession: N833 (Luke)
Prayer of Confession: N834 or C772 (Luke)
Response: C299, EL152, G576, S2275, S2277, WS3133. "Lord, Have Mercy" (Luke)
Sung Benediction: "Let the Peace of God Reign" 1839987 (2 Tim)
Alternate Lessons: Jer 14:7-10, 19-22, Ps 84:1-7
Theme Ideas: Discipleship / Following God, Faithfulness, Holy Spirit, Humility, Joy, Praise

Habakkuk 1:1-4; 2:1-4

[1]The oracle that the prophet Habakkuk saw.
[2]O Lord, how long shall I cry for help,
      and you will not listen?
Or cry to you "Violence!"
      and you will not save?
[3]Why do you make me see wrong-doing
      and look at trouble?
Destruction and violence are before me;
      strife and contention arise.
[4]So the law becomes slack
      and justice never prevails.
The wicked surround the righteous—
      therefore judgment comes forth perverted.
. . . .
2 I will stand at my watchpost,
      and station myself on the rampart;
I will keep watch to see what he will say to me,
      and what he will answer concerning my complaint.
[2]Then the Lord answered me and said:
Write the vision;
      make it plain on tablets,
      so that a runner may read it.
[3]For there is still a vision for the appointed time;
      it speaks of the end, and does not lie.
If it seems to tarry, wait for it;
      it will surely come, it will not delay.
[4]Look at the proud!
      Their spirit is not right in them,
      but the righteous live by their faith.

Psalm 119:137-144 (G64, N701, UM840)

[137]You are righteous, O Lord,
      and your judgments are right.
[138]You have appointed your decrees in righteousness
      and in all faithfulness.
[139]My zeal consumes me
      because my foes forget your words.
[140]Your promise is well tried,
      and your servant loves it.
[141]I am small and despised,
      yet I do not forget your precepts.
[142]Your righteousness is an everlasting righteousness,
      and your law is the truth.
[143]Trouble and anguish have come upon me,
      but your commandments are my delight.
[144]Your decrees are righteous forever;
      give me understanding that I may live.

2 Thessalonians 1:1-4, 11-12

[1]Paul, Silvanus, and Timothy, To the church of the Thessalonians in God our Father and the Lord Jesus Christ:
[2]Grace to you and peace from God our Father and the Lord Jesus Christ.
[3]We must always give thanks to God for you, brothers and sisters, as is right, because your faith is growing abundantly, and the love of every one of you for one another is increasing. [4]Therefore we ourselves boast of you among the churches of God for your steadfastness and faith during all your persecutions and the afflictions that you are enduring. . . .
[11]To this end we always pray for you, asking that our God will make you worthy of his call and will fulfill by his power every good resolve and work of faith, [12]so that the name of our Lord Jesus may be glorified in you, and you in him, according to the grace of our God and the Lord Jesus Christ.

Luke 19:1-10

[1]He entered Jericho and was passing through it. [2]A man was there named Zacchaeus; he was a chief tax collector and was rich. [3]He was trying to see who Jesus was, but on account of the crowd he could not, because he was short in stature. [4]So he ran ahead and climbed a sycamore tree to see him, because he was going to pass that way. [5]When Jesus came to the place, he looked up and said to him, "Zacchaeus, hurry and come down; for I must stay at your house today." [6]So he hurried down and was happy to welcome him. [7]All who saw it began to grumble and said, "He has gone to be the guest of one who is a sinner." [8]Zacchaeus stood there and said to the Lord, "Look, half of my possessions, Lord, I will give to the poor; and if I have defrauded anyone of anything, I will pay back four times as much." [9]Then Jesus said to him, "Today salvation has come to this house, because he too is a son of Abraham. [10]For the Son of Man came to seek out and to save the lost."

Primary Hymns and Songs for the Day

"O God of Every Nation" (Hab) (O)
> C680, CG46, E607, EL713, G756, P289, UM435, VU677
> H-3   Chr-63, 145; Org-102

"Be Thou My Vision" (Hab)
> C595, CG71, E488, EL793, G450, N451, P339, SA573, SH640, UM451, VU642
> H-3   Hbl-15, 48; Chr-36; Org-153
> S-1   #319. Arr. for organ/voices in canon

"Lord, Be Glorified" (2 Thess)
> EL744, G468, S2150, SA593, SH420

"I Am Thine, O Lord" (Luke) (C)
> AH4087, C601, CG504, N455, SA586, UM419 (PD)

Additional Hymn Suggestions

"A Mighty Fortress Is Our God" (Reformation) (O)
> C65, CG418, E687/688, EL503/504/505, G275, N439/440, P259/260, SA1, SH651, UM110 (PD), VU261/262/263

"Be Still, My Soul" (Hab)
> C566, CG57, G819, N488, SH330, UM534, VU652

"Let All Mortal Flesh Keep Silence" (Hab)
> C124, CG81, E324, EL490, G347, N345, P5, UM626 (PD), VU473 (Fr.)

"O Day of God, Draw Nigh" (Hab)
> C700, E601, N611, P452, UM730 (PD), VU688/689 (Fr.)

"O Holy City, Seen of John" (Hab)
> E582/583, G374, N613, P453, UM726, VU709

La Palabra Del Señor Es Recta ("Righteous and Just Is the Word of the Lord") (Pss)
> G40, UM107, SH4

"We'll Understand It Better By and By" (Hab, 2 Thess)
> N444, UM525 (PD)

"I Love Thy Kingdom, Lord" (2 Thess)
> C274, CG262, E524, G310, N312, P441, UM540

"Blest Be the Tie that Binds" (2 Thess)
> C433, CG267, EL656, G306, N393, P438, SA812, SH701, UM557 (PD), VU602

"How Blest Are They Who Trust in Christ" (2 Thess)
> C646, N365, UM654

"Stand Up and Bless the Lord" (2 Thess)
> CG299, P491, SA391, UM662 (PD)

"O Jesus, I Have Promised" (2 Thess, Luke)
> C612, E655, EL810, G724/725, N493, P388/389, SA613, SH623, UM396 (PD), VU120

"Lord Jesus, Think on Me" (Luke)
> E641, EL599 (PD), G417, P301, VU607

"Come, Ye Sinners, Poor and Needy" (Luke)
> CG471, G415, UM340

"Amazing Grace" (Luke)
> AH4091, C546, CG587, E671, EL779, G649, N547/548, P280, SA453, SH523, UM378 (PD), VU266 (Fr.)

"Have Thine Own Way, Lord" (Luke, Stewardship)
> C588, CG493, SA705, SH626, UM382 (PD)

"This Is a Day of New Beginnings" (Luke, Comm.)
> C518, N417, UM383

"Jesus Calls Us" (Luke)
> C337, CG486, E549/550/551, EL696, G720, N171/172, SA653, SH604, UM398, VU562

"Take My Life, and Let It Be" (Luke, Stewardship)
> C609, CG490, E707, EL583/EL685, G697, P391, N448, SA623, SH627/628, UM399 (PD), VU506

Cuando el Pobre ("When the Poor Ones") (Luke)
> C662, EL725, G762, P407, SH240, UM434, VU702

"I Come with Joy" (Luke, Comm.)
> C420, CG456, E304, EL482, G515, N349, P507, SH682, UM617, VU477

"The Summons" ("Will You Come and Follow Me") (Luke)
> CG473, EL798, G726, S2130, SA695, SH598, VU567

"Somebody's Knockin' at Your Door" (Luke)
> G728, P382, SH597, WS3095

"We Give Thee but Thine Own" (Luke)
> C382, EL686, G708, N785, P428, SH643, VU543

Additional Contemporary and Modern Suggestions

"Hungry" ("Falling on My Knees") 2650364 (Hab, Pss, Luke)

"Thy Word Is a Lamp" 14301 (Pss)
> C326, CG38, G458, UM601

"To Know You More" 1767420 (Pss)

"Show Me Your Ways" 1675024 (Pss)

"Ancient Words" 2986399 (Pss)

"Cry of My Heart" 844980 (Pss, Luke)

"He Who Began a Good Work in You" 15238 (2 Thess)

"Lord, Be Glorified" 26368 (2 Thess)
> EL744, G468, S2150, SA593, SH420

"Be Glorified" 429226 (2 Thess)

"Be Glorified" 2732646 (2 Thess)

"Take My Life" 1617154 (2 Thess, Luke)

"Give Thanks" 20285 (2 Thess, Luke)
> C528, CG373, G647, S2036, SA364, SH489

"I'm So Glad Jesus Lifted Me" (Luke)
> C529, EL860 (PD), N474, S2151

"Something Beautiful" 18060 (Luke)

"Shout to the North" 1562261 (Luke)
> G319, SA1009, WS3042

"Amazing Grace" ("My Chains Are Gone") 4768151 (Luke)

"We Fall Down" 2437367 (Luke, All Saints)
> G368, WS3187

"I Will Never Be (the Same Again)" 1874911 (Luke)

"Everyday" 2798154 (Luke)

"Salvation Is Here" 4451327 (Luke)

"Grace Like Rain" 3689877 (Luke)

"Across the Lands" 3709898 (Luke)
> SH654, WS3032

Vocal Solos

"Be Thou My Vision" (Hab)
> V-6   p. 13

"Here I Am" (1 Thess, Luke)
> V-1   p. 19

Anthems

"Be Thou My Vision" (Hab)
Mark Miller, MorningStar MSM-50-6164
SATB, piano (https://bit.ly/50-6164)

"Amazing Grace" (Luke)
Arr. Sandra Eithun; Choristers Guild CGA-1269
Unison, piano (https://bit.ly/CGA1269)

Other Suggestions

The scriptures and service ideas from Nov. 1 may also be used on this day or next Sunday.

Visuals:
> **O**   Praying hands, overturned scales, tower, tablets
> **P**   Open Bible, ten commandments
> **E**   Letter, embrace, love, persecution, prayer
> **G**   Tax form, small man (running, climbing tree), 1/2, 4x, Jesus, Luke 19:9a
> Reformation Sunday: Luther, reformers, 95 theses

Introit: WS3047, st. 3 "God Almighty, We Are Waiting" (Hab)

Sung Benediction: "Let the Peace of God Reign" 1839987 (2 Thess)

Alternate Lessons: Isa 1:10-18, Ps 32:1-7

Theme Ideas: Discipleship / Following God, Faithfulness, Lament, Repentance, Stewardship, Vision, Waiting

Daniel 7:1-3, 15-18

[1]In the first year of King Belshazzar of Babylon, Daniel had a dream and visions of his head as he lay in bed. Then he wrote down the dream: [2]I, Daniel, saw in my vision by night the four winds of heaven stirring up the great sea, [3]and four great beasts came up out of the sea, different from one another. . . .

[15]As for me, Daniel, my spirit was troubled within me, and the visions of my head terrified me. [16]I approached one of the attendants to ask him the truth concerning all this. So he said that he would disclose to me the interpretation of the matter: [17]'As for these four great beasts, four kings shall arise out of the earth. [18]But the holy ones of the Most High shall receive the kingdom and possess the kingdom for ever—for ever and ever.'

Psalm 149 (G550, N722, P257)

[1]Praise the LORD!
Sing to the LORD a new song,
　　his praise in the assembly of the faithful.
[2]Let Israel be glad in its Maker;
　　let the children of Zion rejoice in their King.
[3]Let them praise his name with dancing,
　　making melody to him with tambourine and lyre.
[4]For the LORD takes pleasure in his people;
　　he adorns the humble with victory.
[5]Let the faithful exult in glory;
　　let them sing for joy on their couches.
[6]Let the high praises of God be in their throats
　　and two-edged swords in their hands,
[7]to execute vengeance on the nations
　　and punishment on the peoples,
[8]to bind their kings with fetters
　　and their nobles with chains of iron,
[9]to execute on them the judgment decreed.
　　This is glory for all his faithful ones.
Praise the LORD!

Ephesians 1:11-23

[11]In Christ we have also obtained an inheritance, having been destined according to the purpose of him who accomplishes all things according to his counsel and will, [12]so that we, who were the first to set our hope on Christ, might live for the praise of his glory. [13]In him you also, when you had heard the word of truth, the gospel of your salvation, and had believed in him, were marked with the seal of the promised Holy Spirit; [14]this is the pledge of our inheritance towards redemption as God's own people, to the praise of his glory. [15]I have heard of your faith in the Lord Jesus and your love toward all the saints, and for this reason [16]I do not cease to give thanks for you as I remember you in my prayers. [17]I pray that the God of our Lord Jesus Christ, the Father of glory, may give you a spirit of wisdom and revelation as you come to know him, [18]so that, with the eyes of your heart enlightened, you may know what is the hope to which he has called you, what are the riches of his glorious inheritance among the saints, [19]and what is the immeasurable greatness of his power for us who believe, according to the working of his great power. [20]God put this power to work in Christ when he raised him from the dead and seated him at his right hand in the heavenly places, [21]far above all rule and authority and power and dominion, and above every name that is named, not only in this age but also in the age to come. [22]And he has put all things under his feet and has made him the head over all things for the church, [23]which is his body, the fullness of him who fills all in all.

Luke 6:20-31

[20]Then he looked up at his disciples and said:
"Blessed are you who are poor,
　　for yours is the kingdom of God.
[21]"Blessed are you who are hungry now,
　　for you will be filled.
"Blessed are you who weep now,
　　for you will laugh.
[22]"Blessed are you when people hate you, and when they exclude you, revile you, and defame you on account of the Son of Man. [23]Rejoice on that day and leap for joy, for surely your reward is great in heaven; for that is what their ancestors did to the prophets.
[24]"But woe to you who are rich,
　　for you have received your consolation.
[25]"Woe to you who are full now,
　　for you will be hungry.
"Woe to you who are laughing now,
　　for you will mourn and weep.
[26]"Woe to you when all speak well of you, for that is what their ancestors did to the false prophets.
[27]"But I say to you that listen, Love your enemies, do good to those who hate you, [28]bless those who curse you, pray for those who abuse you. [29]If anyone strikes you on the cheek, offer the other also; and from anyone who takes away your coat do not withhold even your shirt.[30]Give to everyone who begs from you; and if anyone takes away your goods, do not ask for them again. [31]Do to others as you would have them do to you."

Primary Hymns and Songs for the Day
"Come, Thou Almighty King" (Dan) (O)
  C27, CG2, E365, EL408, G2, N275, P139, SA283, SH388, UM61 (PD), VU314
    H-3   Hbl-28, 49, 53; Chr-56; Desc-57; Org-63
    S-1   #185-186. Desc. and harm.
"My Hope Is Built" (Eph)
  AH4105, C537, CG590, EL596/597, G353, N403, P379, SA662, SH324, UM368 (PD)
    H-3   Chr-191
    S-2   #171-172. Trumpet and vocal desc.
"I Sing a Song of the Saints of God" (All Saints)
  E293, G730, N295, P364, UM712 (PD)
"For All the Saints" (Dan, Eph) (C)
  C637, CG567, E287, EL422, G326, N299, P526, SA253, SH231, UM711 (PD), VU705
    H-3   Hbl-58; Chr-65; Org-152
    S-1   #314-318. Various treatments

Additional Hymn Suggestions
"Immortal, Invisible, God Only Wise" (Dan) (O)
  C66, CG58, E423, EL834, G12, N1, P263, SA37, UM103 (PD), VU264
"The God of Abraham Praise" (Dan)
  C24, CG45, E401, EL831, G49, N24, P488, SH50, UM116 (PD), VU255
"Give Thanks for Those Whose Faith Is Firm" (Dan)
  EL428, G731
Cantad al Señor ("O Sing to the Lord") (Pss)
  CG328, EL822, G637, P472, SH429, VU241
"Praise to the Lord, the Almighty" (Dan, Pss) (O)
  C25, CG319, E390, EL858 (PD) and 859, G35, N22, P482, SA56, SH453, UM139, VU220 (Fr.) and VU221
"Open My Eyes, That I May See" (Pss, Eph)
  C586, CG395, G451, P324, SH583, UM454, VU371
"Holy, Holy, Holy" (Eph)
  C4, CG1, E362, EL413, G1, N277, P138, SA31, SH450, UM64/65, VU315
"Holy God, We Praise Thy Name" (Eph)
  CG9, E366, EL414 (PD), G4, N276, P460, SH431, UM79, VU894 (Fr.)
"At the Name of Jesus" (Eph)
  CG424, E435, EL416, G264, P148, SA74, SH657, UM168, VU335
"Hope of the World" (Eph)
  C538, E472, G734, N46, P360, UM178, VU215
"Come, Share the Lord" (Eph, Comm.)
  C408, CG459, G510, S2269, VU469
"Take, O Take Me as I Am" 4562041 (Eph)
  EL814, G698, SH620, WS3119
"Give Me Jesus" (Eph, All Saints)
  CG546, EL770, N409, SH306, WS3140
"If Thou But Suffer God to Guide Thee" (Eph, Luke)
  C565, CG76, E635, EL769, G816, N410, P282, SA40, SH326, UM142 (PD), VU285 (Fr.) and VU286
"Lift Every Voice and Sing" (Eph, Luke)
  AH4055, C631, CG638, E599, EL841, G339, N593, P563, SH36, UM519
"Faith of Our Fathers" (Eph, Luke)
  C635, CG645, EL812/813, N381, UM710 (PD), VU580
"Lord, I Want to be a Christian" (Luke, All Saints)
  C589, CG507, G729, N454, P372 (PD), SH621, UM402
"How Firm a Foundation" (Luke)
  C618, CG425, E636/637, EL796, G463, N407, P361, SA804, SH291, UM529 (PD), VU660
"How Lovely, Lord, How Lovely" (All Saints)
  C285, CG50, G402, P207, S2042, VU801

"Deep in the Shadows of the Past" (All Saints)
  G50, N320, P330, S2246
"As We Gather at Your Table" (All Saints, Comm.)
  EL522, N332, S2268, SH411, VU457
"For the Bread Which You Have Broken" (All Saints, Comm.)
  C411, E340/E341, EL494, G516, P508/P509, UM614/UM615, VU470
"Rejoice in God's Saints" (All Saints)
  C476, EL418, G732, UM708
"By All Your Saints Still Striving" (All Saints)
  EL420, G325

Additional Contemporary and Modern Suggestions
"There's Something About That Name" 14064 (Dan)
  C115, SA80, UM171
"I Could Sing of Your Love Forever" 1043199 (Pss)
"Clap Your Hands" 806674 (Pss)
"Someone Asked the Question" 1640279 (Pss, All Saints)
  N523, S2144
"I Will Enter His Gates" 1493 (Pss)
  S2270, SA337
"Sing Unto the Lord a New Song" 571215 (Pss)
"I Will Celebrate" 21239 (Pss)
"Let Everything That Has Breath" 2430979 (Pss)
"Song of Hope" ("Heaven Come Down") 5111477 (Eph)
"Open the Eyes of My Heart" 2298355 (Eph)
  G452, SA270, SH378, WS3008
"Forever" 3148428 (Eph)
  CG53, SA363, WS3023
"Give Thanks" 20285 (Luke)
  C528, CG373, G647, S2036, SA364, SH489
"Foundation" 706151 (Luke)
"We Fall Down" 2437367 (All Saints)
  G368, WS3187
"Go in Peace" 451022 (All Saints)

Vocal Solos
"Deep River" (All Saints)
  V-3 (1)   p. 4
"Borning Cry" (All Saints, Memorial)
  V-5 (1)   p. 10
"How Long Train Been Gone" (All Saints)
  V-7   p. 17

Anthems
"Bienaventurados" ("Blessed and Beloved") (Luke)
Lourdes C. Montgomery; OCP 30143741
SATB, keyboard, guitar (https://bit.ly/30143741)

"Saints Bound for Heaven" (All Saints)
arr. Parker/Shaw; Lawson-Gould LG00911
SATB *a cappella* (https://bit.ly/LG00911)

Other Suggestions
These scriptures and ideas may be used on Nov 6.
Visuals: Pictures of deceased members
  O   Storm, bed, dreamscape, 4 beasts, 4 crowns, terror
  P   Praise, new song, assembly, dance, instruments
  E   Will, Christ, Bible, seal, flames/dove, jewelry box
  G   Feeding/poor, smile through tears, leaping, prayer, turned cheek, shirt/coat, giving, warning
Greeting: C825 (Luke)
Prayer: UM713 or WSL44 (All Saints)
Litany for Reading Names: WSL45 (All Saints)
Response: WS3010. "Sing of the Lord's Goodness" (Pss, All Saints)
Theme Ideas: Beatitudes/Blessings, Hope, Praise, Saints

Haggai 1:15b–2:9

¹⁵In the second year of King Darius,

2 in the seventh month, on the twenty-first day of the month, the word of the Lord came by the prophet Haggai, saying: ²Speak now to Zerubbabel son of Shealtiel, governor of Judah, and to Joshua son of Jehozadak, the high priest, and to the remnant of the people, and say, ³Who is left among you that saw this house in its former glory? How does it look to you now? Is it not in your sight as nothing? ⁴Yet now take courage, O Zerubbabel, says the Lord; take courage, O Joshua, son of Jehozadak, the high priest; take courage, all you people of the land, says the Lord; work, for I am with you, says the Lord of hosts, ⁵according to the promise that I made you when you came out of Egypt. My spirit abides among you; do not fear. ⁶For thus says the Lord of hosts: Once again, in a little while, I will shake the heavens and the earth and the sea and the dry land; ⁷and I will shake all the nations, so that the treasure of all nations shall come, and I will fill this house with splendor, says the Lord of hosts. ⁸The silver is mine, and the gold is mine, says the Lord of hosts. ⁹The latter splendor of this house shall be greater than the former, says the Lord of hosts; and in this place I will give prosperity, says the Lord of hosts.

Psalm 145:1-5, 17-21 (G42/270/622, N718, P251/252, UM857)

¹I will extol you, my God and King,
   and bless your name forever and ever.
²Every day I will bless you,
   and praise your name forever and ever.
³Great is the Lord, and greatly to be praised;
   his greatness is unsearchable.
⁴One generation shall laud your works to another,
   and shall declare your mighty acts.
⁵On the glorious splendor of your majesty,
   and on your wondrous works, I will meditate.

. . . .

¹⁷The Lord is just in all his ways,
   and kind in all his doings.
¹⁸The Lord is near to all who call on him,
   to all who call on him in truth.
¹⁹He fulfills the desire of all who fear him;
   he also hears their cry, and saves them.
²⁰The Lord watches over all who love him,
   but all the wicked he will destroy.
²¹My mouth will speak the praise of the Lord,
   and all flesh will bless his holy name forever and ever.

2 Thessalonians 2:1-5, 13-17

¹As to the coming of our Lord Jesus Christ and our being gathered together to him, we beg you, brothers and sisters, ²not to be quickly shaken in mind or alarmed, either by spirit or by word or by letter, as though from us, to the effect that the day of the Lord is already here. ³Let no one deceive you in any way; for that day will not come unless the rebellion comes first and the lawless one is revealed, the one destined for destruction. ⁴He opposes and exalts himself above every so-called god or object of worship, so that he takes his seat in the temple of God, declaring himself to be God. ⁵Do you not remember that I told you these things when I was still with you? . . .

¹³But we must always give thanks to God for you, brothers and sisters beloved by the Lord, because God chose you as the first fruits for salvation through sanctification by the Spirit and through belief in the truth. ¹⁴For this purpose he called you through our proclamation of the good news, so that you may obtain the glory of our Lord Jesus Christ. ¹⁵So then, brothers and sisters, stand firm and hold fast to the traditions that you were taught by us, either by word of mouth or by our letter.

¹⁶Now may our Lord Jesus Christ himself and God our Father, who loved us and through grace gave us eternal comfort and good hope, ¹⁷comfort your hearts and strengthen them in every good work and word.

Luke 20:27-38

²⁷Some Sadducees, those who say there is no resurrection, came to him ²⁸and asked him a question, "Teacher, Moses wrote for us that if a man's brother dies, leaving a wife but no children, the man shall marry the widow and raise up children for his brother. ²⁹Now there were seven brothers; the first married, and died childless; ³⁰then the second ³¹and the third married her, and so in the same way all seven died childless. ³²Finally the woman also died. ³³In the resurrection, therefore, whose wife will the woman be? For the seven had married her." ³⁴Jesus said to them, "Those who belong to this age marry and are given in marriage; ³⁵but those who are considered worthy of a place in that age and in the resurrection from the dead neither marry nor are given in marriage. ³⁶Indeed they cannot die anymore, because they are like angels and are children of God, being children of the resurrection. ³⁷And the fact that the dead are raised Moses himself showed, in the story about the bush, where he speaks of the Lord as the God of Abraham, the God of Isaac, and the God of Jacob. ³⁸Now he is God not of the dead, but of the living; for to him all of them are alive."

Primary Hymns and Songs for the Day

"Come, Ye Faithful, Raise the Strain" (2 Thess, Luke) (O)
C215, CG218, E199, EL363, G234, N230, P115, UM315 (PD), VU165
- H-3   Hbl-53; Chr-57; Desc-94; Org-141
- S-2   #161. Descant

"God Is Here" (2 Thess, Luke) (O)
C280, CG298, EL526, G409, N70, P461, UM660, VU389
- H-3   Hbl-61; Chr-132; Org-2
- S-1   #4-5. Instrumental and vocal descants

"Standing on the Promises" (Hag, Luke)
AH4057, C552, CG625, G838, SA522, SH45, UM374 (PD)
- H-3   Chr-177; Org-117

"I Love the Lord" 1168957 (Pss)
CG613, G799, P362, N511, SH343, VU617, WS3142

"O Master, Let Me Walk with Thee" (2 Thess)
C602, CG660, E659/E660, EL818, G738, N503, P357, SA667, SH612, UM430 (PD), VU560
- H-3   Hbl-81; Chr-147; Desc-74; Org-87
- S-2   #118. Descant

Pues Si Vivimos ("When We Are Living") (Luke)
C536, CG265, EL639, G822, N499, P400, SH299, UM356, VU581

"Thine Be the Glory" (Luke) (C)
C218, CG222, EL376, G238, N253, P122, SA276, SH192, UM308, VU173 (Fr.)
- H-3   Hbl-98; Chr-195; Desc-59
- S-1   #190. Arrangement
- S-2   #95. Various treatments and harmonizations

Additional Hymn Suggestions

"Glorious Things of Thee Are Spoken" (Hag)
C709, CG282, E522/523, EL647, G81, N307, P446, SA535, UM731 (PD)

"God of the Ages" (Hag, Luke)
C725, CG62, E718, G331, N592, P262, SA19, UM698

"My Lord, What a Morning" (Hag, 2 Thess)
C708, EL438 (PD), G352, P449, SH356, UM719, VU708

"O God, Our Help in Ages Past" (Hag, Pss) (C)
C67, CG566, E680, EL632, G687, N25, P210, SA47, SH41, UM117 (PD), VU806

"Let All Things Now Living" (Pss, Luke)
C717, CG379, EL881, G37, P554, S2008, SH23, VU242

"Now Thank We All Our God" (2 Thess)
C715, CG371, E396/397, EL839/840, G643, N419, P555, SA45, SH485, UM102 (PD), VU236 (Fr.)

"Holy God, We Praise Thy Name" (2 Thess)
CG9, E366, EL414 (PD), G4, N276, P460, SH431, UM79, VU894 (Fr.)

"O Love That Wilt Not Let Me Go" (2 Thess)
C540, CG631, G833, N485, P384, SA616, SH314, UM480, VU658

"How Firm a Foundation" (2 Thess)
C618, CG425, E636/637, EL796, G463, N407, P361, SA804, SH291, UM529 (PD), VU660

"I Want Jesus to Walk with Me" (2 Thess)
C627, CG635, EL325, G775, N490, P363, SH135, UM521

"Loving Spirit" (2 Thess)
C244, EL397, G293, P323, S2123, VU387

"Sing Praise to God Who Reigns Above" (Luke)
C6, CG315, E408, EL871, G645, N6, UM126 (PD), VU216

"Sent Forth by God's Blessing" (Luke)
CG519, EL547, N76, SH715, UM664, VU481

Additional Contemporary and Modern Suggestions

"Hosanna" 4785835 (Hag)
SH361, WS3188

"Waiting Here for You" 5925663 (Hag, Pss, 2 Thess)

"Blessed Be the Name" 265239 (Pss)

"Praise You" 863806 (Pss)

"I Sing Praises to Your Name" 17061 (Pss)

"He Is Exalted" 17827 (Pss)
AH4082, CG342, S2070, SH423

"God Is Good All the Time" 1729073 (Pss)

"You Are Good" 3383788 (Pss)
AH4018, SH455, WS3014

"I Extol You" 18307 (Pss)

"I Will Celebrate" 21239 (Pss)

"Awesome Is the Lord Most High" 4674159 (Pss)

"Lord, I Lift Your Name on High" 117947 (Pss, Luke)
AH4071, CG606, EL857, S2088, SA379, SH205

"Lord, Be Glorified" 26368 (2 Thess)
EL744, G468, S2150, SA593, SH420

"Give Thanks" 20285 (2 Thess)
C528, CG373, G647, S2036, SA364, SII489

"Here Is Bread, Here Is Wine" 983717 (2 Thess, Comm.)
EL483, S2266

"Wait for the Lord" (2 Thess)
CG644, EL262, G90, SH580, VU22, WS3049

"Today Is the Day" 5200924 (2 Thess)

"Grace Like Rain" 3689877 (2 Thess)

"Foundation" 706151 (2 Thess)

"Spirit of the Living God" 23488 (2 Thess, Luke)
C259, CG233, G288, N283, P322, SA312/313, SH555, UM393, VU376, S-1#212 Vocal desc. idea

"Alive Forever, Amen" 4190176 (Luke)

Vocal Solos

"Thus Saith the Lord" (Hag)
V-2

"Patiently Have I Waited for the Lord" (Hag, 2 Thess)
V-4   p. 24

"Courage, My Heart" (Hag, 2 Thess)
V-9   p. 20

"Redeeming Grace" (2 Thess)
V-4   p. 47

Anthems

"Great Is the Lord" (Pss)
Rosephanye Powell; Gentry 00145523
SATB, percussion (https://bit.ly/G-45523)

"Hark, I Hear the Harps Eternal" (Luke, All Saints)
Arr. Neil Harmon; MorningStar MSM-50-5050
SATB, piano, opt. chamber orchestra (https://bit.ly/50-5050)

Other Suggestions

The scriptures and service ideas from Nov. 1 may be used today as All Saints Sunday.
Daylight Savings Time ends today.
Visuals:
- **O**   Church in ruins/restored, Exodus, quake, sea/desert
- **P**   Crown, teach/learn, light, natural wonders, praise
- **E**   Second Coming, fruit, preaching, letter, 2 Thess 2:16-17
- **G**   Coffin, wedding, seven brothers, bride, resurrection, children in white robes, burning bush, Luke 20:38a

Opening Prayer: N831 (Hag, Pss)
Prayer: UM721. Christ the King (Hag, 2 Thess)
Blessing: N872 (Hag) or C776 (2 Thess)
Alternate scriptures: Job 19:23-27a, Ps 17:1-9
Theme Ideas: Courage, Faithfulness, God: Faithfulness, Resurrection, Saints, Waiting

Isaiah 65:17-25

17For I am about to create new heavens
and a new earth;
the former things shall not be remembered
or come to mind.
18But be glad and rejoice forever
in what I am creating;
for I am about to create Jerusalem as a joy,
and its people as a delight.
19I will rejoice in Jerusalem,
and delight in my people;
no more shall the sound of weeping be heard in it,
or the cry of distress.
20No more shall there be in it
an infant that lives but a few days,
or an old person who does not live out a lifetime;
for one who dies at a hundred years will be considered a youth,
and one who falls short of a hundred will be considered accursed.
21They shall build houses and inhabit them;
they shall plant vineyards and eat their fruit.
22They shall not build and another inhabit;
they shall not plant and another eat;
for like the days of a tree shall the days of my people be,
and my chosen shall long enjoy the work of their hands.
23They shall not labor in vain,
or bear children for calamity;
for they shall be offspring blessed by the Lord—
and their descendants as well.
24Before they call I will answer,
while they are yet speaking I will hear.
25The wolf and the lamb shall feed together,
the lion shall eat straw like the ox;
but the serpent—its food shall be dust!
They shall not hurt or destroy on all my holy mountain,
says the Lord.

Isaiah 12

1You will say in that day:
I will give thanks to you, O Lord,
for though you were angry with me,
your anger turned away,
and you comforted me.
2Surely God is my salvation;
I will trust, and will not be afraid,
for the Lord God is my strength and my might;
he has become my salvation.
3With joy you will draw water from the wells of salvation. 4And you will say in that day:
Give thanks to the Lord,
call on his name;
make known his deeds among the nations;
proclaim that his name is exalted.
5Sing praises to the Lord, for he has done gloriously;
let this be known in all the earth.
6Shout aloud and sing for joy, O royal Zion,
for great in your midst is the Holy One of Israel.

2 Thessalonians 3:6-13

6Now we command you, beloved, in the name of our Lord Jesus Christ, to keep away from believers who are living in idleness and not according to the tradition that they received from us. 7For you yourselves know how you ought to imitate us; we were not idle when we were with you, 8and we did not eat anyone's bread without paying for it; but with toil and labor we worked night and day, so that we might not burden any of you. 9This was not because we do not have that right, but in order to give you an example to imitate. 10For even when we were with you, we gave you this command: Anyone unwilling to work should not eat. 11For we hear that some of you are living in idleness, mere busybodies, not doing any work. 12Now such persons we command and exhort in the Lord Jesus Christ to do their work quietly and to earn their own living. 13Brothers and sisters, do not be weary in doing what is right.

Luke 21:5-19

5When some were speaking about the temple, how it was adorned with beautiful stones and gifts dedicated to God, he said, 6"As for these things that you see, the days will come when not one stone will be left upon another; all will be thrown down." 7They asked him, "Teacher, when will this be, and what will be the sign that this is about to take place?" 8And he said, "Beware that you are not led astray; for many will come in my name and say, 'I am he!' and, 'The time is near!' Do not go after them. 9When you hear of wars and insurrections, do not be terrified; for these things must take place first, but the end will not follow immediately." 10Then he said to them, "Nation will rise against nation, and kingdom against kingdom; 11there will be great earthquakes, and in various places famines and plagues; and there will be dreadful portents and great signs from heaven. 12"But before all this occurs, they will arrest you and persecute you; they will hand you over to synagogues and prisons, and you will be brought before kings and governors because of my name. 13This will give you an opportunity to testify. 14So make up your minds not to prepare your defense in advance; 15for I will give you words and a wisdom that none of your opponents will be able to withstand or contradict. 16You will be betrayed even by parents and brothers, by relatives and friends; and they will put some of you to death. 17You will be hated by all because of my name. 18But not a hair of your head will perish. 19By your endurance you will gain your souls."

Primary Hymns and Songs for the Day

"Sing Praise to God Who Reigns Above" (Isa 12) (O)
 C6, CG315, E408, EL871, G645, N6, UM126 (PD), VU216
 H-3   Hbl-92; Chr-22, 126, 173; Desc-76; Org-91
 S-1   #237. Descant

"O Day of Peace That Dimly Shines" (Isa 65, Luke)
 C711, E597, EL711, G373, P450, UM729, VU682

"The First Song of Isaiah" (Isa 12)
 G71, S2030

"Soon and Very Soon" 11249 (2 Thess, Luke)
 CG562, EL439, G384, SH357, UM706
 S-2   #187. Piano arrangement

"My Lord, What a Morning" (Luke)
 C708, EL438 (PD), G352, P449, SH356, UM719, VU708

"O Master, Let Me Walk with Thee" (Luke) (C)
 C602, CG660, E659/E660, EL818, G738, N503, P357, SA667,
 SH612, UM430 (PD), VU560

"Forth in Thy Name, O Lord" (2 Thess) (C)
 SA642, UM438 (PD), VU416
 H-3   Hbl-29, 57, 58; Chr-117; Desc-31; Org-31
 S-1   #100-103. Various treatments.

Additional Hymn Suggestions

"This Is a Day of New Beginnings" (Isa 65)
 C518, N417, UM383

"Isaiah the Prophet Has Written of Old" (Isa 65)
 G77, N108, P337, VU680

"For the Healing of the Nations" (Isa, 2 Thess, Luke)
 C668, CG698, G346, N576, SA1000, UM428, VU678

"On Jordan's Stormy Banks I Stand" (Isa 65, Luke)
 CG556, EL437, N598, SA542, SH368, UM724 (PD)

"Marching to Zion" (Isa 65, Luke) (O)
 C707, CG550, EL625, N382, SA831, UM733, VU714

"Together We Serve" (2 Thess)
 G767, S2175

"You, Lord, Are Both Lamb and Shepherd" (2 Thess)
 G274, SH210, VU210. WS3043

"Go to the World" (2 Thess)
 CG481, G295, SH720, VU420, WS3158

"Come, Labor On" (2 Thess)
 E541, G719, N532, P415

"Today We All Are Called to Be Disciples" (2 Thess)
 G757, P434, VU507

"Called as Partners in Christ's Service" (2 Thess)
 C453, G761, N495, P343

"It Is Well with My Soul" (2 Thess, Luke)
 C561, CG573, EL785, G840, N438, SA741, SH305, UM377

"A Charge to Keep I Have" (2 Thess, Luke)
 AH4117, CG623, SA946, SH634, UM413 (PD)

"All Who Love and Serve Your City" (2 Thess, Luke)
 C670, CG674, E570/E571, EL724, G351, P413, UM433

"Blessed Quietness" (2 Thess, Luke)
 C267, CG244, N284, S2142

"Bring Forth the Kingdom" (2 Thess, Luke)
 N181, S2190, SH130

"My Hope Is Built" (Luke)
 AH4105, C537, CG590, EL596/597, G353, N403, P379,
 SA662, SH324, UM368 (PD)

"Where Cross the Crowded Ways of Life" (Luke)
 C665, CG657, E609, EL719, G343, N543, P408, UM427 (PD),
 VU681

"Lord, Speak to Me" (Luke)
 CG503, EL676, G722, N531, P426, SA773, SH557, UM463,
 VU589

"Come, Ye Thankful People, Come" (Luke)
 C718, CG372, E290, EL693, G367, N422, P551, SA9, SH355,
 UM694 (PD), VU516

"Mine Eyes Have Seen the Glory" (Luke)
 C705, CG439, EL890, G354, N610, SA263, UM717

"O Day of God, Draw Nigh" (Luke) (C)
 C700, E601, N611, P452, UM730 (PD), VU688/689 (Fr.)

Additional Contemporary and Modern Suggestions

"Forever" 3148428 (Isa 65, Isa 12)
 CG53, SA363, WS3023

"Someone Asked the Question" 1640279 (Isa 65, Isa 12)
 N523, S2144

"Hear our Praises" 2543402 (Isa 65, Isa 12)

"Give Thanks" 20285 (Isa 12)
 C528, CG373, G647, S2036, SA364, SH489

"He Is Exalted" 17827 (Isa 12)
 AH4082, CG342, S2070, SH423

"Shout to the Lord" 1406918 (Isa 12)
 CG348, EL821, S2074, SA264, SH426

"In the Lord I'll Be Ever Thankful" (Isa 12)
 G654, S2195, SH316

"You Are My All in All" 825356 (Isa 12)
 CG571, G519, SH335, WS3040

"I Exalt You" 17803 (Isa 12)

"Be Exalted, O God" ("I Will Give Thanks") 21112 (Isa 12)

"God Is the Strength of My Heart" 80919 (Isa 12)

"Good to Me" 313480 (Isa 12)

"I See the Lord" 1406176 (Isa 12, Luke)

"Freedom Is Coming" 4194244 (Luke)
 G359, S2192, SA29

"Hosanna" 4785835 (Luke)
 SH361, WS3188

"The Battle Belongs to the Lord" 21583 (Luke)

Vocal Solos

"Turn My Heart to You" (Isa)
 V-5 (2)   p. 14

"I'm Goin' Home" (Isa, Luke)
 V-8   p. 325

"It Is Well with My Soul" (2 Thess, Luke)
 V-5 (2)   p. 35

"My Lord, What a Mornin'" (Luke)
 V-3 (1)   p. 39
 V-7   p. 68

Anthems

"I Will Make a Way!" (Isa 65)
Tom Trenney; MorningStar MSM-50-6198
SATB, piano (https://bit.ly/50-6198)

"Sing a Joyful Psalm" (Isa 12)
Joseph M. Martin; Jubilate Music 47209
SATB, piano, opt. claves and maracas (https://bit.ly/J-47209)

Other Suggestions

Visuals:
 O   Space/earth, joy, building, grapes, work, wolf/ lamb
 P   Worship, anger/comfort, arm, water/well, joy
 E   Idleness, bread, work, food
 G   Temple, toppled rock, Jesus, war, whip/chain,
      betrayal, hair
Introit: WS3047, st. 2. "God Almighty, We Are Waiting" (Isa)
Canticle: UM734. "Canticle of Hope" (Isa, Luke)
Prayer: N857. Renewal of Mission (Isa)
Prayer: N856. Eternal Life (Luke)
Alternate Lessons: Mal 4:1-2a, Ps 98
Theme Ideas: Endurance, God: Kingdom of God, New Creation,
 Thanksgiving / Gratitude

Jeremiah 23:1-6

[1]Woe to the shepherds who destroy and scatter the sheep of my pasture! says the LORD. [2]Therefore thus says the LORD, the God of Israel, concerning the shepherds who shepherd my people: It is you who have scattered my flock, and have driven them away, and you have not attended to them. So I will attend to you for your evil doings, says the LORD. [3]Then I myself will gather the remnant of my flock out of all the lands where I have driven them, and I will bring them back to their fold, and they shall be fruitful and multiply. [4]I will raise up shepherds over them who will shepherd them, and they shall not fear any longer, or be dismayed, nor shall any be missing, says the LORD.

[5]The days are surely coming, says the LORD, when I will raise up for David a righteous Branch, and he shall reign as king and deal wisely, and shall execute justice and righteousness in the land. [6]In his days Judah will be saved and Israel will live in safety. And this is the name by which he will be called: "The LORD is our righteousness."

Luke 1:68-79

[68]"Blessed be the Lord God of Israel,
> for he has looked favorably on his people and redeemed them.
[69]He has raised up a mighty savior for us
> in the house of his servant David,
[70]as he spoke through the mouth of his holy prophets from of old,
[71] that we would be saved from our enemies and from the hand of all who hate us.
[72]Thus he has shown the mercy promised to our ancestors,
> and has remembered his holy covenant,
[73]the oath that he swore to our ancestor Abraham,
> to grant us [74]that we, being rescued from the hands of our enemies,
> might serve him without fear, [75]in holiness and righteousness before him all our days.
[76]And you, child, will be called the prophet of the Most High;
> for you will go before the Lord to prepare his ways,
[77]to give knowledge of salvation to his people
> by the forgiveness of their sins.
[78]By the tender mercy of our God,
> the dawn from on high will break upon us,
[79]to give light to those who sit in darkness and in the shadow of death,
> to guide our feet into the way of peace."

Colossians 1:11-20

[11]May you be made strong with all the strength that comes from his glorious power, and may you be prepared to endure everything with patience, while joyfully [12]giving thanks to the Father, who has enabled you to share in the inheritance of the saints in the light. [13]He has rescued us from the power of darkness and transferred us into the kingdom of his beloved Son, [14]in whom we have redemption, the forgiveness of sins.

[15]He is the image of the invisible God, the firstborn of all creation; [16]for in him all things in heaven and on earth were created, things visible and invisible, whether thrones or dominions or rulers or powers—all things have been created through him and for him. [17]He himself is before all things, and in him all things hold together. [18]He is the head of the body, the church; he is the beginning, the firstborn from the dead, so that he might come to have first place in everything. [19]For in him all the fullness of God was pleased to dwell, [20]and through him God was pleased to reconcile to himself all things, whether on earth or in heaven, by making peace through the blood of his cross.

Luke 23:33-43

[33]When they came to the place that is called The Skull, they crucified Jesus there with the criminals, one on his right and one on his left. [34]Then Jesus said, "Father, forgive them; for they do not know what they are doing." And they cast lots to divide his clothing. [35]And the people stood by, watching; but the leaders scoffed at him, saying, "He saved others; let him save himself if he is the Messiah of God, his chosen one!" [36]The soldiers also mocked him, coming up and offering him sour wine, [37]and saying, "If you are the King of the Jews, save yourself!" [38]There was also an inscription over him, "This is the King of the Jews." [39]One of the criminals who were hanged there kept deriding him and saying, "Are you not the Messiah? Save yourself and us!" [40]But the other rebuked him, saying, "Do you not fear God, since you are under the same sentence of condemnation? [41]And we indeed have been condemned justly, for we are getting what we deserve for our deeds, but this man has done nothing wrong." [42]Then he said, "Jesus, remember me when you come into your kingdom." [43]He replied, "Truly I tell you, today you will be with me in Paradise."

Primary Hymns and Songs for the Day
"Immortal, Invisible, God Only Wise" (Col) (O)
  C66, CG58, E423, EL834, G12, N1, P263, SA37, UM103 (PD),
  VU264
      H-3 Hbl-15, 71; Chr-65; Desc-93; Org-135
      S-1 #300. Harm.
"Blessed Be the God of Israel" (Luke 1)
  C135, CG88, E444, EL250/552, G109, P602, UM209, VU901
"Jesus, Remember Me" (Luke)
  C569, CG393, EL616, G227, P599, SH175, UM488, VU148
"Jesus Shall Reign" (Christ the King) (C)
  C95, CG158, E544, EL434, G265, N300, P423, SA258, SH209,
  UM157 (PD), VU330
      H-3 Hbl-29, 57, 58; Chr-117; Desc-31; Org-31
      S-1 #100-103. Various treatments.
"Crown Him with Many Crowns" (Christ the King) (C)
  C234, CG223. E494, EL855, G268, N301, P151, SA358,
  SH208, UM327 (PD), VU211

Additional Hymn Suggestions
"How Great Thou Art" (Jer)
  AH4015, C33, CG323, EL856, G625, N35, P467, SA49, SH14,
  UM77, VU238 (Fr.)
"How Firm a Foundation" (Jer)
  C618, CG425, E636/637, EL796, G463, N407, P361, SA804,
  SH291, UM529 (PD), VU660
"Gather Us In" (Luke 1, Comm.)
  C284, EL532, G401, S2236, SH393
"You, Lord, Are Both Lamb and Shepherd" (Luke 1, Col)
  G274, SH210, VU210. WS3043
"Holy God, We Praise Thy Name" (Col)
  CG9, E366, EL414 (PD), G4, N276, SH431, UM79, VU894
"To God Be the Glory" (Col)
  C72, CG349, G634, P485, SA279, SH545, UM98 (PD)
"In the Cross of Christ I Glory" (Col)
  C207, CG183, E441, EL324, G213, N193, SA174, UM295
"God of Grace and God of Glory" (Col)
  C464, CG285, E594/595, EL705, G307, N436, P420, SA814,
  SH250, UM577, VU686
"I've Got Peace Like a River" (Col)
  C530, G623, N478, P368, S2145, SH276, VU577
"In the Lord I'll Be Ever Thankful" (Col)
  G654, S2195, SH316
"Come, Share the Lord" (Col, Comm.)
  C408, CG459, G510, S2269, VU469
"Blessed Quietness" (Col, Luke 23)
  C267, CG244, N284, S2142
"Sing, My Tongue, the Glorious Battle" (Col, Luke 23)
  E165/166, EL355/356, G225, N220, UM296
"Beneath the Cross of Jesus" (Col, Luke 23)
  C197, CG184, E498, EL338, G216, N190, P92, SA161, SH166,
  UM297 (PD), VU135
"Rejoice, the Lord Is King" (Christ the King)
  C699, CG215, E481, EL430, G363, N303, P155, SA271,
  SH213, UM715/716, VU213

Additional Contemporary and Modern Suggestions
"Foundation" 706151 (Jer)
"I Have a Hope" 5087587 (Jer, Luke 1)
"We Are Marching" ("Siyahamba") 1321512 (Luke 1)
  C442, CG155, EL866, G853, N526, S2235, SA903, SH717,
  VU646
"Here Is Bread, Here Is Wine" 983717 (Luke 1, Comm.)
  EL483, S2266
"Shine, Jesus, Shine" 30426 (Luke 1)
  CG156, EL671, G192, S2173, SA261, SH102
"How Great Is Our God" 4348399 (Luke 1)
  CG322, SH458, WS3003

"God Is Good All the Time" 1729073 (Luke 1)
"Here I Am to Worship" 3266032 (Luke 1, Christ the King)
  CG297, SA114, SH395, WS3177
"Shine on Us" 1754646 (Luke 1)
"Hear our Praises" 2543402 (Luke 1)
"Everyday" 2798154 (Luke 1)
"Marvelous Light" 4491002 (Luke 1, Col)
"You are the Light" 6238098 (Luke 1, Col, Luke 23)
"May You Run and Not Be Weary" 807099 (Col)
"Across the Lands" 3709898 (Col, Christ the King)
  SH654, WS3032
"Lamb of God" 16787 (Luke 23)
  EL336, G518, S2113
"Here at the Cross" 7046292 (Luke 23)
"Awesome God" 41099 (Luke 23, Christ the King)
  G616, S2040
"The Power of the Cross" 4490766 (Luke 23, Christ the King)
  CG190, WS3085
"Our God Reigns" 8458 (Luke 23, Christ the King)
"Blessing, Honour and Glory" 1001179 (Luke 23, Christ the King)
  EL433
"You Are Worthy" ("Eres Digno") (Christ the King)
"All Hail King Jesus" 12877 (Christ the King)
"King of Kings" 23952 (Christ the King)
  S2075, VU167
"Hosanna" 4785835 (Christ the King)
  SH361, WS3188
"Crown Him King of Kings" 206009 (Luke 23, Christ the King)
"My Savior Lives" 4882965 (Luke 23, Christ the King)
"Forever Reign" 5639997 (Luke 23, Christ the King)
"The Highest and the Greatest" 4769758 (Christ the King)
"Prepare Ye the Way" 5286041 (Luke 1, Christ the King)

Vocal Solos
"It Is Well with My Soul" (Col)
  V-5 (2)   p. 35
"Ride On, Jesus" (Christ the King)
  V-7   p. 8
"King of Glory, King of Peace" (Christ the King)
  V-9   p. 24

Anthems
"Ye Choirs of New Jerusalem" (Col, Luke)
C. V. Stanford; GIA Publications G-4188
SATB, organ (https://bit.ly/G-4188)

"Sizohamba Naye" ("We Will Walk with God") (Luke 1)
arr. Terry Taylor; Choristers Guild CGA-1250
Unison (opt. SATB), piano (https://bit.ly/CGA-1250)

Other Suggestions
For Thanksgiving Sunday, see Thanksgiving Day suggestions.
Visuals: Crown, Christus Rex
  O   Scattered/herding sheep, today's shepherds, branch
  P   Christus Rex, rescue, service, child, dawn, feet
  E   Glory, joy, light/dark, rescue, creation, Christ
  G   Skull, blood/lots/cross/clothes, INRI, wine, Luke
      23:42
Introit: WS3047, st. 2. "God Almighty, We Are Waiting" (Jer)
Canticle: C137, UM208, VU900. "Zechariah" (Luke 1)
Greeting: N822 (Luke 1)
Prayer of Confession: N835 (Jer
Prayer: N853. Peace (Luke 1, Col)
Sung Confession: WS3084. "O Christ, You Hang upon a Cross"
  (Luke 23)
Alternate lessons: Jer 23:1-6, Ps 46
Theme Ideas: Cross, Jesus: Return and Reign, Justice, Peace

Deuteronomy 26:1-11

[1]When you have come into the land that the LORD your God is giving you as an inheritance to possess, and you possess it, and settle in it, [2]you shall take some of the first of all the fruit of the ground, which you harvest from the land that the LORD your God is giving you, and you shall put it in a basket and go to the place that the LORD your God will choose as a dwelling for his name. [3]You shall go to the priest who is in office at that time, and say to him, "Today I declare to the LORD your God that I have come into the land that the LORD swore to our ancestors to give us." [4]When the priest takes the basket from your hand and sets it down before the altar of the LORD your God, [5]you shall make this response before the LORD your God: "A wandering Aramean was my ancestor; he went down into Egypt and lived there as an alien, few in number, and there he became a great nation, mighty and populous. [6]When the Egyptians treated us harshly and afflicted us, by imposing hard labor on us, [7]we cried to the LORD, the God of our ancestors; the LORD heard our voice and saw our affliction, our toil, and our oppression. [8]The LORD brought us out of Egypt with a mighty hand and an outstretched arm, with a terrifying display of power, and with signs and wonders; [9]and he brought us into this place and gave us this land, a land flowing with milk and honey. [10]So now I bring the first of the fruit of the ground that you, O LORD, have given me." You shall set it down before the LORD your God and bow down before the LORD your God. [11]Then you, together with the Levites and the aliens who reside among you, shall celebrate with all the bounty that the LORD your God has given to you and to your house.

Psalm 100 (G385, N688, P220, UM821)

[1]Make a joyful noise to the LORD, all the earth.
[2]Worship the LORD with gladness;
come into his presence with singing.
[3]Know that the LORD is God.
It is he that made us, and we are his;
we are his people, and the sheep of his pasture.
[4]Enter his gates with thanksgiving,
and his courts with praise.
Give thanks to him, bless his name.
[5]For the LORD is good;
his steadfast love endures forever,
and his faithfulness to all generations.

Philippians 4:4-9

[4]Rejoice in the Lord always; again I will say, Rejoice. [5]Let your gentleness be known to everyone. The Lord is near. [6]Do not worry about anything, but in everything by prayer and supplication with thanksgiving let your requests be made known to God. [7]And the peace of God, which surpasses all understanding, will guard your hearts and your minds in Christ Jesus.

[8]Finally, beloved, whatever is true, whatever is honorable, whatever is just, whatever is pure, whatever is pleasing, whatever is commendable, if there is any excellence and if there is anything worthy of praise, think about these things. [9]Keep on doing the things that you have learned and received and heard and seen in me, and the God of peace will be with you.

John 6:25-35

[25]When they found him on the other side of the sea, they said to him, "Rabbi, when did you come here?" [26]Jesus answered them, "Very truly, I tell you, you are looking for me, not because you saw signs, but because you ate your fill of the loaves. [27]Do not work for the food that perishes, but for the food that endures for eternal life, which the Son of Man will give you. For it is on him that God the Father has set his seal." [28]Then they said to him, "What must we do to perform the works of God?" [29]Jesus answered them, "This is the work of God, that you believe in him whom he has sent." [30]So they said to him, "What sign are you going to give us then, so that we may see it and believe you? What work are you performing? [31]Our ancestors ate the manna in the wilderness; as it is written, 'He gave them bread from heaven to eat.'" [32]Then Jesus said to them, "Very truly, I tell you, it was not Moses who gave you the bread from heaven, but it is my Father who gives you the true bread from heaven. [33]For the bread of God is that which comes down from heaven and gives life to the world." [34]They said to him, "Sir, give us this bread always." [35]Jesus said to them, "I am the bread of life. Whoever comes to me will never be hungry, and whoever believes in me will never be thirsty."

Primary Hymns and Songs for the Day
"Come, Ye Thankful People, Come" (Deut, Pss) (O)
  C718, CG372, E290, EL693, G367, N422, P551, SA9, SH355,
  UM694 (PD), VU516
    H-3   Hbl-54; Chr-58; Desc-94; Org-137
    S-1   #302-303. Harms. with desc.
"I Will Enter His Gates" 1493 (Pss) (O)
  S2270, SA337
"All People That on Earth Do Dwell" (Pss)
  C18, CG331, E377/378, EL883, G385, N7, P220, SA350,
  SH416, UM75 (PD), VU822 (Fr.)
    H-3   Hbl-45; Chr-24; Desc-84, 85; Org-107
    S-1   #257-259. Various treatments
    S-2   #140. Desc.
"Now Thank We All Our God" (Pss)
  C715, CG371, E396/397, EL839/840, G643, N419, P555,
  SA45, SH485, UM102 (PD), VU236 (Fr.)
    H-3   Hbl-78; Chr-140; Desc 81; Org-98
    S-1   #252-254. Various treatments
"Rejoice, Ye Pure in Heart" (Phil)
  C15, CG312, E556/557, EL873/874, G804, N55/71,
  P145/146, UM160/161
    H-3   Hbl-17, 90; Chr-166; Desc-73; Org-85
    S-1   #228. Desc.
Kum Ba Yah 2749763 (Phil)
  C590, G472, P338, UM494
"For the Beauty of the Earth" (John)
  C56, CG341, E416, EL879, G14, P473, N28, SA14, SH21,
  UM92 (PD), VU226
"Guide Me, O Thou Great Jehovah" (Deut, John) (C)
  C622, CG33, E690, EL618, G65, N18/19, P281, SA27, SH51,
  UM127 (PD), VU651 (Fr.)
    H-3   Hbl-25, 51, 58; Chr-89; Desc-26; Org-23
    S-1   #76-77. Desc. and harm.

Additional Hymn Suggestions
"What Gift Can We Bring" (Deut)
  CG533, N370, UM87
"God Be With You Till We Meet Again" (Deut) (C)
  C434, CG523, EL536, G541/542, N81, P540, SA1027,
  UM672/673, VU422/423
"In the Midst of New Dimensions" (Deut)
  G315, N391, S2238
"Praise God for This Holy Ground" (Deut, Thanks.)
  G405, WS3009
"Hope of the World" (Phil)
  C538, E472, G734, N46, P360, UM178, VU215
"Take My Life, and Let It Be" (Phil) (C)
  C609, CG490, E707, EL583/EL685, G697, P391, N448,
  SA623, SH627/628, UM399 (PD), VU506
"What a Friend We Have in Jesus" (Phil)
  C585, CG409, EL742, G465, N506, P403, SA795, SH585/586,
  UM526 (PD), VU661
"Rejoice, the Lord Is King" (Phil)
  C699, CG215, E481, EL430, G363, N303, P155, SA271,
  SH213, UM715/716, VU213
"Lord of All Hopefulness" (Phil)
  CG678, E482, EL765, G683, S2197, SA772, SH464
"My Life Flows On" (Phil, Thanks.)
  C619, CG592, EL763, G821, N476, S2212, SA663, VU716
"As Those of Old Their First Fruits Brought" (John)
  CG667, E705, G712, P414, VU518
"For the Fruits of This Creation" (John)
  C714, E424, CG376, EL679, G36, N425, P553, SA15, UM97,
  VU227
"For the Healing of the Nations" (John)
  C668, CG698, G346, N576, SA1000, UM428, VU678

"God the Sculptor of the Mountains" (John)
  EL736, G5, S2060
"Eat This Bread" (John, Comm.)
  C414, EL472, G527, N788, SH671, UM628, VU466
"You Satisfy the Hungry Heart" (John, Comm.)
  C429, CG468, EL484, G523, P521, SH672, UM629, VU478
"Let All Things Now Living" (Thanks.)
  C717, CG379, EL881, G37, P554, S2008, SH23, VU242
"Praise Our God Above" (Thanks.)
  N424, P480, S2061

Additional Contemporary and Modern Suggestions
"We Bring the Sacrifice of Praise" 9990 (Deut)
"Forever" 3148428 (Deut, Pss)
  CG53, SA363, WS3023
"You Are Good" 3383788 (Pss)
  AH4018, SH455, WS3014
"Blessed Be the Name" 265239 (Pss)
"Forevermore" 5466830 (Pss)
"Grateful" 7029348 (Pss, Thanks.)
"Hallelujah" ("Your Love Is Amazing") 3091812 (Pss, John)
"Wait for the Lord" (Phil, Advent)
  CG644, EL262, G90, SH580, VU22, WS3049
"I Will Give Thanks" 6266091 (Phil, Thanks.)
"How Can I Keep from Singing" 4822372 (Phil)
"Halle, Halle, Halleluja" 2659190 (John, Thanks.)
  C41, CG433, EL172, G591, N236, S2026, SH694, VU958
"Jesus, Name above All Names" 21291 (John)
  S2071, SA82
"You Who Are Thirsty" 814453 (John)
"Fill My Cup, Lord" 15946 (John, Comm.)
  C351, UM641 (refrain only), WS3093
"There Will Be Bread" 4512352 (John, Comm.)
"I Thank You, Jesus" (Thanks.)
  AH4079, C116, N41, WS3037

Vocal Solos
"Maybe the Rain" (Deut, John)
  V-5 (2)   p. 27
"Now Thank We All Our God" (Thanks.)
  V-6   p. 8
"Thanks to God" (Thanks.)
  V-8   p. 296

Anthems
"What Gift Can We Bring?" (Deut)
Jane Marshall; Hope CY3370
SSAB, keyboard (https://bit.ly/CY3370)

"Thanksgiving" (Thanks.)
Glen Wonacott; Kjos Music Company 6369
2-part, keyboard (https://bit.ly/K-6369)

Other Suggestions
Visuals:
  O   Produce, harvest, basket, altar, bricks, manacles
  P   Praise, singing, sheep, gates
  E   Rejoicing, Phil 4:6, praying hands, Christ, Phil 4:7
  G   Jesus teaching, loaves, John 6:27, manna, John 6:35
Opening Prayer: C771 (John)
Prayer: N858. Providence of God (Deut, Thanks.)
Canticle: UM74. "Canticle of Thanksgiving" (Pss)
Response: G635, WS3007. *Laudate Dominum* (Pss)
Sung Benediction: "Give Us Your Peace" 5767807 (Phil)
Theme Ideas: Bread of Life, God: Hunger / Thirst for
  God, Jesus: Mind of Christ, Peace, Praise, Stewardship,
  Thanksgiving / Gratitude

Isaiah 2:1-5

¹The word that Isaiah son of Amoz saw concerning Judah and Jerusalem.
²In days to come
 the mountain of the Lord's house
shall be established as the highest of the mountains,
 and shall be raised above the hills;
all the nations shall stream to it.
 ³Many peoples shall come and say,
"Come, let us go up to the mountain of the Lord,
 to the house of the God of Jacob;
that he may teach us his ways
 and that we may walk in his paths."
For out of Zion shall go forth instruction,
 and the word of the Lord from Jerusalem.
⁴He shall judge between the nations,
 and shall arbitrate for many peoples;
they shall beat their swords into plowshares,
 and their spears into pruning hooks;
nation shall not lift up sword against nation,
 neither shall they learn war any more.
⁵O house of Jacob,
 come, let us walk
 in the light of the Lord!

Psalm 122 (G400, N705, P235, UM845)

¹I was glad when they said to me,
 "Let us go to the house of the Lord!"
²Our feet are standing
 within your gates, O Jerusalem.
³Jerusalem—built as a city
 that is bound firmly together.
⁴To it the tribes go up,
 the tribes of the Lord,
as was decreed for Israel,
 to give thanks to the name of the Lord.
⁵For there the thrones for judgment were set up,
 the thrones of the house of David.
⁶Pray for the peace of Jerusalem:
 "May they prosper who love you.
⁷Peace be within your walls,
 and security within your towers."
⁸For the sake of my relatives and friends
 I will say, "Peace be within you."
⁹For the sake of the house of the Lord our God,
 I will seek your good.

Romans 13:11-14

¹¹Besides this, you know what time it is, how it is now the moment for you to wake from sleep. For salvation is nearer to us now than when we became believers; ¹²the night is far gone, the day is near. Let us then lay aside the works of darkness and put on the armor of light; ¹³let us live honorably as in the day, not in reveling and drunkenness, not in debauchery and licentiousness, not in quarreling and jealousy. ¹⁴Instead, put on the Lord Jesus Christ, and make no provision for the flesh, to gratify its desires.

Matthew 24:36-44

³⁶"But about that day and hour no one knows, neither the angels of heaven, nor the Son, but only the Father. ³⁷For as the days of Noah were, so will be the coming of the Son of Man. ³⁸For as in those days before the flood they were eating and drinking, marrying and giving in marriage, until the day Noah entered the ark, ³⁹and they knew nothing until the flood came and swept them all away, so too will be the coming of the Son of Man. ⁴⁰Then two will be in the field; one will be taken and one will be left. ⁴¹Two women will be grinding meal together; one will be taken and one will be left. ⁴²Keep awake therefore, for you do not know on what day your Lord is coming. ⁴³But understand this: if the owner of the house had known in what part of the night the thief was coming, he would have stayed awake and would not have let his house be broken into. ⁴⁴Therefore you also must be ready, for the Son of Man is coming at an unexpected hour."

Primary Hymns and Songs for the Day

"Come, Thou Long-Expected Jesus" (Rom, Matt) (O)
    C125, CG83, E66, EL254, G82/83, N122, P1/2, SA104, SH64,
    UM196 (PD), VU2
        H-3   Hbl-46; Chr-26, 134; Desc-53; Org-56
        S-1   #168-171. Various treatments
"You, Lord, Are Both Lamb and Shepherd" (Isa)
    G274, SH210, VU210. WS3043
"Prepare the Way of the Lord" (Isa)
    C121, G95, UM207
"I Want to Walk as a Child of the Light" (Isa, Rom)
    CG96, E490, EL815, G377, SH352, UM206
        S-2   #91. Desc.
Dona Nobis Pacem (Pss)
    C297, E712, EL753, G752, UM376 (PD)
"Come Now, O Prince of Peace" (*"O-So-So"*) (Isa, Matt)
    EL247, G103, S2232, SH235
"Let Us Build a House Where Love Can Dwell" (Pss)
    EL641, G301, SH228 (See also WS3152)
"Watchman, Tell Us of the Night" (Rom)
    E640, G97, N103, P20
"Soon and Very Soon" 11249 (Matt) (C)
    CG562, EL439, G384, SH357, UM706
"Wake, Awake, for Night Is Flying" (Rom, Matt)
    E61, EL436, G349, P17, UM720 (PD), VU711
        H-3   Chr-174, 203; Org-172
"We've a Story to Tell to the Nations" (Isa) (C)
    C484, CG427, SA943, UM569 (PD)

Additional Hymn Suggestions

"O Day of Peace That Dimly Shines" (Isa)
    C711, E597, EL711, G373, P450, UM729, VU682
"O Day of God, Draw Nigh" (Isa)
    C700, E601, N611, P452, UM730 (PD), VU688/689 (Fr.)
"O Holy City, Seen of John" (Isa, Pss)
    E582/583, G374, N613, P453, UM726, VU709
"Lead Me, Guide Me" (Isa, Rom, Advent)
    C583, CG403, EL768, G740, S2214, SH582
"Awake, My Soul, and with the Sun" (Isa, Rom)
    E11, EL557 (PD), G663, P456, SA4
"All Who Love and Serve Your City" (Isa, Matt)
    C670, CG674, E570/E571, EL724, G351, P413, UM433
"Come, We That Love the Lord" (Isa, Matt)
    CG549, E392, N379, SA831, UM732, VU715
"Marching to Zion" (Isa, Matt)
    C707, CG550, EL625, N382, SA831, UM733, VU714
"When Morning Gilds the Skies" (Rom)
    C100, CG345, E427, EL853 (PD), G667, N86, P487, SA403,
    SH466, UM185, VU339 (Fr.)
"People, Look East" (Rom, Matt)
    C142, CG90, EL248, G105, P12, UM202, VU9
"My Lord, What a Morning" (Rom, Matt)
    C708, EL438 (PD), G352, P449, SH356, UM719, VU708
"O Come, O Come, Emmanuel" (Matt)
    C119, CG79, E56, EL257, G88, N116, P9, SA117, SH73,
    UM211, VU1 (Fr.)
"Savior of the Nations, Come" (Matt)
    E54, EL263, G102, P14 (PD), SH67, UM214
"O Lord, How Shall I Meet You?" (Matt)
    EL241, G104, N102, P11, VU31
"Let All Mortal Flesh Keep Silence" (Advent, Comm.)
    C124, CG81, E324, EL490, G347, N345, P5, UM626 (PD),
    VU473 (Fr.)

Additional Contemporary and Modern Suggestions

"Someone Asked the Question" 1640279 (Isa)
    N523, S2144
"Light of the World" 73342 (Isa)
"How Great Is Our God" 4348399 (Isa)
    CG322, SH458, WS3003

"Everyday" 2798154 (Isa)
"Marvelous Light" 4491002 (Isa)
"Give Us Your Peace" 5767807 (Isa, Pss)
"Come True Light" 5767773 (Isa, Rom, Advent)
"We Are Marching" (*"Siyahamba"*) 1321512 (Isa, Matt)
    C442, CG155, EL866, G853, N526, S2235, SH717, VU646
"Lord Jesus Christ, Your Light Shines" (Isa, Matt)
    SH556, WS3137
"Here I Am to Worship" 3266032 (Isa, Matt, Advent)
    CG297, SA114, SH395, WS3177
"I Will Enter His Gates" 1493 (Pss)
    S2270, SA337
"Blessed Be Your Name" 3798438 (Rom)
    SH449, WS3002
"Awaken" 5491647 (Rom)
"The Battle Belongs to the Lord" 21583 (Rom)
"Salvation Is Here" 4451327 (Rom)
"Waiting Here for You" 5925663 (Rom, Advent)
"Ancient of Days" 798108 (Rom, Matt)
"There's Something About That Name" 14064 (Matt)
    C115, SA80, UM171
"Freedom Is Coming" 4194244 (Matt)
    G359, S2192, SA29
"Wait for the Lord" (Matt, Advent)
    CG644, EL262, G90, SH580, VU22, WS3049

Vocal Solos

"Peace, Perfect Peace" (Isa, Pss)
    V-5 (1)   p. 69
"Come, Thou Long Expected Jesus" (Matt, Rom, Advent)
    V-10   p. 11
"For Behold, Darkness Shall Cover the Earth" and
"The People That Walked in Darkness"
"Rejoice Greatly, O Daughter of Zion" (Isa)
    V-2
"My Lord, What a Morning" (Rom, Matt, Advent)
    V-3 (1)   p. 39
    V-7   p. 68

Anthems

"Awake! Awake! Salvation Comes" (Rom.)
Caldara/arr. Hal Hopson; GIA Publications G-9797
SAB, piano (https://bit.ly/G-9797)

"Let All Mortal Flesh Keep Silence" (Advent, Comm.)
Arr. Joel Raney; Hope C6165
SATB, 6 handbells (https://bit.ly/Hope-6165)

Other Suggestions

Visuals:
    O   Mountain/hills/nations, paths, scales/justice, light
    P   Ps. 122:1, feet/gates, Jerusalem, worship, wall/tower
    E   Alarm clock, dawn, dark/light, armor, Rom 13:14
    G   Clock, angels, Christ, Noah/ark/flood, one in field
Introit: C583, CG403, EL768, G740, S2214, SH582. "Lead Me,
    Guide Me" (Matt, Advent)
Call to Worship: N823 (Advent)
Advent Candle Response: C128 or G85 (Advent)
Call to Confession: N832 (Advent)
Response: C119, CG79, E56, EL257, G88, N116, P9, SA117,
    SH73, UM211, VU1 (Fr.), stanza 1. "O Come, O Come
    Emmanuel" (Rom, Matt, Advent)
Call to Prayer: WS3046. "Come, O Redeemer, Come" (Advent)
Theme Ideas: Jesus: Return and Reign, Peace, Preparation,
    Waiting

Isaiah 11:1-10

[1]A shoot shall come out from the stump of Jesse,
and a branch shall grow out of his roots.
[2]The spirit of the LORD shall rest on him,
the spirit of wisdom and understanding,
the spirit of counsel and might,
the spirit of knowledge and the fear of the LORD.
[3]His delight shall be in the fear of the LORD.
He shall not judge by what his eyes see,
or decide by what his ears hear;
[4]but with righteousness he shall judge the poor,
and decide with equity for the meek of the earth;
he shall strike the earth with the rod of his mouth,
and with the breath of his lips he shall kill the wicked.
[5]Righteousness shall be the belt around his waist,
and faithfulness the belt around his loins.
[6]The wolf shall live with the lamb,
the leopard shall lie down with the kid,
the calf and the lion and the fatling together,
and a little child shall lead them.
[7]The cow and the bear shall graze,
their young shall lie down together;
and the lion shall eat straw like the ox.
[8]The nursing child shall play over the hole of the asp,
and the weaned child shall put its hand on the adder's den.
[9]They will not hurt or destroy
on all my holy mountain;
for the earth will be full of the knowledge of the LORD
as the waters cover the sea.
[10]On that day the root of Jesse shall stand as a signal to the peoples; the nations shall inquire of him, and his dwelling shall be glorious.

Psalm 72:1-7, 18-19 (G149, N667, P205, UM795)

[1]Give the king your justice, O God,
and your righteousness to a king's son.
[2]May he judge your people with righteousness,
and your poor with justice.
[3]May the mountains yield prosperity for the people,
and the hills, in righteousness.
[4]May he defend the cause of the poor of the people,
give deliverance to the needy,
and crush the oppressor.
[5]May he live while the sun endures,
and as long as the moon, throughout all generations.
[6]May he be like rain that falls on the mown grass,
like showers that water the earth.
[7]In his days may righteousness flourish
and peace abound, until the moon is no more.
. . . .
[18]Blessed be the LORD, the God of Israel,
who alone does wondrous things.
[19]Blessed be his glorious name forever;
may his glory fill the whole earth.
Amen and Amen.

Romans 15:4-13

[4]For whatever was written in former days was written for our instruction, so that by steadfastness and by the encouragement of the scriptures we might have hope. [5]May the God of steadfastness and encouragement grant you to live in harmony with one another, in accordance with Christ Jesus, [6]so that together you may with one voice glorify the God and Father of our Lord Jesus Christ.
[7]Welcome one another, therefore, just as Christ has welcomed you, for the glory of God. [8]For I tell you that Christ has become a servant of the circumcised on behalf of the truth of God in order that he might confirm the promises given to the patriarchs, [9]and in order that the Gentiles might glorify God for his mercy. As it is written,
"Therefore I will confess you among the Gentiles,
and sing praises to your name";
[10]and again he says,
"Rejoice, O Gentiles, with his people";
[11]and again,
"Praise the Lord, all you Gentiles,
and let all the peoples praise him";
[12]and again Isaiah says,
"The root of Jesse shall come,
the one who rises to rule the Gentiles;
in him the Gentiles shall hope."
[13]May the God of hope fill you with all joy and peace in believing, so that you may abound in hope by the power of the Holy Spirit.

Matthew 3:1-12

[1]In those days John the Baptist appeared in the wilderness of Judea, proclaiming, [2]"Repent, for the kingdom of heaven has come near." [3]This is the one of whom the prophet Isaiah spoke when he said,
"The voice of one crying out in the wilderness:
'Prepare the way of the Lord,
make his paths straight.' "
[4]Now John wore clothing of camel's hair with a leather belt around his waist, and his food was locusts and wild honey. [5]Then the people of Jerusalem and all Judea were going out to him, and all the region along the Jordan, [6]and they were baptized by him in the river Jordan, confessing their sins.
[7]But when he saw many Pharisees and Sadducees coming for baptism, he said to them, "You brood of vipers! Who warned you to flee from the wrath to come? [8]Bear fruit worthy of repentance. [9]Do not presume to say to yourselves, 'We have Abraham as our ancestor'; for I tell you, God is able from these stones to raise up children to Abraham. [10]Even now the axe is lying at the root of the trees; every tree therefore that does not bear good fruit is cut down and thrown into the fire.
[11]"I baptize you with water for repentance, but one who is more powerful than I is coming after me; I am not worthy to carry his sandals. He will baptize you with the Holy Spirit and fire. [12]His winnowing-fork is in his hand, and he will clear his threshing-floor and will gather his wheat into the granary; but the chaff he will burn with unquenchable fire."

Primary Hymns and Songs for the Day

"Hail to the Lord's Anointed" (Isa, Pss, Rom) (O)
    C140, CG98, EL311, G149, N104, P205, SH112, UM203, VU30
        H-3   Hbl-16, 22, 68; Chr-101; Desc-37
        S-1   #114. Desc.
                #115. Harm.
"Lo, How a Rose E'er Blooming" (Isa)
    C160, CG105, E81, EL272, G129, N127, P48 (PD), UM216, VU8
        H-3   Chr-129; Org-38
        S-2   #56-57. Various treatments
"Soon and Very Soon" 11249 (Isa)
    CG562, EL439, G384, SH357, UM706, S-2 #187. Piano arrangement
"O Morning Star, How Fair and Bright" (Isa, Rom)
    C105, E497, EL308, G827, N158, P69, UM247, VU98
        H-3   Chr-147; Desc-104; Org-183
"Wild and Lone the Prophet's Voice" (Matt)
    G163, P409, S2089
"O Come, O Come, Emmanuel" (Isa) (C)
    C119, CG79, E56, EL257, G88, N116, P9, SA117, SH73, UM211, VU1 (Fr.)
        H-3   Hbl-14, 79; Chr-141; Org-168
        S-1   #342. Handbell accompaniment

Additional Hymn Suggestions

"Isaiah the Prophet Has Written of Old" (Isa)
    G77, N108, P337, VU680
"Who Would Think That What Was Needed" (Isa)
    G138, N153
"I Come with Joy" (Isa, Comm.)
    C420, CG456, E304, EL482, G515, N349, P507, SH682, UM617, VU477
"O Day of Peace That Dimly Shines" (Isa)
    C711, E597, EL711, G373, P450, UM729, VU682
"O Day of God, Draw Nigh" (Isa)
    C700, E601, N611, P452, UM730 (PD), VU688/689 (Fr.)
"Come, Thou Almighty King" (Isa, Pss)
    C27, CG2, E365, EL408, G2, N275, P139, SA283, SH388, UM61 (PD), VU314
"Come, Thou Long-Expected Jesus" (Isa, Rom, Matt)
    C125, CG83, E66, EL254, G82/83, N122, P1/2, SA104, SH64, UM196 (PD), VU2
"Savior of the Nations, Come" (Isa, Rom)
    E54, EL263, G102, P14 (PD), SH67, UM214
"Blessed Be the God of Israel" (Isa, Matt)
    C135, CG88, E444, EL250/552, G109, UM209, VU901
Toda la Tierra ("All Earth Is Waiting") (Isa, Matt)
    C139, EL266, N121, SH63, UM210, VU5
"Jesus Shall Reign" (Pss, Rom)
    C95, CG158, E544, EL434, G265, N300, P423, SA258, SH209, UM157 (PD), VU330
"O For a World" (Rom)
    C683, G372, N575, P386, VU697
"I Greet Thee, Who My Sure Redeemer Art" (Rom)
    G624, N251, P457, VU393
"Jesus, the Very Thought of Thee" (Rom)
    C102, CG386, E642, EL754, G629, N507, SA85, UM175
"Hope of the World" (Rom)
    C538, E472, G734, N46, P360, UM178, VU215
"Lord of All Hopefulness" (Rom)
    CG678, E482, EL765, G683, S2197, SA772, SH464
"On Jordan's Bank the Baptist's Cry" (Matt)
    E76, EL249, G96, N115, P10, SA120, SH77, VU20
"Come, Holy Ghost, Our Souls Inspire" (Matt)
    E503/504, N268, G278, P125, UM651, VU201

"God the Sculptor of the Mountains" (Matt)
    EL736, G5, S2060
"There's a Voice in the Wilderness" (Matt)
    E75, EL255, N120, VU18

Additional Contemporary and Modern Suggestions

"Come, Emmanuel" 3999938 (Isa, Advent)
"Come True Light" 5767773 (Isa, Rom, Advent)
"I've Got Peace Like a River" (Isa, Rom)
    C530, G623, N478, P368, S2145, SH276, VU577
"Come and Fill Our Hearts" (*"Confitemini Domino"*) (Isa, Rom)
    EL538, G466, S2157
"Give Us Your Peace" 5767807 (Isa, Rom)
"Blessed Be the Name" 265239 (Pss)
"King of Kings" 23952 (Pss, Advent)
    S2075, VU167
"Glorify Thy Name" 1383 (Rom)
    CG8, S2016, SA582, SH427
"Song of Hope" (*"Canto de Esperanza"*) 5193990 (Rom)
    G765, P432, S2186, SH721, VU424
"Grace Alone" 2335524 (Rom)
    CG43, S2162, SA699.
"Mighty to Save" 4591782 (Rom)
"I Could Sing of Your Love Forever" 1043199 (Rom)
"Song of Hope" ("Heaven Come Down") 5111477 (Rom)
"Waiting Here for You" 5925663 (Rom, Matt, Advent)
"Spirit Song" 27824 (Rom, Matt)
    C352, SH409, UM347
"Jesus, Name above All Names" 21291 (Matt)
    S2071, SA82
"Breathe" 1874117 (Matt)
"Refiner's Fire" 426298 (Matt)
"Prepare Ye the Way" 5286041 (Matt)

Vocal Solos

"In the First Light" (Isa, Rom, Advent)
    V-5 (1)   p. 28
"I Wonder as I Wander" (Pss, Advent)
    V-8   p. 88
"Come Thou Long Expected Jesus" (Rom)
    V-10   p. 11

Anthems

"Come, My Light" (Isa)
Anne Krentz Organ; Augsburg 9780800675813
2-part mixed, piano (https://bit.ly/A-75813)

"The Celtic Rose" (Isa)
Sheldon Curry; Lorenz 10/4404L (https://bit.ly/10-4404L)
SATB, piano, opt. penny whistle, strings

Other Suggestions

Visuals:
    O   Stump/branch/roots, lamp, scales, belt, named animals, child, asp, adder's den, mountain/sea, nations
    P   Crown, scales, mountains/hills, poor/needy, sun/moon, rain, lunar eclipse, Ps 72:18, 19
    E   Bible/OT, circle, welcome, nations/Christ, stump/root
    G   Baptism, ax/root/fire, sandals, fork/wheat/chaff/fire
Introit: C121, G95, UM207. "Prepare the Way of the Lord" (Matt)
Opening Prayer: N816 (Advent)
Canticle: C126. "The Peaceful Realm" (Isa)
Call to Confession: N114. "Return, My People" (Isa)
Advent Candle Response: C128 or G85 (Advent)
For more prayers, see The Abingdon Worship Annual 2022.
Theme Ideas: Jesus: Return and Reign, Justice, Peace, Preparation, Waiting

Isaiah 35:1-10

[1]The wilderness and the dry land shall be glad,
    the desert shall rejoice and blossom;
like the crocus [2]it shall blossom abundantly,
    and rejoice with joy and singing.
The glory of Lebanon shall be given to it,
    the majesty of Carmel and Sharon.
They shall see the glory of the LORD,
    the majesty of our God.
[3]Strengthen the weak hands,
    and make firm the feeble knees.
[4]Say to those who are of a fearful heart,
    "Be strong, do not fear!
Here is your God.
    He will come with vengeance,
with terrible recompense.
    He will come and save you."
[5]Then the eyes of the blind shall be opened,
    and the ears of the deaf unstopped;
[6]then the lame shall leap like a deer,
    and the tongue of the speechless sing for joy.
For waters shall break forth in the wilderness,
    and streams in the desert;
[7]the burning sand shall become a pool,
    and the thirsty ground springs of water;
the haunt of jackals shall become a swamp,
    the grass shall become reeds and rushes.
[8]A highway shall be there,
    and it shall be called the Holy Way;
the unclean shall not travel on it,
    but it shall be for God's people;
no traveler, not even fools, shall go astray.
[9]No lion shall be there,
    nor shall any ravenous beast come up on it;
they shall not be found there,
    but the redeemed shall walk there.
[10]And the ransomed of the LORD shall return,
    and come to Zion with singing;
everlasting joy shall be upon their heads;
    they shall obtain joy and gladness,
    and sorrow and sighing shall flee away.

Luke 1:46b-55

[46b]"My soul magnifies the Lord,
[47]   and my spirit rejoices in God my Savior,
[48]for he has looked with favor on the lowliness of his servant.
    Surely, from now on all generations will call me blessed;
[49]for the Mighty One has done great things for me,
    and holy is his name.
[50]His mercy is for those who fear him
    from generation to generation.
[51]He has shown strength with his arm;
    he has scattered the proud in the thoughts of their hearts.
[52]He has brought down the powerful from their thrones,
    and lifted up the lowly;
[53]he has filled the hungry with good things,
    and sent the rich away empty.
[54]He has helped his servant Israel,
    in remembrance of his mercy,
[55]according to the promise he made to our ancestors,
    to Abraham and to his descendants forever."

James 5:7-10

[7]Be patient, therefore, beloved, until the coming of the Lord. The farmer waits for the precious crop from the earth, being patient with it until it receives the early and the late rains. [8]You also must be patient. Strengthen your hearts, for the coming of the Lord is near. [9]Beloved, do not grumble against one another, so that you may not be judged. See, the Judge is standing at the doors! [10]As an example of suffering and patience, beloved, take the prophets who spoke in the name of the Lord.

Matthew 11:2-11

[2]When John heard in prison what the Messiah was doing, he sent word by his disciples [3]and said to him, "Are you the one who is to come, or are we to wait for another?" [4]Jesus answered them, "Go and tell John what you hear and see: [5]the blind receive their sight, the lame walk, the lepers are cleansed, the deaf hear, the dead are raised, and the poor have good news brought to them. [6]And blessed is anyone who takes no offense at me." [7]As they went away, Jesus began to speak to the crowds about John: "What did you go out into the wilderness to look at? A reed shaken by the wind? [8]What then did you go out to see? Someone dressed in soft robes? Look, those who wear soft robes are in royal palaces. [9]What then did you go out to see? A prophet? Yes, I tell you, and more than a prophet. [10]This is the one about whom it is written,

    'See, I am sending my messenger ahead of you,
    who will prepare your way before you.'

[11]Truly I tell you, among those born of women no one has arisen greater than John the Baptist; yet the least in the kingdom of heaven is greater than he."

Primary Hymns and Songs for the Day

"Come, Thou Long-Expected Jesus" (Jas) (O)
    C125, CG83, E66, EL254, G82/83, N122, P1/2, SA104, SH64,
    UM196 (PD), VU2
        H-3   Hbl-46; Chr-26, 134; Desc-53; Org-56
        S-1   #168-171. Various treatments
"While We Are Waiting, Come" 27525 (Jas)
    G92
"My Soul Gives Glory to My God" (Luke)
    C130, EL251, G99, N119, P600, UM198, VU899
        H-3   Chr-139, 145; Desc-77
        S-1   #241-242. Orff arr. and desc.
"Prepare the Way of the Lord" (Matt)
    C121, G95, UM207
"O For a Thousand Tongues to Sing" (Isa, Matt) (C)
    C5, CG332, E493, EL886, G610, N42, P466, SA89, SH439,
    UM57 (PD), VU326 (See also WS3001)
        H-3   Hbl-79; Chr-142; Desc-17; Org-12
        S-1   #33-38. Various Treatments
"I Want to Walk as a Child of the Light" (Isa, Jas) (C)
    CG96, E490, EL815, G377, SH352, UM206

Additional Hymn Suggestions

"Awake! Awake, and Greet the New Morn" (Isa)
    C138, EL242, G107, N107, SH66
"Lift Up Your Heads, Ye Mighty Gates" (Isa)
    C129, CG173, E436, G93, N117, P8, UM213 (PD)
"Lo, How a Rose E'er Blooming" (Isa)
    C160, CG105, E81, EL272, G129, N127, UM216, VU8
"That Boy-Child of Mary" (Isa, Luke)
    EL293, G139, P55, UM241
"It Came Upon the Midnight Clear" (Isa, Jas, Matt)
    C153, CG132, E89, EL282, G123, N131, P38, SA111, SH89,
    UM218 (PD), VU44
"Hail to the Lord's Anointed" (Isa, Matt)
    C140, CG98, EL311, G149, N104, SH112, UM203, VU30
"Good Christian Friends, Rejoice" (Isa, Matt)
    C164, CG122, E107, EL288, G132, N129, UM224, VU35
"Thou Didst Leave Thy Throne" (Isa, Matt, Advent)
    CG165, S2100, SA153, SH86
"Canticle of the Turning" (Luke)
    EL723, G100, SH68
"The Virgin Mary Had a Baby Boy" 2957081 (Luke)
    AH4037, S2098, SA127, VU73
"Blessed Be the God of Israel" (Luke, Matt)
    C135, CG88, E444, EL250/552, G109, UM209, VU901
"All Who Love and Serve Your City" (Jas)
    C670, CG674, E570/E571, EL724, G351, P413, UM433
"Be Still, My Soul" (Jas)
    C566, CG57, G819, N488, SH330, UM534, VU652
"Watchman, Tell Us of the Night" (Jas)
    E640, G97, N103, P20
"Prepare the Way, O Zion" (Jas)
    CG95, EL264, G106, P13, VU882
"Because You Live, O Christ" (Matt)
    G249, N231, P105
"Once In Royal David's City" (Matt)
    C165, CG104, E102, EL269, G140, N145, P49, SA121, UM250
    (PD), VU62
"Wake, Awake, for Night Is Flying" (Matt)
    E61, EL436, G349, P17, UM720 (PD), VU711
"Wild and Lone the Prophet's Voice" (Matt, Advent)
    G163, P409, S2089

Additional Contemporary and Modern Suggestions

"Come, O Redeemer, Come" 2069663 (Isa, Advent)
"All Who Are Thirsty" 2489542 (Isa, Advent)
"Awaken" 5491647 (Isa, Jas, Advent)
"Give Thanks" 20285 (Isa, Luke)
    C528, CG373, G647, S2036, SA364, SH489

"Awesome in This Place" 847554 (Isa, Luke)
"Please Enter My Heart, Hosanna" 2485371 (Jas, Advent)
    S2154
"Forever" 3148428 (Jas, Luke)
    CG53, SA363, WS3023
"Waiting Here for You" 5925663 (Jas, Luke, Advent)
"Shout to the North" 1562261 (Luke)
    G319, SA1009, WS3042
"Praise to the Lord" (Luke)
    EL844, S2029, VU835
"Shout to the Lord" 1406918 (Luke)
    CG348, EL821, S2074, SA264, SH426
"Make Way" 121074 (Luke, Advent)
    SA148, WS3044
"Your Grace Is Enough" 4477026 (Luke)
"Great and Mighty Is He" 66665 (Luke)
"Good to Me" 313480 (Luke)
"You Are My All in All" 825356 (Luke, Matt)
    CG571, G519, SH335, WS3040
"Welcome to Our World" 2317391 (Matt, Advent)
    V-5 (1)   p. 34. Vocal Solo
"Here I Am to Worship" 3266032 (Matt)
    CG297, SA114, SH395, WS3177
"Emmanuel, Emmanuel" 12949 (Matt)
    C134, CG120, UM204
"Prepare Ye the Way" 5286041 (Matt)

Vocal Solos

"God Will Make a Way" (with "He Leadeth Me") (Isa)
    V-3 (2)   p. 9
"Prepare Thyself, Zion" (Isa, Advent)
    V-9   p. 2
"Lift Up Your Heads" (Isa, Advent)
    V-10   p. 38
"Patiently Have I Waited for the Lord" (Jas)
    V-4   p. 24

Anthems

"Mary's Song" (Luke)
Meg Baker; Choristers Guild CGA1498
Unison, piano (https://bit.ly/CGA1498)

"God's Mother Be" (Luke)
Matthew Culloton; MorningStar MSM-50-0075
SATB *divisi*, harp, guitar or piano (https://bit.ly/MSM-50-0075)

Other Suggestions

Visuals:
    O   Blooms, healing, singing, river/stream, oasis, spring
    P   Mary, joy, arm/scatter, toppled throne, feeding, chest
    E   Second Coming, farmer/cross, gavel, scales, doors
    G   John, prison, Jesus with men, Matt 11:5 imagery
As an alternative to reading the Luke passage, have the choir lead the
    congregation in singing C130, G99, N119, P600, UM198, VU899,
    "My Soul Gives Glory to My God."
Additional Magnificat Settings: C131, CG91, E269, EL314, G100,
    SH68, N732, UM199, VU898 (Luke)
Introit: N142. *"Manglakat na Kita sa Belen"* ("Let Us Even Now
    Go to Bethlehem") (Luke, Advent)
Call to Confession: N832 (Advent)
Canticle: UM199. "Canticle of Mary" ("Magnificat") (Luke)
Advent Candle Response: C128 or G85 (Advent)
Movement or dance can enhance the Luke songs and readings.
Theme Ideas: Hope, Jesus: Return and Reign, Justice, Patience,
    Preparation, Waiting

Isaiah 7:10-16

[10]Again the Lord spoke to Ahaz, saying, [11]Ask a sign of the Lord your God; let it be deep as Sheol or high as heaven. [12]But Ahaz said, I will not ask, and I will not put the Lord to the test. [13]Then Isaiah said: "Hear then, O house of David! Is it too little for you to weary mortals, that you weary my God also? [14]Therefore the Lord himself will give you a sign. Look, the young woman is with child and shall bear a son, and shall name him Immanuel. [15]He shall eat curds and honey by the time he knows how to refuse the evil and choose the good. [16]For before the child knows how to refuse the evil and choose the good, the land before whose two kings you are in dread will be deserted."

Psalm 80:1-7, 17-19 (G355, N672, P206, SH72, UM801)

[1]Give ear, O Shepherd of Israel,
   you who lead Joseph like a flock! You who are enthroned
      upon the cherubim, shine forth
[2]   before Ephraim and Benjamin and Manasseh.
Stir up your might,
   and come to save us!
[3]Restore us, O God;
   let your face shine, that we may be saved.
[4]O Lord God of hosts,
   how long will you be angry with your people's prayers?
[5]You have fed them with the bread of tears,
   and given them tears to drink in full measure.
[6]You make us the scorn of our neighbors;
   our enemies laugh among themselves.
[7]Restore us, O God of hosts;
   let your face shine, that we may be saved.
. . . .
[17]But let your hand be upon the one at your right hand,
   the one whom you made strong for yourself.
[18]Then we will never turn back from you;
   give us life, and we will call on your name.
[19]Restore us, O Lord God of hosts;
   let your face shine, that we may be saved.

Romans 1:1-7

[1]Paul, a servant of Jesus Christ, called to be an apostle, set apart for the gospel of God, [2]which he promised beforehand through his prophets in the holy scriptures, [3]the gospel concerning his Son, who was descended from David according to the flesh [4]and was declared to be Son of God with power according to the spirit of holiness by resurrection from the dead, Jesus Christ our Lord, [5]through whom we have received grace and apostleship to bring about the obedience of faith among all the Gentiles for the sake of his name, [6]including yourselves who are called to belong to Jesus Christ, [7]To all God's beloved in Rome, who are called to be saints: Grace to you and peace from God our Father and the Lord Jesus Christ.

Matthew 1:18-25

[18]Now the birth of Jesus the Messiah took place in this way. When his mother Mary had been engaged to Joseph, but before they lived together, she was found to be with child from the Holy Spirit. [19]Her husband Joseph, being a righteous man and unwilling to expose her to public disgrace, planned to dismiss her quietly. [20]But just when he had resolved to do this, an angel of the Lord appeared to him in a dream and said, "Joseph, son of David, do not be afraid to take Mary as your wife, for the child conceived in her is from the Holy Spirit. [21]She will bear a son, and you are to name him Jesus, for he will save his people from their sins." [22]All this took place to fulfill what had been spoken by the Lord through the prophet:
[23]   "Look, the virgin shall conceive and bear a son,
      and they shall name him Emmanuel,"
   which means, "God is with us." [24]When Joseph awoke from sleep, he did as the angel of the Lord commanded him; he took her as his wife, [25]but had no marital relations with her until she had borne a son; and he named him Jesus.

Primary Hymns and Songs for the Day

"Emmanuel, Emmanuel" 12949 (Isa, Matt) (O)
C134, CG120, UM204

"O Come, O Come, Emmanuel" (Isa, Matt) (O)
C119, CG79, E56, EL257, G88, N116, P9, SA117, SH73, UM211, VU1 (Fr.)
> H-3   Hbl-14, 79; Chr-141; Org-168
> S-1   #342. Handbell accompaniment

"Once in Royal David's City" (Isa, Matt)
C165, CG104, E102, EL269, G140, N145, P49, SA121, UM250 (PD), VU62
> H-3   Hbl-83; Chr-68, 156; Desc-57; Org-63
> S-1   #182-184. Various treatments

"To a Maid Engaged to Joseph" (Isa, Matt)
G98, P19, UM215, VU14

"Joseph Dearest, Joseph Mine" (Matt)
N105, S2099

"Hark! the Herald Angels Sing" (Matt) (C)
C150, CG127, E87, EL270, G119, N144, P31, SA108, SH94, UM240 (PD), VU48
> H-3   Hbl-26, 67; Chr-91; Desc-75; Org-89
> S-1   #234-6. Harms. and desc.

Additional Hymn Suggestions

"It Came Upon the Midnight Clear" (Isa)
C153, CG132, E89, EL282, G123, N131, P38, SA111, SH89, UM218 (PD), VU44

"I Want to Walk as a Child of the Light" (Isa, Pss, Advent)
CG96, E490, EL815, G377, SH352, UM206

Toda la Tierra ("All Earth Is Waiting") (Isa, Matt)
C139, EL266, N121, SH63, UM210, VU5

"Savior of the Nations, Come" (Isa, Matt)
E54, EL263, G102, P14 (PD), SH67, UM214

"Lo, How a Rose E'er Blooming" (Isa, Matt)
C160, CG105, E81, EL272, G129, N127, P48 (PD), UM216, VU8

"Lead Me, Guide Me" (Pss, Advent)
C583, CG403, EL768, G740, S2214, SH582

"People, Look East" (Pss, Advent)
C142, CG90, EL248, G105, P12, UM202, VU9

"Send Your Word" (Pss, Rom Advent)
N317, UM195

"Alleluia, Alleluia" 32376 (Rom)
CG196, E178, G240, P106, SA216, SH189, UM162, VU179

"What Child Is This" (Rom)
C162, CG148, E115, EL296, G145, N148, P53, SH105, UM219 (PD), VU74

"While Shepherds Watched Their Flocks" (Rom)
C154, CG123, G117/118, SA132, UM236, VU75

"O Come, All Ye Faithful" (Rom, Matt)
C148, CG103, E83, EL283, G133, N135, P41, SA116, SH96, UM234 (PD), VU60 (Fr.)

"Come, Thou Long-Expected Jesus" (Matt)
C125, CG83, E66, EL254, G82/83, N122, P1/2, SA104, SH64, UM196 (PD), VU2

"My Soul Gives Glory to My God" (Matt)
C130, EL251, G99, N119, P600, UM198, VU899

"Tell Out, My Soul" (Matt)
CG94, E437/E438, SA393, UM200

"Angels from the Realms of Glory" (Matt)
C149, CG126, E93, EL275, G143, N126, P22, SA100, SH99, UM220 (PD), VU36

"O Little Town of Bethlehem" (Matt) (C)
C144, CG107, E78/79, EL279, G121, N133, P43/44, SA118, SH80, UM230, VU64

"Go, Tell It on the Mountain" (Matt)
C167, CG143, E99, EL290, G136, N154, P29, SA106, SH90, UM251, VU43

"Rise Up, Shepherd, and Follow" (Matt)
G135, P50, S2096, VU70

"O Holy Spirit, Root of Life" (Matt, Advent)
C251, EL399, N57, S2121, VU379

Additional Contemporary and Modern Suggestions

"All Hail King Jesus" 12877 (Isa, Matt)

"Jesus, Name above All Names" 21291 (Isa, Matt)
S2071, SA82

"Glory in the Highest" 4822451 (Isa, Matt)

"Shine, Jesus, Shine" 30426 (Pss)
CG156, EL671, G192, S2173, SA261, SH102

"The Power of Your Love" 917491 (Pss)

"Refresh My Heart" 917518 (Rom, Advent)

"Let the Peace of God Reign" 1839987 (Rom)

"There's Something About That Name" 14064 (Matt)
C115, SA80, UM171

"Jesus, the Light of the World" 6363190 (Matt, Advent)
WS3056 (See also AH4038, CG129, G127, N160, SH103)

"Lord, I Lift Your Name on High" 117947 (Matt, Christmas)
AH4071, CG606, EL857, S2088, SA379, SH205

"Jesus, We Crown You with Praise" 1453284 (Matt)

Vocal Solos

"Behold! A Virgin Shall Conceive" and
"O Thou That Tellest Good Tidings to Zion" (Isa, Matt)
> V-2

"Glory Hallelujah to de New-Born King" (Isa, Matt)
> V-7   p. 80

"Who Is This Boy?" (Matt)
> V-8   p. 223

Anthems

"All Is Well" (Matt)
Arr. Jamey Ray; Excelcia VOC2001
SATB *divisi, a cappella* (https://bit.ly/VOC2001)

"The Hands That First Held Mary's Child" (Matt)
Dan Forrest; Beckenhorst BP1928
SATB, piano (https://bit.ly/BP1928)

Other Suggestions

Visuals:
> **O**   Test, pregnant woman, baby, Immanuel, curds/honey
> **P**   Shepherd, seat, anger/ tears/laughter, returning
> **E**   Letter, Bible, resurrection, Rom 1:7b
> **G**   Pregnant Mary, Joseph, Spirit symbol, birth, angel Emmanuel (God with us), "Jesus"

Introit: N137. *"Hitsuji wa nemureri"* ("Sheep Fast Asleep") (Isa)

Greeting: WSL4 (Matt)

Prayer: WSL6. "Gracious God, your servant Mary" (Matt)

Response: C158. "Her Baby, Newly Breathing" (Matt)

Advent Candle Response: C128 or G85 (Advent)

Prayer: WSL11. "Radiant Morning Star" (Matt)

Offertory Prayer: WS125. "Precious Lord, amid the twinkling lights" (Matt, Advent)

Blessing: WSL7. "The light that enlivens" (Pss)

Theme Ideas: Grace, Jesus: Incarnation, Redemption / Salvation

Isaiah 9:2-7

²The people who walked in darkness
　　have seen a great light;
those who lived in a land of deep darkness—
　　on them light has shined.
³You have multiplied the nation,
　　you have increased its joy;
they rejoice before you
　　as with joy at the harvest,
　　as people exult when dividing plunder.
⁴For the yoke of their burden,
　　and the bar across their shoulders,
　　the rod of their oppressor,
　　you have broken as on the day of Midian.
⁵For all the boots of the tramping warriors
　　and all the garments rolled in blood
　　shall be burned as fuel for the fire.
⁶For a child has been born for us,
　　a son given to us;
authority rests upon his shoulders;
　　and he is named
Wonderful Counselor, Mighty God,
　　Everlasting Father, Prince of Peace.
⁷His authority shall grow continually,
　　and there shall be endless peace
for the throne of David and his kingdom.
　　He will establish and uphold it
with justice and with righteousness
　　from this time onward and forevermore.
The zeal of the LORD of hosts will do this.

Psalm 96 (G304, N684, P216/217, SH648, UM815)

¹O sing to the LORD a new song;
　　sing to the LORD, all the earth.
²Sing to the LORD, bless his name;
　　tell of his salvation from day to day.
³Declare his glory among the nations,
　　his marvelous works among all the peoples.
⁴For great is the LORD, and greatly to be praised;
　　he is to be revered above all gods.
⁵For all the gods of the peoples are idols,
　　but the LORD made the heavens.
⁶Honor and majesty are before him;
　　strength and beauty are in his sanctuary.
⁷Ascribe to the LORD, O families of the peoples,
　　ascribe to the LORD glory and strength.
⁸Ascribe to the LORD the glory due his name;
　　bring an offering, and come into his courts.
⁹Worship the LORD in holy splendor;
　　tremble before him, all the earth.
¹⁰Say among the nations, "The LORD is king!
　　The world is firmly established; it shall never be moved.
　　He will judge the peoples with equity."
¹¹Let the heavens be glad, and let the earth rejoice;
　　let the sea roar, and all that fills it;
¹²let the field exult, and everything in it.
　　Then shall all the trees of the forest sing for joy
¹³before the LORD; for he is coming,
　　for he is coming to judge the earth.
He will judge the world with righteousness,
　　and the peoples with his truth.

Titus 2:11-14

¹¹For the grace of God has appeared, bringing salvation to all, ¹²training us to renounce impiety and worldly passions, and in the present age to live lives that are self-controlled, upright, and godly, ¹³while we wait for the blessed hope and the manifestation of the glory of our great God and Savior, Jesus Christ. ¹⁴He it is who gave himself for us that he might redeem us from all iniquity and purify for himself a people of his own who are zealous for good deeds.

Luke 2:1-14, (15-20)

¹In those days a decree went out from Emperor Augustus that all the world should be registered. ²This was the first registration and was taken while Quirinius was governor of Syria. ³All went to their own towns to be registered. ⁴Joseph also went from the town of Nazareth in Galilee to Judea, to the city of David called Bethlehem, because he was descended from the house and family of David. ⁵He went to be registered with Mary, to whom he was engaged and who was expecting a child. ⁶While they were there, the time came for her to deliver her child. ⁷And she gave birth to her firstborn son and wrapped him in bands of cloth, and laid him in a manger, because there was no place for them in the inn.

⁸In that region there were shepherds living in the fields, keeping watch over their flock by night. ⁹Then an angel of the Lord stood before them, and the glory of the Lord shone around them, and they were terrified. ¹⁰But the angel said to them, "Do not be afraid; for see—I am bringing you good news of great joy for all the people: ¹¹to you is born this day in the city of David a Savior, who is the Messiah, the Lord. ¹²This will be a sign for you: you will find a child wrapped in bands of cloth and lying in a manger." ¹³And suddenly there was with the angel a multitude of the heavenly host, praising God and saying,
¹⁴　"Glory to God in the highest heaven,
　　　and on earth peace among those whom he favors!"

¹⁵When the angels had left them and gone into heaven, the shepherds said to one another, "Let us go now to Bethlehem and see this thing that has taken place, which the Lord has made known to us." ¹⁶So they went with haste and found Mary and Joseph, and the child lying in the manger. ¹⁷When they saw this, they made known what had been told them about this child; ¹⁸and all who heard it were amazed at what the shepherds told them. ¹⁹But Mary treasured all these words and pondered them in her heart. ²⁰The shepherds returned, glorifying and praising God for all they had heard and seen, as it had been told them.

Primary Hymns and Songs for the Day

"Angels We Have Heard on High" (Luke) (O)
C155, CG125, E96, EL289, G113, P23, N125, SII93, UM238, VU38 (Fr.)
- H-3   Hbl-47; Chr-31; Desc-43; Org-45

"On Christmas Night" (Isa, Titus, Luke)
CG133, EL274, G112, N143, WS3064

"Silent Night, Holy Night" (Luke)
C145, CG134, E111, EL281, G122, N134, P60, SA124, SH83, UM239 (PD), VU67 (Fr.)
- H-3   Hbl-92; Chr-171; Desc-99; Org-159
- S-1   #322. Desc.
         #323. Guitar/Autoharp chords
- S-2   #167. Handbell arrangement

"Joy to the World" (Titus, Luke) (C)
C143, CG102, E100, EL267, G134/266, N132, P40, SA113, SH95, UM246 (PD), VU59
- S-1   #19-20. Trumpet desc.

"Go, Tell it on the Mountain" (Luke) (C)
C167, CG143, E99, EL290, G136, N154, P29, SA106, SH90, UM251, VU43
- H-3   Hbl-17; Chr-73; Desc-45; Org-46

Additional Hymn Suggestions

"Born in the Night, Mary's Child" (Isa)
G158, N152, P30, VU95

"Break Forth, O Beauteous Heavenly Light" (Isa)
E91, G130, N140, P26, UM223, VU83

"It Came Upon the Midnight Clear" (Isa, Luke) (O)
C153, CG132, E89, EL282, G123, N131, P38, SA111, SH89, UM218 (PD), VU44

"Angels from the Realms of Glory" (Isa, Luke)
C149, CG126, E93, EL275, G143, N126, P22, SA100, SH99, UM220 (PD), VU36

"Hark! the Herald Angels Sing" (Isa, Luke) (O)
C150, CG127, E87, EL270, G119, N144, P31, SA108, SH94, UM240 (PD), VU48

"Love Has Come" (Isa, Titus, Luke, Christmas)
EL292, G110, WS3059

"In the Bleak Midwinter" (Pss, Titus, Luke)
CG131, E112, EL294, G144, N128, SA110, UM221, VU55

"Love Came Down at Christmas" (Titus, Luke)
CG147, E84, N165, UM242

"Love Has Come" (Titus, Christmas)
EL292, G110, WS3059

"Away in a Manger" (Luke)
C147, CG110/111, E101, EL277, G114/115, N124, P24/P25, SA102, SH79, UM217, VU69

"What Child Is This" (Luke)
C162, CG148, E115, EL296, G145, N148, P53, SH105, UM219 (PD), VU74

"Angels from the Realms of Glory" (Isa, Luke)
C149, CG126, E93, EL275, G143, N126, P22, SA100, SH99, UM220 (PD), VU36

"Infant Holy, Infant Lowly" (Luke)
C163, CG139, EL276, G128, P37, UM229, VU58

"O Come, All Ye Faithful" (Luke)
C148, CG103, E83, EL283, G133, N135, P41, SA116, SH96, UM234 (PD), VU60 (Fr.)

"'Twas in the Moon of Wintertime" (Luke)
C166, E114, EL284, G142, N151, P61, UM244, VU71

"Once in Royal David's City" (Luke)
C165, CG104, E102, EL269, G140, N145, P49, SA121, UM250 (PD), VU62

"Rise Up, Shepherd, and Follow" (Luke)
G135, P50, S2096, VU70

"Still, Still, Still" (Luke)
CG117, G124, P47, VU47, WS3066

Additional Contemporary and Modern Suggestions

"His Name Is Wonderful" 1122230 (Isa)
CG343, SH454, UM174

"How Majestic Is Your Name" 26007 (Isa)
C63, CG326, G613, S2023, SA90

"Jesus, Jesus, Oh, What a Wonderful Child" 4206259 (Isa, Luke)
EL297, G126, N136, WS3060

"Marvelous Light" 4491002 (Isa)

"You are the Light" 6238098 (Isa)

"How Great Is Our God" 4348399 (Isa, Pss)
CG322, SH458, WS3003

"Majesty" 1527 (Pss)
CG346, SA382, SH212, UM176

"Sing Unto the Lord a New Song" 571215 (Pss)

"Sing a New Song to the Lord" 142895 (Pss)

"Shout to the North" 1562261 (Pss)
G319, SA1009, WS3042

"Shout to the Lord" 1406918 (Pss)
CG348, EL821, S2074, SA264, SH426

"Lord, I Lift Your Name on High" 117947 (Luke)
AH4071, CG606, EL857, S2088, SA379, SH205

"Welcome to Our World" 2317391 (Luke)
- V-5 (1)   p. 34. Vocal Solo

"Peace in the Manger" 7104263 (Luke, Christmas)

"What Love Has Done" 5836965 (Luke, Christmas)

Vocal Solos

"O Holy Night" (Luke)
- V-8   p. 93

"Sleep, Little Baby" (Luke)
- V-10   p. 27

"Sing Noel!" (Luke)
- V-1   p. 13

"Glory Hallelujah to de New-Born King" (Luke)
- V-7   p. 80

Anthems

"Hodie!" (Luke)
Matthew J. Armstrong; Alliance AMP1059
SATB, piano (https://bit.ly/AMP1059)

"Silent Night" (Luke)
Arr. Peter Anglea; Beckenhorst Press BP2059
SATB (some *divisi*), piano (https://bit.ly/BP2059)

Other Suggestions

Visuals:
- **O**   Darkness/light, joy, yoke, boots, fire, child, names
- **P**   New song, nations, glory, Ps 96:10a, gavel, nature images
- **E**   Jesus, Second Coming, crucifix
- **G**   Tax register, manger scene, shepherds, angels, Luke 2:14

Introit or Sung Benediction: G158, N152, P30, VU95, stanzas 1-2. "Born in the Night, Mary's Child" (Luke, Christmas)

Introit: EL819, G388, S2274, SH405. "Come, All You People" (Pss)

Introit: C146. "From Heaven Above" (Luke)

Reading: C152, CG108 (Luke)

Response: G584, CG321, N756/758, SH100, VU895. "Gloria" (Luke)

Response: WS3190, stanza 1. "Mary Had a Little Lamb" (Luke)

Communion Hymn: EL487, WS3170. "What Feast of Love" (Same tune as "What Child Is This")

Theme Ideas: Grace, Jesus: Incarnation, Light, Praise

Isaiah 52:7-10

⁷How beautiful upon the mountains
    are the feet of the messenger who announces peace,
who brings good news,
    who announces salvation,
    who says to Zion, "Your God reigns."
⁸Listen! Your sentinels lift up their voices,
    together they sing for joy;
for in plain sight they see
    the return of the LORD to Zion.
⁹Break forth together into singing,
    you ruins of Jerusalem;
for the LORD has comforted his people,
he has redeemed Jerusalem.
¹⁰The LORD has bared his holy arm
    before the eyes of all the nations;
and all the ends of the earth shall see
    the salvation of our God.

Psalm 98 (G276/371, N686, P218-219, UM818)

¹O sing to the LORD a new song,
    for he has done marvelous things.
His right hand and his holy arm
    have gotten him victory.
²The LORD has made known his victory;
    he has revealed his vindication in the sight of the nations.
³He has remembered his steadfast love and faithfulness
    to the house of Israel.
All the ends of the earth have seen
    the victory of our God.
⁴Make a joyful noise to the LORD, all the earth;
    break forth into joyous song and sing praises.
⁵Sing praises to the LORD with the lyre,
    with the lyre and the sound of melody.
⁶With trumpets and the sound of the horn
    make a joyful noise before the King, the LORD.
⁷Let the sea roar, and all that fills it;
    the world and those who live in it.
⁸Let the floods clap their hands;
    let the hills sing together for joy
⁹at the presence of the LORD, for he is coming
    to judge the earth.
He will judge the world with righteousness,
    and the peoples with equity.

Hebrews 1:1-4, (5-12)

¹Long ago God spoke to our ancestors in many and various ways by the prophets, ²but in these last days he has spoken to us by a Son, whom he appointed heir of all things, through whom he also created the worlds. ³He is the reflection of God's glory and the exact imprint of God's very being, and he sustains all things by his powerful word. When he had made purification for sins, he sat down at the right hand of the Majesty on high, ⁴having become as much superior to angels as the name he has inherited is more excellent than theirs.
⁵For to which of the angels did God ever say,
"You are my Son;
    today I have begotten you"?
Or again,
"I will be his Father,
    and he will be my Son"?
⁶And again, when he brings the firstborn into the world, he says,
"Let all God's angels worship him."
⁷ Of the angels he says,
"He makes his angels winds,
    and his servants flames of fire."
⁸But of the Son he says,
"Your throne, O God, is forever and ever,
    and the righteous scepter is the scepter of your kingdom.
⁹ You have loved righteousness and hated wickedness;
therefore God, your God, has anointed you
    with the oil of gladness beyond your companions."
¹⁰And,
"In the beginning, Lord, you founded the earth,
    and the heavens are the work of your hands;
¹¹they will perish, but you remain;
    they will all wear out like clothing;
¹²like a cloak you will roll them up,
    and like clothing they will be changed.
But you are the same,
    and your years will never end."

John 1:1-14

¹In the beginning was the Word, and the Word was with God, and the Word was God. ²He was in the beginning with God. ³All things came into being through him, and without him not one thing came into being. What has come into being ⁴in him was life, and the life was the light of all people. ⁵The light shines in the darkness, and the darkness did not overcome it.
⁶There was a man sent from God, whose name was John. ⁷He came as a witness to testify to the light, so that all might believe through him. ⁸He himself was not the light, but he came to testify to the light. ⁹The true light, which enlightens everyone, was coming into the world.
¹⁰He was in the world, and the world came into being through him; yet the world did not know him. ¹¹He came to what was his own, and his own people did not accept him. ¹²But to all who received him, who believed in his name, he gave power to become children of God, ¹³who were born, not of blood or of the will of the flesh or of the will of man, but of God.
¹⁴And the Word became flesh and lived among us, and we have seen his glory, the glory as of a father's only son, full of grace and truth.

Primary Hymns and Songs for the Day

"Joy to the World" (Isa, Pss) (O)
    C143, CG102, E100, EL267, G134, N132, P40, SA113, SH95,
    UM246 (PD), VU59
        H-3   Hbl-8, 29; Chr-119; Desc-15; Org-6
        S-1   #19-20. Trumpet descants

"O Come, All Ye Faithful" (John) (O)
    C148, CG103, E83, EL283, G133, N135, P41, SA116, SH96,
    UM234 (PD), VU60 (Fr.)
        H-3   Hbl-78; Desc-12; Org-2
        S-1   #7-13. Various treatments

"Good Christian Friends, Rejoice" (Isa)
    C164, CG122, E107 (PD), EL288, G132, N129, P28, UM224,
    VU35
        H-3   Hbl-19, 30; Chr-83; Desc-55; Org-62
        S-1   #180. Rhythm instrument acc.

"Go, Tell It on the Mountain" (Isa)
    C167, CG143, E99, EL290, G136, N154, P29, SA106, SH90,
    UM251, VU43
        H-3   Hbl-17, 28, 61; Chr-73; Desc-45; Org-46

"Love Came Down at Christmas" (John)
    CG147, E84, N165, UM242

"Jesus, Name Above All Names" 21291 (John)
    S2071, SA82

"I Want to Walk as a Child of the Light" (John) (C)
    CG96, E490, EL815, G377, SH352, UM206
        S-2   #91. Descant

"Hark! the Herald Angels Sing" (Heb, John) (C)
    C150, CG127, E87, EL270, G119, N144, P31, SA108, SH94,
    UM240 (PD), VU48
        H-3   Hbl-26, 67; Chr-91; Desc-75; Org-89
        S-1   #234-6. Harmonizations and descant

Additional Hymn Suggestions

"Wake, Awake, for Night is Flying" (Isa)
    E61, EL436, G349, P17, UM720 (PD), VU711

"On This Day Earth Shall Ring" (Isa, John, Comm.)
    E92, G141, P46, UM248 (PD)

"It Came Upon the Midnight Clear" (Heb)
    C153, CG132, E89, EL282, G123, N131, P38, SH89,
    UM218 (PD), VU44

"What Child Is This" (Heb)
    C162, CG148, E115, EL296, G145, N148, P53, SH105, UM219
    (PD), VU74

"Angels from the Realms of Glory" (Heb)
    C149, CG126, E93, EL275, G143, N126, P22, SA100, SH99,
    UM220 (PD), VU36

"Infant Holy, Infant Lowly" (Heb)
    C163, CG139, EL276, G128, P37, UM229, VU58

"Angels We Have Heard on High" (Heb)
    C155, CG125, E96, EL289, G113, P23, N125, SH93, UM238,
    VU38 (Fr.)

"The Snow Lay on the Ground" (Heb, Christmas)
    E110, G116, S2093, P57

"Of the Father's Love Begotten" (John)
    C104, CG113, E82, EL295, G108, N118, P309, SA119, SH81,
    UM184, VU61

"Womb of Life" (John)
    C14, G3, N274, S2046

"Mothering God, You Gave Me Birth" (John)
    C83, EL735, G7, N467, S2050, VU320

"O Holy Spirit, Root of Life" (John)
    C251, EL399, N57, S2121, VU379

"Love Has Come" (John, Christmas)
    EL292, G110, WS3059

"Thou Didst Leave Thy Throne" (John, Christmas)
    CG165, S2100, SA153, SH86

"In the Bleak Midwinter" (Christmas)
    CG131, E112, EL294, G144, N128, P36, SA110, UM221 (PD),
    VU55

"'Twas in the Moon of Wintertime" (Christmas)
    C166, E114, EL284, G142, N151, P61, UM244, VU71

"Deck Thyself, My Soul, With Gladness" (Christmas, Comm.)
    E339, EL488/EL489, G514, P506, UM612 (PD), VU463

Additional Contemporary Suggestions

"Our God Reigns" 8458 (Isa)

"Welcome to Our World" 2317391 (Isa, Heb, John, Christmas)
        V-5(1)   p. 34. Vocal Solo

"Shout to the Lord" 1406918 (Pss)
    CG348, EL821, S2074, SA264, SH426

"Sing Unto the Lord a New Song" 571215 (Pss)

"Jesus, the Light of the World" 6363190 (Heb, John)
    WS3056 (See also AH4038, CG129, G127, N160, SH103)

"Jesus, Jesus, Oh, What a Wonderful Child" 4206259 (Heb)
    AH4039, EL297, G126, N136, WS3060

"Shine, Jesus, Shine" 30426 (John)
    CG156, EL671, G192, S2173, SA261, SH102
        V-3 (2)   p. 48. Vocal Solo

"Shine on Us" 1754646 (John)

"Forevermore" 5466830 (John)

"Glory in the Highest" 4822451 (John, Christmas)

Vocal Solos

"Sing of Mary, Pure and Lowly" (John)
    V-5 (1)   p. 21

"Love Came Down at Christmas" (John)
    V-8   p. 90

"This Christmas Morning" (Christmas)
    V-5 (1)   p. 41

"Glory Hallelujah to de New-Born King" (Christmas)
    V-7   p. 80

Anthems

"Hark! the Herald Angels Sing" (Heb, John)
Arr. Dan Forrest; Beckenhorst BP-2051
SATB, piano 4-hands or organ, opt. handbells
(https://bit.ly/BP-2051)

"Gloria! Angels Sing His Coming" (John)
Richard A. Williamson; Lorenz 10/4977S
SATB, organ (https://bit.ly/10-4977S)

Other Suggestions

Visuals:
    O   Mountains, feet, sheet music, singing, ruins, nations
    P   Singing, hand, creation, musical instruments,
        Ps 98:11, 14
    E   Angels, scepter/crown/royal cloak, oil, flames
    G   Light/darkness, Christ candle, John 1:1, 5, 14

Introit: C184, E277, UM272, st. 1. "Sing of Mary, Pure and
    Lowly" (John)

Introit: E92, G141, P46, UM248 (PD). "On This Day Earth Shall
    Ring" (Pss, Titus, Luke)

Litany of Praise: WSL9. "Sing! Sing to the Lord" (Pss)

Prayer: UM231. Christmas (Heb)

Blessing: WSL7. "The light that enlivens" (John)

Themes: God: Love of God, Jesus: Incarnation, Light, Praise

Ecclesiastes 3:1-13

[1]For everything there is a season, and a time for every matter under heaven:

[2] a time to be born, and a time to die;
a time to plant, and a time to pluck up what is planted;

[3] a time to kill, and a time to heal;
a time to break down, and a time to build up;

[4] a time to weep, and a time to laugh;
a time to mourn, and a time to dance;

[5] a time to throw away stones, and a time to gather stones together;
a time to embrace, and a time to refrain from embracing;

[6] a time to seek, and a time to lose;
a time to keep, and a time to throw away;

[7] a time to tear, and a time to sew;
a time to keep silence, and a time to speak;

[8] a time to love, and a time to hate;
a time for war, and a time for peace.

[9]What gain have the workers from their toil? [10]I have seen the business that God has given to everyone to be busy with. [11]He has made everything suitable for its time; moreover he has put a sense of past and future into their minds, yet they cannot find out what God has done from the beginning to the end. [12]I know that there is nothing better for them than to be happy and enjoy themselves as long as they live; [13]moreover, it is God's gift that all should eat and drink and take pleasure in all their toil.

Psalm 8 (G25, N624, P162/163, SH6, UM743)

[1]O Lord, our Sovereign,
how majestic is your name in all the earth!
You have set your glory above the heavens.

[2] Out of the mouths of babes and infants
you have founded a bulwark because of your foes,
to silence the enemy and the avenger.

[3]When I look at your heavens, the work of your fingers,
the moon and the stars that you have established;

[4]what are human beings that you are mindful of them,
mortals that you care for them?

[5]Yet you have made them a little lower than God,
and crowned them with glory and honor.

[6]You have given them dominion over the works of your hands;
you have put all things under their feet,

[7]all sheep and oxen,
and also the beasts of the field,

[8]the birds of the air, and the fish of the sea,
whatever passes along the paths of the seas.

[9]O Lord, our Sovereign,
how majestic is your name in all the earth!

Revelation 21:1-6a

[1]Then I saw a new heaven and a new earth; for the first heaven and the first earth had passed away, and the sea was no more. [2]And I saw the holy city, the new Jerusalem, coming down out of heaven from God, prepared as a bride adorned for her husband. [3]And I heard a loud voice from the throne saying,

"See, the home of God is among mortals.
He will dwell with them as their God;
they will be his peoples,
and God himself will be with them;

[4] he will wipe every tear from their eyes.
Death will be no more;
mourning and crying and pain will be no more,
for the first things have passed away."

[5]And the one who was seated on the throne said, "See, I am making all things new." Also he said, "Write this, for these words are trustworthy and true." [6a]Then he said to me, "It is done! I am the Alpha and the Omega, the beginning and the end."

Matthew 25:31-46

[31]"When the Son of Man comes in his glory, and all the angels with him, then he will sit on the throne of his glory. [32]All the nations will be gathered before him, and he will separate people one from another as a shepherd separates the sheep from the goats, [33]and he will put the sheep at his right hand and the goats at the left. [34]Then the king will say to those at his right hand, 'Come, you that are blessed by my Father, inherit the kingdom prepared for you from the foundation of the world; [35]for I was hungry and you gave me food, I was thirsty and you gave me something to drink, I was a stranger and you welcomed me, [36]I was naked and you gave me clothing, I was sick and you took care of me, I was in prison and you visited me.' [37]Then the righteous will answer him, 'Lord, when was it that we saw you hungry and gave you food, or thirsty and gave you something to drink? [38]And when was it that we saw you a stranger and welcomed you, or naked and gave you clothing? [39]And when was it that we saw you sick or in prison and visited you?' [40]And the king will answer them, 'Truly I tell you, just as you did it to one of the least of these who are members of my family, you did it to me.' [41]Then he will say to those at his left hand, 'You that are accursed, depart from me into the eternal fire prepared for the devil and his angels; [42]for I was hungry and you gave me no food, I was thirsty and you gave me nothing to drink, [43]I was a stranger and you did not welcome me, naked and you did not give me clothing, sick and in prison and you did not visit me.' [44]Then they also will answer, 'Lord, when was it that we saw you hungry or thirsty or a stranger or naked or sick or in prison, and did not take care of you?' [45]Then he will answer them, 'Truly I tell you, just as you did not do it to one of the least of these, you did not do it to me.' [46]And these will go away into eternal punishment, but the righteous into eternal life."

Primary Hymns and Songs for the Day
"O God, Our Help in Ages Past" (Eccl) (O)
  C67, CG566, E680, EL632, G687, N25, P210, SA47, SH41, UM117 (PD), VU806
      H-3 Hbl-33, 80; Chr-60, 143; Desc-93; Org-132
      S-1 #293-296. Various treatments
"How Great Thou Art" (Pss)
  AH4015, C33, CG323, EL856, G625, N35, P467, SA49, SH14, UM77, VU238 (Fr.)
"O Holy City, Seen of John" (Rev)
  E582/583, G374, N613, P453, UM726, VU709
      H-3 Chr-139, 145; Desc-77
      S-1 #241-242. Orff arr. and desc.
Cuando el Pobre ("When the Poor Ones") (Matt)
  C662, EL725, G762, P407, SH240, UM434, VU702
"Here Am I" (Matt) (C)
  C654, S2178
"Hymn of Promise" (Eccl) (C)
  C638, CG545, G250, N433, UM707, VU703

Additional Hymn Suggestions
"O God, in a Mysterious Way" (Eccl)
  CG39, E677, G30, N412, P270, SA17, SH47
"For the Beauty of the Earth" (Eccl)
  C56, CG341, E416, EL879, G14, P473, N28, SA14, SH21, UM92 (PD), VU226
"Sing Praise to God Who Reigns Above" (Eccl)
  C6, CG315, E408, EL871, G645, N6, UM126 (PD), VU216
"Great Is Thy Faithfulness" (Eccl) (O)
  AH4011, C86, CG48, EL733, G39, N423, P276, SA26, SH48, UM140, VU288
"Many and Great, O God" (Eccl)
  C58, CG28, E385, EL837, G21, N3, N341, P271 (PD), SH5, UM148, VU308
"By Gracious Powers" (Eccl)
  E695/696, EL626, G818, N413, P342, UM517
"For the Fruits of This Creation" (Pss) (O)
  (alternate tune #688)
  C714, E424, CG376, EL679, G36, N425, P553, SA15, UM97, VU227
"Glorious Things of Thee Are Spoken" (Pss)
  C709, CG282, E522/523, EL647, G81, N307, P446, SA535, UM731 (PD)
"Rejoice! Rejoice, Believers" (Rev)
  E68, EL244, G362, P15
"This Is a Day of New Beginnings" (Rev)
  C518, N417, UM383
"For the Healing of the Nations" (Rev)
  C668, CG698, G346, N576, SA1000, UM428, VU678
"Blessed Quietness" (Rev)
  C267, CG244, N284, S2142
"All Who Hunger" (Rev, Matt)
  C419, CG303, EL461, G509, S2126, VU460
"Like a Mother Who Has Borne Us" (Matt)
  G44, N583
"We Praise You, O God, Our Redeemer" (Matt)
  CG356, EL870, G612, N420, VU218
"Where Cross the Crowded Ways of Life" (Matt)
  C665, CG657, E609, EL719, G343, N543, UM427, VU681
"I Come with Joy" (Matt, New Year, Comm.)
  C420, CG456, E304, EL482, G515, N349, P507, SH682, UM617, VU477
"Together We Serve" (Matt)
  G767, S2175

Additional Contemporary and Modern Suggestions
"I Could Sing of Your Love Forever" 1043199 (Eccl)
"Be Glorified" 2732646 (Eccl)
"How Majestic Is Your Name" 26007 (Pss)
  C63, CG326, G613, S2023, SA90

"How Great Is Our God" 4348399 (Pss)
  CG322, SH458, WS3003
"Hallelujah" ("Your Love Is Amazing") 3091812 (Pss)
"Across the Lands" 3709898 (Pss, Christmas)
  SH654, WS3032
"God of Wonders" 3118757 (Pss)
  SH9, WS3034
"Majestic" 4573308 (Pss)
"You Have Saved Us" 5548514 (Pss)
"There's Something About That Name" 14064 (Rev)
  C115, SA80, UM171
"Spirit Song" 27824 (Rev)
  C352, SH409, UM347
"Soon and Very Soon" 11249 (Rev)
  CG562, EL439, G384, SH357, UM706, S-2 #187. Piano arrangement
"We Will Glorify the King of Kings" 19038 (Rev)
  CG360, S2087
"You Who Are Thirsty" 814453 (Rev)
"O Freedom" (Rev)
  S2194
"There Is a Higher Throne" 3994672 (Rev)
"Holy and Anointed One" 164361 (Rev, Matt)
"To Him Who Sits on the Throne" 20429 (Rev, Matt)
"People Need the Lord" 18084 (Matt)
  S2244, SA418
"All of Me" 6290160 (Matt, Covenant, New Year)
"Peace in the Manger" 7104263 (Matt, Christmas)

Vocal Solos
"I Will Sing of Thy Great Mercies" (Eccl, Pss)
  V-4   p. 43
"Sing for Christ Is Born" (Rev, Christmas)
  V-10   p. 16
"Come to the Water" (Rev, Matt)
  S3114
"Reach Out to Your Neighbor" (Matt)
  V-8   p. 372
"Covenant Prayer" (New Year)
  V-1   p. 6

Anthems
"How Great Thou Art" (Pss)
Arr. Eric Nelson; MorningStar MSM-50-7106
SATB, organ, opt. brass quintet, timp. (https://bit.ly/50-7106)

"God Has Work for Us to Do" (Matt)
Mark Miller; Choristers Guild CGA-1288
SATB, piano (https://bit.ly/CGA1288)

Other Suggestions
These scriptures may also be used on Jan. 1.
Visuals:
  O Clock, birth/death, mourn/dance, weep/laugh, etc.
  P Glory, newborns, fingers, moon/stars, humanity, earth
  E Earth/space, heaven, bride, throne, wipe tears, Rev 21:5a
  G Second Coming, nations, goats/sheep, feeding, etc.
Canticle: UM734. "Canticle of Hope" (Rev)
Litany: C157. "For All Who Give You a Face" (Matt)
Response: C638, CG545, G250, N433, UM707, VU703, stanza 3. "Hymn of Promise" (Eccl)
Blessing: WSL27 or WSL159 or WSL169 (Matt)
Theme Ideas: Compassion, God: Glory of God, Justice, New Creation, Patience, Patience

Isaiah 63:7-9

[7]I will recount the gracious deeds of the LORD,
  the praiseworthy acts of the LORD,
because of all that the LORD has done for us,
  and the great favor to the house of Israel
that he has shown them according to his mercy,
  according to the abundance of his steadfast love.
[8]For he said, "Surely they are my people,
  children who will not deal falsely";
and he became their savior
[9] in all their distress.
It was no messenger or angel
  but his presence that saved them;
in his love and in his pity he redeemed them;
  he lifted them up and carried them all the days of old.

Psalm 148 (G16/17, N721, P256, UM861)

[1]Praise the LORD!
Praise the LORD from the heavens;
  praise him in the heights!
[2]Praise him, all his angels;
  praise him, all his host!
[3]Praise him, sun and moon;
  praise him, all you shining stars!
[4]Praise him, you highest heavens,
  and you waters above the heavens!
[5]Let them praise the name of the LORD,
  for he commanded and they were created.
[6]He established them forever and ever;
  he fixed their bounds, which cannot be passed.
[7]Praise the LORD from the earth,
  you sea monsters and all deeps,
[8]fire and hail, snow and frost,
  stormy wind fulfilling his command!
[9]Mountains and all hills,
  fruit trees and all cedars!
[10]Wild animals and all cattle,
  creeping things and flying birds!
[11]Kings of the earth and all peoples,
  princes and all rulers of the earth!
[12]Young men and women alike,
  old and young together!
[13]Let them praise the name of the LORD,
  for his name alone is exalted;
  his glory is above earth and heaven.
[14]He has raised up a horn for his people,
  praise for all his faithful,
for the people of Israel who are close to him.
Praise the LORD!

Hebrews 2:10-18

[10]It was fitting that God, for whom and through whom all things exist, in bringing many children to glory, should make the pioneer of their salvation perfect through sufferings. [11]For the one who sanctifies and those who are sanctified all have one Father. For this reason Jesus is not ashamed to call them brothers and sisters, [12]saying,
  "I will proclaim your name to my brothers and sisters,
    in the midst of the congregation I will praise you."
[13]And again,
  "I will put my trust in him."
And again,
  "Here am I and the children whom God has given me."
[14]Since, therefore, the children share flesh and blood, he himself likewise shared the same things, so that through death he might destroy the one who has the power of death, that is, the devil, [15]and free those who all their lives were held in slavery by the fear of death. [16]For it is clear that he did not come to help angels, but the descendants of Abraham. [17]Therefore he had to become like his brothers and sisters in every respect, so that he might be a merciful and faithful high priest in the service of God, to make a sacrifice of atonement for the sins of the people. [18]Because he himself was tested by what he suffered, he is able to help those who are being tested.

Matthew 2:13-23

[13]Now after they had left, an angel of the Lord appeared to Joseph in a dream and said, "Get up, take the child and his mother, and flee to Egypt, and remain there until I tell you; for Herod is about to search for the child, to destroy him." [14]Then Joseph got up, took the child and his mother by night, and went to Egypt, [15]and remained there until the death of Herod. This was to fulfill what had been spoken by the Lord through the prophet, "Out of Egypt I have called my son."
[16]When Herod saw that he had been tricked by the wise men, he was infuriated, and he sent and killed all the children in and around Bethlehem who were two years old or under, according to the time that he had learned from the wise men. [17]Then was fulfilled what had been spoken through the prophet Jeremiah:
[18] "A voice was heard in Ramah,
    wailing and loud lamentation,
  Rachel weeping for her children;
    she refused to be consoled, because they are no more."
[19]When Herod died, an angel of the Lord suddenly appeared in a dream to Joseph in Egypt and said, [20]"Get up, take the child and his mother, and go to the land of Israel, for those who were seeking the child's life are dead." [21]Then Joseph got up, took the child and his mother, and went to the land of Israel. [22]But when he heard that Archelaus was ruling over Judea in place of his father Herod, he was afraid to go there. And after being warned in a dream, he went away to the district of Galilee. [23]There he made his home in a town called Nazareth, so that what had been spoken through the prophets might be fulfilled, "He will be called a Nazorean."

Primary Hymns and Songs for the Day

"Hark! the Herald Angels Sing" (Isa, Matt) (O)
C150, CG127, E87, EL270, G119, N144, P31, SA108, SH94,
UM240 (PD), VU48
    H-3   Hbl-26, 67; Chr-91; Desc-75; Org-89
    S-1   #234-6. Harms. and desc.
"O Sing a Song of Bethlehem" (Isa, Heb, Matt)
CG164, G159, N51, P308, UM179 (PD)
    H-3   Hbl-15, 20, 34, 84; Chr-150; Org-67
    S-2   #100-103. Various treatments
"Jesus, the Light of the World" 6363190 (Isa, Matt, Epiphany)
WS3056 (See also AH4038, CG129, G127, N160, SH103)
"All Creatures of Our God and King" (Pss) (O)
C22, CG307, E400, EL835, G15, N17, P455, SA2, SH16,
UM62, VU217 (Fr.)
    H-3   Hbl-44; Chr-21; Desc-66; Org-73
    S-1   #198-204. Various treatments
"What Child Is This" (Matt, Christmas, Epiphany) (C)
C162, CG148, E115, EL296, G145, N148, P53, SH105, UM219
(PD), VU74
    H-3   Hbl-102; Chr-210; Desc-46; Org-47
    S-1   #150. Guitar chords
"Joy to the World" (Matt, Christmas, Epiphany) (C)
C143, CG102, E100, EL267, G134/266, N132, P40, SA113,
SH95, UM246 (PD), VU59

Additional Hymn Suggestions

"Great Is Thy Faithfulness" (Isa)
AH4011, C86, CG48, EL733, G39, N423, P276, SA26, SH48,
UM140, VU288
"Children of the Heavenly Father" (Isa)
CG69, EL781, N487, SH42, UM141
"Love Came Down at Christmas" (Isa, Matt) (C)
CG147, E84, N165, UM242
"From All That Dwell Below the Skies" (Pss)
C49, CG330, E380, G327, N27, P229, UM101 (PD)
"Good Christian Friends, Rejoice" (Pss, Heb, Matt)
C164, CG122, E107 (PD), EL288, G132, N129, P28, UM224,
VU35
"O God, We Bear the Imprint of Your Face" (Heb)
C681, G759, N585, P385
"Jesus Entered Egypt" (Heb)
G154
"Holy God, We Praise Thy Name" (Heb) (O)
CG9, E366, EL414 (PD), G4, N276, SH431, UM79, VU894
"To God Be the Glory" (Heb)
C72, CG349, G634, P485, SA279, SH545, UM98 (PD)
"The Friendly Beasts" (Heb)
N138, UM227, VU56
"Break Forth, O Beauteous Heavenly Light" (Heb, Matt)
E91, G130, N140, P26, UM223, VU83
"Infant Holy, Infant Lowly" (Heb, Matt)
C163, CG139, EL276, G128, P37, UM229, VU58
"Once in Royal David's City" (Heb, Matt) (O)
C165, CG104, E102, EL269, G140, N145, P49, SA121, UM250
(PD), VU62
"In Bethlehem a Newborn Boy" (Matt)
E246, G153, P35 (PD), VU77
"Joseph Dearest, Joseph Mine" (Matt)
N105, S2099
"Welcome to Our World" 2317391 (Matt, Christmas)
    V-5 (1)   p. 34. Vocal Solo
"Bread of the World" (Comm.)
C387, E301, G499, N346, P502, UM624, VU461

Additional Contemporary and Modern Suggestions

"Great Is the Lord" 1149 (Isa)
CG325, G614, S2022, SH459
"The Steadfast Love of the Lord" 21590 (Isa)
"Because of Your Love" 4662501 (Isa)

"Glory to God" ("Gloria a Dios") (Pss, Christmas)
CG320, EL164, G585, S2033, SH381
"We Will Glorify the King of Kings" 19038 (Pss)
CG360, S2087
"God of Wonders" 3118757 (Pss)
SH9, WS3034
"Doxology" 5465879 (Pss)
"Let Everything That Has Breath" 2430979 (Pss)
"Glory in the Highest" 4822451 (Pss, Christmas)
"Sing the Praise of God Our Maker" (Heb)
WS3013
"You Are My All in All" 825356 (Heb)
CG571, G519, SH335, WS3040
"You Are My King" ("Amazing Love") 2456623 (Heb)
SH539, WS3102
"He Is Able" 115420 (Heb)
"Before the Throne of God Above" 2306412 (Heb)
"Once Again" 1564362 (Heb)
"Amazing Love" 192553 (Heb)
"That's Why We Praise Him" 2668576 (Heb)
"The Virgin Mary Had a Baby Boy" 2957081 (Matt, Christmas)
AH4037, S2098, SA127, VU73
"Peace in the Manger" 7104263 (Matt, Christmas)

Vocal Solos

"Sing a Song of Joy" (Pss)
    V-4   p. 2
"Little Baby Jesus" (Matt, Christmas)
    V-8   p. 96
"Jesus, What a Wonderful Child" (Matt, Christmas)
    V-5 (1)   p. 48
"Mary Had a Baby" (Matt, Christmas)
    V-7   p. 46
"To Touch His Tiny Hand" (Matt, Christmas)
    V-10   p. 22
"Sing Noel!" (Christmas)
    V-1   p. 13

Anthems

"The Coventry Carol" (Matt)
arr. Victor C. Johnson, Lorenz Corporation 10/3856L
SATB, keyboard, opt. flute (https://bit.ly/10-3856L)

"Love Came Down at Christmas" (Matt)
Arr. Matthew Oldman; Hinshaw Music HMC2381
SATB *divisi, a cappella* (https://bit.ly/HMC-2381)

Other Suggestions

*Today may also be celebrated as Epiphany Sunday using the suggestions
for Jan. 6, or the New Year lections and suggestions for Dec. 31/
Jan. 1 may be used.*
Visuals:
    O   Salvation history, people, children, Christ
    P   Ps 148;1a, angels, sun/moon/stars, nature imagery
    E   Pioneer, crucifix, brothers/sisters, Jesus, manacles
    G   Angel/Joseph, escape, Herod/Wise Men, suffering
           children, return, Nazareth
Prayer: WSL11. "Radiant Morning Star" (Matt)
*For children: N138, UM227, VU56. "The Friendly Beasts."
    Accompanying a soloist with guitar or piano. This tune is also
    recommended for Dec. 31, using another text.*
For more prayers, see The Abingdon Worship Annual 2023.
Theme Ideas: Children / Family of God, Jesus: Childhood,
    Lament, Praise, Redemption / Salvation

Isaiah 60:1-6

[1]Arise, shine; for your light has come,
  and the glory of the LORD has risen upon you.
[2]For darkness shall cover the earth,
  and thick darkness the peoples;
but the LORD will arise upon you,
  and his glory will appear over you.
[3]Nations shall come to your light,
  and kings to the brightness of your dawn.
[4]Lift up your eyes and look around;
  they all gather together, they come to you;
your sons shall come from far away,
  and your daughters shall be carried on their nurses' arms.
[5]Then you shall see and be radiant;
  your heart shall thrill and rejoice,
because the abundance of the sea shall be brought to you,
  the wealth of the nations shall come to you.
[6]A multitude of camels shall cover you,
  the young camels of Midian and Ephah;
  all those from Sheba shall come.
They shall bring gold and frankincense,
  and shall proclaim the praise of the LORD.

Psalm 72:1-7, 10-14 (G149, N667, P205, UM795)

[1]Give the king your justice, O God,
  and your righteousness to a king's son.
[2]May he judge your people with righteousness,
  and your poor with justice.
[3]May the mountains yield prosperity for the people,
  and the hills, in righteousness.
[4]May he defend the cause of the poor of the people,
  give deliverance to the needy,
  and crush the oppressor.
[5]May he live while the sun endures,
  and as long as the moon, throughout all generations.
[6]May he be like rain that falls on the mown grass,
  like showers that water the earth.
[7]In his days may righteousness flourish
  and peace abound, until the moon is no more.
. . . .
[10]May the kings of Tarshish and of the isles
  render him tribute,
may the kings of Sheba and Seba bring gifts.
[11]May all kings fall down before him,
  all nations give him service.
[12]For he delivers the needy when they call,
  the poor and those who have no helper.
[13]He has pity on the weak and the needy,
  and saves the lives of the needy.
[14]From oppression and violence he redeems their life;
  and precious is their blood in his sight.

Ephesians 3:1-12

[1]This is the reason that I Paul am a prisoner for Christ Jesus for the sake of you Gentiles—[2]for surely you have already heard of the commission of God's grace that was given me for you, [3]and how the mystery was made known to me by revelation, as I wrote above in a few words, [4]a reading of which will enable you to perceive my understanding of the mystery of Christ. [5]In former generations this mystery was not made known to humankind, as it has now been revealed to his holy apostles and prophets by the Spirit: [6]that is, the Gentiles have become fellow heirs, members of the same body, and sharers in the promise in Christ Jesus through the gospel.

[7]Of this gospel I have become a servant according to the gift of God's grace that was given me by the working of his power. [8]Although I am the very least of all the saints, this grace was given to me to bring to the Gentiles the news of the boundless riches of Christ, [9]and to make everyone see what is the plan of the mystery hidden for ages in God who created all things; [10]so that through the church the wisdom of God in its rich variety might now be made known to the rulers and authorities in the heavenly places. [11]This was in accordance with the eternal purpose that he has carried out in Christ Jesus our Lord, [12]in whom we have access to God in boldness and confidence through faith in him.

Matthew 2:1-12

[1]In the time of King Herod, after Jesus was born in Bethlehem of Judea, wise men from the East came to Jerusalem, [2]asking, "Where is the child who has been born king of the Jews? For we observed his star at its rising, and have come to pay him homage." [3]When King Herod heard this, he was frightened, and all Jerusalem with him; [4]and calling together all the chief priests and scribes of the people, he inquired of them where the Messiah was to be born. [5]They told him, "In Bethlehem of Judea; for so it has been written by the prophet:
[6] 'And you, Bethlehem, in the land of Judah,
    are by no means least among the rulers of Judah;
  for from you shall come a ruler
    who is to shepherd my people Israel.'"
[7]Then Herod secretly called for the wise men and learned from them the exact time when the star had appeared. [8]Then he sent them to Bethlehem, saying, "Go and search diligently for the child; and when you have found him, bring me word so that I may also go and pay him homage." [9]When they had heard the king, they set out; and there, ahead of them, went the star that they had seen at its rising, until it stopped over the place where the child was. [10]When they saw that the star had stopped, they were overwhelmed with joy. [11]On entering the house, they saw the child with Mary his mother; and they knelt down and paid him homage. Then, opening their treasure chests, they offered him gifts of gold, frankincense, and myrrh. [12]And having been warned in a dream not to return to Herod, they left for their own country by another road.

Primary Hymns and Songs for the Day

"Hail to the Lord's Anointed" (Pss) (O)
C140, CG98, EL311, G149, N104, P205, SII112, UM203, VU30

"We Three Kings" (Matt, Pss)
C172, CG151, E128, G151, P66, SA129, SH107, UM254
H-3   Chr-208; Org-65
S-2   #97-98. Various treatments

"O Morning Star, How Fair and Bright" (Isa, Pss, Eph, Matt)
C105, E497, EL308, G827, N158, P69, UM247, VU98

"Star-Child" (Matt)
CG145, S2095

"We Are Marching" ("Siyahamba") 1321512 (Matt, Epiphany)
C442, CG155, EL866, G853, N526, S2235, SA903, SH717, VU646

"Jesus Shall Reign" (Isa, Pss, Eph) (C)
C95, CG158, E544, EL434, G265, N300, P423, SA258, SH209, UM157 (PD), VU330

"Go, Tell It on the Mountain" (Eph, Christmas) (C)
C167, CG143, E99, EL290, G136, N154, P29, SA106, SH90, UM251, VU43
H-3   Hbl-17, 28, 61; Chr-73; Desc-45; Org-46

Additional Hymn Suggestions

"Awake! Awake, and Greet the New Morn" (Isa)
C138, EL242, G107, N107, SH66

"Arise, Your Light Is Come" (Isa)
CG87, EL314, G744, N164, P411, VU79

"Break Forth, O Beauteous Heavenly Light" (Isa)
E91, G130, N140, P26, UM223, VU83

"This Little Light of Mine" (Isa)
N525, SH257, UM585 (See also AH4150, EL677, N524)

"Deck Thyself, My Soul, with Gladness" (Isa, Comm.)
E339, EL488/EL489, G514, P506, UM612 (PD), VU463

"From All That Dwell Below the Skies" (Pss)
C49, CG330, E380, G327, N27, P229, UM101 (PD)

"Christ, Whose Glory Fills the Skies" (Eph)
EL553, G662, P462/463, SA249, UM173, VU336

"Ye Servants of God" (Eph)
C110, CG420, E535, EL825 (PD), G299, N305, P477, SA97, UM181 (PD), VU342

"Blessed Jesus, At Thy Word" (Eph)
E440, EL520, G395, N74, P454, UM596 (PD), VU500

"I'm Gonna Live So God Can Use Me" (Eph)
C614, G700, P369, S2153, SH632, VU575

"Joy to the World" (Eph, Matt)
C143, CG102, E100, EL267, G134/266, N132, P40, SA113, SH95, UM246 (PD), VU59

"What Star Is This, with Beams So Bright" (Matt)
E124, G152, P68

"What Child Is This" (Matt)
C162, CG148, E115, EL296, G145, N148, P53, SH105, UM219 (PD), VU74

"Angels from the Realms of Glory" (Matt)
C149, CG126, E93, EL275, G143, N126, P22, SA100, SH99, UM220 (PD), VU36

"In the Bleak Midwinter" (Matt)
CG131, E112, EL294, G144, N128, P36, SA110, UM221 (PD), VU55

"Silent Night, Holy Night" (Matt)
C145, CG134, E111, EL281, G122, N134, P60, SA124, SH83, UM239 (PD), VU67 (Fr.)

"Love Came Down at Christmas" (Matt)
CG147, E84, N165, UM242

"The First Noel" (Matt)
C151, CG124, E109, EL300, G147, N139, P56, SA126, UM245 (PD), VU90 (Fr.) and VU91

"On This Day Earth Shall Ring" (Matt)
E92, G141, P46, UM248 (PD)

"Rise Up, Shepherd, and Follow" (Matt)
G135, P50, S2096, VU70

"Love Has Come" (Matt, Epiphany)
EL292, G110, WS3059

Additional Contemporary and Modern Suggestions

"Shine, Jesus, Shine" 30426 (Isa, Epiphany)
CG156, EL671, G192, S2173, SA261, SH102

"Mighty to Save" 4591782 (Isa)

"Arise, Shine" 13797 (Isa)

"Let It Rise" 2240585 (Isa)

"Shine on Us" 1754646 (Isa, Epiphany)

"You Are the Light" 6238098 (Isa, Epiphany)

"Holy Spirit, Come to Us" ("Veni Sancte Spiritus") (Pss)
EL406, G281, S2118

"Grace Alone" 2335524 (Eph)
CG43, S2162, SA699.

"Alleluia" 16811 (Matt)
C106, N765, SH699, UM186

"All Hail King Jesus" 12877 (Matt, Epiphany)

"Here I Am to Worship" 3266032 (Matt, Epiphany)
CG297, SA114, SH395, WS3177

Vocal Solos

"For Behold, Darkness Shall Cover the Earth" and "The People That Walked in Darkness" (Isa)
V-2

"Jesus, What a Wonderful Child" (Eph, Matt, Christmas)
V-5 (1)   p. 48

"Love Came Down at Christmas" (Matt)
V-8   p. 90

"A Scottish Christmas Song" (Matt, Epiphany)
V-4   p. 4

"Let De Heb'n-Light Shine on Me" (Matt, Epiphany)
V-7   p. 66

"The Kings" (Matt, Epiphany)
V-9   p. 13

"Fit for a King" (Matt, Epiphany)
V-10   p. 32

Anthems

"A Light Shines in the Darkness" (Isa)
Michael John Trotta; GIA Music HRMG1835.4
SATB, keyboard (https://bit.ly/1835-4)

"Canticle of Peace (Nunc Dimittis)" (Luke)
John Purifoy; Jubilate Music 47212
SATB, keyboard (https://bit.ly/J-47212)

Other Suggestions

These scriptures and ideas can be used on Jan 1.
Visuals:
O   Light, glory, darkness, daughters/nurses, sea, camels
P   Scales of justice, Christ, mountains/hills, poor/needy
E   Manacles, letter, Christ, all nations
G   Herod, Wise Men, star, Bethlehem, Mary/baby, gifts
Introit: C160, CG105, E81, EL272, G129, N127, P48 (PD), UM216, VU8. "Lo, How a Rose E'er Blooming" (Matt)
Canticle: N808. "Song of Simeon" (Pss, Matt)
Canticle: UM225. "Canticle of Simeon" (Pss, Matt)
Prayer: UM255 (Isa, Epiphany)
Response: C175. "Lovely Star in the Sky" (Matt)
Sung Benediction: WS3062. "Spirit-Child Jesus" (Matt)
Theme Ideas: God: Wisdom, Grace, Jesus: Childhood, Justice, Light

Isaiah 42:1-9

[1]Here is my servant, whom I uphold,
  my chosen, in whom my soul delights;
I have put my spirit upon him;
  he will bring forth justice to the nations.
[2]He will not cry or lift up his voice,
  or make it heard in the street;
[3]a bruised reed he will not break,
  and a dimly burning wick he will not quench;
  he will faithfully bring forth justice.
[4]He will not grow faint or be crushed
  until he has established justice in the earth;
  and the coastlands wait for his teaching.
[5]Thus says God, the LORD,
  who created the heavens and stretched them out,
  who spread out the earth and what comes from it,
who gives breath to the people upon it
  and spirit to those who walk in it:
[6]I am the LORD, I have called you in righteousness,
  I have taken you by the hand and kept you;
I have given you as a covenant to the people,
  a light to the nations,
  [7]to open the eyes that are blind,
to bring out the prisoners from the dungeon,
  from the prison those who sit in darkness.
[8]I am the LORD, that is my name;
  my glory I give to no other,
  nor my praise to idols.
[9]See, the former things have come to pass,
  and new things I now declare;
before they spring forth,
  I tell you of them.

Psalm 29 (G10, N638, P180, UM761)

[1]Ascribe to the LORD, O heavenly beings,
  ascribe to the LORD glory and strength.
[2]Ascribe to the LORD the glory of his name;
  worship the LORD in holy splendor.
[3]The voice of the LORD is over the waters;
  the God of glory thunders,
  the LORD, over mighty waters.
[4]The voice of the LORD is powerful;
  the voice of the LORD is full of majesty.
[5]The voice of the LORD breaks the cedars;
  the LORD breaks the cedars of Lebanon.
[6]He makes Lebanon skip like a calf,
  and Sirion like a young wild ox.
[7]The voice of the LORD flashes forth flames of fire.
[8]The voice of the LORD shakes the wilderness;
  the LORD shakes the wilderness of Kadesh.
[9]The voice of the LORD causes the oaks to whirl,
  and strips the forest bare;
  and in his temple all say, "Glory!"
[10]The LORD sits enthroned over the flood;
  the LORD sits enthroned as king forever.
[11]May the LORD give strength to his people!
  May the LORD bless his people with peace!

Acts 10:34-43

[34]Then Peter began to speak to them: "I truly understand that God shows no partiality, [35]but in every nation anyone who fears him and does what is right is acceptable to him. [36]You know the message he sent to the people of Israel, preaching peace by Jesus Christ—he is Lord of all. [37]That message spread throughout Judea, beginning in Galilee after the baptism that John announced: [38]how God anointed Jesus of Nazareth with the Holy Spirit and with power; how he went about doing good and healing all who were oppressed by the devil, for God was with him. [39]We are witnesses to all that he did both in Judea and in Jerusalem. They put him to death by hanging him on a tree; [40]but God raised him on the third day and allowed him to appear, [41]not to all the people but to us who were chosen by God as witnesses, and who ate and drank with him after he rose from the dead. [42]He commanded us to preach to the people and to testify that he is the one ordained by God as judge of the living and the dead. [43]All the prophets testify about him that everyone who believes in him receives forgiveness of sins through his name."

Matthew 3:13-17

[13]Then Jesus came from Galilee to John at the Jordan, to be baptized by him. [14]John would have prevented him, saying, "I need to be baptized by you, and do you come to me?" [15]But Jesus answered him, "Let it be so now; for it is proper for us in this way to fulfill all righteousness." Then he consented. [16]And when Jesus had been baptized, just as he came up from the water, suddenly the heavens were opened to him and he saw the Spirit of God descending like a dove and alighting on him. [17]And a voice from heaven said, "This is my Son, the Beloved, with whom I am well pleased."

Primary Hymns and Songs for the Day
"Fairest Lord Jesus" (Isa, Matt) (O)
    C97, CG159, E383, EL838, G630, N44, P306, SA77, SH7,
    UM189 (PD), VU341
        H-3   Hbl-57; Chr-63; Desc-25, 94; Org-22, 135
        S-1   #301. Descant
        S-2   #158. Choral harmonization
"When Jesus Came to Jordan" (Isa, Matt)
    CG152, EL305, P72, SH113, UM252
        H-3   Chr-211
"Spirit Song" 27824 (Matt)
    C352, SH409, UM347
"Wash, O God, Our Sons and Daughters" (Matt)
    C365, EL445, G490, SH669, UM605, VU442
        H-3   Hbl-14, 64; Chr-132, 203
        S-2   #22. Desc.
"Spirit of God, Descend upon My Heart" (Matt)
    C265, CG243, EL800, G688, N290, P326, SA290, SH277,
    UM500 (PD), VU378
"Take Me to the Water" (Matt, Baptism)
    AH4045, C367, G480, N322, SH665, WS3165
"Song of Hope" ("*Canto de Esperanza*") 5193990 (Isa) (C)
    G765, P432, S2186, SH721, VU424

Additional Hymn Suggestions
"Today We All Are Called to Be Disciples" (Isa)
    G757, P434, VU507
"Jesus Shall Reign" (Isa)
    C95, CG158, E544, EL434, G265, N300, P423, SA258, SH209,
    UM157 (PD), VU330
"Jesus, the Very Thought of Thee" (Isa)
    C102, CG386, E642, EL754, G629, N507, SA85, UM175
"Breathe on Me, Breath of God" (Isa)
    C254, CG235, E508, G286, N292, P316, SA294, SH224/273,
    UM420 (PD), VU382 (Fr.)
"The Church of Christ, in Every Age" (Isa) (C)
    C475, EL729, G320, N306, P421, UM589, VU601
"Gather Us In" (Isa)
    C284, EL532, G401, S2236, SH393
"For the Healing of the Nations" (Isa, Acts)
    C668, CG698, G346, N576, SA1000, UM428, VU678
"O For a Thousand Tongues to Sing" (Isa, Pss) (O)
    C5, CG332, E493, EL886, G610, N42, P466, SA89, SH439,
    UM57 (PD), VU326 (See also WS3001)
"Come, Ye Faithful, Raise the Strain" (Acts)
    C215, CG218, E199, EL363, G234, N230, P115, UM315 (PD),
    VU165
"This Is My Song" (Acts)
    C722, CG697, EL887, G340, N591, UM437
"Filled with the Spirit's Power" (Acts)
    N266, UM537, VU194
"In Christ There Is No East or West" (Acts, Matt)
    C687, CG273, E529, EL650 (PD), G317/318, N394/395,
    P439/440, SA1006, SH226, UM548, VU606
"On Jordan's Bank the Baptist's Cry" (Acts, Matt)
    E76, EL249, G96, N115, P10, SA120, SH77, VU20
"I Come with Joy" (Acts, Comm.)
    C420, CG456, E304, EL482, G515, N349, P507, SH682,
    UM617, VU477
"Wild and Lone the Prophet's Voice" (Acts, Matt)
    G163, P409, S2089
"At the Font We Start Our Journey" (Acts, Baptism)
    N308, S2114
"We Know That Christ Is Raised" (Acts, Baptism)
    E296, EL449, G485, P495, UM610, VU448
"Sweet, Sweet Spirit" (Matt)
    C261, CG241, G408, N293, P398, SH410, UM334

"Down Galilee's Slow Roadways"
    G164
"I Was There to Hear Your Borning Cry" (Matt)
    C75, EL732, G488, N351, S2051, VU644
"Loving Spirit" (Matt, Baptism)
    C244, EL397, G293, P323, S2123, VU387
"Wonder of Wonders" (Matt, Baptism)
    C378, G489, N328, P499, S2247
"Baptized in Water" (Matt, Baptism)
    CG449, E294, EL456, P492, S2248, SH666
"Water, River, Spirit, Grace" (Matt, Baptism)
    C366, N169, S2253
"*Soplo de Dios*" ("Breath of the Living God") (Matt)
    EL407, N56, SH8

Additional Contemporary and Modern Suggestions
"From Ashes to Beauty" 5288953 (Isa)
"I'm Goin'a Sing When the Spirit Says Sing" (Isa, Matt)
    AH4073, UM333
"Holy" ("*Santo*") (Isa)
    EL762, G594, SH39, S2019
"Light of the World" 73342 (Isa)
"We Are Marching" ("*Siyahamba*") 1321512 (Isa)
    C442, CG155, EL866, G853, N526, S2235, SA903, SH717,
    VU646
"Awesome God" 41099 (Pss)
    G616, S2040
"God Is the Strength of My Heart" 80919 (Pss)
"Ah, Lord God" 17896 (Pss)
"Great and Mighty Is He" 66665 (Pss, Matt)
"Holy and Anointed One" 164361 (Acts)
"Surely the Presence of the Lord" 7909 (Matt)
    C263, UM328; S-2 #200. Stanzas for soloist
"Wade in the Water" (Matt, Baptism)
    AH4046, C371, EL459 (PD), S2107
"Jesus, Name above All Names" 21291 (Matt)
    S2071, SA82
"Breathe" 1874117 (Matt)

Vocal Solos
"Wash, O God, Our Sons and Daughters" (Matt, Baptism)
    V-5 (1)   p. 64
"This Is de Healin' Water" (Matt, Baptism)
    V-7   p. 52

Anthems
"With This Water" (Matt, Baptism)
Frad Gramman; E. C. Schirmer 8540
SATB *a cappella* (https://bit.ly/ECS8540)

"Gracious Spirit, Dwell with Me" (Matt, Baptism)
Arr. K. Lee Scott; Augsburg 0800646134
2-part mixed, organ (https://bit.ly/A-46134)

Other Suggestions
Visuals:
    O   Christ, dove, scales, bent reed, lighted wick, earth
    P   Ps 29:1-2, worship, sea, storm, cedars, calf, ox, flames
    E   Jesus/baptism/dove, healing, risen Christ, witness
    G   John baptizing Jesus, dove, Matt 3:17
Baptism reaffirmation resources: UM608, CG451, S2252, S2249,
    WS3164, SH665, WS3165
Call to Worship: SA148, WS3044. "Make Way" (Isa)
Opening Prayer: N829 (Matt)
Sung Confession: WS3111. "Redemption" (Isa)
Baptism Readings: C370, C372, C377
Theme Ideas: Baptism, Covenant, God: Glory of God, Holy
    Spirit, Inclusion, Light, New Creation

Isaiah 49:1-7

[1]Listen to me, O coastlands,
    pay attention, you peoples from far away!
The LORD called me before I was born,
    while I was in my mother's womb he named me.
[2]He made my mouth like a sharp sword,
    in the shadow of his hand he hid me;
he made me a polished arrow,
    in his quiver he hid me away.
[3]And he said to me, "You are my servant,
    Israel, in whom I will be glorified."
[4]But I said, "I have labored in vain,
    I have spent my strength for nothing and vanity;
yet surely my cause is with the LORD,
    and my reward with my God."
[5]And now the LORD says,
    who formed me in the womb to be his servant,
to bring Jacob back to him,
    and that Israel might be gathered to him,
for I am honored in the sight of the LORD,
    and my God has become my strength—
[6]he says,
"It is too light a thing that you should be my servant
    to raise up the tribes of Jacob
    and to restore the survivors of Israel;
I will give you as a light to the nations,
    that my salvation may reach to the end of the earth."
[7]Thus says the LORD,
    the Redeemer of Israel and his Holy One,
to one deeply despised, abhorred by the nations,
    the slave of rulers,
"Kings shall see and stand up,
    princes, and they shall prostrate themselves,
because of the LORD, who is faithful,
    the Holy One of Israel, who has chosen you."

Psalm 40:1-11 (G651, N647, SH607, UM774)

[1]I waited patiently for the LORD;
    he inclined to me and heard my cry.
[2]He drew me up from the desolate pit,
    out of the miry bog,
and set my feet upon a rock,
    making my steps secure.
[3]He put a new song in my mouth,
    a song of praise to our God.
Many will see and fear,
    and put their trust in the LORD.
[4]Happy are those who make
    the LORD their trust,
who do not turn to the proud,
    to those who go astray after false gods.
[5]You have multiplied, O LORD my God,
    your wondrous deeds and your thoughts toward us;
    none can compare with you.
Were I to proclaim and tell of them,
    they would be more than can be counted.
[6]Sacrifice and offering you do not desire,
    but you have given me an open ear.
Burnt offering and sin offering
    you have not required.
[7]Then I said, "Here I am;
    in the scroll of the book it is written of me.
[8]I delight to do your will, O my God;
    your law is within my heart."
[9]I have told the glad news of deliverance
    in the great congregation;
see, I have not restrained my lips,
    as you know, O LORD.

[10]I have not hidden your saving help within my heart,
    I have spoken of your faithfulness and your salvation;
I have not concealed your steadfast love and your faithfulness
    from the great congregation.
[11]Do not, O LORD, withhold
    your mercy from me;
let your steadfast love and your faithfulness
    keep me safe forever.

1 Corinthians 1:1-9

[1]Paul, called to be an apostle of Christ Jesus by the will of God, and our brother Sosthenes,

[2]To the church of God that is in Corinth, to those who are sanctified in Christ Jesus, called to be saints, together with all those who in every place call on the name of our Lord Jesus Christ, both their Lord and ours:

[3]Grace to you and peace from God our Father and the Lord Jesus Christ.

[4]I give thanks to my God always for you because of the grace of God that has been given you in Christ Jesus, [5]for in every way you have been enriched in him, in speech and knowledge of every kind—[6]just as the testimony of Christ has been strengthened among you—[7]so that you are not lacking in any spiritual gift as you wait for the revealing of our Lord Jesus Christ. [8]He will also strengthen you to the end, so that you may be blameless on the day of our Lord Jesus Christ. [9]God is faithful; by him you were called into the fellowship of his Son, Jesus Christ our Lord.

John 1:29-42

[29]The next day he saw Jesus coming toward him and declared, "Here is the Lamb of God who takes away the sin of the world! [30]This is he of whom I said, 'After me comes a man who ranks ahead of me because he was before me.' [31]I myself did not know him; but I came baptizing with water for this reason, that he might be revealed to Israel." [32]And John testified, "I saw the Spirit descending from heaven like a dove, and it remained on him. [33]I myself did not know him, but the one who sent me to baptize with water said to me, 'He on whom you see the Spirit descend and remain is the one who baptizes with the Holy Spirit.' [34]And I myself have seen and have testified that this is the Son of God."

[35]The next day John again was standing with two of his disciples, [36]and as he watched Jesus walk by, he exclaimed, "Look, here is the Lamb of God!" [37]The two disciples heard him say this, and they followed Jesus. [38]When Jesus turned and saw them following, he said to them, "What are you looking for?" They said to him, "Rabbi" (which translated means Teacher), "where are you staying?" [39]He said to them, "Come and see." They came and saw where he was staying, and they remained with him that day. It was about four o'clock in the afternoon. [40]One of the two who heard John speak and followed him was Andrew, Simon Peter's brother. [41]He first found his brother Simon and said to him, "We have found the Messiah" (which is translated Anointed). [42]He brought Simon to Jesus, who looked at him and said, "You are Simon son of John. You are to be called Cephas" (which is translated Peter).

Primary Hymns and Songs for the Day
"Great Is Thy Faithfulness" (Isa, 1 Cor) (O)
  AH4011, C86, CG48, EL733, G39, N423, P276, SA26, SH48,
  UM140, VU288
    H-3 Chr-87; Desc-39; Org-39
    S-2 #59. Piano arrangement
"O Jesus, I Have Promised" (1 Cor)
  C612, E655, EL810, G724/725, N493, P388/389, SA613,
  SH623, UM396 (PD), VU120
"Lord God, Your Love Has Called Us Here" (1 Cor, John)
  EL358. P353, SA335, UM579, S-1 #57-61. Various treatments
"The Summons" ("Will You Come and Follow Me") (John)
  CG473, EL798, G726, S2130, SA695, SH598, VU567
"We Are Marching" ("Siyahamba") 1321512 (Isa) (C)
  C442, CG155, EL866, G853, N526, S2235, SA903, SH717,
  VU646

Additional Hymn Suggestions
"Holy God, We Praise Thy Name" (Isa) (O)
  CG9, E366, EL414 (PD), G4, N276, P460, SH431, UM79,
  VU894 (Fr.)
"Ye Servants of God" (Rom)
  C110, CG420, E535, EL825 (PD), G299, N305, P477, SA97,
  UM181 (PD), VU342
"Womb of Life" (Isa)
  C14, G3, N274, S2046
"I Was There to Hear Your Borning Cry" (Isa)
  C75, EL732, G488, N351, S2051, VU644
"This Little Light of Mine" (Isa, Epiphany)
  N525, SH257, UM585 (See also AH4150, EL677, N524)
"Mothering God, You Gave Me Birth" (Isa, Comm.)
  C83, EL735, G7, N467, S2050, VU320
"What Does the Lord Require of You" 456859 (Pss)
  C661, CG690, G70, S2174, VU701
"Jesus, Thou Joy of Loving Hearts" (1 Cor)
  C101, CG394, E649, G494, N329, P510, SA340, SH688,
  VU472
"How Great Thou Art" (1 Cor)
  AH4015, C33, CG323, EL856, G625, N35, P467, SH14,
  UM77, VU238 (Fr.)
"Leaning on the Everlasting Arms" (1 Cor)
  AH4100, C560, CG640, EL774, G837, N471, SA906, UM133
"Blessed Be the God of Israel" (1 Cor)
  C135, CG88, E444, EL250/552, G109, UM209, VU901
"Amazing Grace" (1 Cor)
  AH4091, C546, CG587, E671, EL779, G649, N547/548, P280,
  SA453, SH523, UM378 (PD), VU266 (Fr.)
"I Sing a Song of the Saints of God" (1 Cor, John)
  E293, G730, N295, P364, UM712 (PD)
"Come, Holy Spirit, Heavenly Dove" (John)
  C248, E510, G279, N281, P126
"I Love to Tell the Story" (John)
  C480, CG581, EL661, G462, N522, SA846, SH569, UM156,
  VU343
"Sweet, Sweet Spirit" (John)
  C261, CG241, G408, N293, P398, SH410, UM334
"Tú Has Venido a la Orilla" ("Lord, You Have Come to the
Lakeshore") (John)
  C342, EL817, G721, N173, P377, SH599, UM344, VU563
"Just as I Am" (John)
  C339, CG500, E693, EL592, G442, N207, P370, SA503,
  SH500, UM357 (PD), VU508
"Spirit of God, Descend upon My Heart" (John)
  C265, CG243, EL800, G688, N290, P326, SA290, SH277,
  UM500 (PD), VU378

"Lead On, O King Eternal" (John)
  C632, CG63, E555, EL805, G269, N573, P447/ P448, SA964,
  UM580
"Take, O Take Me as I Am" 4562041 (John)
  EL814, G698, SH620, WS3119

Additional Contemporary and Modern Suggestions
"Lord, Be Glorified" 26368 (Isa)
  EL744, G468, S2150, SA593, SH420
"Be Glorified" 429226 (Isa)
"Be Glorified" 2732646 (Isa)
"Good to Me" 313480 (Isa)
"You Are My All in All" 825356 (Isa, John)
  CG571, G519, SH335, WS3040
"Light of the World" 73342 (Isa, Epiphany)
"You Are Good" 3383788 (Pss)
  AH4018, SH455, WS3014
"Your Love, Oh Lord" 1894255 (Pss)
"You Are My Hiding Place" 21442 (Pss)
  C554, S2055, SH46
"Waiting Here for You" 5925663 (Pss)
"Amazing Grace" ("My Chains Are Gone") 4768151 (1 Cor)
"Let the Peace of God Reign" 1839987 (1 Cor)
"Grace Like Rain" 3689877 (1 Cor)
"Spirit Song" 27824 (John)
  C352, SH409, UM347
"Cry of My Heart" 844980 (John)
"Step by Step" 696994 (John)
  CG495, G743, WS3004
"Now Behold the Lamb" (John)
  EL341, WS3081
"Agnus Dei" 626713 (John)
  CG351
"Come Just As You Are" 1189479 (John)

Vocal Solos
"Patiently Have I Waited for the Lord" (Pss)
  V-4 p. 24
"Holy Is the Lamb" (John)
  V-5 (1) p. 5

Anthems
"I Waited for the Lord" (Pss)
F. Mendelssohn; Theodore Presser 312-10269
SATB, keyboard (https://bit.ly/TP-10269)

"Just as I Am, I Come" (John)
Victor Johnson; Lorenz Music 10/4078L
SATB, piano, opt. clarinet (https://bit.ly/10-4078L)

Other Suggestions
Consider including observances of Martin Luther King Jr. Day.
Visuals:
    O Coast, pregnancy, hand, arrow, light, earth, Christ
    P Clasped hands, pit, bog, feet/rock, sing, preach
    E People, speak, learning, Bible, gifts, Second Coming
    G Jesus, Lamb, baptism, Spirit, John, witnessing
Prayer: N863. Justice (Martin Luther King Jr. Day)
Litany: C664. Litany for the World (Martin Luther King Jr. Day)
Medley: "Take This Moment, Sign, and Space" (WS3118) and
  "Take, O Take Me As I Am" (EL814, G698, SH620, WS3119)
  (John)
For more resources, see The Abingdon Worship Annual 2023.
Theme Ideas: Call of God, Discipleship / Following God, Light,
  Spiritual Gifts, Waiting

Isaiah 9:1-4

[1]But there will be no gloom for those who were in anguish. In the former time he brought into contempt the land of Zebulun and the land of Naphtali, but in the latter time he will make glorious the way of the sea, the land beyond the Jordan, Galilee of the nations.

[2]   The people who walked in darkness
       have seen a great light;
   those who lived in a land of deep darkness—
       on them light has shined.
[3]   You have multiplied the nation,
       you have increased its joy;
   they rejoice before you
       as with joy at the harvest,
       as people exult when dividing plunder.
[4]   For the yoke of their burden,
       and the bar across their shoulders,
       the rod of their oppressor,
       you have broken as on the day of Midian.

Psalm 27:1, 4-9 (G90/841/842, N637, P179, UM758)

[1]The LORD is my light and my salvation;
   whom shall I fear?
The LORD is the stronghold of my life;
   of whom shall I be afraid?
. . . .
[4]One thing I asked of the LORD,
   that will I seek after:
to live in the house of the LORD
   all the days of my life,
to behold the beauty of the LORD,
   and to inquire in his temple.
[5]For he will hide me in his shelter
   in the day of trouble;
he will conceal me under the cover of his tent;
   he will set me high on a rock.
[6]Now my head is lifted up
   above my enemies all around me,
and I will offer in his tent
   sacrifices with shouts of joy;
I will sing and make melody to the LORD.
[7]Hear, O LORD, when I cry aloud,
   be gracious to me and answer me!
[8]"Come," my heart says, "seek his face!"
   Your face, LORD, do I seek.
[9]   Do not hide your face from me.
Do not turn your servant away in anger,
   you who have been my help.
Do not cast me off, do not forsake me,
   O God of my salvation!

1 Corinthians 1:10-18

[10]Now I appeal to you, brothers and sisters, by the name of our Lord Jesus Christ, that all of you be in agreement and that there be no divisions among you, but that you be united in the same mind and the same purpose. [11]For it has been reported to me by Chloe's people that there are quarrels among you, my brothers and sisters. [12]What I mean is that each of you says, "I belong to Paul," or "I belong to Apollos," or "I belong to Cephas," or "I belong to Christ." [13]Has Christ been divided? Was Paul crucified for you? Or were you baptized in the name of Paul?

[14]I thank God that I baptized none of you except Crispus and Gaius, [15]so that no one can say that you were baptized in my name. [16](I did baptize also the household of Stephanas; beyond that, I do not know whether I baptized anyone else.) [17]For Christ did not send me to baptize but to proclaim the gospel, and not with eloquent wisdom, so that the cross of Christ might not be emptied of its power.

[18]For the message about the cross is foolishness to those who are perishing, but to us who are being saved it is the power of God.

Matthew 4:12-23

[12]Now when Jesus heard that John had been arrested, he withdrew to Galilee. [13]He left Nazareth and made his home in Capernaum by the sea, in the territory of Zebulun and Naphtali, [14]so that what had been spoken through the prophet Isaiah might be fulfilled:
[15]   "Land of Zebulun, land of Naphtali,
       on the road by the sea, across the Jordan, Galilee of the
          Gentiles—
[16]   the people who sat in darkness
       have seen a great light,
   and for those who sat in the region and shadow of death
       light has dawned."
[17]From that time Jesus began to proclaim, "Repent, for the kingdom of heaven has come near."

[18]As he walked by the Sea of Galilee, he saw two brothers, Simon, who is called Peter, and Andrew his brother, casting a net into the sea—for they were fishermen. [19]And he said to them, "Follow me, and I will make you fish for people." [20]Immediately they left their nets and followed him. [21]As he went from there, he saw two other brothers, James son of Zebedee and his brother John, in the boat with their father Zebedee, mending their nets, and he called them. [22]Immediately they left the boat and their father, and followed him.

[23]Jesus went throughout Galilee, teaching in their synagogues and proclaiming the good news of the kingdom and curing every disease and every sickness among the people.

Primary Hymns and Songs for the Day
"The Church's One Foundation" (1 Cor) (O)
 C272, CG246, E525, EL654, G321, N386, P442, SH233,
 UM545/546, VU332 (Fr.)
  H-3 Hbl-94; Chr-180; Desc-16; Org-9
  S-1 #25-26. Desc. and harm.
"We Are One in Christ Jesus" ("*Somos Uno en Cristo*") 6368975
(1 Cor)
 C493, EL643, G322, S2229, SH227
"Fight the Good Fight" (1 Cor)
 E552, G846, P307 (PD), SA952, VU674
"*Tú Has Venido a la Orilla*" ("Lord, You Have Come to the
Lakeshore") (Matt)
 C342, EL817, G721, N173, P377, SH599, UM344, VU563
  H-3 Chr-133; Org-114
"Jesus Calls Us" (Matt)
 C337, CG486, E551, EL696, G720, N172, SA653, SH604,
 UM398, VU562
  H-3 Chr-115
  S-2 #65. Harmonization
 E549/550, N171
"I Have Decided to Follow Jesus" (Matt) (C)
 C344, CG497, S2129, SH610

Additional Hymn Suggestions
"Christ, Whose Glory Fills the Skies" (Isa, Matt)
 EL553, G662, P462/463, SA249, UM173, VU336
"I Want to Walk as a Child of the Light" (Isa, Matt)
 CG96, E490, EL815, G377, SH352, UM206
"How Firm a Foundation" (Isa)
 C618, CG425, E636/637, EL796, G463, N407, P361, SA804,
 SH291, UM529 (PD), VU660
"Goodness Is Stronger than Evil" (Isa, Matt)
 EL721, G750, S2219
"Praise, My Soul, the King of Heaven" (Pss)
 C23, CG337, E410, EL864/865, G619/620, P478/479, SA55,
 SH418, UM66 (PD), VU240
"Where Charity and Love Prevail" (1 Cor)
 CG264, E581, EL359, G316, N396, SH271, UM549
"In the Cross of Christ I Glory" (1 Cor)
 C207, CG183, E441, EL324, G213, N193, SA174, UM295
"When I Survey the Wondrous Cross" (1 Cor)
 C195, CG186, E474, EL803, G223/224, N224, P100/101,
 SA208, SH163/164, UM298/299, VU149 (Fr.)
"Blest Be the Tie that Binds" (1 Cor) (C)
 C433, CG267, EL656, G306, N393, P438, SA812, SH701,
 UM557 (PD), VU602
"Help Us Accept Each Other" (1 Cor)
 C487, G754, N388, P358, UM560
"Lord of the Dance" 78529 (Matt)
 G157, P302, SA141, UM261, VU352
"Softly and Tenderly Jesus Is Calling" (Matt)
 C340, CG474, EL608, G418, N449, SA435, SH601, UM348
"Dear Lord and Father of Mankind" (Matt)
 (*Alternate Text–"Parent of Us All"*)
 C594, CG413, E652/563, G169, N502, P345, SA456, UM358
 (PD), VU608
"O Jesus, I Have Promised" (Matt)
 C612, E655, EL810, G724/725, N493, P388/389, SA613,
 SH623, UM396 (PD), VU120
"Where Cross the Crowded Ways of Life" (Matt)
 C665, CG657, E609, EL719, G343, N543, UM427, VU681
"O Master, Let Me Walk with Thee" (Matt)
 C602, CG660, E659/E660, EL818, G738, N503, P357, SA667,
 SH612, UM430 (PD), VU560
"The Summons" ("Will You Come and Follow Me") (Matt)
 CG473, EL798, G726, S2130, SA695, SH598, VU567
"Somebody's Knockin' at Your Door" (Matt)
 G728, P382, SH597, WS3095

Additional Contemporary and Modern Suggestions
"Foundation" 706151 (Isa, 1 Cor)
"How Great Is Our God" 4348399 (Isa, Pss, Matt)
 CG322, SH458, WS3003
"Here I Am to Worship" 3266032 (Isa, Pss, Matt)
 CG297, SA114, SH395, WS3177
"Shine, Jesus, Shine" 30426 (Isa, Pss, Matt)
 CG156, EL671, G192, S2173, SA261, SH102
"Light of the World" 73342 (Isa, Pss, Matt)
"Shine on Us" 1754646 (Isa, Pss, Matt)
"You Are the Light" 6238098 (Isa, Pss, Matt)
"I Will Call upon the Lord" 11263 (Pss)
 G621, S2002
"We Bring the Sacrifice of Praise" 9990 (Pss)
"Oh Lord, You're Beautiful" 14514 (Pss)
"Shout to the Lord" 1406918 (Pss)
 CG348, EL821, S2074, SA264, SH426
"Today" 5775617 (Pss)
"The Lord Is My Light" 41240 (Pss)
"All Heaven Declares" 120556 (Pss)
"Better Is One Day" 1097451 (Pss)
"Marvelous Light" 4491002 (Pss, Matt)
"We Are Marching" ("*Siyahamba*") 1321512 (Pss, Matt)
 C442, CG155, EL866, G853, N526, S2235, SA903, SH717,
 VU646
"Step by Step" 696994 (Pss, Matt)
 CG495, G743, WS3004
"I Stand Amazed" 769450 (Pss, Matt)
"Let It Be Said of Us" 1855882 (1 Cor)
"The Wonderful Cross" 3148435 (1 Cor)
"I Will Boast" 4662350 (1 Cor)
"Everyday" 2798154 (Matt)
"Cry of My Heart" 844980 (Matt)

Vocal Solos
"The People That Walked in Darkness" (Isa)
 V-2
"The Lord Is My Light" (Pss)
 V-8   p. 57
"Softly and Tenderly" (Matt)
 V-5 (3)   p. 52

Anthems
"Lord of the Dance" (Matt)
Arr. Neil Harmon; MorningStar MSM-50-4365
SATB, piano or flute, Orff inst. (https://bit.ly/50-4365)

"Who At My Door Is Standing?" (Matt)
arr. K. Lee Scott; Hinshaw HMC728
2-part mixed, keyboard (https://bit.ly/KLS-728)

Other Suggestions
Visuals:
 O Light/darkness, sea/land, joy, harvest, yoke, rod
 P Light, church, seekers, tent/rock, joy, singing
 E Walls torn down, baptism, crucifix, stone
 G John, sea, light/darkness, dawn, fishnet, net with
    people, mending nets, boat, Jesus teaching
Prayer of Confession: N835 (Matt)
Response: SH556, WS3137. "Lord Jesus Christ, Your Light
 Shines" (Isa, Pss)
Litany: N880 (Isa, Matt)
Litany: C664. A Litany for the World (Isa, Matt)
Theme Ideas: Call of God, Cross, Discipleship / Following God,
 Inclusion, Light, Unity

Micah 6:1-8

[1]Hear what the LORD says:
    Rise, plead your case before the mountains,
      and let the hills hear your voice.
[2]Hear, you mountains, the controversy of the LORD,
    and you enduring foundations of the earth;
for the LORD has a controversy with his people,
    and he will contend with Israel.
[3]"O my people, what have I done to you?
    In what have I wearied you? Answer me!
[4]For I brought you up from the land of Egypt,
    and redeemed you from the house of slavery;
and I sent before you Moses,
    Aaron, and Miriam.
[5]O my people, remember now what King Balak of Moab devised,
    what Balaam son of Beor answered him,
and what happened from Shittim to Gilgal,
    that you may know the saving acts of the LORD."
[6]"With what shall I come before the LORD,
    and bow myself before God on high?
Shall I come before him with burnt offerings,
    with calves a year old?
[7]Will the LORD be pleased with thousands of rams,
    with ten thousands of rivers of oil?
Shall I give my firstborn for my transgression,
    the fruit of my body for the sin of my soul?"
[8]He has told you, O mortal, what is good;
    and what does the LORD require of you
but to do justice, and to love kindness,
    and to walk humbly with your God?

Psalm 15 (G419, N627, P164, UM747)

[1]O LORD, who may abide in your tent?
    Who may dwell on your holy hill?
[2]Those who walk blamelessly, and do what is right,
    and speak the truth from their heart;
[3]who do not slander with their tongue,
    and do no evil to their friends,
    nor take up a reproach against their neighbors;
[4]in whose eyes the wicked are despised,
    but who honor those who fear the LORD;
who stand by their oath even to their hurt;
[5]who do not lend money at interest,
    and do not take a bribe against the innocent.
Those who do these things shall never be moved.

1 Corinthians 1:18-31

[18]For the message about the cross is foolishness to those who are perishing, but to us who are being saved it is the power of God. [19]For it is written,
    "I will destroy the wisdom of the wise,
      and the discernment of the discerning I will thwart."
[20]Where is the one who is wise? Where is the scribe? Where is the debater of this age? Has not God made foolish the wisdom of the world? [21]For since, in the wisdom of God, the world did not know God through wisdom, God decided, through the foolishness of our proclamation, to save those who believe. [22]For Jews demand signs and Greeks desire wisdom, [23]but we proclaim Christ crucified, a stumbling block to Jews and foolishness to Gentiles, [24]but to those who are the called, both Jews and Greeks, Christ the power of God and the wisdom of God. [25]For God's foolishness is wiser than human wisdom, and God's weakness is stronger than human strength.

[26]Consider your own call, brothers and sisters: not many of you were wise by human standards, not many were powerful, not many were of noble birth. [27]But God chose what is foolish in the world to shame the wise; God chose what is weak in the world to shame the strong; [28]God chose what is low and despised in the world, things that are not, to reduce to nothing things that are, [29]so that no one might boast in the presence of God. [30]He is the source of your life in Christ Jesus, who became for us wisdom from God, and righteousness and sanctification and redemption, [31]in order that, as it is written, "Let the one who boasts, boast in the Lord."

Matthew 5:1-12

[1]When Jesus saw the crowds, he went up the mountain; and after he sat down, his disciples came to him. [2]Then he began to speak, and taught them, saying:
[3]"Blessed are the poor in spirit, for theirs is the kingdom of heaven.
[4]"Blessed are those who mourn, for they will be comforted.
[5]"Blessed are the meek, for they will inherit the earth.
[6]"Blessed are those who hunger and thirst for righteousness, for they will be filled.
[7]"Blessed are the merciful, for they will receive mercy.
[8]"Blessed are the pure in heart, for they will see God.
[9]"Blessed are the peacemakers, for they will be called children of God.
[10]"Blessed are those who are persecuted for righteousness' sake, for theirs is the kingdom of heaven.
[11]"Blessed are you when people revile you and persecute you and utter all kinds of evil against you falsely on my account. [12]Rejoice and be glad, for your reward is great in heaven, for in the same way they persecuted the prophets who were before you."

Primary Hymns and Songs for the Day

"Rejoice in God's Saints" (Matt) (O)
  C476, EL418, G732, UM708
        H-3   Hbl-90, 105; Chr-221; Desc-49; Org-51
        S-2   #71-74. Intro. and harms.

"What Does the Lord Require of You" 456859 (Mic)
  C661, CG690, G70, S2174, VU701

"Be Thou My Vision" (1 Cor, Matt)
  C595, CG71, E488, EL793, G450, N451, P339, SA573, SH640,
  UM451, VU642
        H-3   Hbl-15, 48; Chr-36; Org-153
        S-1   #319. Arr. for organ and voices in canon

"Lord, You Give the Great Commission" (Mic, Pss) (C)
  C459, CG651, S2176, EL579, G298, P429, UM584, VU512
        H-3   Hbl-61; Chr-132; Org-2
        S-1   #4-5. Instrumental and vocal desc.

"Sent Out in Jesus' Name" ("Enviado Soy de Dios") 6290823 (Mic) (C)
  EL538, G747, S2184, SH718

Additional Hymn Suggestions

"O for a Closer Walk with God" (Mic)
  CG679, E684, G739, N450, P396, SA612

"Softly and Tenderly Jesus Is Calling" (Mic)
  C340, CG474, EL608 (PD), G418, N449, SA435, SH601,
  UM348

"I'm Gonna Live So God Can Use Me" (Mic)
  C614, G700, P369, S2153, SH632, VU575

"Healer of Our Every Ill" (Mic)
  C506, EL612, G795, S2213, SH339, VU619

"What Gift Can We Bring" (Mic, Matt)
  CG533, N370, UM87

"All Who Love and Serve Your City" (Mic, Matt)
  C670, CG674, E570/E571, EL724, G351, P413, UM433

"Cuando el Pobre" ("When the Poor Ones") (Mic, Matt)
  C662, EL725, G762, P407, SH240, UM434, VU702

"Lift Up Your Heads, Ye Mighty Gates" (Pss, Matt)
  C129, CG173, E436, G93, N117, P8, UM213 (PD)

"Fairest Lord Jesus" (1 Cor)
  C97, CG159, E383, EL838, G630, N44, P306, SA77, SH7,
  UM189 (PD), VU341

"In the Cross of Christ I Glory" (1 Cor)
  C207, CG183, E441, EL324, G213, N193, P84, SA174, UM295

"When I Survey the Wondrous Cross" (1 Cor)
  C195, CG186, E474, EL803, G223/ 224, N224, P100/101,
  SA208, SH163/164, UM298/299, VU149 (Fr.)

"Help Us Accept Each Other" (1 Cor)
  C487, G754, N388, P358, UM560

"O For a World" (1 Cor)
  C683, G372, N575, P386, VU697

"My Faith Looks Up to Thee" (1 Cor, Matt)
  C576, CG407, E691, EL759, G829, P383, SA726, UM452,
  VU663

"Holy Spirit, Truth Divine" (1 Cor, Matt)
  C241, EL398, N63, P321, SA285, UM465, VU368

"O Love That Wilt Not Let Me Go" (1 Cor, Matt)
  C540, CG631, G833, N485, P384, SA616, SH314, UM480,
  VU658

"Lord, I Want to be a Christian" (Matt)
  C589, CG507, G729, N454, P372 (PD), SH621, UM402

"Near to the Heart of God" (Matt)
  C581, CG383, G824, P527, UM472 (PD)

"Holy" ("Santo") (Matt)
  EL762, G594, SH39, S2019

"All Who Hunger" (Matt)
  C419, CG303, EL461, G509, S2126, VU460

"Goodness Is Stronger than Evil" (Matt)
  EL721, G750, S2219

"Purify My Heart" (Matt)

"Purify My Heart" 1314323 (Matt)

Additional Contemporary and Modern Suggestions

"Live in Charity" ("Ubi Caritas") (Mic)
  C523, EL642, G205, S2179

"Come to the Water" 5272842 (Mic)

"Rule of Life" (Mic, Matt)
  AH4056, WS3117

"Here I Am to Worship" 3266032 (Mic, 1 Cor)
  CG297, SA114, SH395, WS3177

"All I Need Is You" 488384 (1 Cor)

"You Are My All in All" 825356 (1 Cor)
  CG571, G519, SH335, WS3040

"Shout to the North" 1562261 (1 Cor)
  G319, SA1009, WS3042

"Let It Be Said of Us" 1855882 (1 Cor)

"The Wonderful Cross" 3148435 (1 Cor)

"I Will Boast" 4662350 (1 Cor)

"Here Is Bread, Here Is Wine" 983717 (1 Cor, Comm.)
  EL483, S2266

"Give Thanks" 20285 (1 Cor, Matt)
  C528, CG373, G647, S2036, SA364, SH489

"Open Our Eyes, Lord" 1572 (Matt)
  CG392, S2086, SA386, SH562

"You Who Are Thirsty" 814453 (Matt)

"Blessed Be Your Name" 3798438 (Matt)
  SH449, WS3002

"Open the Eyes of My Heart" 2298355 (Matt)
  G452, SA270, SH378, WS3008

"Restless" 5775569 (Matt)

Vocal Solos

"Fit for a King" (Mic)
  V-10   p. 32

"Maybe the Rain" (Matt)
  V-5 (2)   p. 27

"This Is My Commandment" (Matt)
  V-8   p. 284

Anthems

"Let Us Not Become Weary" (Mic)
Benjamin Kornelis; Musicspoke.com MS50755
SATB, piano (https://bit.ly/MS50755)

"The Old Rugged Cross" (1 Cor)
arr. Joel Raney; Hope C5175
SATB, keyboard (https://bit.ly/C-5175)

Other Suggestions

Visuals:
  O   Briefcase, Exodus, prayer, scales of justice, ministry
  P   tent, hill, walking, speaking, destructive behavior,
         ministry, justice, money
  E   Empty cross, clown, debate, crucifix, block, Christ,
         world upside down
  G   Jesus teaching, examples of ministry described

Prayer: N860. Those in Need (Mic)
Prayer: UM392 (Matt) (1 Cor, Matt)
Response: WS3103. "Purify My Heart" (Matt)
Canticle: C185. "The Beatitudes" (Matt)
Dance Solo: N180. "Blessed Are the Poor in Spirit" (Matt)
Blessing: WSL160. "What does the Lord require" (Mic)

Theme Ideas: Beatitudes/Blessings, Cross, Faithfulness, God:
  Hunger / Thirst for God, God: Wisdom, Humility, Justice,
  Saints

Isaiah 58:1-9a (9b-12)

¹Shout out, do not hold back!
Lift up your voice like a trumpet!
Announce to my people their rebellion,
   to the house of Jacob their sins.
²Yet day after day they seek me
   and delight to know my ways,
as if they were a nation that practiced righteousness
   and did not forsake the ordinance of their God;
they ask of me righteous judgments,
   they delight to draw near to God.
³ "Why do we fast, but you do not see?
   Why humble ourselves, but you do not notice?"
Look, you serve your own interest on your fast day,
   and oppress all your workers.
⁴Look, you fast only to quarrel and to fight
   and to strike with a wicked fist.
Such fasting as you do today
   will not make your voice heard on high.
⁵Is such the fast that I choose,
   a day to humble oneself?
Is it to bow down the head like a bulrush,
   and to lie in sackcloth and ashes?
Will you call this a fast,
   a day acceptable to the Lord?
⁶Is not this the fast that I choose:
   to loose the bonds of injustice,
   to undo the thongs of the yoke,
to let the oppressed go free,
   and to break every yoke?
⁷Is it not to share your bread with the hungry,
   and bring the homeless poor into your house;
when you see the naked, to cover them,
   and not to hide yourself from your own kin?
⁸Then your light shall break forth like the dawn,
   and your healing shall spring up quickly;
your vindicator shall go before you,
   the glory of the Lord shall be your rear guard.
⁹Then you shall call, and the Lord will answer;
   you shall cry for help, and he will say, Here I am.
If you remove the yoke from among you,
   the pointing of the finger, the speaking of evil,
¹⁰if you offer your food to the hungry
   and satisfy the needs of the afflicted,
then your light shall rise in the darkness
   and your gloom be like the noonday.
¹¹The Lord will guide you continually,
   and satisfy your needs in parched places,
   and make your bones strong;
and you shall be like a watered garden,
   like a spring of water,
   whose waters never fail.
¹²Your ancient ruins shall be rebuilt;
   you shall raise up the foundations of many generations;
you shall be called the repairer of the breach,
   the restorer of streets to live in.

Psalm 112:1-9 (10) (G755, N697, UM833)

¹Praise the Lord!
   Happy are those who fear the Lord,
   who greatly delight in his commandments.
²Their descendants will be mighty in the land;
   the generation of the upright will be blessed.
³Wealth and riches are in their houses,
   and their righteousness endures forever.
⁴They rise in the darkness as a light for the upright;
   they are gracious, merciful, and righteous.
⁵It is well with those who deal generously and lend,
   who conduct their affairs with justice.
⁶For the righteous will never be moved;
   they will be remembered forever.
⁷They are not afraid of evil tidings;
   their hearts are firm, secure in the Lord.
⁸Their hearts are steady, they will not be afraid;
   in the end they will look in triumph on their foes.
⁹They have distributed freely, they have given to the poor;
   their righteousness endures forever; their horn is exalted in
      honor.
¹⁰The wicked see it and are angry;
   they gnash their teeth and melt away;
   the desire of the wicked comes to nothing.

1 Corinthians 2:1-12 (13-16)

¹When I came to you, brothers and sisters, I did not come proclaiming the mystery of God to you in lofty words or wisdom. ²For I decided to know nothing among you except Jesus Christ, and him crucified. ³And I came to you in weakness and in fear and in much trembling. ⁴My speech and my proclamation were not with plausible words of wisdom, but with a demonstration of the Spirit and of power, ⁵so that your faith might rest not on human wisdom but on the power of God.

⁶Yet among the mature we do speak wisdom, though it is not a wisdom of this age or of the rulers of this age, who are doomed to perish. ⁷But we speak God's wisdom, secret and hidden, which God decreed before the ages for our glory. ⁸None of the rulers of this age understood this; for if they had, they would not have crucified the Lord of glory. ⁹But, as it is written,
   "What no eye has seen, nor ear heard,
      nor the human heart conceived,
   what God has prepared for those who love him"—
¹⁰these things God has revealed to us through the Spirit; for the Spirit searches everything, even the depths of God. ¹¹For what human being knows what is truly human except the human spirit that is within? So also no one comprehends what is truly God's except the Spirit of God. ¹²Now we have received not the spirit of the world, but the Spirit that is from God, so that we may understand the gifts bestowed on us by God. ¹³And we speak of these things in words not taught by human wisdom but taught by the Spirit, interpreting spiritual things to those who are spiritual.

¹⁴Those who are unspiritual do not receive the gifts of God's Spirit, for they are foolishness to them, and they are unable to understand them because they are spiritually discerned. ¹⁵Those who are spiritual discern all things, and they are themselves subject to no one else's scrutiny.
¹⁶ "For who has known the mind of the Lord
      so as to instruct him?"
   But we have the mind of Christ.

Matthew 5:13-20

¹³"You are the salt of the earth; but if salt has lost its taste, how can its saltiness be restored? It is no longer good for anything, but is thrown out and trampled under foot.

¹⁴"You are the light of the world. A city built on a hill cannot be hid. ¹⁵No one after lighting a lamp puts it under the bushel basket, but on the lampstand, and it gives light to all in the house. ¹⁶In the same way, let your light shine before others, so that they may see your good works and give glory to your Father in heaven.

¹⁷"Do not think that I have come to abolish the law or the prophets; I have come not to abolish but to fulfill. ¹⁸For truly I tell you, until heaven and earth pass away, not one letter, not one stroke of a letter, will pass from the law until all is accomplished. ¹⁹Therefore, whoever breaks one of the least of these commandments, and teaches others to do the same, will be called least in the kingdom of heaven; but whoever does them and teaches them will be called great in the kingdom of heaven. ²⁰For I tell you, unless your righteousness exceeds that of the scribes and Pharisees, you will never enter the kingdom of heaven."

Primary Hymns and Songs for the Day

"Gather Us In" (Isa, Matt, Comm.) (O)
    C284, EL532, G401, S2236, SH393
"For the Healing of the Nations" (Isa) (O)
    C668, CG698, G346, N576, SA1000, UM428, VU678
"Awake, My Soul, and with the Sun" (Isa)
    E11, EL557 (PD), G663, P456, SA4
"All Who Love and Serve Your City" (Isa)
    C670, CG674, E570/E571, EL724, G351, P413, UM433
      H-3   Chr-26, 65; Org-19
      S-1   #62. Desc.
"I Want to Walk as a Child of the Light" (Matt)
    CG96, E490, EL815, G377, SH352, UM206
      S-2   #91. Desc.
"*Sois la Semilla*" ("You Are the Seed") (Matt) (C)
    C478, N528, UM583
"This Little Light of Mine" (Matt, Black History) (C)
    N525, SH257, UM585 (See also AH4150, EL677, N524)

Additional Hymn Suggestions

"O For a Thousand Tongues to Sing" (Isa)
    C5, CG332, E493, EL886, G610, N42, P466, SA89, SH439,
    UM57 (PD), UM58, VU326 (See also WS3001)
"Guide Me, O Thou Great Jehovah" (Isa)
    C622, CG33, E690, EL618, G65, N18/19, P281, SA27, SH51,
    UM127 (PD), VU651 (Fr.)
"*Cuando el Pobre*" ("When the Poor Ones") (Isa)
    C662, EL725, G762, P407, SH240, UM434, VU702
"Here I Am, Lord" (Isa)
    C452, CG482, EL574, G69, P525, SA1002, SH608, UM593,
    VU509
"God Is So Good" 4956994 (Isa)
    G658, S2056, SH461
"What Does the Lord Require of You" 456859 (Isa)
    C661, CG690, G70, S2174, VU701
"Draw Us in the Spirit's Tether" (Isa, Comm.)
    C392, EL470, G529, N337, P504, UM632, VU479
"Mine Eyes Have Seen the Glory" (Isa)
    C705, CG439, EL890, G354, N610, SA263, UM717
"Guide My Feet" (Isa, Black History)
    CG637, G741, N497, P354, S2208, SH54
"Christ, Be Our Light" ("*Cristo, la Luz*") (Isa, Matt)
    EL715, G314, SH242
"All Praise to Thee, for Thou, O King Divine" (Pss, 1 Cor)
    CG352, E477, SA351, UM166, VU327
"Lord, Speak to Me" (Pss, 1 Cor)
    CG503, EL676, G722, N531, P426, SA773, SH557, UM463,
    VU589
"Ask Ye What Great Thing I Know" (1 Cor)
    CG443, N49, UM163 (PD), VU338
"Jesus, the Very Thought of Thee" (1 Cor)
    C102, CG386, E642, EL754, G629, N507, P310, SA85, UM175
    (PD)
"Be Thou My Vision" (1 Cor)
    C595, CG71, E488, EL793, G450, N451, P339, SA573, SH640,
    UM451, VU642
"Woke Up This Morning" (1 Cor)
    C623, N85, S2082
"Christ Beside Me" (1 Cor)
    G702, S2166
"Blessed Jesus, At Thy Word" (Matt)
    E440, EL520, G395, N74, P454, UM596 (PD), VU500
"I'm Gonna Live So God Can Use Me" (Matt)
    C614, G700, P369, S2153, SH632, VU575
"Bring Forth the Kingdom" (Matt)
    N181, S2190, SH130

"Lead Me, Guide Me" (Matt)
    C583, CG403, EL768, G740, S2214, SH582
"We All Are One in Mission" (Matt)
    CG269, EL576, G733, P435, S2243

Additional Contemporary and Modern Suggestions

"Shout to the Lord" 1406918 (Isa)
    CG348, EL821, S2074, SA264, SH426
"Something Beautiful" 18060 (1 Cor)
"To Know You More" 1767420 (1 Cor)
"More Like You" 2145051 (1 Cor)
"Knowing You" 1045238 (1 Cor)
"Let It Be Said of Us" 1855882 (1 Cor)
"Take My Life" 1617154 1 Cor)
"I Will Boast" 4662350 (1 Cor)
"I Have a Hope" 5087587 (1 Cor)
"Here I Am to Worship" 3266032 (Matt)
"Shine, Jesus, Shine" 30426 (Matt)
    CG156, EL671, G192, S2173, SA261, SH102
"Light of the World" 73342 (Matt)
"We Are Marching" ("*Siyahamba*") 1321512 (Matt)
    C442, CG155, EL866, G853, N526, S2235, SA903, SH717,
    VU646
"Mighty to Save" 4591782 (Matt)
"Lord Jesus Christ, Your Light Shines" (Matt)
    SH556, WS3137
"Carry the Light" 126402 (Matt)
"Song for the Nations" 20340 (Matt)
"Everyday" 2798154 (Matt)
"Freedom in the Spirit" 7127886 (Matt)

Vocal Solos

"God Will Make a Way" (with "He Leadeth Me") (Isa)
    V-3 (2)   p. 9
"A Song of Joy" (Isa)
    V-1   p. 2
"Christ Living Within You" (1 Cor)
    V-8   p. 177
"Here I Am" (1 Cor)
    V-1   p. 19

Anthems

"Teach Me, O Lord" (Pss)
Thomas Atwood; MorningStar MSM-50-3425
SATB *a cappella* (https://bit.ly/MSM-50-3425)

"Light of My Soul" (Matt)
Tchaikovsky/arr. Tom Fettke; Hal Leonard 00129787
SATB, piano (https://bit.ly/HL129787)

Other Suggestions

This day may include an observance of Boy Scout Sunday.
*February is Black History Month, which can be reflected in your choice of
    music and liturgy.*
Visuals:
    O   Trumpet, fist, open shackles, yoke, bread, light, water
    P   Bible, light/dark, justice, heart, ministry to poor,
           anger
    E   Bible, heart, emotion, praise, walking
    G   Salt/light, globe, city, lamp/basket/lampstand, Bible,
           teaching
Canticle: UM125. Canticle of Covenant Faithfulness (Isa)
Prayer: UM456. For Courage to Do Justice (Isa)
Theme Ideas: Discipleship / Following God, Faithfulness, God:
    Wisdom, Jesus: Mind of Christ, Justice, Light, Redemption /
    Salvation

Deuteronomy 30:15-20

[15]See, I have set before you today life and prosperity, death and adversity. [16]If you obey the commandments of the LORD your God that I am commanding you today, by loving the LORD your God, walking in his ways, and observing his commandments, decrees, and ordinances, then you shall live and become numerous, and the LORD your God will bless you in the land that you are entering to possess. [17]But if your heart turns away and you do not hear, but are led astray to bow down to other gods and serve them, [18]I declare to you today that you shall perish; you shall not live long in the land that you are crossing the Jordan to enter and possess. [19]I call heaven and earth to witness against you today that I have set before you life and death, blessings and curses. Choose life so that you and your descendants may live, [20]loving the LORD your God, obeying him, and holding fast to him; for that means life to you and length of days, so that you may live in the land that the LORD swore to give to your ancestors, to Abraham, to Isaac, and to Jacob.

Psalm 119:1-8 (G64, N701, UM840)

[1] Happy are those whose way is blameless,
    who walk in the law of the LORD.
[2]Happy are those who keep his decrees,
    who seek him with their whole heart,
[3]who also do no wrong,
    but walk in his ways.
[4]You have commanded your precepts
    to be kept diligently.
[5]O that my ways may be steadfast
    in keeping your statutes!
[6]Then I shall not be put to shame,
    having my eyes fixed on all your commandments.
[7]I will praise you with an upright heart,
    when I learn your righteous ordinances.
[8]I will observe your statutes;
    do not utterly forsake me.

1 Corinthians 3:1-9

[1]And so, brothers and sisters, I could not speak to you as spiritual people, but rather as people of the flesh, as infants in Christ. [2]I fed you with milk, not solid food, for you were not ready for solid food. Even now you are still not ready, [3]for you are still of the flesh. For as long as there is jealousy and quarreling among you, are you not of the flesh, and behaving according to human inclinations? [4]For when one says, "I belong to Paul," and another, "I belong to Apollos," are you not merely human?

[5]What then is Apollos? What is Paul? Servants through whom you came to believe, as the Lord assigned to each. [6]I planted, Apollos watered, but God gave the growth. [7]So neither the one who plants nor the one who waters is anything, but only God who gives the growth. [8]The one who plants and the one who waters have a common purpose, and each will receive wages according to the labor of each. [9]For we are God's servants, working together; you are God's field, God's building.

Matthew 5:21-37

[21]"You have heard that it was said to those of ancient times, 'You shall not murder'; and 'whoever murders shall be liable to judgment.' [22]But I say to you that if you are angry with a brother or sister, you will be liable to judgment; and if you insult a brother or sister, you will be liable to the council; and if you say, 'You fool,' you will be liable to the hell of fire. [23]So when you are offering your gift at the altar, if you remember that your brother or sister has something against you, [24]leave your gift there before the altar and go; first be reconciled to your brother or sister, and then come and offer your gift. [25]Come to terms quickly with your accuser while you are on the way to court with him, or your accuser may hand you over to the judge, and the judge to the guard, and you will be thrown into prison. [26]Truly I tell you, you will never get out until you have paid the last penny.

[27]"You have heard that it was said, 'You shall not commit adultery.' [28]But I say to you that everyone who looks at a woman with lust has already committed adultery with her in his heart. [29]If your right eye causes you to sin, tear it out and throw it away; it is better for you to lose one of your members than for your whole body to be thrown into hell. [30]And if your right hand causes you to sin, cut it off and throw it away; it is better for you to lose one of your members than for your whole body to go into hell.

[31]"It was also said, 'Whoever divorces his wife, let him give her a certificate of divorce.' [32]But I say to you that anyone who divorces his wife, except on the ground of unchastity, causes her to commit adultery; and whoever marries a divorced woman commits adultery.

[33]"Again, you have heard that it was said to those of ancient times, 'You shall not swear falsely, but carry out the vows you have made to the Lord.' [34]But I say to you, Do not swear at all, either by heaven, for it is the throne of God, [35]or by the earth, for it is his footstool, or by Jerusalem, for it is the city of the great King. [36]And do not swear by your head, for you cannot make one hair white or black. [37]Let your word be 'Yes, Yes' or 'No, No'; anything more than this comes from the evil one."

Primary Hymns and Songs for the Day
"The Church's One Foundation" (1 Cor) (O)
    C272, CG246, E525, EL654, G321, N386, P442, SH233,
    UM545/546, VU332 (Fr.)
        H-3   Hbl-94; Chr-180; Desc-16; Org-9
        S-1   #25-26. Desc. and harm.
"Kum Ba Yah" 2749763 (Matt)
    C590, G472, P338, UM494
"God, How Can We Forgive" (Matt)
    G445, S2169
        H-3   Hbl-62, 95; Chr-59; Org-77
        S-1   #211. Harm.
"Christ for the World We Sing" (1 Cor) (C)
    E537, SA917, UM568 (PD)
        H-3   Hbl-28, 49, 53; Chr-56; Desc-57; Org-63
        S-1   #185-186. Desc. and harm.

Additional Hymn Suggestions
"Spirit of God, Descend upon My Heart" (Deut)
    C265, CG243, EL800, G688, N290, P326, SA290, SH277,
    UM500 (PD) VU378
"Love the Lord Your God" 1400093 (Deut)
    G62, S2168
"As We Gather at Your Table" (Deut, Comm.)
    EL522, N332, S2268, SH411, VU457
"O Master, Let Me Walk with Thee" (Deut, Pss)
    C602, CG660, E659/E660, EL818, G738, N503, P357, SA667,
    SH612, UM430 (PD), VU560
"Like the Murmur of the Dove's Song" (1 Cor)
    C245, CG233, E513, EL403, G285, N270, P314, SH407,
    UM544, VU205
"In Christ There Is No East or West" (1 Cor)
    C687, CG273, E529, EL650 (PD), G317/318, N394/395,
    P439/440, SA1006, SH226, UM548, VU606
"Sois la Semilla" ("You Are the Seed") (1 Cor)
    C478, N528, UM583
"Together We Serve" (1 Cor)
    G767, S2175
"We All Are One in Mission" (1 Cor)
    CG269, EL576, G733, P435, S2243
"God Made from One Blood" (1 Cor, Matt)
    C500, CG686, N427, S2170, VU554
"Come, Share the Lord" (1 Cor, Matt, Comm.)
    C408, CG459, G510, S2269, VU469
"The Lord's Prayer" (Matt)
    C307-C310, G464, P589, S2278, SH595, UM271, WS3068-
    WS3071
"Forgive Our Sins as We Forgive" (Matt)
    CG694 E674, EL605, G444, P347, SH504, UM390, VU364
"The Gift of Love" (Matt)
    C526, CG440, G693, P335, UM408, VU372
"Breathe on Me, Breath of God" (Matt)
    C254, CG235, E508, G286, N292, P316, SA294, SH224/273,
    UM420 (PD), VU382 (Fr.)
"Blest Be the Tie That Binds" (Matt)
    C433, CG267, EL656, G306, N393, P438, SA812, SH701,
    UM557 (PD), VU602
"Help Us Accept Each Other" (Matt)
    C487, G754, N388, P358, UM560
"Purify My Heart" (Matt)
"Purify My Heart" 1314323 (Matt)
"Tell Me the Story of Jesus" (Matt)
    SA152, SH122
"Si Fui Motio de Dolor" ("If I Have Been the Source of Pain")
    N544, SH134

Additional Contemporary and Modern Suggestions
"To Know You More" 1767420 (Deut)
"The Family Prayer Song" 1680466 (Deut)
"Love the Lord" 4572938 (Deut)
"Cry of My Heart" 844980 (Deut, Pss)
"Step by Step" 696994 (Deut, Pss)
    CG495, G743, WS3004
"More Love, More Power" 60661 (Deut. Pss)
"You're Worthy of My Praise" 487976 (Deut, Pss)
"Take This Life" 2563365 (Deut, Pss)
"The Dark Is Not Your Home" 7132934 (Deut, Pss)
"Let It Be Said of Us" 1855882 (Deut, 1 Cor)
"Ancient Words" 2986399 (Pss)
"In the Secret" 1810119 (Pss)
"Show Me Your Ways" 1675024 (Pss)
"Thy Word Is a Lamp" 14301 (Pss)
    C326, CG38, G458, UM601
"They'll Know We Are Christians" 26997 (1 Cor)
    AH4074, C494, CG272, G300, S2223, SH232
"A Wilderness Wandering People" 7068566 (1 Cor, Matt)
"Draw the Circle Wide" (1 Cor, Matt)
    WS3154
"Seek Ye First" 1352 (Matt)
    C354, CG436, E711, G175, P333, SA675, SH126, UM405,
    VU356
"Give Me a Clean Heart" 314764 (Matt)
    AH4125, C515, N188, S2133
"Make Me a Channel of Your Peace" (Matt)
    G753, S2171, SA608, SH616 VU684
"Make Me a Channel of Your Peace" 6399315 (Matt)

Vocal Solos
"Turn My Heart to You" (Deut)
    V-5 (2)   p. 14
"My Heart Is Steadfast" (Deut, Pss)
    V-5 (2)   p. 40
"If With All Your Hearts" (Deut, Pss)
    V-8   p. 277
"This Is My Commandment" (Matt)
    V-8   p. 284
"He Breaks the Bread, He Pours the Wine" (Matt, Comm.)
    V-10   p. 43

Anthems
"Walking With God" (Deut)
Paul Basler; Colla Voce 36-22001
SATB, keyboard (https://bit.ly/36-22001)

"Forgive Our Sins as We Forgive" (Matt)
Nancy Raabe; Augsburg 9781506408644
SAB, piano (https://bit.ly/A-08644)

Other Suggestions
Visuals:
    O   Ten commandments, heart, river, "choose life"
    P   Bible, heart, devotion, praise, walking
    E   Infants, milk, quarrel, plant/water/growth, work,
         field, building
    G   Anger, fire, gift/altar, reconcile, jail, eye, hand,
         divorce certificate, stool
Call to Confession: WSL84. "We cannot come" (Matt)
Prayer of Confession: UM892 (Deut)
Sung Confession: WS3138. "Confession" (Matt)
Response: EL814, G698, SH620, WS3119. "Take, O Take Me As I
    Am" (Deut)
Theme Ideas: Faithfulness, Reconciliation, Sin and Forgiveness,
    Unity

Exodus 24:12-18

[12]The Lord said to Moses, "Come up to me on the mountain, and wait there; and I will give you the tablets of stone, with the law and the commandment, which I have written for their instruction." [13]So Moses set out with his assistant Joshua, and Moses went up into the mountain of God. [14]To the elders he had said, "Wait here for us, until we come to you again; for Aaron and Hur are with you; whoever has a dispute may go to them." [15]Then Moses went up on the mountain, and the cloud covered the mountain. [16]The glory of the Lord settled on Mount Sinai, and the cloud covered it for six days; on the seventh day he called to Moses out of the cloud. [17]Now the appearance of the glory of the Lord was like a devouring fire on the top of the mountain in the sight of the people of Israel. [18]Moses entered the cloud, and went up on the mountain. Moses was on the mountain for forty days and forty nights.

Psalm 99 (G57, N687, UM819)

[1]The Lord is king; let the peoples tremble!
   He sits enthroned upon the cherubim; let the earth quake!
[2]The Lord is great in Zion;
   he is exalted over all the peoples.
[3]Let them praise your great and awesome name.
   Holy is he!
[4]Mighty King, lover of justice,
   you have established equity;
you have executed justice
   and righteousness in Jacob.
[5]Extol the Lord our God;
   worship at his footstool.
   Holy is he!
[6]Moses and Aaron were among his priests,
   Samuel also was among those who called on his name.
   They cried to the Lord, and he answered them.
[7]He spoke to them in the pillar of cloud;
   they kept his decrees,
   and the statutes that he gave them.
[8]O Lord our God, you answered them;
   you were a forgiving God to them,
   but an avenger of their wrongdoings.
[9]Extol the Lord our God,
   and worship at his holy mountain;
   for the Lord our God is holy.

2 Peter 1:16-21

[16]For we did not follow cleverly devised myths when we made known to you the power and coming of our Lord Jesus Christ, but we had been eyewitnesses of his majesty. [17]For he received honor and glory from God the Father when that voice was conveyed to him by the Majestic Glory, saying, "This is my Son, my Beloved, with whom I am well pleased." [18]We ourselves heard this voice come from heaven, while we were with him on the holy mountain.

[19]So we have the prophetic message more fully confirmed. You will do well to be attentive to this as to a lamp shining in a dark place, until the day dawns and the morning star rises in your hearts. [20]First of all you must understand this, that no prophecy of scripture is a matter of one's own interpretation, [21]because no prophecy ever came by human will, but men and women moved by the Holy Spirit spoke from God.

Matthew 17:1-9

[1]Six days later, Jesus took with him Peter and James and his brother John and led them up a high mountain, by themselves. [2]And he was transfigured before them, and his face shone like the sun, and his clothes became dazzling white. [3]Suddenly there appeared to them Moses and Elijah, talking with him. [4]Then Peter said to Jesus, "Lord, it is good for us to be here; if you wish, I will make three dwellings here, one for you, one for Moses, and one for Elijah." [5]While he was still speaking, suddenly a bright cloud overshadowed them, and from the cloud a voice said, "This is my Son, the Beloved; with him I am well pleased; listen to him!" [6]When the disciples heard this, they fell to the ground and were overcome by fear. [7]But Jesus came and touched them, saying, "Get up and do not be afraid." [8]And when they looked up, they saw no one except Jesus himself alone.

[9]As they were coming down the mountain, Jesus ordered them, "Tell no one about the vision until after the Son of Man has been raised from the dead."

Primary Hymns and Songs for the Day
"Christ, Whose Glory Fills the Skies" (2 Pet, Matt) (O)
   EL553, G662, P462/463, SA249, UM173, VU336
      H-3   Hbl-51; Chr-206; Desc-89; Org-120
      S-1   #278-279. Harms.
"Open the Eyes of My Heart" 2298355 (2 Pet)
   G452, SA270, SH378, WS3008
"O Wondrous Sight! O Vision Fair" (2 Pet, Matt)
   E137, UM258 (PD)
      H-3   Hbl-93; Chr-84; Desc-102; Org-175
      S-2   #191. Harm.
   E136, EL316 (PD), G189, N184, P75
"Swiftly Pass the Clouds of Glory" (Matt)
   G190, P73, S2102
      H-3   Chr-98; Org-43
"Holy Ground" 21198 (Matt)
   C112, G406, S2272, SA400
"You, Lord, Are Both Lamb and Shepherd" (Matt)
   G274, SH210, VU210. WS3043
"Immortal, Invisible, God Only Wise" (Exod) (C)
   C66, CG58, E423, EL834, G12, N1, P263, SA37, UM103 (PD),
   VU264
      H-3   Hbl-15, 71; Chr-65; Desc-93; Org-135
      S-1   #300. Harm.

Additional Hymn Suggestions
"O Worship the King" (Exod)
   C17, CG52, E388, EL842, G41, N26, P476, SA52, SH2, UM73
   (PD), VU235
"Source and Sovereign, Rock and Cloud" (Exod)
   C12, G11, UM113
"Guide Me, O Thou Great Jehovah" (Exod)
   C622, CG33, E690, EL618, G65, N18/19, P281, SA27, SH51,
   UM127 (PD), VU651 (Fr.)
"Glorious Things of Thee Are Spoken" (Exod)
   C709, CG282, E522/523, EL647, G81, N307, P446, SA535,
   UM731 (PD)
"Spirit, Spirit of Gentleness" (Exod)
   C249, EL396, G291, N286, P319, S2120, VU375 (Fr.)
"Praise God for This Holy Ground" (Exod, Matt)
   G405, WS3009
"The God of Abraham Praise" (Exod, Matt)
   C24, CG45, E401, EL831, G49, N24, P488, SH50, UM116
   (PD), VU255
"Every Time I Feel the Spirit" (Exod, Matt)
   C592, G66, N282, P315, UM404
"Be Thou My Vision" (Exod, Matt, Transfig.)
   C595, CG71, E488, EL793, G450, N451, P339, SA573, SH640,
   UM451, VU642
"La Palabra Del Señor Es Recta" ("Righteous and Just Is the Word
   of the Lord") (Pss)
   G40, UM107, SH4
"A Hymn of Glory Let Us Sing" (2 Pet)
   E218, G258, N259, P141
"Lord of All Hopefulness" (2 Pet)
   CG678, E482, EL765, G683, S2197, SA772, SH464
"Deep in the Shadows of the Past" (2 Pet)
   G50, N320, P330, S2246
"Jesus, the Light of the World" 6363190 (2 Pet)
   WS3056 (See also AH4038, CG129, G127, N160, SH103)
"O Morning Star, How Fair and Bright" (2 Pet, Matt)
   C105, E497, EL308, G827, N158, P69, UM247, VU98
"Jesus, Take Us to the Mountain" (Matt)
   N183, G193
"Here, O My Lord, I See Thee" (Matt, Comm.)
   C416, CG460, E318, G517, N336, P520, UM623, VU459
"Let Us with a Joyful Mind" (Matt)
   E389, G31, N16, P244, S2012, SA42, VU234

"We Have Come at Christ's Own Bidding" (Matt)
   CG162, G191, N182, S2103, VU104
"How Good, Lord, to Be Here!" (*"Es bueno estar aquí"*) (Matt)
   EL315, SH133, VU103

Additional Contemporary and Modern Suggestions
"Awesome God" 41099 (Exod, Pss)
   G616, S2040
"Doxology" 5465879 (Exod, Pss)
"Majesty" 1527 (Pss)
   CG346, SA382, SH212, UM176
"Awesome Is the Lord Most High" 4674159 (Pss)
"Famous One" 3599431 (Pss, 2 Pet)
"Ancient Words" 2986399 (2 Pet)
"All Hail King Jesus" 12877 (Matt, Transfig.)
"He Is Exalted" 17827 (Matt, Transfig.)
   AH4082, CG342, S2070, SH423
"Shine, Jesus, Shine" 30426 (Matt, Transfig.)
   CG156, F1.671, G192, S2173, SA261, SH102; V-3 (2) p. 48
   Vocal Solo
"Turn Your Eyes upon Jesus" 15960 (Matt)
   CG472, SA445, UM349
"We Fall Down" 2437367 (Matt, Transfig.)
   G368, WS3187
"Awesome in This Place" 847554 (Matt, Transfig.)
"We Declare Your Majesty" 121483 (Matt, Transfig.)
"Great and Mighty Is He" 66665 (Transfig.)
"Honor and Praise" 1867485 (Transfig.)
"Hosanna" 4785835 (Transfig.)
   SH361, WS3188

Vocal Solos
"Be Thou My Vision" (Exod, Matt, Transfig.)
   V-6   p. 13
"I Saw the Lord, and All Beside Was Darkness" (Exod, Matt)
   V-8   p. 268
"Ev'ry Time I Feel De Spirit" (Exod, Matt)
   V-7   p. 78

Anthems
"Christ Whose Glory Fills the Skies" (Matt)
Eleanor Daley; Alliance Music AMP0162
SATB *a cappella* (https://bit.ly/AMP0162)

"My God, How Wonderful Thou Art" (Exod, Matt)
arr. René Clausen; Augsburg 0-8006-7699-8
SATB *a cappella* (https://bit.ly/7699-8)

Other Suggestions
Visuals:
   O   Exod.24:12b, mountain, tablets, cloud, glory, volcano
   P   Throne, quake, Ps 99:3, scales, footstool, cloud, tablet
   E   Majesty, 2 Pet 1:17b, mountain, lamp, dawn, star
   G   Mountain, three figures/booths, cloud, Matt 17:5b
Introit: EL819, G388, S2274, SH405. "Come, All You People"
   (Pss)
Introit: N742. "Gathered Here in the Mystery" (Transfig.)
Sung Confession: UM82 "Canticle of God's Glory" (Exod, Matt)
Call to Prayer: EL529, G392, S2273, SH611. "Jesus, We Are
   Here" (Matt)
Prayer: UM259 and WSL13 (Matt, Transfig.)
Prayer: WSL11 (2 Pet)
Prayer: N831 (Matt, Transfig.)
Blessing: N872 (Exod, Matt, Transfig.)
Alternate Lesson: Ps 2
Theme Ideas: God: Glory of God, God: Wisdom, Praise

Joel 2:1-2, 12-17

[1] Blow the trumpet in Zion;
   sound the alarm on my holy mountain!
Let all the inhabitants of the land tremble,
   for the day of the LORD is coming, it is near—
[2] a day of darkness and gloom,
   a day of clouds and thick darkness!
Like blackness spread upon the mountains
   a great and powerful army comes;
their like has never been from of old,
   nor will be again after them
   in ages to come.

. . . .

[12] Yet even now, says the LORD,
   return to me with all your heart,
with fasting, with weeping, and with mourning;
   [13] rend your hearts and not your clothing.
Return to the LORD, your God,
   for he is gracious and merciful,
slow to anger, and abounding in steadfast love,
   and relents from punishing.
[14] Who knows whether he will not turn and relent,
   and leave a blessing behind him,
a grain offering and a drink offering
   for the LORD, your God?
[15] Blow the trumpet in Zion;
   sanctify a fast;
call a solemn assembly;
   [16] gather the people.
Sanctify the congregation;
   assemble the aged;
gather the children,
   even infants at the breast.
Let the bridegroom leave his room,
   and the bride her canopy.
[17] Between the vestibule and the altar
   let the priests, the ministers of the LORD, weep.
Let them say, "Spare your people, O LORD,
   and do not make your heritage a mockery,
   a byword among the nations.
Why should it be said among the peoples,
   'Where is their God?'"

Psalm 51:1-17 (G421/422/423, N657, P195/196, UM785)

[1] Have mercy on me, O God,
   according to your steadfast love;
according to your abundant mercy
   blot out my transgressions.
[2] Wash me thoroughly from my iniquity,
   and cleanse me from my sin.
[3] For I know my transgressions,
   and my sin is ever before me.
[4] Against you, you alone, have I sinned,
   and done what is evil in your sight,
so that you are justified in your sentence
   and blameless when you pass judgment.
[5] Indeed, I was born guilty,
   a sinner when my mother conceived me.
[6] You desire truth in the inward being;
   therefore teach me wisdom in my secret heart.
[7] Purge me with hyssop, and I shall be clean;
   wash me, and I shall be whiter than snow.
[8] Let me hear joy and gladness;
   let the bones that you have crushed rejoice.
[9] Hide your face from my sins,
   and blot out all my iniquities.
[10] Create in me a clean heart, O God,
   and put a new and right spirit within me.

[11] Do not cast me away from your presence,
   and do not take your holy spirit from me.
[12] Restore to me the joy of your salvation,
   and sustain in me a willing spirit.
[13] Then I will teach transgressors your ways,
   and sinners will return to you.
[14] Deliver me from bloodshed, O God,
   O God of my salvation,
   and my tongue will sing aloud of your deliverance.
[15] O Lord, open my lips,
   and my mouth will declare your praise.
[16] For you have no delight in sacrifice;
   if I were to give a burnt offering, you would not be pleased.
[17] The sacrifice acceptable to God is a broken spirit;
   a broken and contrite heart, O God, you will not despise.

2 Corinthians 5:20b–6:10

[20b] we entreat you on behalf of Christ, be reconciled to God. [21] For our sake he made him to be sin who knew no sin, so that in him we might become the righteousness of God.

6 As we work together with him, we urge you also not to accept the grace of God in vain. [2] For he says,
   "At an acceptable time I have listened to you,
      and on a day of salvation I have helped you."
See, now is the acceptable time; see, now is the day of salvation! [3] We are putting no obstacle in anyone's way, so that no fault may be found with our ministry, [4] but as servants of God we have commended ourselves in every way: through great endurance, in afflictions, hardships, calamities, [5] beatings, imprisonments, riots, labors, sleepless nights, hunger; [6] by purity, knowledge, patience, kindness, holiness of spirit, genuine love, [7] truthful speech, and the power of God; with the weapons of righteousness for the right hand and for the left; [8] in honor and dishonor, in ill repute and good repute. We are treated as impostors, and yet are true; [9] as unknown, and yet are well known; as dying, and see—we are alive; as punished, and yet not killed; [10] as sorrowful, yet always rejoicing; as poor, yet making many rich; as having nothing, and yet possessing everything.

Matthew 6:1-6, 16-21

[1] "Beware of practicing your piety before others in order to be seen by them; for then you have no reward from your Father in heaven. [2] So whenever you give alms, do not sound a trumpet before you, as the hypocrites do in the synagogues and in the streets, so that they may be praised by others. Truly I tell you, they have received their reward. [3] But when you give alms, do not let your left hand know what your right hand is doing, [4] so that your alms may be done in secret; and your Father who sees in secret will reward you. [5] "And whenever you pray, do not be like the hypocrites; for they love to stand and pray in the synagogues and at the street corners, so that they may be seen by others. Truly I tell you, they have received their reward. [6] But whenever you pray, go into your room and shut the door and pray to your Father who is in secret; and your Father who sees in secret will reward you. . . .

[16] "And whenever you fast, do not look dismal, like the hypocrites, for they disfigure their faces so as to show others that they are fasting. Truly I tell you, they have received their reward. [17] But when you fast, put oil on your head and wash your face, [18] so that your fasting may be seen not by others but by your Father who is in secret; and your Father who sees in secret will reward you.

[19] "Do not store up for yourselves treasures on earth, where moth and rust consume and where thieves break in and steal; [20] but store up for yourselves treasures in heaven, where neither moth nor rust consumes and where thieves do not break in and steal. [21] For where your treasure is, there your heart will be also."

Primary Hymns and Songs for the Day

"Take Time to Be Holy" (Matt) (O)
C572, SA790, UM395 (PD), VU672
H-3   Chr-178
S-1   #159. Harm.

"Give Me a Clean Heart" 314764 (Pss, Ash Wed.)
AH4125, C515, N188, S2133

"Sunday's Palms Are Wednesday's Ashes" (Pss, Ash Wed.)
S2138, VU107
H-3   Hbl-14, 64; Chr-132, 203
S-2   #22. Desc.

"Come and Find the Quiet Center" (Matt, Ash Wed.)
C575, S2128, VU374

"Lord, I Want to Be a Christian" (Joel, Matt) (C)
C589, CG507, G729, N454, P372 (PD), SH621, UM402
H-3   Chr-130

Additional Hymn Suggestions

"There's a Wideness in God's Mercy" (Joel)
C73, CG41, E470, EL587/88G435, N23, P298, SH526,
UM121, VU271

"Come Back Quickly to the Lord" (Joel)
G416, P381, UM343

"O Master, Let Me Walk with Thee" (Joel)
C602, CG660, E659/E660, EL818, G738, N503, P357, SA667,
SH612, UM430 (PD), VU560

"Today We All Are Called to Be Disciples" (Joel)
G757, P434, VU507

"O for a Closer Walk with God" (Pss)
CG679, E684, G739, N450, P396, SA612

"Give Me Jesus" (Pss, Matt)
CG546, EL770, N409, SH306, WS3140

"Jesus, the Very Thought of Thee" (2 Cor)
C102, CG386, E642, EL754, G629, N507, P310, SA85, UM175
(PD)

"What Wondrous Love Is This" (2 Cor)
C200, CG171, E439, EL666, G215, N223, P85, SA207, SH177,
UM292, VU147 (Fr.)

"Alas! and Did My Savior Bleed" (2 Cor, Lent)
AH4067, C204, CG182/595, EL337, G212, N199/200, P78,
SA159, UM294/359, SH172/173

"Lord, Speak to Me" (2 Cor)
CG503, EL676, G722, N531, P426, SA773, SH557, UM463,
VU589

"We Walk by Faith" (2 Cor, Matt)
CG634, E209, EL635, G817, N256, P399, S2196, SH660

"Lord, Who Throughout These Forty Days" (Matt, Lent) (C)
C180, CG169, E142, EL319, G166, N211, P81, UM269

"Amazing Grace" (Matt, Comm.)
AH4091, C546, CG587, E671, EL779, G649, N547/548, P280,
SA453, SH523, UM378 (PD), VU266 (Fr.)

"Be Thou My Vision" (Matt)
C595, CG71, E488, EL793, G450, N451, P339, SA573, SH640,
UM451, VU642

"Near to the Heart of God" (Matt)
C581, CG383, G824, P527, UM472 (PD)

"Lord of All Hopefulness" (Matt)
CG678, E482, EL765, G683, S2197, SA772, SH464

"The Glory of These Forty Days" (Matt)
E143, EL320, G165, P87

"Forty Days and Forty Nights" (Matt)
C179, E150, G167, N205, P77, SH116, VU114

"The Lord's Prayer" (Matt, Lent)
C307-C310, G464, P589, S2278, SH595, UM271, WS3068-
WS3071

Additional Contemporary and Modern Suggestions

"You Are My Hiding Place" 21442 (Pss)
C554, S2055, SH46

"Open Our Eyes, Lord" 1572 (Pss)
CG392, S2086, SA386, SH562

"Please Enter My Heart, Hosanna" 2485371 (Pss)
S2154

"Change My Heart, O God" 1565 (Pss)
EL801, G695, S2152, SA409, SH507

"Open the Eyes of My Heart" 2298355 (Pss)
G452, SA270, SH378, WS3008

"Purify My Heart" 1314323 (Pss)

"The Power of Your Love" 917491 (Pss)

"Refresh My Heart" 917518 (Pss)

"Refiner's Fire" 426298 (Pss)

"Purified" 3409710 (Pss)

"Today" 5775617 (Pss)

"I Give You My Heart" 1866132 (Pss)

"Give Us Clean Hands" 2060208 (Pss)

"Because of Your Love" 4662501 (Pss)

"Come, Emmanuel" 3999938 (Pss, 2 Cor, Ash Wed.)

"This is My Story" 7046375 (2 Cor)

"We Want to See Jesus Lifted High" 1033408 (2 Cor)

"That's Why We Praise Him" 2668576 (2 Cor)

"The Battle Belongs to the Lord" 21583 (2 Cor)

"Amazing Grace" ("My Chains Are Gone") 4768151 (Matt)

"Grace Like Rain" 3689877 (Matt)

"In the Silence" 6182357 (Matt)

"In the Secret" 1810119 (Matt)

"When It's All Been Said and Done" 2788353 (Matt)

"You Are My All in All" 825356 (Matt, Lent)
CG571, G519, SH335, WS3040

Vocal Solos

"If With All Your Hearts" (Joel)
V-8   p. 277

"A Contrite Heart" (Pss)
V-4   p. 10

"Turn My Heart to You" (Pss, Ash Wed.)
V-5 (2)   p. 14

"How Quiet Is the Night" (Matt, Ash Wed.)
V-8   p. 158

Anthems

"Wondrous Love" (2 Cor)
Arr. Eric Nelson; MorningStar MSM-50-3902
SATB *divisi*, piano (https://bit.ly/50-3902)

"That Priceless Grace" (John)
Arr. John Helgen; Augsburg 0800658590
Unison, piano, opt. descant (https://bit.ly/A-58590)

Other Suggestions

Visuals: Ashes, rough fabrics
- **O**   Black cloth, grain, trumpet, empty plate, weeping
- **P**   Water, snow, rejoicing, Ps 51:10, 15, 17, heart
- **E**   Clock, calendar with today's date, black/gold
- **G**   Praying hands, oil/water, closed door, empty plate, rusty items, Matt 6:21, ashes of last year's palms, oil

Isa 58:1-12 gives another interpretation of fasting.

Call to Prayer: EL538, G466, S2157. "Come and Fill Our Hearts" (Pss)

Call to Confession: N833 or WSL93 (Pss, Healing)

Response: WS3122. "Christ Has Broken Down the Wall" (2 Cor)

Responsive Reading: CG166. (Lent)

Prayer: N846 or UM353 (Pss, Ash Wed.)

Theme Ideas: Patience, Prayer, Redemption / Salvation, Repentance, Sin and Forgiveness

Genesis 2:15-17; 3:1-7

[15]The LORD God took the man and put him in the garden of Eden to till it and keep it. [16]And the LORD God commanded the man, "You may freely eat of every tree of the garden; [17]but of the tree of the knowledge of good and evil you shall not eat, for in the day that you eat of it you shall die." . . .

[3] Now the serpent was more crafty than any other wild animal that the LORD God had made. He said to the woman, "Did God say, 'You shall not eat from any tree in the garden'?" [2]The woman said to the serpent, "We may eat of the fruit of the trees in the garden; [3]but God said, 'You shall not eat of the fruit of the tree that is in the middle of the garden, nor shall you touch it, or you shall die.'" [4]But the serpent said to the woman, "You will not die; [5]for God knows that when you eat of it your eyes will be opened, and you will be like God, knowing good and evil." [6]So when the woman saw that the tree was good for food, and that it was a delight to the eyes, and that the tree was to be desired to make one wise, she took of its fruit and ate; and she also gave some to her husband, who was with her, and he ate. [7]Then the eyes of both were opened, and they knew that they were naked; and they sewed fig leaves together and made loincloths for themselves.

Psalm 32 (G446, N642, P184, SH527, UM766)

[1]Happy are those whose transgression is forgiven,
 whose sin is covered.
[2]Happy are those to whom the LORD imputes no iniquity,
 and in whose spirit there is no deceit.
[3]While I kept silence, my body wasted away
 through my groaning all day long.
[4]For day and night your hand was heavy upon me;
 my strength was dried up as by the heat of summer.   *[Selah]*
[5]Then I acknowledged my sin to you,
 and I did not hide my iniquity;
I said, "I will confess my transgressions to the LORD,"
 and you forgave the guilt of my sin.   *[Selah]*
[6]Therefore let all who are faithful
 offer prayer to you;
at a time of distress, the rush of mighty waters
 shall not reach them.
[7]You are a hiding place for me;
 you preserve me from trouble;
 you surround me with glad cries of deliverance.   *[Selah]*
[8]I will instruct you and teach you the way you should go;
 I will counsel you with my eye upon you.
[9]Do not be like a horse or a mule, without understanding,
 whose temper must be curbed with bit and bridle,
 else it will not stay near you.
[10]Many are the torments of the wicked,
 but steadfast love surrounds those who trust in the LORD.
[11]Be glad in the LORD and rejoice, O righteous,
 and shout for joy, all you upright in heart.

Romans 5:12-19

[12]Therefore, just as sin came into the world through one man, and death came through sin, and so death spread to all because all have sinned—[13]sin was indeed in the world before the law, but sin is not reckoned when there is no law. [14]Yet death exercised dominion from Adam to Moses, even over those whose sins were not like the transgression of Adam, who is a type of the one who was to come.

[15]But the free gift is not like the trespass. For if the many died through the one man's trespass, much more surely have the grace of God and the free gift in the grace of the one man, Jesus Christ, abounded for the many. [16]And the free gift is not like the effect of the one man's sin. For the judgment following one trespass brought condemnation, but the free gift following many trespasses brings justification. [17]If, because of the one man's trespass, death exercised dominion through that one, much more surely will those who receive the abundance of grace and the free gift of righteousness exercise dominion in life through the one man, Jesus Christ.

[18]Therefore just as one man's trespass led to condemnation for all, so one man's act of righteousness leads to justification and life for all. [19]For just as by the one man's disobedience the many were made sinners, so by the one man's obedience the many will be made righteous.

Matthew 4:1-11

[1]Then Jesus was led up by the Spirit into the wilderness to be tempted by the devil. [2]He fasted forty days and forty nights, and afterwards he was famished. [3]The tempter came and said to him, "If you are the Son of God, command these stones to become loaves of bread." [4]But he answered, "It is written,
 'One does not live by bread alone,
  but by every word that comes from the mouth of God.'"
[5]Then the devil took him to the holy city and placed him on the pinnacle of the temple, [6]saying to him, "If you are the Son of God, throw yourself down; for it is written,
 'He will command his angels concerning you,'
and 'On their hands they will bear you up,
  so that you will not dash your foot against a stone.'"
[7]Jesus said to him, "Again it is written, 'Do not put the Lord your God to the test.'"
[8]Again, the devil took him to a very high mountain and showed him all the kingdoms of the world and their splendor; [9]and he said to him, "All these I will give you, if you will fall down and worship me." [10]Jesus said to him, "Away with you, Satan! for it is written,
 'Worship the Lord your God,
  and serve only him.'"
[11]Then the devil left him, and suddenly angels came and waited on him.

Primary Hymns and Songs for the Day
"Lord, Who Throughout These Forty Days" (Matt) (O)
   C180, CG169, E142, G166, N211, P81
     H-3   Chr-132; Desc-94; Org-137
   UM269
     H-3   Chr-106; Desc-65; Org-72
     S-2   #105. Flute/violin desc.
             #106. Harm.
   EL319
"Jesus, Tempted in the Desert" (Matt)
   S2105, VU115
     H-3   Chr-53; Org-33
     S-1   #109-10. Desc. and harm.
"Jesus Walked This Lonesome Valley" (Matt)
   C211, P80, S2112
"Amazing Grace" (Pss, Rom, Comm.) (C)
   AH4091, C546, CG587, E671, EL779, G649, N547/548, P280,
   SA453, SH523, UM378 (PD), VU266 (Fr.)
     H-3   Hbl-14, 46; Chr-27; Desc-14; Org-4
     S-2   #5-7. Various treatments

Additional Hymn Suggestions
"All My Hope Is Firmly Grounded" (Gen)
   C88, E665, EL757, N408, SA530, UM132, VU654/655
"God Who Stretched the Spangled Heavens" (Gen)
   C651, CG21, E580, EL771, G24, N556, P268, UM150
"O Love That Wilt Not Let Me Go" (Gen)
   C540, CG631, G833, N485, P384, SA616, SH314, UM480,
   VU658
"Creator of the Stars of Night" (Gen)
   C127, E60, EL245, G84, N111, P4, SH74, UM692 (PD)
"God Made from One Blood" (Gen)
   C500, CG686, N427, S2170, VU554
"There in God's Garden" (Gen)
   EL342, G226, VU346
"Today We All Are Called to Be Disciples" (Gen)
   G757, P434, VU507
"O Worship the King" (Gen, Rom)
   C17, CG52, E388, EL842, G41, N26, P476, SA52, SH2, UM73
   (PD), VU235
"A Mighty Fortress Is Our God" (Rom)
   C65, CG418, E687/688, EL503/504/505, G275, N439/440,
   P259/260, SA1, SH651, UM110 (PD), VU261/262/263
"Alas! and Did My Savior Bleed" (Rom)
   AH4067, C204, CG182/595, EL337, G212, N199/200, P78,
   SA159, UM294/359, SH172/173
"When I Survey the Wondrous Cross" (Rom) (C)
   C195, CG186, E474, EL803, G223/ 224, N224, P100/101,
   SA208, SH163/164, UM298/299, VU149 (Fr.)
"Cristo Vive" ("Christ Is Risen") (Rom)
   N235, P109, SH184, UM313
"Lord, Dismiss Us With Thy Blessing" (Rom) (C)
   C439, E344, EL545, G546, N77, UM671 (PD), VU425
"In the Singing" (Rom, Comm.)
   EL466, G533, S2255
"Bread of the World" (Rom, Matt, Comm.)
   C387, E301, G499, N346, P502, UM624, VU461
"O Love, How Deep" (Matt)
   E448/449, EL322, G618, N209, P83, SH115, UM267, VU348
"It Is Well with My Soul" (Matt)
   C561, CG573, EL785, G840, N438, SA741, SH305, UM377
"Be Still, My Soul" (Matt)
   C566, CG57, G819, N488, SH330, UM534, VU652
"I Was There to Hear Your Borning Cry" (Matt)
   C75, EL732, G488, N351, S2051, VU644
"My Song Is Love Unknown" (Matt, Lent)
   E458, EL343, G209, N222, P76, S2083, SA149, VU143

"Praise God for This Holy Ground" (Matt, Lent)
   G405, WS3009
"The Glory of These Forty Days" (Matt)
   E143, EL320, G165, P87
"Forty Days and Forty Nights" (Matt)
   C179, E150, G167, N205, P77, SH116, VU114
"Wild and Lone the Prophet's Voice" (Lent)
   G163, P409, S2089

Additional Contemporary and Modern Suggestions
"Daughter of God" 4509781 (Gen)
"Able" 1256560 (Gen, Pss, Lent)
"You Are My Hiding Place" 21442 (Pss)
   C554, S2055, SH46
"All Things Are Possible" 2245140 (Pss)
"My Redeemer Lives" 2397964 (Pss, Lent)
"Hallelujah" ("Your Love Is Amazing") 3091812 (Pss, Lent)
"Amazing Grace" ("My Chains Are Gone") 4768151 (Pss, Rom)
"Grace Like Rain" 3689877 (Pss, Rom)
"We Fall Down" 2437367 (Rom)
   G368, WS3187
"Oh Lord, You're Beautiful" 14514 (Rom)
"Sing Alleluia to the Lord" (Rom)
   C32, S2258, SH685
"Restored" 5894615 (Rom, Lent)
"Lamb of God" 16787 (Matt, Lent)
   EL336, G518, S2113
"Lord, I Lift Your Name on High" 117947 (Matt, Lent)
   AH4071, CG606, EL857, S2088, SA379, SH205
"We Walk His Way" (Matt, Lent)
   WS3073

Vocal Solos
"In the Image of God" (Gen, Rom, Lent)
   V-8   p. 362
"Amazing Grace" (Rom)
   V-8   p. 56
"Grace Greater Than Our Sin" (Rom)
   V-8   p. 180
"Holy Is the Lamb" (Matt)
   V-5 (1)   p. 5

Anthems
"Jesus, Full of Grace" (Pss, Rom)
Nicole Elsey & Robert Sterling, Shawnee Press HL-35032179
SATB, piano (https://bit.ly/HL32179)

"Lord, Who Throughout These Forty Days" (Matt)
Zebulon M. Highben; MorningStar MSM-50-5121
SATB *a cappella* (https://bit.ly/50-5121)

Other Suggestions
Visuals:
   O   Garden, fruit tree, serpent, fig leaves/loin cloth
   P   Hand, dry/heat, praying hands, waterfall, hiding
          place, teaching, bit/bridle, joy, Ps. 32:11
   E   Target/arrows (sin), gift, Christ, crucifix
   G   Dove/flames, 40/40, stones/bread, Bible, pinnacle,
          angels ministering, Matt 4:7, mountain, vista
Introit: G274, SH210, VU210. WS3043, stanza 3. "You, Lord, are
   Both Lamb and Shepherd" (Matt, Lent)
Prayer: UM366. For Guidance (Gen, Rom)
Prayer: WSL16 or WSL19 (Matt, Lent)
Canticle: UM167. "Canticle of Christ's Obedience" (Rom, Matt)
Blessing: WSL18. "May the blessing of God" (Matt, Lent)
Theme Ideas: Covenant, Grace, Jesus: Temptation, Sin and
   Forgiveness

Genesis 12:1-4a

[1]Now the LORD said to Abram, "Go from your country and your kindred and your father's house to the land that I will show you. [2]I will make of you a great nation, and I will bless you, and make your name great, so that you will be a blessing. [3]I will bless those who bless you, and the one who curses you I will curse; and in you all the families of the earth shall be blessed."

[4a]So Abram went, as the LORD had told him; and Lot went with him.

Psalm 121 (P45/845, N704, P234, UM844)

[1]I lift up my eyes to the hills—
    from where will my help come?
[2]My help comes from the LORD,
    who made heaven and earth.
[3]He will not let your foot be moved;
    he who keeps you will not slumber.
[4]He who keeps Israel
    will neither slumber nor sleep.
[5]The LORD is your keeper;
    the LORD is your shade at your right hand.
[6]The sun shall not strike you by day,
    nor the moon by night.
[7]The LORD will keep you from all evil;
    he will keep your life.
[8]The LORD will keep
    your going out and your coming in
    from this time on and forevermore.

Romans 4:1-5, 13-17

[1]What then are we to say was gained by Abraham, our ancestor according to the flesh? [2]For if Abraham was justified by works, he has something to boast about, but not before God. [3]For what does the scripture say? "Abraham believed God, and it was reckoned to him as righteousness." [4]Now to one who works, wages are not reckoned as a gift but as something due. [5]But to one who without works trusts him who justifies the ungodly, such faith is reckoned as righteousness. . . .

[13]For the promise that he would inherit the world did not come to Abraham or to his descendants through the law but through the righteousness of faith. [14]If it is the adherents of the law who are to be the heirs, faith is null and the promise is void. [15]For the law brings wrath; but where there is no law, neither is there violation.

[16]For this reason it depends on faith, in order that the promise may rest on grace and be guaranteed to all his descendants, not only to the adherents of the law but also to those who share the faith of Abraham (for he is the father of all of us, [17]as it is written, "I have made you the father of many nations")—in the presence of the God in whom he believed, who gives life to the dead and calls into existence the things that do not exist.

John 3:1-17

[1]Now there was a Pharisee named Nicodemus, a leader of the Jews. [2]He came to Jesus by night and said to him, "Rabbi, we know that you are a teacher who has come from God; for no one can do these signs that you do apart from the presence of God." [3]Jesus answered him, "Very truly, I tell you, no one can see the kingdom of God without being born from above." [4]Nicodemus said to him, "How can anyone be born after having grown old? Can one enter a second time into the mother's womb and be born?" [5]Jesus answered, "Very truly, I tell you, no one can enter the kingdom of God without being born of water and Spirit. [6]What is born of the flesh is flesh, and what is born of the Spirit is spirit. [7]Do not be astonished that I said to you, 'You must be born from above.' [8]The wind blows where it chooses, and you hear the sound of it, but you do not know where it comes from or where it goes. So it is with everyone who is born of the Spirit." [9]Nicodemus said to him, "How can these things be?" [10]Jesus answered him, "Are you a teacher of Israel, and yet you do not understand these things?

[11]"Very truly, I tell you, we speak of what we know and testify to what we have seen; yet you do not receive our testimony. [12]If I have told you about earthly things and you do not believe, how can you believe if I tell you about heavenly things? [13]No one has ascended into heaven except the one who descended from heaven, the Son of Man. [14]And just as Moses lifted up the serpent in the wilderness, so must the Son of Man be lifted up, [15]that whoever believes in him may have eternal life.

[16]"For God so loved the world that he gave his only Son, so that everyone who believes in him may not perish but may have eternal life.

[17]"Indeed, God did not send the Son into the world to condemn the world, but in order that the world might be saved through him."

Primary Hymns and Songs for the Day

"The God of Abraham Praise" (Gen) (O)
  C24, CG45, E401, EL831, G49, N24, P488, SH50, UM116
  (PD), VU255
    H-3   Hbl-62, 95; Chr-59; Org-77
    S-1   #211. Harm.
"To God Be the Glory" (John)
  C72, CG349, G634, P485, SA279, SH545, UM98 (PD)
    H-3   Chr-201
    S-2   #176. Piano arrangement
"Lift High the Cross" (John)
  C108, CG415, E473, EL660, G826, N198, P371, SH162,
  UM159, VU151
    H-3   Hbl-75; Chr-128; Desc-25; Org-21
    S-1   #71-75. Various treatments
"He Came Down" 4679219 (John)
  EL253, G137, S2085, SH88

Additional Hymn Suggestions

"Let All Things Now Living" (Gen)
  C717, CG379, EL881, G37, P554, S2008, SH23, VU242
"Deep in the Shadows of the Past" (Gen)
  G50, N320, P330, S2246
"O God, Our Help in Ages Past" (Gen, Pss)
  C67, CG566, E680, EL632, G687, N25, P210, SA47, SH41,
  UM117 (PD), VU806
"If Thou But Suffer God to Guide Thee" (Gen, Pss)
  C565, CG76, E635, EL769, G816, N410, P282, SA40, SH326,
  UM142 (PD), VU285 (Fr.) and VU286
"Immortal, Invisible, God Only Wise" (Pss, Rom)
  C66, CG58, E423, EL834, G12, N1, P263, SA37, UM103 (PD),
  VU264
"Sing Praise to God Who Reigns Above" (Pss)
  C6, CG315, E408, EL871, G645, N6, P483, UM126 (PD),
  VU216
"Jesus, Lover of My Soul" (Pss, Rom)
  C542, CG406, E699, G440, N546, P303, SA257, SH542/543,
  UM479, VU669
"My Faith Looks Up to Thee" (Rom)
  C576, CG407, E691, EL759, G829, P383, SA726, UM452,
  VU663
"Faith of Our Fathers" (Rom)
  C635, CG645, EL812/813, N381, UM710 (PD), VU580
"We Walk by Faith" (Rom)
  CG634, E209, EL635, G817, N256, P399, S2196, SH660
"In the Singing" (Rom, Comm.)
  EL466, G533, S2255
"Of the Father's Love Begotten" (John)
  C104, CG113, E82, EL295, G108, N118, P309, SA119, SH81,
  UM184, VU61
"Blessed Assurance" (John)
  AH4083, C543, CG619, EL638, G839, N473, P341, SA455,
  SH320, UM369 (PD), VU337
"Wash, O God, Our Sons and Daughters" (John, Baptism)
  C365, EL445, G490, SH669, UM605, VU442
"We Know That Christ Is Raised" (John, Baptism)
  E296, EL449, G485, P495, UM610, VU448
"You Satisfy the Hungry Heart" (John, Comm.)
  C429, CG468, EL484, G523, P521, SH672, UM629, VU478
"How Blest Are They Who Trust in Christ" (John)
  C646, N365, UM654
"Womb of Life" (John, Comm.)
  C14, G3, N274, S2046
"Mothering God, You Gave Me Birth" (John, Comm.)
  C83, EL735, G7, N467, S2050, VU320
"O Holy Spirit, Root of Life" (John)
  C251, EL399, N57, S2121, VU379

"Gather Us In" (John)
  C284, EL532, G401, S2236, SH393
"Dearest Jesus, We Are Here" (John)
  EL443, G483, P493

Additional Contemporary and Modern Suggestions

"Love Moves You" ("Love Alone") 5775514 (Gen, John)
"Shout to the Lord" 1406918 (Pss)
  CG348, EL821, S2074, SA264, SH426
"Holy Spirit, Come to Us" (*Veni Sancte Spiritus*) (Pss)
  EL406, G281, S2118
"Here Is Bread, Here Is Wine" 983717 (Rom, Comm.)
  EL483, S2266
"Celebrate Love" 155246 (John)
"O How He Loves You and Me" 15850 (John)
  CG600, S2108, SH535
"Lord, I Lift Your Name on High" 117947 (John, Lent)
  AH4071, CG606, EL857, S2088, SA379, SH205
"There Is a Redeemer" 11483 (John)
  CG377, G443, SA204, SH495
"You Are My All in All" 825356 (John)
  CG571, G519, SH335, WS3040
"I Believe in Jesus" 61282 (John)
"No Greater Love" 930887 (John, Lent)
"God Is Good All the Time" 1729073 (John)
"I Could Sing of Your Love Forever" 1043199 (John)
"You Are My King" ("Amazing Love") 2456623 (John)
  SH539, WS3102
"That's Why We Praise Him" 2668576 (John)
"I Come to the Cross" 1965249 (John, Lent)

Vocal Solos

"I Will Lift Up Mine Eyes" (Pss)
    V-1   p. 27
"Redeeming Grace" (Rom)
    V-4   p. 47
"The Gospel of Grace" (Rom, John)
    V-3 (1)   p.44
"Wash Me in Your Water" (John, Baptism)
    V-5 (2)   p. 18
"Born Again" (John)
    V-8   p. 8

Anthems

"Lift Your Eyes" (Pss)
Michael Moose; Hinshaw HMC2566
SATB, piano (https://bit.ly/HMC2566)

"I Lift My Eyes" (Pss)
Dan Forrest; Beckenhorst BP2222
SATB, piano, opt. brass (https://bit.ly/BP2222)

Other Suggestions

Visuals:
  O   Luggage, multitude, farewell, walking
  P   Hills, foot, sleep, sun/moon, evils, open door
  E   Abraham, paycheck, will, trust
  G   Cloak/night, newborn, water/Spirit, wind, serpent
       lifted, crucifix, John 3:16, Ascension, world
*The scripture from John makes today an excellent day to schedule
  baptisms.*
Greeting: N819 (Pss)
Call to Prayer: G782, WS3131, stanza 1. "Hear My Prayer, O
  God" (Pss)
For more prayers, see The Abingdon Worship Annual 2023.
Theme Ideas: Covenant, Faith, God: Providence / God our
  Help, Holy Spirit, Resurrection

Exodus 17:1-7

[1]From the wilderness of Sin the whole congregation of the Israelites journeyed by stages, as the LORD commanded. They camped at Rephidim, but there was no water for the people to drink. [2]The people quarreled with Moses, and said, "Give us water to drink." Moses said to them, "Why do you quarrel with me? Why do you test the LORD?" [3]But the people thirsted there for water; and the people complained against Moses and said, "Why did you bring us out of Egypt, to kill us and our children and livestock with thirst?" [4]So Moses cried out to the LORD, "What shall I do with this people? They are almost ready to stone me." [5]The LORD said to Moses, "Go on ahead of the people, and take some of the elders of Israel with you; take in your hand the staff with which you struck the Nile, and go. [6]I will be standing there in front of you on the rock at Horeb. Strike the rock, and water will come out of it, so that the people may drink." Moses did so, in the sight of the elders of Israel. [7]He called the place Massah and Meribah, because the Israelites quarreled and tested the LORD, saying, "Is the LORD among us or not?"

Psalm 95 (G386/638, N683, P214/215, SH401, UM814)

[1]O come, let us sing to the LORD;
 let us make a joyful noise to the rock of our salvation!
[2]Let us come into his presence with thanksgiving;
 let us make a joyful noise to him with songs of praise!
[3]For the LORD is a great God,
 and a great King above all gods.
[4]In his hand are the depths of the earth;
 the heights of the mountains are his also.
[5]The sea is his, for he made it,
 and the dry land, which his hands have formed.
[6]O come, let us worship and bow down,
 let us kneel before the LORD, our Maker!
[7]For he is our God,
 and we are the people of his pasture,
 and the sheep of his hand.
O that today you would listen to his voice!
 [8]Do not harden your hearts,
 as at Meribah, as on the day at Massah in the wilderness,
[9]when your ancestors tested me,
 and put me to the proof, though they had seen my work.
[10]For forty years I loathed that generation
 and said, "They are a people whose hearts go astray,
 and they do not regard my ways."
[11]Therefore in my anger I swore,
 "They shall not enter my rest."

Romans 5:1-11

[1]Therefore, since we are justified by faith, we have peace with God through our Lord Jesus Christ, [2]through whom we have obtained access to this grace in which we stand; and we boast in our hope of sharing the glory of God. [3]And not only that, but we also boast in our sufferings, knowing that suffering produces endurance, [4]and endurance produces character, and character produces hope, [5]and hope does not disappoint us, because God's love has been poured into our hearts through the Holy Spirit that has been given to us.

[6]For while we were still weak, at the right time Christ died for the ungodly. [7]Indeed, rarely will anyone die for a righteous person—though perhaps for a good person someone might actually dare to die. [8]But God proves his love for us in that while we still were sinners Christ died for us. [9]Much more surely then, now that we have been justified by his blood, will we be saved through him from the wrath of God. [10]For if while we were enemies, we were reconciled to God through the death of his Son, much more surely, having been reconciled, will we be saved by his life. [11]But more than that, we even boast in God through our Lord Jesus Christ, through whom we have now received reconciliation.

John 4:5-42

[5]So he came to a Samaritan city called Sychar, near the plot of ground that Jacob had given to his son Joseph. [6]Jacob's well was there, and Jesus, tired out by his journey, was sitting by the well. It was about noon.

[7]A Samaritan woman came to draw water, and Jesus said to her, "Give me a drink." [8](His disciples had gone to the city to buy food.) [9]The Samaritan woman said to him, "How is it that you, a Jew, ask a drink of me, a woman of Samaria?" (Jews do not share things in common with Samaritans.) [10]Jesus answered her, "If you knew the gift of God, and who it is that is saying to you, 'Give me a drink,' you would have asked him, and he would have given you living water." [11]The woman said to him, "Sir, you have no bucket, and the well is deep. Where do you get that living water? [12]Are you greater than our ancestor Jacob, who gave us the well, and with his sons and his flocks drank from it?" [13]Jesus said to her, "Everyone who drinks of this water will be thirsty again, [14]but those who drink of the water that I will give them will never be thirsty. The water that I will give will become in them a spring of water gushing up to eternal life." [15]The woman said to him, "Sir, give me this water, so that I may never be thirsty or have to keep coming here to draw water."

[16]Jesus said to her, "Go, call your husband, and come back." [17]The woman answered him, "I have no husband." Jesus said to her, "You are right in saying, 'I have no husband'; [18]for you have had five husbands, and the one you have now is not your husband. What you have said is true!" [19]The woman said to him, "Sir, I see that you are a prophet. [20]Our ancestors worshiped on this mountain, but you say that the place where people must worship is in Jerusalem." [21]Jesus said to her, "Woman, believe me, the hour is coming when you will worship the Father neither on this mountain nor in Jerusalem. [22]You worship what you do not know; we worship what we know, for salvation is from the Jews. [23]But the hour is coming, and is now here, when the true worshipers will worship the Father in spirit and truth, for the Father seeks such as these to worship him. [24]God is spirit, and those who worship him must worship in spirit and truth." [25]The woman said to him, "I know that Messiah is coming" (who is called Christ). "When he comes, he will proclaim all things to us." [26]Jesus said to her, "I am he, the one who is speaking to you."

[27]Just then his disciples came. They were astonished that he was speaking with a woman, but no one said, "What do you want?" or, "Why are you speaking with her?" [28]Then the woman left her water jar and went back to the city. She said to the people, [29]"Come and see a man who told me everything I have ever done! He cannot be the Messiah, can he?" [30]They left the city and were on their way to him.

[31]Meanwhile the disciples were urging him, "Rabbi, eat something." [32]But he said to them, "I have food to eat that you do not know about." [33]So the disciples said to one another, "Surely no one has brought him something to eat?" [34]Jesus said to them, "My food is to do the will of him who sent me and to complete his work. [35]Do you not say, 'Four months more, then comes the harvest'? But I tell you, look around you, and see how the fields are ripe for harvesting. [36]The reaper is already receiving wages and is gathering fruit for eternal life, so that sower and reaper may rejoice together. [37]For here the saying holds true, 'One sows and another reaps.' [38]I sent you to reap that for which you did not labor. Others have labored, and you have entered into their labor."

[39]Many Samaritans from that city believed in him because of the woman's testimony, "He told me everything I have ever done." [40]So when the Samaritans came to him, they asked him to stay with them; and he stayed there two days. [41]And many more believed because of his word. [42]They said to the woman, "It is no longer because of what you said that we believe, for we have heard for ourselves, and we know that this is truly the Savior of the world."

Primary Hymns and Songs for the Day

"Guide Me, O Thou Great Jehovah" (Exod, John) (O)
C622, CG33, E690, EL618, G65, N18/19, P281, SA27, SH51, UM127 (PD), VU651 (Fr.)
    H-3   Hbl-25, 51, 58; Chr-89; Desc-26; Org-23
    S-1   #76-77. Desc. and harm.
"O How He Loves You and Me" 15850 (Rom)
CG600, S2108, SH535
"When I Survey the Wondrous Cross" (Rom) (C)
C195, CG186, EL803, G223, N224, SH163/164, UM298
    H-3   Hbl-6, 102; Chr-213; Desc-49; Org-49
    S-1   #155. Descant
E474, G224, P100, SA208, UM299 (PD), VU149 (Fr.)
    H-3   Hbl-47; Chr-214; Desc-90; Org-127
    S-1   #288. Transposition to E-flat major

Additional Hymn Suggestions

"All My Hope Is Firmly Grounded" (Exod)
C88, E665, EL757, N408, SA530, UM132, VU654/655
"Rock of Ages, Cleft for Me" (Exod)
C214, E685, EL623, G438, N596, SA671, SH301, UM361 (PD)
"Jesus, Thou Joy of Loving Hearts" (Exod, John)
C101, CG394, E649, G494, N329, SA340, SH6688, VU472
"Glorious Things of Thee Are Spoken" (Exod, John)
C709, CG282, E522/523, EL647, G81, N307, P446, SA535, UM731 (PD)
"We Walk by Faith" (Pss, Rom)
CG634, E209, EL635, G817, N256, P399, S2196, SH660
"O Love That Wilt Not Let Me Go" (Rom)
C540, CG631, G833, N485, P384, SA616, SH314, UM480, VU658
"Spirit of God, Descend upon My Heart" (Rom)
C265, CG243, EL800, G688, N290, P326, SA290, SH277, UM500 (PD), VU378
"You, Lord, are Both Lamb and Shepherd" (Rom, Lent)
G274, SH210, VU210. WS3043
"Hope of the World" (Rom, John)
C538, E472, G734, N46, P360, UM178, VU215
"Healer of Our Every Ill" (Rom, John)
C506, EL612, G795, S2213, SH339, VU619
"The King of Love, My Shepherd Is" (John)
CG64, E645, EL502, G802, P171, SA61, SH359, UM138 (PD), VU273
"Jesus, Lover of My Soul" (John)
C542, CG406, E699, G440, N546, P303, SA257, SH542/543, UM479, VU669
"You Satisfy the Hungry Heart" (John, Comm.)
C429, CG468, EL484, G523, P521, SH672, UM629, VU478
"O Splendor of God's Glory Bright" (John)
E5, G666, N87, P474, UM679, VU413
"Come, Labor On" (John)
E541, G719, N532, P415
"Gather Us In" (John)
C284, EL532, G401, S2236, SH393
"All Who Hunger" (John, Comm.)
C419, CG303, EL461, G509, S2126, VU460
"Feed Us, Lord" 4636207 (John, Comm.)
G501, WS3167

Additional Contemporary and Modern Suggestions

"Forever" 3148428 (Exod, Pss)
CG53, SA363, WS3023
"God of Wonders" 3118757 (Exod, Pss)
SH9, WS3034
"Restless" 5775569 (Exod, Pss, John)
"I Will Call upon the Lord" 11263 (Pss)
G621, S2002

"Great Is the Lord" 1149 (Pss)
CG325, G614, S2022, SH459
"Come, All You People" ("Uyai Mose") (Pss)
EL819, G388, S2274, SH405
"Rock of Ages" 2240547 (Pss)
"I Could Sing of Your Love Forever" 1043199 (Pss, Rom)
"Celebrate Love" 155246 (Rom)
"O Lord, Your Tenderness" 38136 (Rom)
"Sing Alleluia to the Lord" (Rom)
C32, S2258, SH685
"Something Beautiful" 18060 (Rom)
"You Are My King" ("Amazing Love") 2456623 (Rom)
SH539, WS3102
"That's Why We Praise Him" 2668576 (Rom)
"Love Moves You" ("Love Alone") 5775514 (Rom, John)
"Song of Hope" ("Heaven Come Down") 5111477 (Rom, John)
"Here Is Bread, Here Is Wine" 983717 (Rom, John, Comm.)
EL483, S2266
"Jesus, Name above All Names" 21291 (John)
S2071, SA82
"Fill My Cup, Lord" 15946 (John, Comm.)
C351, UM641 (refrain only), WS3093
"Hungry" ("Falling on My Knees") 2650364 (John)
"Here at the Cross" 7046292 (John, Lent)
"The River Is Here" 1475231 (John)
"Who Can Satisfy My Soul Like You?" 208492 (John)
"More Love, More Power" 60661 (John)
"Come Just As You Are" 1189479 (John)
"All Who Are Thirsty" 2489542 (John)
"Just to Be with You" 5585120 (John)

Vocal Solos

"Leanin' on Dat Lamb" (Exod, Lent)
    V-7   p. 42
"Redeeming Grace" (Rom)
    V-4   p. 47
"Maybe the Rain" (John)
    V-5 (2)   p. 27
"Life Indeed" (John)
    V-8   p. 271

Anthems

"Uyai Mose" (Pss)
Arr. Kevin Holland; Choristers Guild CGA-1373
SATB, opt. percussion (https://bit.ly/CGA-1373)

"I Love You, O My Lord Most High" (John)
Anthony Giamanco; Lorenz 10/4851L
SATB, piano (https://bit.ly/10-4851L)

Other Suggestions

This day may include an observance of Girl Scout Sunday.
Daylight Savings Time begins today.
Visuals:
    O   Wilderness, quarrel, stones, staff, rock, water, Exod 17:7c
    P   Singing, rock, instruments, mountain, sea, dry land
    E   Christ, glory/suffering, hearts/Spirit, crucifix
    G   Well, noon, water jar, living water, clock
Canticle: UM91. "Canticle of Praise to God" (Pss)
Greeting: N820 (John) or N821 (Psalm)
Call to Confession: N833 (Lent)
Words of Assurance: Rom 5:8
For more prayers, see The Abingdon Worship Annual 2023.
Theme Ideas: Faith, God: Hunger / Thirst for God, God: Love of God, God: Shepherd, Hope, Praise, Sin and Forgiveness

1 Samuel 16:1-13

[1]The Lord said to Samuel, "How long will you grieve over Saul? I have rejected him from being king over Israel. Fill your horn with oil and set out; I will send you to Jesse the Bethlehemite, for I have provided for myself a king among his sons." [2]Samuel said, "How can I go? If Saul hears of it, he will kill me." And the Lord said, "Take a heifer with you, and say, 'I have come to sacrifice to the Lord.' [3]Invite Jesse to the sacrifice, and I will show you what you shall do; and you shall anoint for me the one whom I name to you." [4]Samuel did what the Lord commanded, and came to Bethlehem. The elders of the city came to meet him trembling, and said, "Do you come peaceably?" [5]He said, "Peaceably; I have come to sacrifice to the Lord; sanctify yourselves and come with me to the sacrifice." And he sanctified Jesse and his sons and invited them to the sacrifice.

[6]When they came, he looked on Eliab and thought, "Surely the Lord's anointed is now before the Lord." [7]But the Lord said to Samuel, "Do not look on his appearance or on the height of his stature, because I have rejected him; for the Lord does not see as mortals see; they look on the outward appearance, but the Lord looks on the heart." [8]Then Jesse called Abinadab, and made him pass before Samuel. He said, "Neither has the Lord chosen this one." [9]Then Jesse made Shammah pass by. And he said, "Neither has the Lord chosen this one." [10]Jesse made seven of his sons pass before Samuel, and Samuel said to Jesse, "The Lord has not chosen any of these." [11]Samuel said to Jesse, "Are all your sons here?" And he said, "There remains yet the youngest, but he is keeping the sheep." And Samuel said to Jesse, "Send and bring him; for we will not sit down until he comes here." [12]He sent and brought him in. Now he was ruddy, and had beautiful eyes, and was handsome. The Lord said, "Rise and anoint him; for this is the one." [13]Then Samuel took the horn of oil, and anointed him in the presence of his brothers; and the spirit of the Lord came mightily upon David from that day forward. Samuel then set out and went to Ramah.

Psalm 23 (G473/801-803, N633, P170-175, SH295/307, UM134/754)

[1]The Lord is my shepherd, I shall not want.
[2] He makes me lie down in green pastures;
he leads me beside still waters;
[3] he restores my soul.
He leads me in right paths
  for his name's sake.
[4]Even though I walk through the darkest valley,
  I fear no evil;
for you are with me;
  your rod and your staff—
  they comfort me.
[5]You prepare a table before me
  in the presence of my enemies;
you anoint my head with oil;
  my cup overflows.
[6]Surely goodness and mercy shall follow me
  all the days of my life,
and I shall dwell in the house of the Lord
  my whole life long.

Ephesians 5:8-14

[8]For once you were darkness, but now in the Lord you are light. Live as children of light—[9]for the fruit of the light is found in all that is good and right and true. [10]Try to find out what is pleasing to the Lord. [11]Take no part in the unfruitful works of darkness, but instead expose them. [12]For it is shameful even to mention what such people do secretly; [13]but everything exposed by the light becomes visible, [14]for everything that becomes visible is light. Therefore it says,
  "Sleeper, awake!
  Rise from the dead,
    and Christ will shine on you."

John 9:1-41

[1]As he walked along, he saw a man blind from birth. [2]His disciples asked him, "Rabbi, who sinned, this man or his parents, that he was born blind?" [3]Jesus answered, "Neither this man nor his parents sinned; he was born blind so that God's works might be revealed in him. [4]We must work the works of him who sent me while it is day; night is coming when no one can work. [5]As long as I am in the world, I am the light of the world." [6]When he had said this, he spat on the ground and made mud with the saliva and spread the mud on the man's eyes, [7]saying to him, "Go, wash in the pool of Siloam" (which means Sent). Then he went and washed and came back able to see.

[8]The neighbors and those who had seen him before as a beggar began to ask, "Is this not the man who used to sit and beg?" [9]Some were saying, "It is he." Others were saying, "No, but it is someone like him." He kept saying, "I am the man." [10]But they kept asking him, "Then how were your eyes opened?" [11]He answered, "The man called Jesus made mud, spread it on my eyes, and said to me, 'Go to Siloam and wash.' Then I went and washed and received my sight." [12]They said to him, "Where is he?" He said, "I do not know."

[13]They brought to the Pharisees the man who had formerly been blind. [14]Now it was a sabbath day when Jesus made the mud and opened his eyes. [15]Then the Pharisees also began to ask him how he had received his sight. He said to them, "He put mud on my eyes. Then I washed, and now I see." [16]Some of the Pharisees said, "This man is not from God, for he does not observe the sabbath." But others said, "How can a man who is a sinner perform such signs?" And they were divided. [17]So they said again to the blind man, "What do you say about him? It was your eyes he opened." He said, "He is a prophet."

[18]The Jews did not believe that he had been blind and had received his sight until they called the parents of the man who had received his sight [19]and asked them, "Is this your son, who you say was born blind? How then does he now see?" [20]His parents answered, "We know that this is our son, and that he was born blind; [21]but we do not know how it is that now he sees, nor do we know who opened his eyes. Ask him; he is of age. He will speak for himself." [22]His parents said this because they were afraid of the Jews; for the Jews had already agreed that anyone who confessed Jesus to be the Messiah would be put out of the synagogue. [23]Therefore his parents said, "He is of age; ask him."

[24]So for the second time they called the man who had been blind, and they said to him, "Give glory to God! We know that this man is a sinner." [25]He answered, "I do not know whether he is a sinner. One thing I do know, that though I was blind, now I see." [26]They said to him, "What did he do to you? How did he open your eyes?" [27]He answered them, "I have told you already, and you would not listen. Why do you want to hear it again? Do you also want to become his disciples?" [28]Then they reviled him, saying, "You are his disciple, but we are disciples of Moses. [29]We know that God has spoken to Moses, but as for this man, we do not know where he comes from." [30]The man answered, "Here is an astonishing thing! You do not know where he comes from, and yet he opened my eyes. [31]We know that God does not listen to sinners, but he does listen to one who worships him and obeys his will. [32]Never since the world began has it been heard that anyone opened the eyes of a person born blind. [33]If this man were not from God, he could do nothing." [34]They answered him, "You were born entirely in sins, and are you trying to teach us?" And they drove him out.

[35]Jesus heard that they had driven him out, and when he found him, he said, "Do you believe in the Son of Man?" [36]He answered, "And who is he, sir? Tell me, so that I may believe in him." [37]Jesus said to him, "You have seen him, and the one speaking with you is he." [38]He said, "Lord, I believe." And he worshiped him. [39]Jesus said, "I came into this world for judgment so that those who do not see may see, and those who do see may become blind." [40]Some of the Pharisees near him heard this and said to him, "Surely we are not blind, are we?" [41]Jesus said to them, "If you were blind, you would not have sin. But now that you say, 'We see,' your sin remains."

Primary Hymns and Songs for the Day

"Savior, Like a Shepherd Lead Us" (1 Sam, Pss) (O)
C558, CG405, E708, EL789, G187, N252, P387, SH538, UM381 (PD)
        H-3   Chr-167; Org-15
        S-2   #29. Harmonization
"Open My Eyes, That I May See" (John) (O)
C586, CG395, G451, P324, SH583, UM454, VU371
        H-3   Chr-157; Org-108
"Shepherd Me, O God" (1 Sam, Pss)
EL780, G473, S2058, SH365
"We Are Marching" ("*Siyahamba*") 1321512 (Eph)
C442, CG155, EL866, G853, N526, S2235, SA903, SH717, VU646
"Open Our Eyes, Lord" 1572 (John)
CG392, S2086, SA386, SH562
"I Want to Walk as a Child of the Light" (Eph, John) (C)
CG96, E490, EL815, G377, SH352, UM206
        S-2   #91. Desc.
"He Leadeth Me: O Blessed Thought" (1 Sam, Pss) (C)
C545, CG68, SA645, SH304, UM128 (PD), VU657

Additional Hymn Suggestions

"O God, in a Mysterious Way" (1 Sam)
CG39, E677, G30, N412, P270, SA17, SH47
"Awake, My Soul, and with the Sun" (1 Sam)
E11, EL557 (PD), G663, P456, SA4
"Great Is Thy Faithfulness" (1 Sam)
AH4011, C86, CG48, EL733, G39, N423, P276, SA26, SH48, UM140, VU288
"I Sing the Almighty Power of God" (1 Sam)
C64, CG19, E398, G32, N12, P288, SA36, SH15, UM152, VU231
"Spirit of the Living God" 23488 (1 Sam)
C259, CG233, G288, N283, P322, SA312/313, SH555, UM393, VU376
"Take My Life, and Let It Be" (1 Sam)
C609, CG490, E707, EL583/EL685, G697, P391
"Take, O Take Me as I Am" 4562041 (1 Sam)
EL814, G698, SH620, WS3119
"Precious Lord, Take My Hand" (1 Sam, Pss)
C628, CG400, EL773, G834, N472, P404, SH336, UM474, VU670
"O Master, Let Me Walk with Thee" (1 Sam, Pss)
C602, CG660, E659/E660, EL818, G738, N503, P357, SA667, SH612, UM430 (PD), VU560
"The Lord's My Shepherd" (Pss)
C78/79, CG65, EL778, G801, N479, P170, SA62, SH375, UM136, VU747/748
"The King of Love My Shepherd Is" (Pss)
CG64, E645, EL502, G802, P171, SA61, SH359, UM138 (PD), VU273
"My Shepherd Will Supply My Need" (Pss)
C80, CG66, E664, EL782 (PD), G803, N247, P172, SH44
"Lead Me, Guide Me" (Pss, Eph)
C583, CG403, EL768, G740, S2214, SH582
"O for a Closer Walk with God" (Eph)
CG679, E684, G739, N450, P396, SA612
"O Christ, the Healer" (John)
C503. EL610, G793, N175, P380, UM265
"All Who Love and Serve Your City" (John)
C670, CG674, E570/E571, EL724, G351, P413, UM433
"Wash, O God, Our Sons and Daughters" (John)
C365, EL445, G490, SH669, UM605, VU442
"Come, Labor On" (John)
E541, G719, N532, P415
"In Remembrance of Me" 25156 (John, Comm.)
C403, CG462, G521, S2254, SH667

Additional Contemporary and Modern Suggestions

"Nothing Can Trouble" ("*Nada Te Turbe*") (Pss)
CG73, G820, N772, S2054, SH292, VU290
"For Us" 7119349 (Pss, Lent)
"God Will Make a Way" 458620 (Pss)
SA492, SH57
"Gentle Shepherd" 15609 (Pss, Lent)
"Your Grace Is Enough" 4477026 (Pss, Lent)
"The King of Love My Shepherd Is" 7023979 (Pss)
"I Stand Amazed" 769450 (Pss, Lent)
"You Never Let Go" 4674166 (Pss, Eph, John)
"I Have a Hope" 5087587 (Pss, Eph, John)
"Awaken" 5491647 (Eph)
"Shine on Us" 1754646 (Eph)
"Everyday" 2798154 (Eph)
"Shine, Jesus, Shine" 30426 (Eph, John)
CG156, EL671, G192, S2173, SA261, SH102
"Light of the World" 73342 (Eph, John)
"Here I Am to Worship" 3266032 (Eph, John)
CG297, SA114, SH395, WS3177
"Turn Your Eyes upon Jesus" 15960 (John)
CG472, SA445, UM349
"Open the Eyes of My Heart" 2298355 (John)
G452, SA270, SH378, WS3008
"Restored" 5894615 (John, Lent)
"The Power of Your Love" 917491 (John)
"Good to Me" 313480 (John)
"You Hear" 6005063 (John, Lent)

Vocal Solos

"God, Our Ever Faithful Shepherd" (Pss)
    V-4   p. 15
"The Lord is My Shepherd" (Pss)
    V-5 (3)   p. 30
"Shepherd of Love" (Pss)
    V-8   p. 142
"My Shepherd Will Supply My Need" (Pss)
    V-10   p. 4

Anthems

"The 23rd Psalm" (Pss)
Bobby McFerrin; Hal Leonard 08596598
SATB *a cappella* (https://bit.ly/HL-96598)

"I Believe" (John)
Mark Miller; Choristers Guild CGA-1310
SATB, piano (https://bit.ly/CGA-1310)

Other Suggestions

Visuals:
    O   Oil/horn, crown, heifer, washing hands, seven sons
    P   Shepherd/sheep, pasture, water, path, dark valley, rod/ staff, banquet, oil, overflowing cup, house of God
    E   Dark/light, children, ministry, waking, Christ
    G   Mud, dark glasses, day/night, light/dark, water
Introit: C593, N774, UM473 (PD), VU662. "Lead Me, Lord" (Pss)
Bilingual Sung Response: SH294/613. "*El Señor es mi pastor*" ("The Lord Is My Shepherd") (Pss)
Canticle: UM137 (Pss)
Prayer: C81. Knee-bowed and Body-Bent (Pss, John)
Litany: N880. A Litany of Darkness and Light (Eph)
Theme Ideas: Call of God, God: Shepherd, Healing, Light, Vision

Ezekiel 37:1-14

[1]The hand of the Lord came upon me, and he brought me out by the spirit of the Lord and set me down in the middle of a valley; it was full of bones. [2]He led me all around them; there were very many lying in the valley, and they were very dry. [3]He said to me, "Mortal, can these bones live?" I answered, "O Lord God, you know." [4]Then he said to me, "Prophesy to these bones, and say to them: O dry bones, hear the word of the Lord. [5]Thus says the Lord God to these bones: I will cause breath to enter you, and you shall live. [6]I will lay sinews on you, and will cause flesh to come upon you, and cover you with skin, and put breath in you, and you shall live; and you shall know that I am the Lord."

[7]So I prophesied as I had been commanded; and as I prophesied, suddenly there was a noise, a rattling, and the bones came together, bone to its bone. [8]I looked, and there were sinews on them, and flesh had come upon them, and skin had covered them; but there was no breath in them. [9]Then he said to me, "Prophesy to the breath, prophesy, mortal, and say to the breath: Thus says the Lord God: Come from the four winds, O breath, and breathe upon these slain, that they may live." [10]I prophesied as he commanded me, and the breath came into them, and they lived, and stood on their feet, a vast multitude.

[11]Then he said to me, "Mortal, these bones are the whole house of Israel. They say, 'Our bones are dried up, and our hope is lost; we are cut off completely.' [12]Therefore prophesy, and say to them, Thus says the Lord God: I am going to open your graves, and bring you up from your graves, O my people; and I will bring you back to the land of Israel. [13]And you shall know that I am the Lord, when I open your graves, and bring you up from your graves, O my people. [14]I will put my spirit within you, and you shall live, and I will place you on your own soil; then you shall know that I, the Lord, have spoken and will act," says the Lord.

Psalm 130 (G424/791, N709, P240, SH573, UM848)

[1]Out of the depths I cry to you, O Lord.
[2]   Lord, hear my voice!
Let your ears be attentive
     to the voice of my supplications!
[3]If you, O Lord, should mark iniquities,
     Lord, who could stand?
[4]But there is forgiveness with you,
     so that you may be revered.
[5]I wait for the Lord, my soul waits,
     and in his word I hope;
[6]my soul waits for the Lord
     more than those who watch for the morning,
     more than those who watch for the morning.
[7]O Israel, hope in the Lord!
     For with the Lord there is steadfast love,
     and with him is great power to redeem.
[8]It is he who will redeem Israel
     from all its iniquities.

Romans 8:6-11

[6]To set the mind on the flesh is death, but to set the mind on the Spirit is life and peace. [7]For this reason the mind that is set on the flesh is hostile to God; it does not submit to God's law—indeed it cannot, [8]and those who are in the flesh cannot please God. [9]But you are not in the flesh; you are in the Spirit, since the Spirit of God dwells in you. Anyone who does not have the Spirit of Christ does not belong to him. [10]But if Christ is in you, though the body is dead because of sin, the Spirit is life because of righteousness. [11]If the Spirit of him who raised Jesus from the dead dwells in you, he who raised Christ from the dead will give life to your mortal bodies also through his Spirit that dwells in you.

John 11:1-45

[1]Now a certain man was ill, Lazarus of Bethany, the village of Mary and her sister Martha. [2]Mary was the one who anointed the Lord with perfume and wiped his feet with her hair; her brother Lazarus was ill. [3]So the sisters sent a message to Jesus, "Lord, he whom you love is ill." [4]But when Jesus heard it, he said, "This illness does not lead to death; rather it is for God's glory, so that the Son of God may be glorified through it." [5]Accordingly, though Jesus loved Martha and her sister and Lazarus, [6]after having heard that Lazarus was ill, he stayed two days longer in the place where he was.

[7]Then after this he said to the disciples, "Let us go to Judea again." [8]The disciples said to him, "Rabbi, the Jews were just now trying to stone you, and are you going there again?" [9]Jesus answered, "Are there not twelve hours of daylight? Those who walk during the day do not stumble, because they see the light of this world. [10]But those who walk at night stumble, because the light is not in them." [11]After saying this, he told them, "Our friend Lazarus has fallen asleep, but I am going there to awaken him." [12]The disciples said to him, "Lord, if he has fallen asleep, he will be all right." [13]Jesus, however, had been speaking about his death, but they thought that he was referring merely to sleep. [14]Then Jesus told them plainly, "Lazarus is dead. [15]For your sake I am glad I was not there, so that you may believe. But let us go to him." [16]Thomas, who was called the Twin, said to his fellow disciples, "Let us also go, that we may die with him."

[17]When Jesus arrived, he found that Lazarus had already been in the tomb four days. [18]Now Bethany was near Jerusalem, some two miles away, [19]and many of the Jews had come to Martha and Mary to console them about their brother. [20]When Martha heard that Jesus was coming, she went and met him, while Mary stayed at home. [21]Martha said to Jesus, "Lord, if you had been here, my brother would not have died. [22]But even now I know that God will give you whatever you ask of him." [23]Jesus said to her, "Your brother will rise again." [24]Martha said to him, "I know that he will rise again in the resurrection on the last day." [25]Jesus said to her, "I am the resurrection and the life. Those who believe in me, even though they die, will live, [26]and everyone who lives and believes in me will never die. Do you believe this?" [27]She said to him, "Yes, Lord, I believe that you are the Messiah, the Son of God, the one coming into the world."

[28]When she had said this, she went back and called her sister Mary, and told her privately, "The Teacher is here and is calling for you." [29]And when she heard it, she got up quickly and went to him. [30]Now Jesus had not yet come to the village, but was still at the place where Martha had met him. [31]The Jews who were with her in the house, consoling her, saw Mary get up quickly and go out. They followed her because they thought that she was going to the tomb to weep there. [32]When Mary came where Jesus was and saw him, she knelt at his feet and said to him, "Lord, if you had been here, my brother would not have died." [33]When Jesus saw her weeping, and the Jews who came with her also weeping, he was greatly disturbed in spirit and deeply moved. [34]He said, "Where have you laid him?" They said to him, "Lord, come and see." [35]Jesus began to weep. [36]So the Jews said, "See how he loved him!" [37]But some of them said, "Could not he who opened the eyes of the blind man have kept this man from dying?"

[38]Then Jesus, again greatly disturbed, came to the tomb. It was a cave, and a stone was lying against it. [39]Jesus said, "Take away the stone." Martha, the sister of the dead man, said to him, "Lord, already there is a stench because he has been dead four days." [40]Jesus said to her, "Did I not tell you that if you believed, you would see the glory of God?" [41]So they took away the stone. And Jesus looked upward and said, "Father, I thank you for having heard me. [42]I knew that you always hear me, but I have said this for the sake of the crowd standing here, so that they may believe that you sent me." [43]When he had said this, he cried with a loud voice, "Lazarus, come out!" [44]The dead man came out, his hands and feet bound with strips of cloth, and his face wrapped in a cloth. Jesus said to them, "Unbind him, and let him go."

[45]Many of the Jews therefore, who had come with Mary and had seen what Jesus did, believed in him.

Primary Hymns and Songs for the Day
"Lord of the Dance" 78529 (John, Lent) (O)
  G157, P302, SA141, UM261, VU352
"Now the Green Blade Riseth" (Ezek, John)
  C230, E204, EL379, G247, N238, SH187, UM311, VU186
"This Is a Day of New Beginnings" (Ezek, John, Comm.)
  C518, N417, UM383
      H-3   Chr-196
"Spirit of the Living God" (Rom, Comm.)
  C259, CG233, G288, N283, P322, SA312/313, SH555,
  UM393, VU376, S-1#212 Vocal desc. idea
"Why Has God Forsaken Me?" (Pss, John)
  G809, P406, S2110, VU154
      H-3   Chr-220
"Every Time I Feel the Spirit" (Rom)
  C592, G66, N282, P315, UM404
"Let Us Build a House Where Love Can Dwell" (John)
  EL641, G301, SH228 (See also WS3152)
"Somebody's Knockin' at Your Door" (John)
  G728, P382, SH597, WS3095
"Breathe on Me, Breath of God" (Ezek) (C)
  C254, CG235, E508, G286, N292, P316, SA294, SH224/273,
  UM420 (PD), VU382 (Fr.)

Additional Hymn Suggestions
"Let It Breathe on Me" (Ezek)
  C260, N288, UM503
"Hope of the World" (Ezek, John)
  C538, E472, G734, N46, P360, UM178, VU215
Camina, Pueblo de Dios ("Walk On, O People of God") (Ezek, John)
  N614, P296, UM305
"Christ Is Risen" (Ezek, John)
  C222, CG206, P104, UM307
"Come, Ye Faithful, Raise the Strain" (Ezek, John)
  C215, CG218, E199, EL363, G234, N230, P115, UM315 (PD), VU165
"To God Be the Glory" (Rom)
  C72, CG349, G634, P485, SA279, SH545, UM98 (PD)
"Alas! and Did My Savior Bleed" (Rom)
  AH4067, C204, CG182/595, EL337, G212, N199/200, P78,
  SA159, UM294/359, SH172/173
"Spirit Divine, Attend Our Prayers" (Rom)
  E509, G407, P325, SA210, VU385
"Holy Spirit, Truth Divine" (Rom)
  C241, EL398, N63, P321, SA285, UM465, VU368
"Christ Beside Me" (Rom)
  G702, S2166
"Trust and Obey" (Rom, John)
  C556, CG509, SA690, SH636, UM467 (PD)
"Spirit of God, Descend upon My Heart" (Rom, John)
  C265, CG243, EL800, G688, N290, P326, SA290, SH277,
  UM500 (PD), VU378
"O Christ, the Healer" (John)
  C503, EL610, G793, N175, P380, UM265
"Woman in the Night" (John)
  C188, G161, UM274
"Love Divine, All Loves Excelling" (John, Comm.)
  C517, CG281, E657, EL631, G366, N43, P376, SA262,
  SH353/354, UM384 (PD), VU333
"Hymn of Promise" (John)
  C638, CG545, G250, N433, UM707, VU703
"Womb of Life" (John, Comm.)
  C14, G3, N274, S2046
"When Jesus Wept" (John)
  C199, E715, G194, N192, P312, S2106, VU146
"Just a Closer Walk with Thee" (John, Lent)
  C557, EL697, G835, S2158, SH584
"Lead Me, Guide Me" (John, Lent)
  C583, CG403, EL768, G740, S2214, SH582

Additional Contemporary and Modern Suggestions
"Holy Spirit, Come to Us" (*"Veni Sancte Spiritus"*) (Ezek)
  EL406, G281, S2118
"Days of Elijah" 1537904 (Ezek)
"Oh, I Know the Lord's Laid His Hands on Me" (Ezekiel, John)
  S2139
"Lord, I Lift Your Name on High" 117947 (Ezek, Rom, John, Lent)
  AH4071, CG606, EL857, S2088, SA379, SH205
"Restored" 5894615 (Ezekiel, Pss, Rom, John, Lent)
"Let Your Spirit Rise Within Me" 15355 (Ezek, Rom, John)
"Hungry" ("Falling on My Knees") 2650364 (Pss)
"Lord, Be Glorified" 26368 (Rom, John)
  EL744, G468, S2150, SA593, SH420
"Cares Chorus" 25974 (John)
"Halle, Halle, Halleluja" 2659190 (John)
  C41, CG433, EL172, G591, N236, S2026, SH694, VU958
"Light of the World" 73342 (John)
"We Are Marching" (*"Siyahumba"*) 1321512 (John)
  C442, CG155, EL866, G853, N526, S2235, SA903, SH717,
  VU646
"I Believe in Jesus" 61282 (John)
"Everyday" 2798154 (John)
"Awaken" 5491647 (John)
"The Dark Is Not Your Home" 7132934 (John)

Vocal Solos
"Like a Child" (Pss)
  V-8   p. 356
"Out of the Depths I Cry to Thee" (Pss)
  V-9   p. 16
"Just a Closer Walk with Thee" (John, Lent)
  V-5 (2)   p. 31
  V-8   p. 323

Anthems
"Out of the Depths I Cry to Thee" (Pss)
Arr. K. Lee Scott; Augsburg 9780800647322
2-part mixed, keyboard (https://bit.ly/A-47322)

"*Lacrymosa*: Do not stand at my grave and weep" (John)
Howard Goodall; MorningStar MSM-56-0053
Baritone solo, SATB, piano (https://bit.ly/56-0053)

Other Suggestions
Visuals:
  O   Valley/bones, wilderness, multitude, open graves
  P   Listening, praying hands/waiting, rescue
  E   Coffin, Spirit symbols, Christ, open tomb
  G   Jar/woman, hair/feet, message, night/stumbling
        block, woman/Jesus/kneeling, tears, tomb, strips of
        cloth
Plan this service so that it moves from the quietness of the tomb and the Psalm to the joy of Lazarus's resurrection.
Introit: N231, stanza 1. "Because You Live" (Ezek, John)
Opening Prayer: N831 (John) or WSL52 (Ezek, Rom)
Sung Confession: WS3111. "Redemption" (Rom, Lent)
Canticle: UM516. "Canticle of Redemption" (Pss)
Prayer: UM461. For Those Who Mourn (John)
Blessing: WSL178. "May the God who made heaven" (John)
Theme Ideas: Healing, Jesus: Mind of Christ, Lament, New
  Creation, Repentance, Resurrection

Palm Readings
Matthew 21:1-11

¹When they had come near Jerusalem and had reached Bethphage, at the Mount of Olives, Jesus sent two disciples, ²saying to them, "Go into the village ahead of you, and immediately you will find a donkey tied, and a colt with her; untie them and bring them to me. ³If anyone says anything to you, just say this, 'The Lord needs them.' And he will send them immediately." ⁴This took place to fulfill what had been spoken through the prophet, saying,

⁵"Tell the daughter of Zion,
Look, your king is coming to you,
    humble, and mounted on a donkey,
    and on a colt, the foal of a donkey."

⁶The disciples went and did as Jesus had directed them; ⁷they brought the donkey and the colt, and put their cloaks on them, and he sat on them. ⁸A very large crowd spread their cloaks on the road, and others cut branches from the trees and spread them on the road. ⁹The crowds that went ahead of him and that followed were shouting,

"Hosanna to the Son of David!
    Blessed is the one who comes in the name of the Lord!
Hosanna in the highest heaven!"

¹⁰When he entered Jerusalem, the whole city was in turmoil, asking, "Who is this?" ¹¹The crowds were saying, "This is the prophet Jesus from Nazareth in Galilee."

Psalm 118:1-2, 19-29 (G391/6681, N700, P232, UM839)

¹O give thanks to the LORD, for he is good;
    his steadfast love endures forever!
²Let Israel say,
    "His steadfast love endures forever."
. . . .
¹⁹Open to me the gates of righteousness,
    that I may enter through them
    and give thanks to the LORD.
²⁰This is the gate of the LORD;
    the righteous shall enter through it.
²¹I thank you that you have answered me
    and have become my salvation.
²²The stone that the builders rejected
    has become the chief cornerstone.
²³This is the Lord's doing;
    it is marvelous in our eyes.
²⁴This is the day that the LORD has made;
    let us rejoice and be glad in it.
²⁵Save us, we beseech you, O LORD!
    O LORD, we beseech you, give us success!
²⁶Blessed is the one who comes in the name of the LORD.
    We bless you from the house of the LORD.
²⁷The LORD is God,
    and he has given us light.
Bind the festal procession with branches,
    up to the horns of the altar.
²⁸You are my God, and I will give thanks to you;
    you are my God, I will extol you.
²⁹O give thanks to the LORD, for he is good,
    for his steadfast love endures forever.

Passion Readings
Isaiah 50:4-9a

⁴The Lord GOD has given me
    the tongue of a teacher,
that I may know how to sustain
    the weary with a word.
Morning by morning he wakens—
    wakens my ear
    to listen as those who are taught.
⁵The Lord GOD has opened my ear,
    and I was not rebellious,
    I did not turn backward.
⁶I gave my back to those who struck me,
    and my cheeks to those who pulled out the beard;
I did not hide my face
    from insult and spitting.
⁷The Lord GOD helps me;
    therefore I have not been disgraced;
therefore I have set my face like flint,
    and I know that I shall not be put to shame;
⁸ he who vindicates me is near.
Who will contend with me?
    Let us stand up together.
Who are my adversaries?
    Let them confront me.
⁹ªIt is the Lord GOD who helps me.

Psalm 31:9-16 (G214/814, N641, P182, UM764)

⁹Be gracious to me, O LORD, for I am in distress;
    my eye wastes away from grief,
    my soul and body also.
¹⁰For my life is spent with sorrow,
    and my years with sighing;
my strength fails because of my misery,
    and my bones waste away.
¹¹I am the scorn of all my adversaries,
    a horror to my neighbors,
an object of dread to my acquaintances;
    those who see me in the street flee from me.
¹²I have passed out of mind like one who is dead;
    I have become like a broken vessel.
¹³For I hear the whispering of many—
    terror all around!—
as they scheme together against me,
    as they plot to take my life.
¹⁴But I trust in you, O LORD;
    I say, "You are my God."
¹⁵My times are in your hand;
    deliver me from the hand of my enemies and persecutors.
¹⁶Let your face shine upon your servant;
    save me in your steadfast love.

Philippians 2:5-11

⁵Let the same mind be in you that was in Christ Jesus,
⁶who, though he was in the form of God,
  did not regard equality with God
  as something to be exploited,
⁷but emptied himself,
  taking the form of a slave,
  being born in human likeness.
And being found in human form,
⁸he humbled himself
  and became obedient to the point of death—
  even death on a cross.
⁹Therefore God also highly exalted him
  and gave him the name
  that is above every name,
¹⁰so that at the name of Jesus
  every knee should bend,
  in heaven and on earth and under the earth,
¹¹and every tongue should confess
  that Jesus Christ is Lord,
  to the glory of God the Father.

Matthew 26:14–27:66 (27:11-54)

¹⁴Then one of the twelve, who was called Judas Iscariot, went to the chief priests ¹⁵and said, "What will you give me if I betray him to you?" They paid him thirty pieces of silver. ¹⁶And from that moment he began to look for an opportunity to betray him.

¹⁷On the first day of Unleavened Bread the disciples came to Jesus, saying, "Where do you want us to make the preparations for you to eat the Passover?" ¹⁸He said, "Go into the city to a certain man, and say to him, 'The Teacher says, My time is near; I will keep the Passover at your house with my disciples.'" ¹⁹So the disciples did as Jesus had directed them, and they prepared the Passover meal.

²⁰When it was evening, he took his place with the twelve; ²¹and while they were eating, he said, "Truly I tell you, one of you will betray me." ²²And they became greatly distressed and began to say to him one after another, "Surely not I, Lord?" ²³He answered, "The one who has dipped his hand into the bowl with me will betray me. ²⁴The Son of Man goes as it is written of him, but woe to that one by whom the Son of Man is betrayed! It would have been better for that one not to have been born." ²⁵Judas, who betrayed him, said, "Surely not I, Rabbi?" He replied, "You have said so."

²⁶While they were eating, Jesus took a loaf of bread, and after blessing it he broke it, gave it to the disciples, and said, "Take, eat; this is my body." ²⁷Then he took a cup, and after giving thanks he gave it to them, saying, "Drink from it, all of you; ²⁸for this is my blood of the covenant, which is poured out for many for the forgiveness of sins. ²⁹I tell you, I will never again drink of this fruit of the vine until that day when I drink it new with you in my Father's kingdom."

³⁰When they had sung the hymn, they went out to the Mount of Olives. ³¹Then Jesus said to them, "You will all become deserters because of me this night; for it is written,
'I will strike the shepherd,
  and the sheep of the flock will be scattered.'
³²But after I am raised up, I will go ahead of you to Galilee." ³³Peter said to him, "Though all become deserters because of you, I will never desert you." ³⁴Jesus said to him, "Truly I tell you, this very night, before the cock crows, you will deny me three times." ³⁵Peter said to him, "Even though I must die with you, I will not deny you." And so said all the disciples.

³⁶Then Jesus went with them to a place called Gethsemane; and he said to his disciples, "Sit here while I go over there and pray." ³⁷He took with him Peter and the two sons of Zebedee, and began to be grieved and agitated. ³⁸Then he said to them, "I am deeply grieved, even to death; remain here, and stay awake with me." ³⁹And going a little farther, he threw himself on the ground and prayed, "My Father, if it is possible, let this cup pass from me; yet not what I want but what you want." ⁴⁰Then he came to the disciples and found them sleeping; and he said to Peter, "So, could you not stay awake with me one hour? ⁴¹Stay awake and pray that you may not come into the time of trial; the spirit indeed is willing, but the flesh is weak." ⁴²Again he went away for the second time and prayed, "My Father, if this cannot pass unless I drink it, your will be done." ⁴³Again he came and found them sleeping, for their eyes were heavy. ⁴⁴So leaving them again, he went away and prayed for the third time, saying the same words. ⁴⁵Then he came to the disciples and said to them, "Are you still sleeping and taking your rest? See, the hour is at hand, and the Son of Man is betrayed into the hands of sinners. ⁴⁶Get up, let us be going. See, my betrayer is at hand."

⁴⁷While he was still speaking, Judas, one of the twelve, arrived; with him was a large crowd with swords and clubs, from the chief priests and the elders of the people. ⁴⁸Now the betrayer had given them a sign, saying, "The one I will kiss is the man; arrest him." ⁴⁹At once he came up to Jesus and said, "Greetings, Rabbi!" and kissed him. ⁵⁰Jesus said to him, "Friend, do what you are here to do." Then they came and laid hands on Jesus and arrested him. ⁵¹Suddenly, one of those with Jesus put his hand on his sword, drew it, and struck the slave of the high priest, cutting off his ear. ⁵²Then Jesus said to him, "Put your sword back into its place; for all who take the sword will perish by the sword. ⁵³Do you think that I cannot appeal to my Father, and he will at once send me more than twelve legions of angels? ⁵⁴But how then would the scriptures be fulfilled, which say it must happen in this way?" ⁵⁵At that hour Jesus said to the crowds, "Have you come out with swords and clubs to arrest me as though I were a bandit? Day after day I sat in the temple teaching, and you did not arrest me. ⁵⁶But all this has taken place, so that the scriptures of the prophets may be fulfilled." Then all the disciples deserted him and fled.

⁵⁷Those who had arrested Jesus took him to Caiaphas the high priest, in whose house the scribes and the elders had gathered. ⁵⁸But Peter was following him at a distance, as far as the courtyard of the high priest; and going inside, he sat with the guards in order to see how this would end. ⁵⁹Now the chief priests and the whole council were looking for false testimony against Jesus so that they might put him to death, ⁶⁰but they found none, though many false witnesses came forward. At last two came forward ⁶¹and said, "This fellow said, 'I am able to destroy the temple of God and to build it in three days.'" ⁶²The high priest stood up and said, "Have you no answer? What is it that they testify against you?" ⁶³But Jesus was silent. Then the high priest said to him, "I put you under oath before the living God, tell us if you are the Messiah, the Son of God." ⁶⁴Jesus said to him, "You have said so. But I tell you,
From now on you will see the Son of Man
  seated at the right hand of Power
  and coming on the clouds of heaven."
⁶⁵Then the high priest tore his clothes and said, "He has blasphemed! Why do we still need witnesses? You have now heard his blasphemy. ⁶⁶What is your verdict?" They answered, "He deserves death." ⁶⁷Then they spat in his face and struck him; and some slapped him, ⁶⁸saying, "Prophesy to us, you Messiah! Who is it that struck you?"

⁶⁹Now Peter was sitting outside in the courtyard. A servant-girl came to him and said, "You also were with Jesus the Galilean." ⁷⁰But he denied it before all of them, saying, "I do not know what you are talking about." ⁷¹When he went out to the porch, another servant-girl saw him, and she said to the bystanders, "This man was with Jesus of Nazareth." ⁷²Again he denied it with an oath, "I do not know the man." ⁷³After a little while the bystanders came up and said to Peter, "Certainly you are also one of them, for your accent betrays you." ⁷⁴Then he began to curse, and he swore an oath, "I do not know the man!" At that

moment the cock crowed. ⁷⁵Then Peter remembered what Jesus had said: "Before the cock crows, you will deny me three times." And he went out and wept bitterly.

27 When morning came, all the chief priests and the elders of the people conferred together against Jesus in order to bring about his death. ²They bound him, led him away, and handed him over to Pilate the governor.

³When Judas, his betrayer, saw that Jesus was condemned, he repented and brought back the thirty pieces of silver to the chief priests and the elders. ⁴He said, "I have sinned by betraying innocent blood." But they said, "What is that to us? See to it yourself." ⁵Throwing down the pieces of silver in the temple, he departed; and he went and hanged himself. ⁶But the chief priests, taking the pieces of silver, said, "It is not lawful to put them into the treasury, since they are blood money." ⁷After conferring together, they used them to buy the potter's field as a place to bury foreigners. ⁸For this reason that field has been called the Field of Blood to this day. ⁹Then was fulfilled what had been spoken through the prophet Jeremiah, "And they took the thirty pieces of silver, the price of the one on whom a price had been set, on whom some of the people of Israel had set a price, ¹⁰and they gave them for the potter's field, as the Lord commanded me."

¹¹Now Jesus stood before the governor; and the governor asked him, "Are you the King of the Jews?" Jesus said, "You say so." ¹²But when he was accused by the chief priests and elders, he did not answer. ¹³Then Pilate said to him, "Do you not hear how many accusations they make against you?" ¹⁴But he gave him no answer, not even to a single charge, so that the governor was greatly amazed.

¹⁵Now at the festival the governor was accustomed to release a prisoner for the crowd, anyone whom they wanted. ¹⁶At that time they had a notorious prisoner, called Jesus Barabbas. ¹⁷So after they had gathered, Pilate said to them, "Whom do you want me to release for you, Jesus Barabbas or Jesus who is called the Messiah?" ¹⁸For he realized that it was out of jealousy that they had handed him over. ¹⁹While he was sitting on the judgment seat, his wife sent word to him, "Have nothing to do with that innocent man, for today I have suffered a great deal because of a dream about him." ²⁰Now the chief priests and the elders persuaded the crowds to ask for Barabbas and to have Jesus killed. ²¹The governor again said to them, "Which of the two do you want me to release for you?" And they said, "Barabbas." ²²Pilate said to them, "Then what should I do with Jesus who is called the Messiah?" All of them said, "Let him be crucified!" ²³Then he asked, "Why, what evil has he done?" But they shouted all the more, "Let him be crucified!"

²⁴So when Pilate saw that he could do nothing, but rather that a riot was beginning, he took some water and washed his hands before the crowd, saying, "I am innocent of this man's blood; see to it yourselves." ²⁵Then the people as a whole answered, "His blood be on us and on our children!" ²⁶So he released Barabbas for them; and after flogging Jesus, he handed him over to be crucified.

²⁷Then the soldiers of the governor took Jesus into the governor's headquarters, and they gathered the whole cohort around him. ²⁸They stripped him and put a scarlet robe on him, ²⁹and after twisting some thorns into a crown, they put it on his head. They put a reed in his right hand and knelt before him and mocked him, saying, "Hail, King of the Jews!" ³⁰They spat on him, and took the reed and struck him on the head. ³¹After mocking him, they stripped him of the robe and put his own clothes on him. Then they led him away to crucify him.

³²As they went out, they came upon a man from Cyrene named Simon; they compelled this man to carry his cross. ³³And when they came to a place called Golgotha (which means Place of a Skull), ³⁴they offered him wine to drink, mixed with gall; but when he tasted it, he would not drink it. ³⁵And when they had crucified him, they divided his clothes among themselves by casting lots; ³⁶then they sat down there and kept watch over him. ³⁷Over his head they put the charge against him, which read, "This is Jesus, the King of the Jews."

³⁸Then two bandits were crucified with him, one on his right and one on his left. ³⁹Those who passed by derided him, shaking their heads ⁴⁰and saying, "You who would destroy the temple and build it in three days, save yourself! If you are the Son of God, come down from the cross." ⁴¹In the same way the chief priests also, along with the scribes and elders, were mocking him, saying, ⁴²"He saved others; he cannot save himself. He is the King of Israel; let him come down from the cross now, and we will believe in him. ⁴³He trusts in God; let God deliver him now, if he wants to; for he said, 'I am God's Son.'" ⁴⁴The bandits who were crucified with him also taunted him in the same way.

⁴⁵From noon on, darkness came over the whole land until three in the afternoon. ⁴⁶And about three o'clock Jesus cried with a loud voice, "*Eli, Eli, lema sabachthani?*" that is, "My God, my God, why have you forsaken me?" ⁴⁷When some of the bystanders heard it, they said, "This man is calling for Elijah." ⁴⁸At once one of them ran and got a sponge, filled it with sour wine, put it on a stick, and gave it to him to drink. ⁴⁹But the others said, "Wait, let us see whether Elijah will come to save him." ⁵⁰Then Jesus cried again with a loud voice and breathed his last. ⁵¹At that moment the curtain of the temple was torn in two, from top to bottom. The earth shook, and the rocks were split. ⁵²The tombs also were opened, and many bodies of the saints who had fallen asleep were raised. ⁵³After his resurrection they came out of the tombs and entered the holy city and appeared to many. ⁵⁴Now when the centurion and those with him, who were keeping watch over Jesus, saw the earthquake and what took place, they were terrified and said, "Truly this man was God's Son!"

⁵⁵Many women were also there, looking on from a distance; they had followed Jesus from Galilee and had provided for him. ⁵⁶Among them were Mary Magdalene, and Mary the mother of James and Joseph, and the mother of the sons of Zebedee.

⁵⁷When it was evening, there came a rich man from Arimathea, named Joseph, who was also a disciple of Jesus. ⁵⁸He went to Pilate and asked for the body of Jesus; then Pilate ordered it to be given to him. ⁵⁹So Joseph took the body and wrapped it in a clean linen cloth ⁶⁰and laid it in his own new tomb, which he had hewn in the rock. He then rolled a great stone to the door of the tomb and went away. ⁶¹Mary Magdalene and the other Mary were there, sitting opposite the tomb.

⁶²The next day, that is, after the day of Preparation, the chief priests and the Pharisees gathered before Pilate ⁶³and said, "Sir, we remember what that impostor said while he was still alive, 'After three days I will rise again.' ⁶⁴Therefore command the tomb to be made secure until the third day; otherwise his disciples may go and steal him away, and tell the people, 'He has been raised from the dead,' and the last deception would be worse than the first." ⁶⁵Pilate said to them, "You have a guard of soldiers; go, make it as secure as you can." ⁶⁶So they went with the guard and made the tomb secure by sealing the stone.

Primary Hymns and Songs for the Day

"All Glory, Laud, and Honor" (Palms Gospel) (O)
    C192, CG175, E154/ E155, EL344, G196, N216/N217, P88,
    SA135, SH143, UM280 (PD), VU122
        H-3   Hbl-45; Chr-22; Desc-96; Org-144
        S-1   #309-310. Harmonization with descant
"Tell Me the Stories of Jesus" (Palms Gospel)
    C190, SA151, UM277 (PD), VU357
Mantos y Palmas ("Filled with Excitement") (Palms Gospel)
    G199, N214, SH144, UM279
        S-2   #90. Performance note
                #89. Harm.
"Lamb of God" 16787 (Passion Gospel)
    EL336, G518, S2113
"Stay with Me" (*Nohu pû*) (Passion Gospel)
    EL348, G204, S2198, SH157
"O Sacred Head, Now Wounded" (Passion)
    C202, CG191, E168/169, EL351/352, G221, N226, P98,
    SA190, SH168, UM286, VU145 (Fr.)
        H-3   Hbl-82; Chr-148; Desc-86; Org-111
"Lord Whose Love Through Humble Service" (C) (Passion)
    C461, CG650, E610, EL712, P427, SH239, UM581

Additional Hymn Suggestions

"Hosanna, Loud Hosanna" (Palms Gospel)
    CG172, G197, N213, P89, SH146, UM278 (PD), VU123
"Ride On! Ride On in Majesty!" (Palms Gospel)
    C191, EL346, G198, N215, P90/91, SA196, VU127
"Holy" (*Santo*) (Palms Gospel)
    EL762, G594, SH39, S2019
"Bring Many Names" (Palms)
    C10, G760, N11, S2047, VU268
"Great Is Thy Faithfulness" (Isa)
    AH4011, C86, CG48, EL733, G39, N423, P276, SA26, SH48,
    UM140, VU288
"He Never Said a Mumbalin' Word" (Isa, Passion)
    C208, EL350, G219, P95 (PD), UM291, VU141
"At the Name of Jesus" (Phil)
    CG424, E435, EL416, G264, P148, SA74, SH657, UM168,
    VU335
"Christ Beside Me" (Phil)
    G702, S2166
"Ah, Holy Jesus" (Passion Gospel)
    C210, E158, EL349, G218, N218, P93, UM289, VU138
"Sing, My Tongue, the Glorious Battle" (Passion)
    E165/166, EL355/356, G225, N220, UM296
"Bread of the World" (Passion, Comm.)
    C387, E301, G499, N346, P502, UM624, VU461
"The Bread of Life for All Is Broken" (Passion, Comm.)
    E342, N333, UM633
"My Song Is Love Unknown" (Palms/Passion)
    E458, EL343, G209, N222, P76, S2083, SA149, VU143
"An Upper Room Did Our Lord Prepare" (Passion Gospel)
    C385, G202, P94, VU130
"An Outcast Among Outcasts" (Passion Gospel)
    N201, S2104
"Why Has God Forsaken Me?" (Passion Gospel)
    G809, P406, S2110, VU154
"How Long, O Lord" (Passion Gospel)
    G777, S2209
"You, Lord, are Both Lamb and Shepherd" (Passion)
    G274, SH210, VU210. WS3043

Additional Contemporary and Modern Suggestions

"All Hail King Jesus" 12877 (Palms Gospel)
    S2069
"King of Kings" 23952 (Palms Gospel)
    S2075, VU167

"The King of Glory Comes" (Palms Gospel)
    CG177, S2091, SH206
"Make Way" 121074 (Palms Gospel)
    SA148, WS3044
"Hosanna" 4785835 (Palms Gospel)
    SH361, WS3188
"Alleluia" (Ps 118)
    EL174, G587, S2043
"I Will Enter His Gates" 1493 (Ps 118)
    S2270, SA337
"Forever" 3148428 (Ps 118)
    CG53, SA363, WS3023
"Hallelujah" ("Your Love Is Amazing") 3091812 (Pss)
    WS3027
"Shout to the North" 1562261 (Phil)
    G319, SA1009, WS3042
"He Is Lord" 1515225 (Phil)
    C117, CG208, SA222, SH657, UM177
"How Majestic Is Your Name" 26007 (Phil)
    C63, CG326, G613, S2023, SA90
"I Exalt You" 17803 (Phil)
"Ancient of Days" 798108 (Phil)
"Majestic" 4573308 (Phil)
"Jesus, We Crown You with Praise" 1453284 (Passion Gospel)
"Once Again" 1564362 (Passion Gospel)
"You Hear" 6005063 (Passion Gospel, Holy Week)

Vocal Solos

"Ride On, Ride On in Majesty!" (Palm Sunday)
    V-5 (2)   p. 57
"Ride On, Jesus" (Palm Sunday)
    V-7   p. 8
"The Shepherd Became a Lamb" (Palm/Passion)
    V-10   p. 48

Anthems

"Hosanna to the King" (Palms Liturgy)
arr. Jack Schrader; Hope C5178
SATB, piano, opt. children's choir (https://bit.ly/C5178)

"Hosanna!" (Palms Liturgy)
Lynn Russell; Celebrating Grace 622022205
Unison, piano, opt. chimes (https://bit.ly/CG-22205)

Other Suggestions

Visuals:

Palms Gospel	Donkey, colt/cloaks/crowd/branches
Ps 188	Gate, cornerstone, branches, joy
O	Jesus teaching, morning, Christ, passion, flint
Ps 31	Tears, praying/comforting hands, broken pottery
E	Manacles, wood cross, crucifix, resurrection
Passion Gospel	Thirty coins, Praying hands, sword, robe, crucifix, crown of thorns, INRI, dice/robe, tombstone

For additional Passion ideas, consult Good Friday suggestions.
Introit: WS3078. "Hosanna" (Palms Gospel, Ps 118)
Greeting: WSL21. "Hosanna!" (Palms Gospel, Ps 118)
Canticle: UM167. "Canticle of Christ's Obedience" (Phil)
Affirmation of Faith: WSL76 or WSL 80. "We believe" (Phil)
Prayer: UM281. Passion/Palm Sunday
Offertory Prayer: WSL141. "Holy One" (Holy Week)
Theme Ideas: God: Glory of God, Jesus: Crucifixion, Jesus: Mind of Christ, Lament, Praise, Thanksgiving / Gratitude

Exodus 12:1-4, (5-10), 11-14

¹The Lord said to Moses and Aaron in the land of Egypt: ²This month shall mark for you the beginning of months; it shall be the first month of the year for you. ³Tell the whole congregation of Israel that on the tenth of this month they are to take a lamb for each family, a lamb for each household. ⁴If a household is too small for a whole lamb, it shall join its closest neighbor in obtaining one; the lamb shall be divided in proportion to the number of people who eat of it. ⁵Your lamb shall be without blemish, a year-old male; you may take it from the sheep or from the goats. ⁶You shall keep it until the fourteenth day of this month; then the whole assembled congregation of Israel shall slaughter it at twilight. ⁷They shall take some of the blood and put it on the two doorposts and the lintel of the houses in which they eat it. ⁸They shall eat the lamb that same night; they shall eat it roasted over the fire with unleavened bread and bitter herbs. ⁹Do not eat any of it raw or boiled in water, but roasted over the fire, with its head, legs, and inner organs. ¹⁰You shall let none of it remain until the morning; anything that remains until the morning you shall burn. ¹¹This is how you shall eat it: your loins girded, your sandals on your feet, and your staff in your hand; and you shall eat it hurriedly. It is the passover of the Lord. ¹²For I will pass through the land of Egypt that night, and I will strike down every firstborn in the land of Egypt, both human beings and animals; on all the gods of Egypt I will execute judgments: I am the Lord. ¹³The blood shall be a sign for you on the houses where you live: when I see the blood, I will pass over you, and no plague shall destroy you when I strike the land of Egypt.

¹⁴This day shall be a day of remembrance for you. You shall celebrate it as a festival to the Lord; throughout your generations you shall observe it as a perpetual ordinance.

Psalm 116:1-2, 12-19 (G655, N699, P228, SH344, UM837)

¹I love the Lord, because he has heard
   my voice and my supplications.
²Because he inclined his ear to me,
   therefore I will call on him as long as I live.
. . . .
¹²What shall I return to the Lord
   for all his bounty to me?
¹³I will lift up the cup of salvation
   and call on the name of the Lord,
¹⁴I will pay my vows to the Lord
   in the presence of all his people.
¹⁵Precious in the sight of the Lord
   is the death of his faithful ones.
¹⁶O Lord, I am your servant;
   I am your servant, the child of your serving girl.
   You have loosed my bonds.
¹⁷I will offer to you a thanksgiving sacrifice
   and call on the name of the Lord.
¹⁸I will pay my vows to the Lord
   in the presence of all his people,
¹⁹in the courts of the house of the Lord,
   in your midst, O Jerusalem.
Praise the Lord!

1 Corinthians 11:23-26

²³For I received from the Lord what I also handed on to you, that the Lord Jesus on the night when he was betrayed took a loaf of bread, ²⁴and when he had given thanks, he broke it and said, "This is my body that is for you. Do this in remembrance of me." ²⁵In the same way he took the cup also, after supper, saying, "This cup is the new covenant in my blood. Do this, as often as you drink it, in remembrance of me." ²⁶For as often as you eat this bread and drink the cup, you proclaim the Lord's death until he comes.

John 13:1-17, 31b-35

¹Now before the festival of the Passover, Jesus knew that his hour had come to depart from this world and go to the Father. Having loved his own who were in the world, he loved them to the end. ²The devil had already put it into the heart of Judas son of Simon Iscariot to betray him. And during supper ³Jesus, knowing that the Father had given all things into his hands, and that he had come from God and was going to God, ⁴got up from the table, took off his outer robe, and tied a towel around himself. ⁵Then he poured water into a basin and began to wash the disciples' feet and to wipe them with the towel that was tied around him. ⁶He came to Simon Peter, who said to him, "Lord, are you going to wash my feet?" ⁷Jesus answered, "You do not know now what I am doing, but later you will understand." ⁸Peter said to him, "You will never wash my feet." Jesus answered, "Unless I wash you, you have no share with me." ⁹Simon Peter said to him, "Lord, not my feet only but also my hands and my head!" ¹⁰Jesus said to him, "One who has bathed does not need to wash, except for the feet, but is entirely clean. And you are clean, though not all of you." ¹¹For he knew who was to betray him; for this reason he said, "Not all of you are clean."

¹²After he had washed their feet, had put on his robe, and had returned to the table, he said to them, "Do you know what I have done to you? ¹³You call me Teacher and Lord—and you are right, for that is what I am. ¹⁴So if I, your Lord and Teacher, have washed your feet, you also ought to wash one another's feet. ¹⁵For I have set you an example, that you also should do as I have done to you. ¹⁶Very truly, I tell you, servants are not greater than their master, nor are messengers greater than the one who sent them. ¹⁷If you know these things, you are blessed if you do them. . . .

³¹ᵇ"Now the Son of Man has been glorified, and God has been glorified in him. ³²If God has been glorified in him, God will also glorify him in himself and will glorify him at once. ³³Little children, I am with you only a little longer. You will look for me; and as I said to the Jews so now I say to you, 'Where I am going, you cannot come.' ³⁴I give you a new commandment, that you love one another. Just as I have loved you, you also should love one another. ³⁵By this everyone will know that you are my disciples, if you have love for one another."

Primary Hymns and Songs for the Day
"What Wondrous Love Is This" (Pss, John) (O)
  C200, CG171, E439, EL666, G215, N223, P85, SA207, SH177,
  UM292, VU147 (Fr.)
    H-3   Hbl-102; Chr-212; Org-185
    S-1   #347. Harm.
"In Remembrance of Me" 25156 (Pss, 1 Cor, Comm.)
  C403, CG462, G521, S2254, SH667
"Jesu, Jesu" 3049039 (John, Footwashing) (C)
    S-1   #63. Vocal part
  C600, CG656, E602, EL708, G203, N498, P367, SH155,
  UM432, VU593, S-1 #63. Vocal part

Additional Hymn Suggestions
"O God, Our Help in Ages Past" (Exod)
  C67, CG566, E680, EL632, G687, N25, P210, SA47, SH41,
  UM117 (PD), VU806
"God the Sculptor of the Mountains" (Exod)
  EL736, G5, S2060
"Deep in the Shadows of the Past" (Exod)
  G50, N320, P330, S2246
"Saranam, Saranam" ("Refuge") (Exod, Pss)
  G789, UM523
"Out of the Depths I Cry to You" (Pss)
  EL600, G424, N483, P240, SH513, UM515
"I Love the Lord" 1168957 (Pss)
  CG613, G799, P362, N511, SH343, VU617, WS3142
"The Church of Christ, in Every Age" (1 Cor)
  C475, EL729, G320, N306, P421, UM589, VU601
"For the Bread Which You Have Broken" (1 Cor, Comm.)
  C411, E340/E341, EL494, G516, P508/P509, UM614/
  UM615, VU470
"Una Espiga" ("Sheaves of Summer") (1 Cor, Comm.)
  C396, G532, N338, UM637
"Mothering God, You Gave Me Birth" (1 Cor, Comm.)
  C83, EL735, G7, N467, S2050, VU320
"In the Singing" (1 Cor, Comm.)
  EL466, G533, S2255
"Come, Share the Lord" (1 Cor, Comm.)
  C408, CG459, G510, S2269, VU469
"Ah, Holy Jesus" (John)
  C210, E158, EL349, G218, N218, P93, UM289, VU138
"O Master, Let Me Walk with Thee" (John)
  C602, CG660, E659/E660, EL818, G738, N503, P357, SA667,
  SH612, UM430 (PD), VU560
"Lord God, Your Love Has Called Us Here" (John)
  EL358, P353, SA335, UM579
"Lavapés" ("The Washing of Feet") (John, Foot Washing)
  SH154
"Draw Us in the Spirit's Tether" (John, Comm.)
  C392, EL470, G529, N337, P504, UM632, VU479
"Together We Serve" (John)
  G767, S2175
"Healer of Our Every Ill" (John)
  C506, EL612, G795, S2213, SH339, VU619
"As We Gather at Your Table" (John, Comm.)
  EL522, N332, S2268, SH411, VU457

Additional Contemporary and Modern Suggestions
"I Will Call upon the Lord" 11263 (Pss)
  G621, S2002
"We Bring the Sacrifice of Praise" 9990 (Pss)
  S2031
"I Love You, Lord" 25266 (Pss)
  CG362, G627, S2068, SA369, SH417
"I Stand Amazed" 769450 (Pss, Lent)
"I Will Not Forget You" 2694306 (Pss)
"Beautiful Savior" 2492216 (Pss, Holy Week)

"This Is My Story" 7046375 (Pss, John)
"Eat This Bread" (1 Cor, Comm.)
  C414, EL472, G527, N788, SH671, UM628, VU466
"Take Our Bread" (1 Cor, John, Comm.)
  C413, UM640
"We Remember We Believe" 5767711 (1 Cor, John, Comm.)
"Here Is Bread, Here Is Wine" 983717 (1 Cor, Comm.)
  EL483, S2266
"Father, I Adore You" 26557 (John)
  CG4, S2038, SH587
"Make Me a Servant" 33131 (John)
  CG651, S2176
"Live in Charity" (*"Ubi Caritas"*) (John)
  C523, EL642, G205, S2179
"The Servant Song" 72673 (John)
  C490, CG289, EL659, G727, N539, S2222, SA1005, SH264,
  VU595
"They'll Know We Are Christians" 26997 (John)
  AH4074, C494, CG272, G300, S2223, SH232
"Make Us One" 695737 (John)
"Bind Us Together" 1228 (John)
"There's a Spirit of Love in This Place" (John)
  WS3148
"The Jesus in Me" (John)
  AH4109, WS3151
"For Us" 7119349 (John, Holy Week)
"There Will Be Bread" 4512352 (John, Comm.)

Vocal Solos
"In Remembrance" (John, Comm.)
  V-5 (2)   p. 7
"He Breaks the Bread, He Pours the Wine" (John)
  V-10   p. 43
"Now the Silence" (Comm.)
  C415, E333, EL460, G534, UM619, VU475

Anthems
"Midnight on Olive's Brow" (John)
David Rasbach; Hinshaw Music HMC2504
SATB, piano (https://bit.ly/HMC2504)

"How Beautiful" (John)
arr. Lloyd Larson; Hope C5258
SAB, keyboard (https://bit.ly/C5258)

Other Suggestions
Visuals:
  O   Goat/lamb, blood/doorposts, unleavened bread,
          sandals, staff, Exod 12:11b, 14a
  P   Praying hands, lifted cup, death, open manacles
  E   Broken loaf, cup, Last Supper
  G   Robe/towel/water/basin, John 13:12b or 13:34ab,
          Last Supper, Jesus speaking, acts of love
For additional Passion ideas, consult Good Friday suggestions.
Consider a quiet service of acoustic or a cappella music.
Prayer: UM283. Holy Thursday
Reading: C388. Remember Me (1 Cor)
Offertory Prayer: WSL154. "Heavenly Father" (John)
Invitation to Communion: WS3152. "Welcome" (John)
Sung Communion: WS3171. "Communion Setting" (1 Cor)
Closing Prayer: WSL17. "A wilderness beckons" (Holy Week)
Blessing: WSL27. "May the Christ who walks" (John, Holy Week)
Theme Ideas: Communion, Love, Servanthood / Service

Isaiah 52:13–53:12

¹³See, my servant shall prosper;
    he shall be exalted and lifted up,
    and shall be very high.
¹⁴Just as there were many who were astonished at him
    —so marred was his appearance, beyond human semblance,
    and his form beyond that of mortals—
¹⁵so he shall startle many nations;
    kings shall shut their mouths because of him;
for that which had not been told them they shall see,
    and that which they had not heard they shall contemplate.
53 Who has believed what we have heard?
    And to whom has the arm of the LORD been revealed?
²For he grew up before him like a young plant,
    and like a root out of dry ground;
he had no form or majesty that we should look at him,
    nothing in his appearance that we should desire him.
³He was despised and rejected by others;
    a man of suffering and acquainted with infirmity;
and as one from whom others hide their faces
    he was despised, and we held him of no account.
⁴Surely he has borne our infirmities
    and carried our diseases;
yet we accounted him stricken,
    struck down by God, and afflicted.
⁵But he was wounded for our transgressions,
    crushed for our iniquities;
upon him was the punishment that made us whole,
    and by his bruises we are healed.
⁶All we like sheep have gone astray;
    we have all turned to our own way,
and the LORD has laid on him
    the iniquity of us all.
⁷He was oppressed, and he was afflicted,
    yet he did not open his mouth;
like a lamb that is led to the slaughter,
    and like a sheep that before its shearers is silent,
    so he did not open his mouth.
⁸By a perversion of justice he was taken away.
    Who could have imagined his future?
For he was cut off from the land of the living,
    stricken for the transgression of my people.
⁹They made his grave with the wicked
    and his tomb with the rich,
although he had done no violence,
    and there was no deceit in his mouth.
¹⁰Yet it was the will of the LORD to crush him with pain.
When you make his life an offering for sin,
    he shall see his offspring, and shall prolong his days;
through him the will of the LORD shall prosper.
    ¹¹Out of his anguish he shall see light;
he shall find satisfaction through his knowledge.
    The righteous one, my servant, shall make many righteous,
    and he shall bear their iniquities.
¹²Therefore I will allot him a portion with the great,
    and he shall divide the spoil with the strong;
because he poured out himself to death,
    and was numbered with the transgressors;
yet he bore the sin of many,
    and made intercession for the transgressors.

Psalm 22 (G210/631, N632, SH178, UM752)

¹My God, my God, why have you forsaken me?
    Why are you so far from helping me, from the words of my
        groaning?
²O my God, I cry by day, but you do not answer;
    and by night, but find no rest.
³Yet you are holy,
    enthroned on the praises of Israel.
⁴In you our ancestors trusted;
    they trusted, and you delivered them.
⁵To you they cried, and were saved;
    in you they trusted, and were not put to shame.
⁶But I am a worm, and not human;
    scorned by others, and despised by the people.
⁷All who see me mock at me;
    they make mouths at me, they shake their heads;
⁸"Commit your cause to the LORD; let him deliver—
    let him rescue the one in whom he delights!"
⁹Yet it was you who took me from the womb;
    you kept me safe on my mother's breast.
¹⁰On you I was cast from my birth,
    and since my mother bore me you have been my God.
¹¹Do not be far from me,
    for trouble is near
    and there is no one to help.
¹²Many bulls encircle me,
    strong bulls of Bashan surround me;
¹³they open wide their mouths at me,
    like a ravening and roaring lion.
¹⁴I am poured out like water,
    and all my bones are out of joint;
    my heart is like wax;
        it is melted within my breast;
¹⁵my mouth is dried up like a potsherd,
    and my tongue sticks to my jaws;
    you lay me in the dust of death.
¹⁶For dogs are all around me;
    a company of evildoers encircles me.
My hands and feet have shriveled;
¹⁷I can count all my bones.
They stare and gloat over me;
¹⁸they divide my clothes among themselves,
    and for my clothing they cast lots.
¹⁹But you, O LORD, do not be far away!
    O my help, come quickly to my aid!
²⁰Deliver my soul from the sword,
    my life from the power of the dog!
²¹   Save me from the mouth of the lion!
From the horns of the wild oxen you have rescued me.
²²I will tell of your name to my brothers and sisters;
    in the midst of the congregation I will praise you:
²³You who fear the LORD, praise him!
    All you offspring of Jacob, glorify him;
    stand in awe of him, all you offspring of Israel!
²⁴For he did not despise or abhor
    the affliction of the afflicted;
he did not hide his face from me,
    but heard when I cried to him.
²⁵From you comes my praise in the great congregation;
    my vows I will pay before those who fear him.
²⁶The poor shall eat and be satisfied;
    those who seek him shall praise the LORD.
May your hearts live forever!
²⁷All the ends of the earth shall remember
    and turn to the LORD;
and all the families of the nations
    shall worship before him.
²⁸For dominion belongs to the LORD,
    and he rules over the nations.

[29]To him, indeed, shall all who sleep in the earth bow down;
    before him shall bow all who go down to the dust,
    and I shall live for him.
[30]Posterity will serve him;
    future generations will be told about the Lord,
[31]and proclaim his deliverance to a people yet unborn,
    saying that he has done it.

Hebrews 10:16-25

[16] "This is the covenant that I will make with them
        after those days, says the Lord:
    I will put my laws in their hearts,
        and I will write them on their minds,"
[17]he also adds,
    "I will remember their sins and their lawless deeds no more."
[18]Where there is forgiveness of these, there is no longer any offering for sin.

[19]Therefore, my friends, since we have confidence to enter the sanctuary by the blood of Jesus, [20]by the new and living way that he opened for us through the curtain (that is, through his flesh), [21]and since we have a great priest over the house of God, [22]let us approach with a true heart in full assurance of faith, with our hearts sprinkled clean from an evil conscience and our bodies washed with pure water. [23]Let us hold fast to the confession of our hope without wavering, for he who has promised is faithful. [24]And let us consider how to provoke one another to love and good deeds, [25]not neglecting to meet together, as is the habit of some, but encouraging one another, and all the more as you see the Day approaching.

John 18:1–19:42

[1]After Jesus had spoken these words, he went out with his disciples across the Kidron valley to a place where there was a garden, which he and his disciples entered. [2]Now Judas, who betrayed him, also knew the place, because Jesus often met there with his disciples. [3]So Judas brought a detachment of soldiers together with police from the chief priests and the Pharisees, and they came there with lanterns and torches and weapons. [4]Then Jesus, knowing all that was to happen to him, came forward and asked them, "Whom are you looking for?" [5]They answered, "Jesus of Nazareth." Jesus replied, "I am he." Judas, who betrayed him, was standing with them. [6]When Jesus said to them, "I am he," they stepped back and fell to the ground. [7]Again he asked them, "Whom are you looking for?" And they said, "Jesus of Nazareth." [8]Jesus answered, "I told you that I am he. So if you are looking for me, let these men go." [9]This was to fulfill the word that he had spoken, "I did not lose a single one of those whom you gave me." [10]Then Simon Peter, who had a sword, drew it, struck the high priest's slave, and cut off his right ear. The slave's name was Malchus. [11]Jesus said to Peter, "Put your sword back into its sheath. Am I not to drink the cup that the Father has given me?"

[12]So the soldiers, their officer, and the Jewish police arrested Jesus and bound him. [13]First they took him to Annas, who was the father-in-law of Caiaphas, the high priest that year. [14]Caiaphas was the one who had advised the Jews that it was better to have one person die for the people.

[15]Simon Peter and another disciple followed Jesus. Since that disciple was known to the high priest, he went with Jesus into the courtyard of the high priest, [16]but Peter was standing outside at the gate. So the other disciple, who was known to the high priest, went out, spoke to the woman who guarded the gate, and brought Peter in. [17]The woman said to Peter, "You are not also one of this man's disciples, are you?" He said, "I am not." [18]Now the slaves and the police had made a charcoal fire because it was cold, and they were standing around it and warming themselves. Peter also was standing with them and warming himself.

[19]Then the high priest questioned Jesus about his disciples and about his teaching. [20]Jesus answered, "I have spoken openly to the world; I have always taught in synagogues and in the temple, where all the Jews come together. I have said nothing in secret. [21]Why do you ask me? Ask those who heard what I said to them; they know what I said." [22]When he had said this, one of the police standing nearby struck Jesus on the face, saying, "Is that how you answer the high priest?" [23]Jesus answered, "If I have spoken wrongly, testify to the wrong. But if I have spoken rightly, why do you strike me?" [24]Then Annas sent him bound to Caiaphas the high priest.

[25]Now Simon Peter was standing and warming himself. They asked him, "You are not also one of his disciples, are you?" He denied it and said, "I am not." [26]One of the slaves of the high priest, a relative of the man whose ear Peter had cut off, asked, "Did I not see you in the garden with him?" [27]Again Peter denied it, and at that moment the cock crowed.

[28]Then they took Jesus from Caiaphas to Pilate's headquarters. It was early in the morning. They themselves did not enter the headquarters, so as to avoid ritual defilement and to be able to eat the Passover. [29]So Pilate went out to them and said, "What accusation do you bring against this man?" [30]They answered, "If this man were not a criminal, we would not have handed him over to you." [31]Pilate said to them, "Take him yourselves and judge him according to your law." The Jews replied, "We are not permitted to put anyone to death." [32](This was to fulfill what Jesus had said when he indicated the kind of death he was to die.)

[33]Then Pilate entered the headquarters again, summoned Jesus, and asked him, "Are you the King of the Jews?" [34]Jesus answered, "Do you ask this on your own, or did others tell you about me?" [35]Pilate replied, "I am not a Jew, am I? Your own nation and the chief priests have handed you over to me. What have you done?" [36]Jesus answered, "My kingdom is not from this world. If my kingdom were from this world, my followers would be fighting to keep me from being handed over to the Jews. But as it is, my kingdom is not from here." [37]Pilate asked him, "So you are a king?" Jesus answered, "You say that I am a king. For this I was born, and for this I came into the world, to testify to the truth. Everyone who belongs to the truth listens to my voice." [38]Pilate asked him, "What is truth?"

After he had said this, he went out to the Jews again and told them, "I find no case against him. [39]But you have a custom that I release someone for you at the Passover. Do you want me to release for you the King of the Jews?" [40]They shouted in reply, "Not this man, but Barabbas!" Now Barabbas was a bandit.

19 Then Pilate took Jesus and had him flogged. [2]And the soldiers wove a crown of thorns and put it on his head, and they dressed him in a purple robe. [3]They kept coming up to him, saying, "Hail, King of the Jews!" and striking him on the face. [4]Pilate went out again and said to them, "Look, I am bringing him out to you to let you know that I find no case against him." [5]So Jesus came out, wearing the crown of thorns and the purple robe. Pilate said to them, "Here is the man!" [6]When the chief priests and the police saw him, they shouted, "Crucify him! Crucify him!" Pilate said to them, "Take him yourselves and crucify him; I find no case against him." [7]The Jews answered him, "We have a law, and according to that law he ought to die because he has claimed to be the Son of God."

[8]Now when Pilate heard this, he was more afraid than ever. [9]He entered his headquarters again and asked Jesus, "Where are you from?" But Jesus gave him no answer. [10]Pilate therefore said to him, "Do you refuse to speak to me? Do you not know that I have power to release you, and power to crucify you?" [11]Jesus answered him, "You would have no power over me unless it had been given you from above; therefore the one who handed me over to you is guilty of a greater sin." [12]From then on Pilate tried to release him, but the Jews cried out, "If you release this man, you are no friend of the emperor. Everyone who claims to be a king sets himself against the emperor."

[13]When Pilate heard these words, he brought Jesus outside and sat on the judge's bench at a place called The Stone Pavement, or in Hebrew Gabbatha. [14]Now it was the day of Preparation for the Passover; and it was about noon. He said to the Jews, "Here is your King!" [15]They cried out, "Away with him! Away with him! Crucify him!" Pilate asked them, "Shall I crucify your King?" The chief priests answered, "We have no king but the emperor." [16]Then he handed him over to them to be crucified.

So they took Jesus; [17]and carrying the cross by himself, he went out to what is called The Place of the Skull, which in Hebrew is called Golgotha. [18]There they crucified him, and with him two others, one on either side, with Jesus between them.

[19]Pilate also had an inscription written and put on the cross. It read, "Jesus of Nazareth, the King of the Jews." [20]Many of the Jews read this inscription, because the place where Jesus was crucified was near the city; and it was written in Hebrew, in Latin, and in Greek. [21]Then the chief priests of the Jews said to Pilate, "Do not write, 'The King of the Jews,' but, 'This man said, I am King of the Jews.'" [22]Pilate answered, "What I have written I have written." [23]When the soldiers had crucified Jesus, they took his clothes and divided them into four parts, one for each soldier. They also took his tunic; now the tunic was seamless, woven in one piece from the top. [24]So they said to one another, "Let us not tear it, but cast lots for it to see who will get it." This was to fulfill what the scripture says,

"They divided my clothes among themselves,
    and for my clothing they cast lots."

[25]And that is what the soldiers did. Meanwhile, standing near the cross of Jesus were his mother, and his mother's sister, Mary the wife of Clopas, and Mary Magdalene. [26]When Jesus saw his mother and the disciple whom he loved standing beside her, he said to his mother, "Woman, here is your son." [27]Then he said to the disciple, "Here is your mother." And from that hour the disciple took her into his own home.

[28]After this, when Jesus knew that all was now finished, he said (in order to fulfill the scripture), "I am thirsty." [29]A jar full of sour wine was standing there. So they put a sponge full of the wine on a branch of hyssop and held it to his mouth. [30]When Jesus had received the wine, he said, "It is finished." Then he bowed his head and gave up his spirit.

[31]Since it was the day of Preparation, the Jews did not want the bodies left on the cross during the sabbath, especially because that sabbath was a day of great solemnity. So they asked Pilate to have the legs of the crucified men broken and the bodies removed. [32]Then the soldiers came and broke the legs of the first and of the other who had been crucified with him. [33]But when they came to Jesus and saw that he was already dead, they did not break his legs. [34]Instead, one of the soldiers pierced his side with a spear, and at once blood and water came out. [35](He who saw this has testified so that you also may believe. His testimony is true, and he knows that he tells the truth.) [36]These things occurred so that the scripture might be fulfilled, "None of his bones shall be broken." [37]And again another passage of scripture says, "They will look on the one whom they have pierced."

[38]After these things, Joseph of Arimathea, who was a disciple of Jesus, though a secret one because of his fear of the Jews, asked Pilate to let him take away the body of Jesus. Pilate gave him permission; so he came and removed his body. [39]Nicodemus, who had at first come to Jesus by night, also came, bringing a mixture of myrrh and aloes, weighing about a hundred pounds. [40]They took the body of Jesus and wrapped it with the spices in linen cloths, according to the burial custom of the Jews. [41]Now there was a garden in the place where he was crucified, and in the garden there was a new tomb in which no one had ever been laid. [42]And so, because it was the Jewish day of Preparation, and the tomb was nearby, they laid Jesus there.

Primary Hymns and Songs for the Day

"Were You There" (John)
C198, CG192, E172, EL353, G228, N229, P102, SA206, SH176, UM288, VU144
    H-3   Hbl-101; Chr-209
    S-2   #195-196. Desc. and harm.
    V-7   p. 60 Vocal Solo
"O Sacred Head, Now Wounded" (John)
C202, CG191, E168/169, EL351/352, G221, N226, P98, SA190, SH168, UM286, VU145 (Fr.)
    H-3   Hbl-82; Chr-148; Desc-86; Org-111
"When I Survey the Wondrous Cross" (John) (C)
C195, CG186, EL803, G223, N224, P101, SH163/164, UM298
    H-3   Hbl-6, 102; Chr-213; Desc-49; Org-49
    S-1   #155. Descant
E474, G224, P100, SA208, UM299 (PD), VU149 (Fr.)
    H-3   Hbl-47; Chr-214; Desc-90; Org-127
    S-1   #288. Transposition to E-flat major

Additional Hymn Suggestions

"He Never Said a Mumbalin' Word" (Isa, John)
C208, EL350, G219, P95 (PD), UM291, VU141
"Alas! and Did My Savior Bleed" (Isa, John)
AH4067, C204, CG182/595, EL337, G212, N199/200, P78, SA159, UM294/359, SH172/173
"You, Lord, Are Both Lamb and Shepherd" (Isa, John)
G274, SH210, VU210. WS3043
"Out of the Depths I Cry to You" (Pss)
EL600, G424, N483, P240, SH513, UM515
"Why Stand So Far Away, My God?" (Pss, John)
C671, G786, S2180
"How Long, O Lord" (Pss, Good Friday)
G777, S2209
"Taste and See" (Pss, Comm.)
EL493, G520, S2267, SH691
"I Am Thine, O Lord" (Heb)
AH4087, C601, CG504, N455, SA586, UM419 (PD)
"Near to the Heart of God" (Heb)
C581, CG383, G824, P527, UM472 (PD)
"Ah, Holy Jesus" (John)
C210, E158, EL349, G218, N218, P93, UM289, VU138
"Go to Dark Gethsemane" (John)
C196, CG180, E171, EL347, G220, N219, P97, SH171, UM290 (PD), VU133
"Bread of the World" (John, Comm.)
C387, E301, G499, N346, P502, UM624, VU461
"The Bread of Life for All Is Broken" (John, Comm.)
E342, N333, UM633
"My Song Is Love Unknown" (Good Friday)
E458, EL343, G209, N222, P76, S2083, SA149, VU143
"When Jesus Wept" (John)
C199, E715, G194, N192, P312, S2106, VU146
"Why Has God Forsaken Me?" (John)
G809, P406, S2110, VU154

Additional Contemporary and Modern Suggestions

"Our God Reigns" 8458 (Isa)
"O How He Loves You and Me" 15850 (Isa, John)
CG600, S2108, SH535
"There Is a Redeemer" 11483 (Isa, John)
CG377, G443, SA204, SH495
"Stand in Awe" (Pss)
WS3162
"Here at the Cross" 7046292 (Pss, Heb, Lent)
"You Are My King" ("Amazing Love") 2456623 (Heb)
SH539, WS3102
"Take Our Bread" (Heb, Comm.)
C413, UM640

"Before the Throne of God Above" 2306412 (Heb)
"Amazing Love" 192553 (Heb, Good Friday)
"Because of Your Love" 4662501 (Heb, Good Friday)
"I Come to the Cross" 1965249 (Heb, Good Friday)
"This Is My Story" 7046375 (John, Good Friday)
"Jesus, Remember Me" (John, Good Friday)
C569, CG393, EL616, G227, P599, SH175, UM488, VU148
"Stay with Me" ("Nohu pû") (Good Friday)
EL348, G204, S2198, SH157
"Lamb of God" 16787 (Good Friday)
EL336, G518, S2113
"The Power of the Cross" 4490766 (John, Good Friday)
CG190, WS3085
"The Wonderful Cross" 3148435 (Good Friday)
"Above All" 2672885 (John, Good Friday)
    V-3 (2) p. 17 Vocal Solo
"Revelation Song" 4447960 (Good Friday)

Vocal Solos

"He was Cut Off Out of the Land of the Living" (recitative) and
"But Thou Didst Not Leave His Soul in Hell" (aria) (John)
    V-2
"Sing of Mary, Pure and Lowly" (John, Good Friday)
    V-5 (1)   p. 21
"Lamb of God" (John, Good Friday)
    V-5 (2)   p. 5
"Ah, Holy Jesus" (John, Good Friday)
    V-6   p. 24
"He Carried My Cross" (John, Good Friday)
    V-8   p. 213
"They Led Him Away" (John)
    V-8   p. 245

Anthems

"*Recordare*: Drop, drop slow tears" (John, Good Friday)
Howard Goodall; MorningStar MSM-56-0055
Soprano solo, SATB, piano (https://bit.ly/56-0055)

"Lenten Contemplation" (Good Friday)
Jonathan Shippey; Hinshaw HMC1786
SATB *a cappella* (https://bit.ly/HMC1786)

Other Suggestions

Visuals: Black-draped cross, altar stripped
    O   Plant, root, suffering, crucifix, lamb/shears
    P   Crucifix, Exodus, nursing, water, bones, sword, dog/lion/ox, feeding the poor
    E   Heb 10:16b, eraser, crucifix, curtain, worship
    G   Sword, fire, cock, whip, robe, rugged cross, crucifix nails, crown (thorns), ladder, sponge, spear, shroud
For additional ideas, consult Palm/Passion Sunday suggestions.
Opening Prayer: WSL25. "Today the carpenter's hands" (John)
Psalm: SH178. Ps 22 with stanzas of "What Wondrous Love Is This" (Pss)
Offertory Prayer: WSL155. "God of the Crucified Jesus" (John)
Prayers: N833, N880, and UM284 (John)
Litany: C201 or C209 (John)
Reading: C205, UM293 (John, Good Friday)
Reading: C196, CG180, E171, EL347, G220, N219, P97, SH171, UM290 (PD), VU133. "Go to Dark Gethsemane." Use this hymn to supplement the reading of the John passage. Stanza 1 before beginning 18:1. Sing stanza 2 after 19:3. Sing stanza 3 after 19:30. Sing UM288, stanza 5 at the conclusion of the reading.
Blessing: N872 (Holy Week)
Theme Ideas: Covenant, Cross, Jesus: Crucifixion, Lament

Acts 10:34-43

³⁴Then Peter began to speak to them: "I truly understand that God shows no partiality, ³⁵but in every nation anyone who fears him and does what is right is acceptable to him. ³⁶You know the message he sent to the people of Israel, preaching peace by Jesus Christ—he is Lord of all. ³⁷That message spread throughout Judea, beginning in Galilee after the baptism that John announced: ³⁸how God anointed Jesus of Nazareth with the Holy Spirit and with power; how he went about doing good and healing all who were oppressed by the devil, for God was with him. ³⁹We are witnesses to all that he did both in Judea and in Jerusalem. They put him to death by hanging him on a tree; ⁴⁰but God raised him on the third day and allowed him to appear, ⁴¹not to all the people but to us who were chosen by God as witnesses, and who ate and drank with him after he rose from the dead. ⁴²He commanded us to preach to the people and to testify that he is the one ordained by God as judge of the living and the dead. ⁴³All the prophets testify about him that everyone who believes in him receives forgiveness of sins through his name."

Psalm 118:1-2, 14-24 (G391/681, N700, P230/232, UM839)

¹O give thanks to the Lᴏʀᴅ, for he is good;
  his steadfast love endures forever!
²Let Israel say,
  "His steadfast love endures forever."
. . . .
¹⁴The Lᴏʀᴅ is my strength and my might;
  he has become my salvation.
¹⁵There are glad songs of victory in the tents of the righteous:
  "The right hand of the Lᴏʀᴅ does valiantly;
¹⁶the right hand of the Lᴏʀᴅ is exalted;
  the right hand of the Lᴏʀᴅ does valiantly."
¹⁷I shall not die, but I shall live,
  and recount the deeds of the Lᴏʀᴅ.
¹⁸The Lᴏʀᴅ has punished me severely,
  but he did not give me over to death.
¹⁹Open to me the gates of righteousness,
  that I may enter through them
  and give thanks to the Lᴏʀᴅ.
²⁰This is the gate of the Lᴏʀᴅ;
  the righteous shall enter through it.
²¹I thank you that you have answered me
  and have become my salvation.
²²The stone that the builders rejected
  has become the chief cornerstone.
²³This is the Lord's doing;
  it is marvelous in our eyes.
²⁴This is the day that the Lᴏʀᴅ has made;
  let us rejoice and be glad in it.

Colossians 3:1-4

¹So if you have been raised with Christ, seek the things that are above, where Christ is, seated at the right hand of God. ²Set your minds on things that are above, not on things that are on earth, ³for you have died, and your life is hidden with Christ in God. ⁴When Christ who is your life is revealed, then you also will be revealed with him in glory.

John 20:1-18 (or Matthew 28:1-10)

¹Early on the first day of the week, while it was still dark, Mary Magdalene came to the tomb and saw that the stone had been removed from the tomb. ²So she ran and went to Simon Peter and the other disciple, the one whom Jesus loved, and said to them, "They have taken the Lord out of the tomb, and we do not know where they have laid him." ³Then Peter and the other disciple set out and went toward the tomb. ⁴The two were running together, but the other disciple outran Peter and reached the tomb first. ⁵He bent down to look in and saw the linen wrappings lying there, but he did not go in. ⁶Then Simon Peter came, following him, and went into the tomb. He saw the linen wrappings lying there, ⁷and the cloth that had been on Jesus' head, not lying with the linen wrappings but rolled up in a place by itself. ⁸Then the other disciple, who reached the tomb first, also went in, and he saw and believed; ⁹for as yet they did not understand the scripture, that he must rise from the dead. ¹⁰Then the disciples returned to their homes.

¹¹But Mary stood weeping outside the tomb. As she wept, she bent over to look into the tomb; ¹²and she saw two angels in white, sitting where the body of Jesus had been lying, one at the head and the other at the feet. ¹³They said to her, "Woman, why are you weeping?" She said to them, "They have taken away my Lord, and I do not know where they have laid him." ¹⁴When she had said this, she turned around and saw Jesus standing there, but she did not know that it was Jesus. ¹⁵Jesus said to her, "Woman, why are you weeping? Whom are you looking for?" Supposing him to be the gardener, she said to him, "Sir, if you have carried him away, tell me where you have laid him, and I will take him away." ¹⁶Jesus said to her, "Mary!" She turned and said to him in Hebrew, "Rabbouni!" (which means Teacher). ¹⁷Jesus said to her, "Do not hold on to me, because I have not yet ascended to the Father. But go to my brothers and say to them, 'I am ascending to my Father and your Father, to my God and your God.'" ¹⁸Mary Magdalene went and announced to the disciples, "I have seen the Lord"; and she told them that he had said these things to her.

[Matthew 28:1-10]

¹After the sabbath, as the first day of the week was dawning, Mary Magdalene and the other Mary went to see the tomb. ²And suddenly there was a great earthquake; for an angel of the Lord, descending from heaven, came and rolled back the stone and sat on it. ³His appearance was like lightning, and his clothing white as snow. ⁴For fear of him the guards shook and became like dead men. ⁵But the angel said to the women, "Do not be afraid; I know that you are looking for Jesus who was crucified. ⁶He is not here; for he has been raised, as he said. Come, see the place where he lay. ⁷Then go quickly and tell his disciples, 'He has been raised from the dead, and indeed he is going ahead of you to Galilee; there you will see him.' This is my message for you." ⁸So they left the tomb quickly with fear and great joy, and ran to tell his disciples. ⁹Suddenly Jesus met them and said, "Greetings!" And they came to him, took hold of his feet, and worshiped him. ¹⁰Then Jesus said to them, "Do not be afraid; go and tell my brothers to go to Galilee; there they will see me."

Primary Hymns and Songs for the Day

"Christ the Lord Is Risen Today" (John, Matt) (O)
C216, CG194, N233, SA218, SH181, UM302 (PD), VU155
and VU157
  H-3 Hbl-8, 51; Chr-49; Desc-31; Org-32
  S-1 #104-108. Various treatments
G245, P113
  H-3 Hbl-72; Chr-50; Desc-69; Org-78
  S-1 #213. Desc.
EL373
"The Day of Resurrection" (John, Matt)
C228, CG214, E210, EL361, G233, N245, P118, SH186,
UM303 (PD), VU164
  H-3 Hbl-74; Chr-123; Desc-64; Org-71
  S-1 #195-197. Various treatments
"The Easter Song" 12279 (John, Matt, Easter)
"Crown Him with Many Crowns" (John) (C)
C234, CG223. E494, EL855, G268, N301, P151, SA358,
SH208, UM327 (PD), VU211
  H-3 Hbl-55; Chr-60; Desc-30; Org-27
  S-1 #86-88. Various treatments

Additional Hymn Suggestions

"At the Font We Start Our Journey" (Acts, Baptism)
N308, S2114
"Ask Ye What Great Thing I Know" (Acts, Easter)
CG443, N49, UM163 (PD), VU338
"Lord of the Dance" 78529 (Acts)
G157, P302, SA141, UM261, VU352
"The Strife Is O'er, the Battle Done" (Acts)
C221, E208, EL366, G236, N242, P119, SA233, SH193,
UM306, VU159
"This Is the Day" 32754 (Pss)
AH4149, C286, N84, SA398, SH379, UM657, VU412
"This Is the Day the Lord Hath Made" (Pss)
G681, P230, UM658
"O Sons and Daughters, Let Us Sing" (Pss, John)
C220, CG212, E203, EL386/E387, G235/255, N244, P116
(PD), SH190, UM317, VU170
"Woke Up This Morning" (Col)
C623, N85, S2082
"Woman in the Night" (John)
C188, G161, UM274
"Thine Be the Glory" (John, Matt)
C218, CG222, EL376, G238, N253, P122, SA276, SH192,
UM308, VU173 (Fr.)
"He Lives" (John, Matt)
C226, CG622, SA847, SH198, UM310
Cristo Vive ("Christ Is Risen") (John, Matt)
N235, P109, SH184, UM313
"In the Garden" (John)
C227, CG200, N237, UM314
"Come, Ye Faithful, Raise the Strain" (John, Matt)
C215, CG218, E199, EL363, G234, N230, P115, UM315 (PD),
VU165
"He Rose" (John, Matt)
N239, UM316
"Christ Is Alive" (John, Matt)
CG205, E182, EL389, G246, P108, SA217, UM318, VU158
"Up from the Grave He Arose" (John, Matt)
C224, CG207, SA228, SH185, UM322 (PD)
"You, Lord, Are Both Lamb and Shepherd" (John)
G274, SH210, VU210. WS3043
"Deck Thyself, My Soul, with Gladness" (Easter, Comm.)
E339, EL488/EL489, G514, P506, UM612 (PD), VU463

Additional Contemporary and Modern Suggestions

"Halle, Halle, Halleluja" 2659190 (Easter, Opening)
C41, CG433, EL172, G591, N236, S2026, SH694, VU958

"Holy and Anointed One" 164361 (Acts)
"In the Lord I'll Be Ever Thankful" (Pss)
G654, S2195, SH316
"I Will Enter His Gates" 1493 (Pss)
S2270, SA337
"You Are Good" 3383788 (Pss)
AH4018, SH455, WS3014
"Forever" 3148428 (Pss)
CG53, SA363, WS3023
"Hallelujah" ("Your Love Is Amazing") 3091812 (Pss)
"To Know You More" 1767420 (Col)
"Lord, I Lift Your Name on High" 117947 (Col, Easter)
AH4071, CG606, EL857, S2088, SA379, SH205
"Christ the Lord Is Risen" 230240 (John, Matt, Easter)
"Alleluia" 16811 (John, Matt, Easter)
C106, N765, SH699, UM186
"Our God Reigns" 8458 (John, Matt, Easter)
"Celebrate Jesus" 16859 (John, Matt, Easter)
"Jesus Is Alive" 550652 (John, Matt, Easter)
"See What a Morning" ("Resurrection Hymn") 4108797 (John)
"Blessing, Honour and Glory" 1001179 (Easter)
EL433
"My Redeemer Lives" 2397964 (Easter)
"Alive Forever, Amen" 4190176 (Easter)
"Holy, Holy" 18792 (Easter)
P140, S2039
"Alleluia" (Easter)
EL174, G587, S2043
"Sing Alleluia to the Lord" (Easter, Comm.)
C32, S2258, SH685
"Amen, Amen" (Easter, Closing)
N161, P299, S2072

Vocal Solos

"I Know That My Redeemer Liveth" (Easter)
V-2
V-8   p. 202
"I Know That My Redeemer Lives" (Easter)
V-5 (2)   p. 22

Anthems

"Day of Delight and Beauty Unbonded" (John, Easter)
Thomas Keesecker; MorningStar MSM-50-4068
Unison/2-part, keyboard, opt. tamb. / hand drum
  (https://bit.ly/50-4068)

"This Is the Day the Lord Has Made" (Pss)
Allen Pote; Hope C5187
SATB, keyboard (https://bit.ly/C-5187)

Other Suggestions

Visuals:
  O Crucifix, resurrection, Acts 10:39a
  P Ps 118:29, singing, tents, gates, cornerstone
  E Butterfly, empty cross, open tomb, Christ returning
  G Basket/spices, open tomb, grave clothes, napkin,
     runners, tears, risen Christ, "I have seen..."
Introit: SA148, WS3044. "Make Way" (Pss, Easter)
Call to Worship: WSL29. "Christ is risen" (John, Easter)
Opening Prayer: WSL28. "Eternal God, rock (John, Easter)
Litany: C217. Easter Affirmations
Response: AH4081, C531, SH496, UM84. "Thank You, Lord"
  (Pss)
Benediction: N872 (John)
Theme Ideas: God: Glory of God, Inclusion, Jesus: Mind of
  Christ, Resurrection, Thanksgiving / Gratitude

Acts 2:14a, 22-32

[14a]But Peter, standing with the eleven, raised his voice and addressed them, . . .

[22]"You that are Israelites, listen to what I have to say: Jesus of Nazareth, a man attested to you by God with deeds of power, wonders, and signs that God did through him among you, as you yourselves know—[23]this man, handed over to you according to the definite plan and foreknowledge of God, you crucified and killed by the hands of those outside the law. [24]But God raised him up, having freed him from death, because it was impossible for him to be held in its power. [25]For David says concerning him,

'I saw the Lord always before me,
    for he is at my right hand so that I will not be shaken;
[26]therefore my heart was glad, and my tongue rejoiced;
    moreover my flesh will live in hope.
[27]For you will not abandon my soul to Hades,
    or let your Holy One experience corruption.
[28]You have made known to me the ways of life;
    you will make me full of gladness with your presence.'

[29]"Fellow Israelites, I may say to you confidently of our ancestor David that he both died and was buried, and his tomb is with us to this day. [30]Since he was a prophet, he knew that God had sworn with an oath to him that he would put one of his descendants on his throne. [31]Foreseeing this, David spoke of the resurrection of the Messiah, saying,

'He was not abandoned to Hades,
    nor did his flesh experience corruption.'

[32]This Jesus God raised up, and of that all of us are witnesses."

Psalm 16 (G810, N628, P165, UM748)

[1]Protect me, O God, for in you I take refuge.
[2]I say to the LORD, "You are my Lord;
    I have no good apart from you."
[3]As for the holy ones in the land, they are the noble,
    in whom is all my delight.
[4]Those who choose another god multiply their sorrows;
    their drink offerings of blood I will not pour out
    or take their names upon my lips.
[5]The LORD is my chosen portion and my cup;
    you hold my lot.
[6]The boundary lines have fallen for me in pleasant places;
    I have a goodly heritage.
[7]I bless the LORD who gives me counsel;
    in the night also my heart instructs me.
[8]I keep the LORD always before me;
    because he is at my right hand, I shall not be moved.
[9]Therefore my heart is glad, and my soul rejoices;
    my body also rests secure.
[10]For you do not give me up to Sheol,
    or let your faithful one see the Pit.
[11]You show me the path of life.
    In your presence there is fullness of joy;
    in your right hand are pleasures forevermore.

1 Peter 1:3-9

[3]Blessed be the God and Father of our Lord Jesus Christ! By his great mercy he has given us a new birth into a living hope through the resurrection of Jesus Christ from the dead, [4]and into an inheritance that is imperishable, undefiled, and unfading, kept in heaven for you, [5]who are being protected by the power of God through faith for a salvation ready to be revealed in the last time. [6]In this you rejoice, even if now for a little while you have had to suffer various trials, [7]so that the genuineness of your faith—being more precious than gold that, though perishable, is tested by fire—may be found to result in praise and glory and honor when Jesus Christ is revealed. [8]Although you have not seen him, you love him; and even though you do not see him now, you believe in him and rejoice with an indescribable and glorious joy, [9]for you are receiving the outcome of your faith, the salvation of your souls.

John 20:19-31

[19]When it was evening on that day, the first day of the week, and the doors of the house where the disciples had met were locked for fear of the Jews, Jesus came and stood among them and said, "Peace be with you." [20]After he said this, he showed them his hands and his side. Then the disciples rejoiced when they saw the Lord. [21]Jesus said to them again, "Peace be with you. As the Father has sent me, so I send you." [22]When he had said this, he breathed on them and said to them, "Receive the Holy Spirit. [23]If you forgive the sins of any, they are forgiven them; if you retain the sins of any, they are retained."

[24]But Thomas (who was called the Twin), one of the twelve, was not with them when Jesus came. [25]So the other disciples told him, "We have seen the Lord." But he said to them, "Unless I see the mark of the nails in his hands, and put my finger in the mark of the nails and my hand in his side, I will not believe."

[26]A week later his disciples were again in the house, and Thomas was with them. Although the doors were shut, Jesus came and stood among them and said, "Peace be with you." [27]Then he said to Thomas, "Put your finger here and see my hands. Reach out your hand and put it in my side. Do not doubt but believe." [28]Thomas answered him, "My Lord and my God!" [29]Jesus said to him, "Have you believed because you have seen me? Blessed are those who have not seen and yet have come to believe."

[30]Now Jesus did many other signs in the presence of his disciples, which are not written in this book. [31]But these are written so that you may come to believe that Jesus is the Messiah, the Son of God, and that through believing you may have life in his name.

Primary Hymns and Songs for the Day

"Hail the Day That Sees Him Rise" (Acts) (O)
    CG219, E214, N260, SA221, SH203, UM312, VU189
        H-3   Hbl-72; Chr-50; Desc-69; Org-78
        S-1   #213. Descant
"Alleluia, Alleluia" 32376 (Acts)
    CG196, E178, G240, P106, SA216, SH189, UM162, VU179
        H-3   Hbl-46; Chr-26
        S-1   #14. Desc.
"We Walk by Faith" (1 Pet, John)
    CG634, E209, EL635, G817, N256, P399, S2196, SH660
"That Easter Day with Joy Was Bright" (John, Easter)
    C229, CG204, E193, EL384 (PD), G254, P121
        H-3   Chr-19
"Dona Nobis Pacem" (John)
    C297, E712, EL753, G752, UM376 (PD)
"Thine Be the Glory" (Acts, John) (C)
    C218, CG222, EL376, G238, N253, P122, SA276, SH192,
    UM308, VU173 (Fr.)
        H-3   Hbl-98; Chr-195; Desc-59
        S-1   #190. Arrangement
        S-2   #95. Various treatments

Additional Hymn Suggestions

"This Joyful Eastertide" (Acts)
    E192, EL391, G244, N232, SA234, VU177
"Hail Thee, Festival Day" (Acts)
    E175, EL394, G277, N262, UM324, VU163
"How Firm a Foundation" (Acts, 1 Pet)
    C618, CG425, E636/637, EL796, G463, N407, P361, SA804,
    SH291, UM529 (PD), VU660
"To God Be the Glory" (1 Pet)
    C72, CG349, G634, P485, SA279, SH545, UM98 (PD)
"Jesus, the Very Thought of Thee" (1 Pet)
    C102, CG386, E642, EL754, G629, N507, P310, SA85, UM175
    (PD)
"Hope of the World" (1 Pet)
    C538, E472, G734, N46, P360, UM178, VU215
"Mothering God, You Gave Me Birth" (1 Pet, Comm.)
    C83, EL735, G7, N467, S2050, VU320
"The Day of Resurrection" (1 Pet, John, Easter)
    C228, CG214, E210, EL361, G233, N245, P118, SH186,
    UM303 (PD), VU164
"Depth of Mercy" 5412781 (1 Pet, John)
"O Sons and Daughters, Let Us Sing" (John)
    C220, CG212, E203, EL386/E387, G235/255, N244, P116
    (PD), SH190, UM317, VU170
"Christ Jesus Lay in Death's Strong Band" (John)
    E186, EL370, G237, P110, UM319 (PD)
"Breathe on Me, Breath of God" (John)
    C254, CG235, E508, G286, N292, P316, SA294, SH224/273,
    UM420 (PD), VU382 (Fr.)
"Holy Spirit, Truth Divine" (John)
    C241, EL398, N63, P321, SA285, UM465, VU368
"Let It Breathe on Me" (John)
    C260, N288, UM503
"Praise the Source of Faith and Learning" (John)
    N411, S2004
"God, How Can We Forgive" (John)
    G445, S2169
"In the Singing" (John, Comm.)
    EL466, G533, S2255
"Come, Share the Lord" (John, Comm.)
    C408, CG459, G510, S2269, VU469
"I Know that My Redeemer Lives!" (John)
    CG210, EL619 (PD), SA224, SH199

Additional Contemporary and Modern Suggestions

"I Will Enter His Gates" 1493 (Acts)
    S2270, SA337
"Foundation" 706151 (Acts, 1 Pet)
"Surely the Presence of the Lord" 7909 (Acts, John)
    C263, UM328; S-2 #200. Stanzas for soloist
"Holy Ground" 21198 (Acts, John)
    C112, G406, S2272, SA400
"Awesome in This Place" 847554 (Acts, John)
"I Believe In Jesus" 61282 (Acts, John)
"All Things Are Possible" 2245140 (Pss)
"More Precious than Silver" 11335 (Pss, 1 Pet)
"Knowing You" 1045238 (Pss, 1 Pet, John)
"Song of Hope" ("Heaven Come Down") 5111477 (1 Pet)
"My Tribute" 11218 (1 Pet)
    AH4080, C39, CG574, N14, SH434, UM99; V-8 p. 5. Vocal
    Solo
"Please Enter My Heart, Hosanna" 2485371 (1 Pet, John)
"I'm So Glad Jesus Lifted Me" (1 Pet, John)
    C529, EL860 (PD), N474, S2151
"God Is Good All the Time" 1729073 (1 Pet, John)
"Blessing, Honour and Glory" 1001179 (1 Pet, John, Easter)
    EL433
"There Is a Redeemer" 11483 (1 Pet, John)
    CG377, G443, SA204, SH495
"Our God Reigns" 8458 (John)
"My Life Is in You, Lord" 17315 (John)
"Open Our Eyes, Lord" 1572 (John)
    CG392, S2086, SA386, SH562
"Where the Spirit of the Lord Is" 27484 (John, Comm.)
    C264, S2119
"Here Is Bread, Here Is Wine" 983717 (John, Comm.)
    EL483, S2266
"Open the Eyes of My Heart" 2298355 (John)
    G452, SA270, SH378, WS3008
"The Power of Your Love" 917491 (John)
"In the Secret" 1810119 (John)

Vocal Solos

"Crown Him, the Risen King" (Acts, 1 Peter, Easter)
    V-10   p. 55
"The First Day of My Life" (John, Easter)
    V-1   p. 22

Anthems

"The Strife Is O'er" (Acts)
Arr. Robert J. Powell; MorningStar MSM-50-4019
SATB, organ, opt brass quartet, timp. (https://bit.ly/50-4019)

"A Better Resurrection" (1 Pet, John)
Craig Courtney; Beckenhorst CU1000
SATB *divisi, a cappella* (https://bit.ly/B-CU1000)

Other Suggestions

Visuals:
    O   Eleven men, preaching, crucifix, open tomb, heart,
            joy
    P   Cup, boundary line, prayer, joy, rest, path, hand
    E   Newborn, butterfly/chrysalis, gold/fire, joy
    G   Locked door, Jesus, "Peace . . . ," wind, wounds,
            John 20:29b
Litany: WSL33. "This is the good news" (1 Pet, Easter)
Prayers: N827 and N847 (John)
Offertory: WSL131. "Blessed One, the resurrection" (1 Pet)
Blessing: WSL27. "May the Christ who walks" (John, Easter)
Response: UM376. *"Dona Nobis Pacem"* (John)
Theme Ideas: Doubt, Faith, Holy Spirit, Hope, New Creation,
    Resurrection

Acts 2:14a, 36-41

14aBut Peter, standing with the eleven, raised his voice and addressed them, . . .

36"Therefore let the entire house of Israel know with certainty that God has made him both Lord and Messiah, this Jesus whom you crucified."

37Now when they heard this, they were cut to the heart and said to Peter and to the other apostles, "Brothers, what should we do?" 38Peter said to them, "Repent, and be baptized every one of you in the name of Jesus Christ so that your sins may be forgiven; and you will receive the gift of the Holy Spirit. 39For the promise is for you, for your children, and for all who are far away, everyone whom the Lord our God calls to him." 40And he testified with many other arguments and exhorted them, saying, "Save yourselves from this corrupt generation." 41So those who welcomed his message were baptized, and that day about three thousand persons were added.

Psalm 116:1-4, 12-19 (G655, N699, P228, SH344, UM837)

1I love the LORD, because he has heard
    my voice and my supplications.
2Because he inclined his ear to me,
    therefore I will call on him as long as I live.
3The snares of death encompassed me;
    the pangs of Sheol laid hold on me;
    I suffered distress and anguish.
4Then I called on the name of the LORD:
    "O LORD, I pray, save my life!"
. . . .
12What shall I return to the LORD
    for all his bounty to me?
13I will lift up the cup of salvation
    and call on the name of the LORD,
14I will pay my vows to the LORD
    in the presence of all his people.
15Precious in the sight of the LORD
    is the death of his faithful ones.
16O LORD, I am your servant;
    I am your servant, the child of your serving girl.
    You have loosed my bonds.
17I will offer to you a thanksgiving sacrifice
    and call on the name of the LORD.
18I will pay my vows to the LORD
    in the presence of all his people,
19in the courts of the house of the LORD,
    in your midst, O Jerusalem.
Praise the LORD!

1 Peter 1:17-23

17If you invoke as Father the one who judges all people impartially according to their deeds, live in reverent fear during the time of your exile. 18You know that you were ransomed from the futile ways inherited from your ancestors, not with perishable things like silver or gold, 19but with the precious blood of Christ, like that of a lamb without defect or blemish. 20He was destined before the foundation of the world, but was revealed at the end of the ages for your sake. 21Through him you have come to trust in God, who raised him from the dead and gave him glory, so that your faith and hope are set on God.

22Now that you have purified your souls by your obedience to the truth so that you have genuine mutual love, love one another deeply from the heart. 23You have been born anew, not of perishable but of imperishable seed, through the living and enduring word of God.

Luke 24:13-35

13Now on that same day two of them were going to a village called Emmaus, about seven miles from Jerusalem, 14and talking with each other about all these things that had happened. 15While they were talking and discussing, Jesus himself came near and went with them, 16but their eyes were kept from recognizing him. 17And he said to them, "What are you discussing with each other while you walk along?" They stood still, looking sad. 18Then one of them, whose name was Cleopas, answered him, "Are you the only stranger in Jerusalem who does not know the things that have taken place there in these days?" 19He asked them, "What things?" They replied, "The things about Jesus of Nazareth, who was a prophet mighty in deed and word before God and all the people, 20and how our chief priests and leaders handed him over to be condemned to death and crucified him. 21But we had hoped that he was the one to redeem Israel. Yes, and besides all this, it is now the third day since these things took place. 22Moreover, some women of our group astounded us. They were at the tomb early this morning, 23and when they did not find his body there, they came back and told us that they had indeed seen a vision of angels who said that he was alive. 24Some of those who were with us went to the tomb and found it just as the women had said; but they did not see him." 25Then he said to them, "Oh, how foolish you are, and how slow of heart to believe all that the prophets have declared! 26Was it not necessary that the Messiah should suffer these things and then enter into his glory?" 27Then beginning with Moses and all the prophets, he interpreted to them the things about himself in all the scriptures.

28As they came near the village to which they were going, he walked ahead as if he were going on. 29But they urged him strongly, saying, "Stay with us, because it is almost evening and the day is now nearly over." So he went in to stay with them. 30When he was at the table with them, he took bread, blessed and broke it, and gave it to them. 31Then their eyes were opened, and they recognized him; and he vanished from their sight. 32They said to each other, "Were not our hearts burning within us while he was talking to us on the road, while he was opening the scriptures to us?" 33That same hour they got up and returned to Jerusalem; and they found the eleven and their companions gathered together. 34They were saying, "The Lord has risen indeed, and he has appeared to Simon!" 35Then they told what had happened on the road, and how he had been made known to them in the breaking of the bread.

Primary Hymns and Songs for the Day

"We Know That Christ Is Raised" (Acts) (O)
E296, EL449, G485, P495, UM610, VU448
- H-3   Hbl-100; Chr-214; Desc-38; Org-37
- S-1   #118-127. Various treatments

"I Love the Lord" 1168957 (Pss)
CG613, G799, P362, N511, SH343, VU617, WS3142

"Jesus, the Very Thought of Thee" (1 Pet)
C102, CG386, E642, EL754, G629, N507, P310, SA85, UM175 (PD)

"Christ Is Alive" (Luke)
CG205, E182, EL389, G246, P108, SA217, UM318, VU158
- H-3   Hbl-91; Chr-129, 176; Desc-101; Org-167
- S-1   #334-5. Descant and harmonization

"Day of Arising" (Luke, Comm.)
CG203, G252, EL374, WS3086
- H-3   Hbl-77; Chr-136; Desc-21; Org-16
- S-1   #50-51. Flute and vocal desc.

"Open My Eyes, That I May See" (Luke)
C586, CG395, G451, P324, SH583, UM454, VU371
- H-3   Chr-157; Org-108

"Lord, I Want to Be a Christian" (1 Pet)
C589, CG507, G729, N454, P372 (PD), SH621, UM402
- H-3   Chr-130

Additional Hymn Suggestions

"What Is This Place" (Acts)
C289, EL524, G404

"Let Us Talents and Tongues Employ" (Acts)
C422, CG458, EL674, G526, N347, P514, VU468

"Let Us Break Bread Together" (Acts, Comm.)
AH4140, C425, CG461, EL471 (PD), G525, N330, P513, SH674, UM618, VU480

"Blessed Assurance" (1 Pet)
AH4083, C543, CG619, EL638, G839, N473, P341, SA455, SH320, UM369 (PD), VU337

"Amazing Grace" (1 Pet)
AH4091, C546, CG587, E671, EL779, G649, N547/548, P280, SA453, SH523, UM378 (PD), VU266 (Fr.)

"Jesus, Priceless Treasure" (1 Pet)
E701, EL775, G830, N480 P365, UM532 (PD), VU667 and VU668 (Fr.)

"Healer of Our Every Ill" (1 Pet)
C506, EL612, G795, S2213, SH339, VU619

"The King Shall Come When Morning Dawns" (1 Pet)
CG97, E73, EL260, SH346

"Baptized in Water" (1 Pet, Baptism)
CG449, E294, EL456, G482, P492, S2248, SH666

"Leaning on the Everlasting Arms" (Luke)
AH4100, C560, CG640, EL774, G837, N471, SA906, UM133

"Cuando el Pobre" ("When the Poor Ones") (Luke)
C662, EL725, G762, P407, SH240, UM434, VU702

"By Gracious Powers" (Luke)
E695/696, EL626, G818, N413, P342, UM517

"The Bread of Life for All Is Broken" (Luke)
E342, N333, UM633

"God the Sculptor of the Mountains" (Luke)
EL736, G5, S2060

"Just a Closer Walk with Thee" (Luke)
C557, EL697, G835, S2158, SH584

"We Walk by Faith" (Luke)
CG634, E209, EL635, G817, N256, P399, S2196, SH660

"Come, Share the Lord" (Luke, Comm.)
C408, CG459, G510, S2269, VU469

"Feed Us, Lord" 4636207 (Luke, Comm.)
G501, WS3167

"Be Known to Us in Breaking Bread" (Luke)
C398, G500, N342, P505

Additional Contemporary and Modern Suggestions

"Able" 1256560 (Acts, 1 Pet)

"Come, Be Baptized" 239485 (Acts, Baptism)
CG451, S2252

"I Will Call upon the Lord" 11263 (Pss)
G621, S2002

"We Bring the Sacrifice of Praise" 9990 (Pss)

"I Love You, Lord" 25266 (Pss)
CG362, G627, S2068, SA369, SH417

"Amazing Grace" ("My Chains Are Gone") 4768151 (1 Pet)

"Take, O Take Me as I Am" 4562041 (1 Pet)
EL814, G698, SH620, WS3119

"More Precious than Silver" 11335 (1 Pet)

"Live in Charity" ("Ubi Caritas") (1 Pet)
C523, EL642, G205, S2179

"They'll Know We Are Christians" 26997 (1 Pet)
AH4074, C494, CG272, G300, S2223, SH232

"Bind Us Together" 1228 (1 Pet)

"Agnus Dei" 626713 (1 Pet, Easter)
CG351

"Hallelujah to the Lamb" 2316323 (1 Pet, Easter)

"We Will Worship the Lamb" 208409 (1 Pet, Easter)

"Grace Like Rain" 3689877 (1 Pet)

"Turn Your Eyes upon Jesus" 15960 (Luke)
CG472, SA445, UM349

"Open Our Eyes, Lord" 1572 (Luke)
CG392, S2086, SA386, SH562

"The Servant Song" 72673 (Luke)
C490, CG289, EL659, G727, N539, S2222, SA1005, SH264, VU595

"Open the Eyes of My Heart" 2298355 (Luke)
G452, SA270, SH378, WS3008

Vocal Solos

"Wash, O God, Our Sons and Daughters" (Acts, Baptism)
V-5 (1)   p. 64

"Worthy Is the Lamb" (1 Pet, Easter)
V-8   p. 228

"Just a Closer Walk with Thee" (Luke)
V-5 (2)   p. 31
V-8   p. 323

Anthems

"Assurance" (1 Pet)
arr. John Ness Beck; Beckenhorst BP1097
SATB, keyboard (https://bit.ly/BP1097)

"Alleluia! Jesus Is Risen!" (Luke)
Michael Burkhardt; MorningStar MSM-50-4066
SATB, organ, opt. brass (https://bit.ly/MSM-50-4066)

Other Suggestions

Visuals:
- **O**   Christus Rex, repent, baptism, gift, Spirit, 3000
- **P**   Ear, snare, anguish, prayer, cup, shackles, gifts
- **E**   Silver/gold, blood, lamb, Jesus, baptism, Bible
- **G**   Jesus, three men walking, Bible, broken bread, burning heart, blindness/vision

Introit: 2273, EL529, G392, S2273, SH611. "Jesus, We Are Here" (Luke)

Call to Worship: WSL31. "The Risen Savior" (1 Pet)

Opening Prayer: N831 (Luke)

Call to Communion: C418. Behold These Emblems (Luke)

Theme Ideas: Assurance, Baptism, Bread of Life, Communion, Grace, Holy Spirit, Resurrection

BOOKS FOR BUILDING BETTER WORSHIP

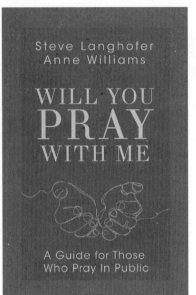

WILL YOU PRAY WITH ME: A Guide for Those Who Pray in Public
by Steve Langhofer and Anne Williams
Teaches all who lead others in prayer new methods and techniques for writing and leading prayers in traditional church services and many other less conventional circumstances.

9781791013431

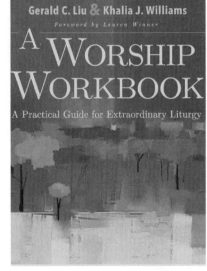

A WORSHIP WORKBOOK: A Practical Guide for Extraordinary Liturgy
by Gerald C. Liu and Khalia J. Williams
This book introduc[es] crucial and under-examined liturgica[l] and social concept[s] for students and leaders of worship.

9781501896569

LITURGIES FROM BELOW: Praying with People at the Ends of the World
by Cláudio Carvalhaes
This collection of prayers and liturgies express love, hope, anger, questions, and pain for pastors and other leaders to use in worship services and other gatherings.

9781791007355

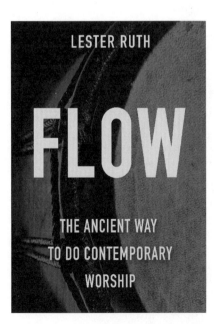

FLOW: The Ancient Way to Do Contemporary Worship
by Lester Ruth
Flow teaches leade[rs] how to create worship services using classic worsh[ip] order in a way tha[t] feels legitimately and authentically contemporary.

9781501898990

AbingdonPress.com

Cokesbury.com

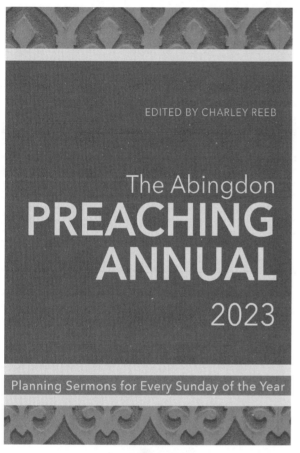

Acts 2:42-47

[42]They devoted themselves to the apostles' teaching and fellowship, to the breaking of bread and the prayers.

[43]Awe came upon everyone, because many wonders and signs were being done by the apostles. [44]All who believed were together and had all things in common; [45]they would sell their possessions and goods and distribute the proceeds to all, as any had need. [46]Day by day, as they spent much time together in the temple, they broke bread at home and ate their food with glad and generous hearts, [47]praising God and having the goodwill of all the people. And day by day the Lord added to their number those who were being saved.

Psalm 23 (G473/801-803, N633, P170-175, SH295/307, UM134/754)

[1]The LORD is my shepherd, I shall not want.
[2]   He makes me lie down in green pastures;
he leads me beside still waters;
[3]   he restores my soul.
He leads me in right paths
    for his name's sake.
[4]Even though I walk through the darkest valley,
    I fear no evil;
for you are with me;
    your rod and your staff—
    they comfort me.
[5]You prepare a table before me
    in the presence of my enemies;
you anoint my head with oil;
    my cup overflows.
[6]Surely goodness and mercy shall follow me
    all the days of my life,
and I shall dwell in the house of the LORD
    my whole life long.

1 Peter 2:19-25

[19]For it is a credit to you if, being aware of God, you endure pain while suffering unjustly. [20]If you endure when you are beaten for doing wrong, what credit is that? But if you endure when you do right and suffer for it, you have God's approval. [21]For to this you have been called, because Christ also suffered for you, leaving you an example, so that you should follow in his steps.
[22]   "He committed no sin,
        and no deceit was found in his mouth."
[23]When he was abused, he did not return abuse; when he suffered, he did not threaten; but he entrusted himself to the one who judges justly. [24]He himself bore our sins in his body on the cross, so that, free from sins, we might live for righteousness; by his wounds you have been healed. [25]For you were going astray like sheep, but now you have returned to the shepherd and guardian of your souls.

John 10:1-10

[1]"Very truly, I tell you, anyone who does not enter the sheepfold by the gate but climbs in by another way is a thief and a bandit. [2]The one who enters by the gate is the shepherd of the sheep. [3]The gatekeeper opens the gate for him, and the sheep hear his voice. He calls his own sheep by name and leads them out. [4]When he has brought out all his own, he goes ahead of them, and the sheep follow him because they know his voice. [5]They will not follow a stranger, but they will run from him because they do not know the voice of strangers." [6]Jesus used this figure of speech with them, but they did not understand what he was saying to them.

[7]So again Jesus said to them, "Very truly, I tell you, I am the gate for the sheep. [8]All who came before me are thieves and bandits; but the sheep did not listen to them. [9]I am the gate. Whoever enters by me will be saved, and will come in and go out and find pasture. [10]The thief comes only to steal and kill and destroy. I came that they may have life, and have it abundantly."

Primary Hymns and Songs for the Day

"The Lord's My Shepherd, I'll Not Want" (Pss, John) (O)
C78/79, CG65, EL778, G801, N479, P170, SA62, SH375, UM136, VU747/748

"Where Charity and Love Prevail" (Acts)
CG264, EL359, G316, N396, SH271
     H-3   Hbl-71, 104; Chr-111-112, 219; Desc-95; Org-143
     S-2   #162. Harmonization
E581, UM549

"The King of Love My Shepherd Is" (Pss, 1 Pet)
CG64, E645, EL502, G802, P171, SA61, SH359, UM138 (PD), VU273
     S-1   #298-299. Harms.

"Shepherd Me, O God" (Pss, John)
EL780, G473, S2058, SH365

"They'll Know We Are Christians" 26997 (Acts) (C)
AH4074, C494, CG272, G300, S2223, SH232

Additional Hymn Suggestions

"Let Us Talents and Tongues Employ" (Acts)
C422, CG458, EL674, G526, N347, P514, VU468

"O For a World" (Acts)
C683, G372, N575, P386, VU697

"Great Is Thy Faithfulness" (Acts)
AH4011, C86, CG48, EL733, G39, N423, P276, SA26, SH48, UM140, VU288

"Together We Serve" (Acts)
G767, S2175

"When God Restored Our Common Life" (Acts)
G74, S2182

"In the Midst of New Dimensions" (Acts)
G315, N391, S2238

"We All Are One in Mission" (Acts)
CG269, EL576, G733, P435, S2243

"Sweet, Sweet Spirit" (Acts, 1 Pet)
C261, CG241, G408, N293, P398, SH410, UM334

"I Come with Joy" (Acts, Comm.)
C420, CG456, E304, EL482, G515, N349, P507, SH682, UM617, VU477

"Let Us Break Bread Together" (Acts, Comm.)
AH4140, C425, CG461, EL471 (PD), G525, N330, P513, SH674, UM618, VU480

"Come, Share the Lord" (Acts, Comm.)
C408, CG459, G510, S2269, VU469

"Precious Lord, Take My Hand" (Pss)
C628, CG400, EL773, G834, N472, P404, SH336, UM474, VU670

"Send Me, Lord" (Pss)
C447, EL809, G746, N360, SH723, UM497, VU572

"My Shepherd Will Supply My Need" (Pss)
C80, CG66, E664, EL782 (PD), G803, N247, P172, SH44

"Savior, Like a Shepherd Lead Us" (Pss, John) (O)
C558, CG405, E708, EL789, G187, N252, P387, SH538, UM381 (PD)

"Lead Me, Guide Me" (Pss, John)
C583, CG403, EL768, G740, S2214, SH582

"In the Cross of Christ I Glory" (1 Pet)
C207, CG183, E441, EL324, G213, N193, P84, SA174, UM295

"Christ Is Alive" (1 Pet)
CG205, E182, EL389, G246, P108, SA217, UM318, VU158

"O Jesus, I Have Promised" (1 Pet)
C612, E655, EL810, G724/725, N493, P388/389, SA613, SH623, UM396 (PD), VU120

"Take Up Thy Cross" (1 Pet)
E675, EL667, G718, N204, P393, SH605, UM415, VU561

"God of Grace and God of Glory" (1 Pet)
C464, CG285, E594/595, EL705, G307, N436, P420, SA814, SH250, UM577, VU686

"Lord of the Dance" 78529 (John, Easter)
G157, P302, SA141, UM261, VU352

"You Satisfy the Hungry Heart" (John, Comm.)
C429, CG468, EL484, G523, P521, SH672, UM629, VU478

"God Be With You Till We Meet Again" (John) (C)
C434, CG523, EL536, G541/542, N81, P540, SA1027, UM672/673, VU422/423

Additional Contemporary and Modern Suggestions

"If You Believe and I Believe" 3273104 (Acts)

"One Bread, One Body" (Acts, Comm.)
C393, EL496, G530, SH678, UM620, VU467

"Make Us One" 695737 (Acts)

"One God and Father of Us All" 3417678 (Acts)

"Nothing Can Trouble" ("*Nada Te Turbe*") (Pss)
CG73, G820, N772, S2054, SH292, VU290

"God Is Good All the Time" 1729073 (Pss)

"Gentle Shepherd" 15609 (Pss)

"Your Grace Is Enough" 4477026 (Pss)

"God Will Make a Way" 458620 (Pss)
SA492, SH57

"For Us" 7119349 (Pss)

"The King of Love My Shepherd Is" 7023979 (Pss)

"Lead Me, Lord" 1609045 (Pss, 1 Pet)

"His Name Is Wonderful" 1122230 (Pss, John)
CG343, SH454, UM174

"Jesus, Name above All Names" 21291 (1 Pet)
S2071, SA82

"Amen, Amen" (1 Pet)
N161, P299, S2072

"The Power of the Cross" 4490766 (1 Pet, Easter)
CG190, WS3085

"People Need the Lord" 18084 (John)
S2244, SA418

"Who Can Satisfy My Soul Like You?" 208492 (John)

Vocal Solos

"The Lord Is My Shepherd" (Pss, John)
V-5 (3)   p. 30

"My Shepherd Will Supply My Need" (Pss, John)
V-10   p. 4

"Maybe the Rain" (Pss, John)
V-5 (2)   p. 27

"In the Image of God" (1 Pet)
V-8   p. 362

Anthems

"My Song in the Night" (Pss, 1 Pet, John)
Terre Johnson; MorningStar MSM-50-3104
SATB, cello, piano (https://bit.ly/50-3104)

"Savior, Like a Shepherd Lead Us" (Pss, John)
Arr. Heather Sorenson; Hal Lenoard 00195516
SATB, piano, opt. bluegrass ens. (https://bit.ly/HL95516)

Other Suggestions

Visuals:
     O   Teaching, fellowship, broken bread, prayer, meal
     P   Shepherd/sheep, pasture, lake, path, valley, rod, staff, banquet table, cup, sanctuary
     E   Whip/club, Passion, crucifix, healing, sheep
     G   Sheepfold, gate, robber's mask, sheep/shepherd

Canticle: UM137. Ps 23 (Pss, John)
Litany: UM556. Litany for Christian Unity (Acts)
Theme Ideas: Discipleship / Following God, Endurance, God: Shepherd, Holy Spirit, Unity

Acts 7:55-60

[55]But filled with the Holy Spirit, he gazed into heaven and saw the glory of God and Jesus standing at the right hand of God. [56]"Look," he said, "I see the heavens opened and the Son of Man standing at the right hand of God!" [57]But they covered their ears, and with a loud shout all rushed together against him. [58]Then they dragged him out of the city and began to stone him; and the witnesses laid their coats at the feet of a young man named Saul. [59]While they were stoning Stephen, he prayed, "Lord Jesus, receive my spirit." [60]Then he knelt down and cried out in a loud voice, "Lord, do not hold this sin against them." When he had said this, he died.

Psalm 31:1-5, 15-16 (G214/811, N640/641, P182/183, UM764)

[1]In you, O Lord, I seek refuge;
 do not let me ever be put to shame;
 in your righteousness deliver me.
[2]Incline your ear to me;
 rescue me speedily.
Be a rock of refuge for me,
 a strong fortress to save me.
[3]You are indeed my rock and my fortress;
 for your name's sake lead me and guide me,
[4]take me out of the net that is hidden for me,
 for you are my refuge.
[5]Into your hand I commit my spirit;
 you have redeemed me, O Lord, faithful God.

. . . .

[15]My times are in your hand;
 deliver me from the hand of my enemies and persecutors.
[16]Let your face shine upon your servant;
 save me in your steadfast love.

1 Peter 2:2-10

[2]Like newborn infants, long for the pure, spiritual milk, so that by it you may grow into salvation—[3]if indeed you have tasted that the Lord is good.

[4]Come to him, a living stone, though rejected by mortals yet chosen and precious in God's sight, and [5]like living stones, let yourselves be built into a spiritual house, to be a holy priesthood, to offer spiritual sacrifices acceptable to God through Jesus Christ. [6]For it stands in scripture:

 "See, I am laying in Zion a stone,
 a cornerstone chosen and precious;
 and whoever believes in him will not be put to shame."

[7]To you then who believe, he is precious; but for those who do not believe,

 "The stone that the builders rejected
 has become the very head of the corner,"

[8]and

 "A stone that makes them stumble,
 and a rock that makes them fall."

They stumble because they disobey the word, as they were destined to do.

[9]But you are a chosen race, a royal priesthood, a holy nation, God's own people, in order that you may proclaim the mighty acts of him who called you out of darkness into his marvelous light.

[10]Once you were not a people,
 but now you are God's people;
 once you had not received mercy,
 but now you have received mercy.

John 14:1-14

[1]"Do not let your hearts be troubled. Believe in God, believe also in me. [2]In my Father's house there are many dwelling places. If it were not so, would I have told you that I go to prepare a place for you? [3]And if I go and prepare a place for you, I will come again and will take you to myself, so that where I am, there you may be also. [4]And you know the way to the place where I am going." [5]Thomas said to him, "Lord, we do not know where you are going. How can we know the way?" [6]Jesus said to him, "I am the way, and the truth, and the life. No one comes to the Father except through me. [7]If you know me, you will know my Father also. From now on you do know him and have seen him."

[8]Philip said to him, "Lord, show us the Father, and we will be satisfied." [9]Jesus said to him, "Have I been with you all this time, Philip, and you still do not know me? Whoever has seen me has seen the Father. How can you say, 'Show us the Father'? [10]Do you not believe that I am in the Father and the Father is in me? The words that I say to you I do not speak on my own; but the Father who dwells in me does his works. [11]Believe me that I am in the Father and the Father is in me; but if you do not, then believe me because of the works themselves. [12]Very truly, I tell you, the one who believes in me will also do the works that I do and, in fact, will do greater works than these, because I am going to the Father. [13]I will do whatever you ask in my name, so that the Father may be glorified in the Son. [14]If in my name you ask me for anything, I will do it."

Primary Hymns and Songs for the Day

"The Church's One Foundation" (1 Pet, John) (O)
    C272, CG246, E525, EL654, G321, N386, P442, SH233,
    UM545/546, VU332 (Fr.)
        H-3   Hbl-94; Chr-180; Desc-16; Org-9
        S-1   #25-26. Desc. and harm.
"Be Still, My Soul" (Acts, Pss)
    C566, CG57, G819, N488, SH330, UM534, VU652
        H-3   Chr-36
"Nothing Can Trouble" (*"Nada Te Turbe"*) (John)
    CG73, G820, N772, S2054, SH292, VU290
"His Eye Is on the Sparrow" (John)
    C82, G661, N475, S2146, SH322
"Christ Is Made the Sure Foundation" (1 Pet, Comm.) (C)
    C275, CG248, E518, EL645, G394, N400, P416/417, SA246,
    SH225, UM559 (PD), VU325
        H-3   Chr-49; Desc-103; Org-180
        S-1   #346. Desc.

Additional Hymn Suggestions

"I'll Praise My Maker While I've Breath" (Acts)
    C20, CG336, E429 (PD), G806, P253, UM60, VU867
"God of Grace and God of Glory" (Acts)
    C464, CG285, E594/595, EL705, G307, N436, P420, SA814,
    SH250, UM577, VU686
"The Head That Once Was Crowned" (Acts)
    CG209, E483, EL432, P149, SA232, UM326 (PD), VU190
"Deep in the Shadows of the Past" (Acts)
    G50, N320, P330, S2246
"Guide My Feet" (Acts, Pss)
    CG637, G741, N497, P354, S2208, SH54
"Lead Me, Guide Me" (Acts, Pss)
    C583, CG403, EL768, G740, S2214, SH582
"How Firm a Foundation" (Acts, 1 Pet)
    C618, CG425, E636/637, EL796, G463, N407, P361, SA804,
    SH291, UM529 (PD), VU660
"From All That Dwell Below the Skies" (1 Pet)
    C49, CG330, E380, G327, N27, P229, UM101 (PD)
"Sing Praise to God Who Reigns Above" (1 Pet)
    C6, CG315, E408, EL871, G645, N6, P483, UM126 (PD),
    VU216
"God Is Here" (1 Pet)
    C280, CG298, EL526, G409, N70, P461, UM660, VU389
"Christ, the Great Foundation" (1 Pet)
    G361, P443
"Come, O Spirit, Dwell Among Us" (1 Pet)
    G280, N267, P129, VU198
"Spirit Divine, Attend Our Prayers" (John)
    E509, G407, P325, SA310, SH571, VU385
"Come, My Way, My Truth, My Life" (John)
    E487, EL816, N331, UM164 (PD), VU628
"Prayer Is the Soul's Sincere Desire" (John)
    CG391, N508, SA784, UM492
"Here, O Lord, Your Servants Gather" (John)
    C278, EL530, G311, N72, P465, UM552, VU362
"Womb of Life" (John, Comm.)
    C14, G3, N274, S2046
"Healer of Our Every Ill" (John)
    C506, EL612, G795, S2213, SH339, VU619
"In Remembrance of Me" 25156 (John, Comm.)
    C403, CG462, G521, S2254, SH667
"In God Alone" (John)
    G814, WS3135
"Let Us Break Bread Together" (Comm.)
    AH4140, C425, CG461, EL471 (PD), G525, N330, P513,
    SH674, UM618, VU480

Additional Contemporary and Modern Suggestions

"Holy Ground" 21198 (Acts)
    C112, G406, S2272, SA400
"Foundation" 706151 (Acts, 1 Pet)
"You Are the Light" 6238098 (Acts, 1 Pet)
"Guide My Feet" (Acts, Pss)
    CG637, G741, N497, P354, S2208, SH54
"I Will Call upon the Lord" 11263 (Pss)
    G621, S2002
"Praise Him" 684779 (Pss)
"Rock of Ages" 2240547 (Pss)
"Lead Me, Lord" 1609045 (Pss)
"God Will Make a Way" 458620 (Pss)
    SA492, SH57
"More Precious than Silver" 11335 (1 Pet)
"Grace Alone" 2335524 (1 Pet)
    CG43, S2162, SA699.
"Light of the World" 73342 (1 Pet)
"Cornerstone" 6158927 (1 Pet)
"Knowing You" 1045238 (1 Pet)
"Marvelous Light" 4491002 (1 Pet)
"Here I Am to Worship" 3266032 (1 Pet)
    CG297, SA114, SH395, WS3177
"Be Glorified" 429226 (John)
"Be Glorified" 2732646 (John)
"Behold, What Manner of Love" 1596 (John)
"Someone Asked the Question" 1640279 (John)
    N523, S2144
"Halle, Halle, Halleluja" 2659190 (John, Easter)
    C41, CG433, EL172, G591, N236, S2026, SH694, VU958
"That's Why We Praise Him" 2668576 (John, Easter)
"For All You've Done" 4254689 (John, Easter)
"Give Us Your Peace" 5767807 (John)
"Jesus I Trust in You 4510828 (John)
"My Savior Lives" 4882965 (John, Easter)

Vocal Solos

"How Firm a Foundation" (1 Pet)
    V-6   p. 31
"Because He Lives" (1 Pet, Easter)
    V-8   p. 24
"The Call" (John)
    V-4   p. 31
"In Bright Mansions Above" (John)
    V-4   p. 39

Anthems

"I'll Fly Away" (John)
Arr. Brandon A. Boyd; MorningStar MSM-50-5117
SATB *divisi*, piano, opt. bass, perc. (https://bit.ly/50-5117)

"As Tenderly as a Father" (John, Christian Home)
John Shepherd; Hinshaw Music HMC-472
2-part, keyboard (https://bit.ly/H-472)

Other Suggestions

Visuals:
    O   Spirit/flames/dove, Christ, heavens opened, stones,
            coats, Acts 7:59b, 60b, life/death
    P   Rock, Ps 31:3a, fortress, net, hands, Ps 31:16ab
    E   Newborn, milk, stone(s), cornerstone, stumbling
            blocks, 1 Pet 2:9a, crowd, nations, dark/light
    G   Hearts, mourning, dwellings, Christ, works,
            John 14:13, 14
Prayer: N856. Eternal Life (John)
Prayer of Confession: N836 (Christian Home)
Theme Ideas: Comfort, God: Providence / God our Help, Holy
    Spirit, Jesus: Cornerstone, Lament

Acts 17:22-31

[22]Then Paul stood in front of the Areopagus and said, "Athenians, I see how extremely religious you are in every way. [23]For as I went through the city and looked carefully at the objects of your worship, I found among them an altar with the inscription, 'To an unknown god.' What therefore you worship as unknown, this I proclaim to you. [24]The God who made the world and everything in it, he who is Lord of heaven and earth, does not live in shrines made by human hands, [25]nor is he served by human hands, as though he needed anything, since he himself gives to all mortals life and breath and all things. [26]From one ancestor he made all nations to inhabit the whole earth, and he allotted the times of their existence and the boundaries of the places where they would live, [27]so that they would search for God and perhaps grope for him and find him—though indeed he is not far from each one of us. [28]For 'In him we live and move and have our being'; as even some of your own poets have said,
'For we too are his offspring.'

[29]Since we are God's offspring, we ought not to think that the deity is like gold, or silver, or stone, an image formed by the art and imagination of mortals. [30]While God has overlooked the times of human ignorance, now he commands all people everywhere to repent, [31]because he has fixed a day on which he will have the world judged in righteousness by a man whom he has appointed, and of this he has given assurance to all by raising him from the dead."

Psalm 66:8-20 (G54, N662, UM790)

[8]Bless our God, O peoples,
    let the sound of his praise be heard,
[9]who has kept us among the living,
    and has not let our feet slip.
[10]For you, O God, have tested us;
    you have tried us as silver is tried.
[11]You brought us into the net;
    you laid burdens on our backs;
[12]you let people ride over our heads;
    we went through fire and through water;
yet you have brought us out to a spacious place.
[13]I will come into your house with burnt offerings;
    I will pay you my vows,
[14]those that my lips uttered
    and my mouth promised when I was in trouble.
[15]I will offer to you burnt offerings of fatlings,
    with the smoke of the sacrifice of rams;
I will make an offering of bulls and goats.   *[Selah]*
[16]Come and hear, all you who fear God,
    and I will tell what he has done for me.
[17]I cried aloud to him,
    and he was extolled with my tongue.
[18]If I had cherished iniquity in my heart,
    the Lord would not have listened.
[19]But truly God has listened;
    he has given heed to the words of my prayer.
[20]Blessed be God,
    because he has not rejected my prayer
    or removed his steadfast love from me.

1 Peter 3:13-22

[13]Now who will harm you if you are eager to do what is good? [14]But even if you do suffer for doing what is right, you are blessed. Do not fear what they fear, and do not be intimidated, [15]but in your hearts sanctify Christ as Lord. Always be ready to make your defense to anyone who demands from you an accounting for the hope that is in you; [16]yet do it with gentleness and reverence. Keep your conscience clear, so that, when you are maligned, those who abuse you for your good conduct in Christ may be put to shame. [17]For it is better to suffer for doing good, if suffering should be God's will, than to suffer for doing evil. [18]For Christ also suffered for sins once for all, the righteous for the unrighteous, in order to bring you to God. He was put to death in the flesh, but made alive in the spirit, [19]in which also he went and made a proclamation to the spirits in prison, [20]who in former times did not obey, when God waited patiently in the days of Noah, during the building of the ark, in which a few, that is, eight persons, were saved through water. [21]And baptism, which this prefigured, now saves you—not as a removal of dirt from the body, but as an appeal to God for a good conscience, through the resurrection of Jesus Christ, [22]who has gone into heaven and is at the right hand of God, with angels, authorities, and powers made subject to him.

John 14:15-21

[15]"If you love me, you will keep my commandments. [16]And I will ask the Father, and he will give you another Advocate, to be with you forever. [17]This is the Spirit of truth, whom the world cannot receive, because it neither sees him nor knows him. You know him, because he abides with you, and he will be in you.

[18]"I will not leave you orphaned; I am coming to you. [19]In a little while the world will no longer see me, but you will see me; because I live, you also will live. [20]On that day you will know that I am in my Father, and you in me, and I in you. [21]They who have my commandments and keep them are those who love me; and those who love me will be loved by my Father, and I will love them and reveal myself to them."

Primary Hymns and Songs for the Day
"I Sing the Almighty Power of God" (Acts, John) (O)
  C64, G32, N12, P288 (PD), SA36
    H-3   Hbl-16, 22, 68; Chr-101; Desc-37
    S-1   #115. Harmonization
  CG19, E398, UM152 (PD)
    H-3   Hbl-44; Chr-21; Desc-40; Org-40
    S-1   #131-132. Introduction and descant
  VU231 (PD)
    H-3   Hbl-44; Chr-21; Desc-40; Org-40
    S-1   #131-132. Intro. and desc.
"Spirit of the Living God" 23488 (Acts, John)
    S-1   #212. Vocal desc. idea
  C259, CG233, G288, N283, P322, SA312/313, SH555,
  UM393, VU376
"Love Divine, All Loves Excelling" (John) (C)
  C517, CG281, E657, EL631, G366, N43, P376, SA262,
  SH353/354, UM384 (PD), VU333
    H-3   Chr-134; Desc-18; Org-13
    S-1   #41-42. Desc. and harm.

Additional Hymn Suggestions
"All Creatures of Our God and King" (Acts)
  C22, CG307, E400, EL835, G15, N17, P455, SA2, SH16,
  UM62, VU217 (Fr.)
"For the Beauty of the Earth" (Acts, Comm.)
  C56, CG341, E416, EL879, G14, P473, N28, SA14, SH21,
  UM92 (PD), VU226
"From All That Dwell Below the Skies" (Acts)
  C49, CG330, E380, G327, N27, P229, UM101 (PD)
"I Need Thee Every Hour" (Acts)
  C578, CG404, G735, N517, SA707, UM397, VU671
"Near to the Heart of God" (Acts)
  C581, CG383, G824, P527, UM472 (PD)
"O for a Closer Walk with God" (Acts)
  CG679, E684, G739, N450, P396, SA612
"I Greet Thee, Who My Sure Redeemer Art" (Acts, 1 Pet)
  G624, N251, P457, VU393
"Rejoice, the Lord Is King" (Acts, 1 Pet)
  C699, CG215, E481, EL430, G363, N303, P155, SA271,
  SH213, UM715/716, VU213
"O For a World" (1 Pet)
  C683, G372, N575, P386, VU697
"To God Be the Glory" (1 Pet)
  C72, CG349, G634, P485, SA279, SH545, UM98 (PD)
"Rejoice, Ye Pure in Heart" (1 Pet)
  C15, CG312, E556/557, EL873/874, G804, N55/71,
  P145/146, UM160/161
"Wash, O God, Our Sons and Daughters" (1 Pet, Baptism)
  C365, EL445, G490, SH669, UM605, VU442
"We Know That Christ Is Raised" (1 Pet, Baptism)
  E296, EL449, G485, P495, UM610, VU448
"Wonder of Wonders" (1 Pet, Baptism)
  C378, G489, N328, P499, S2247
"Spirit Divine, Attend Our Prayers" (John)
  E509, G407, P325, SA210, VU385
"Joyful, Joyful, We Adore Thee" (John)
  C2, CG310, E376, EL836, G611, N4, P464, SA39, SH390,
  UM89 (PD), VU232
"Pues Si Vivimos" ("When We Are Living") (John)
  C536, CG265, EL639, G822, N499, P400, SH299, UM356,
  VU581
"Because He Lives" (John, Easter)
  AH4070, C562, CG620, SA219, SH200, UM364
"Lord, I Want to Be a Christian" (John)
  C589, CG507, G729, N454, P372 (PD), SH621, UM402
"Holy Spirit, Truth Divine" (John)
  C241, EL398, N63, P321, SA285, UM465, VU368

"Come Down, O Love Divine" (John)
  C582, E516, EL804, G282, N289, P313, SA295, UM475,
  VU367
"Blessed Jesus, At Thy Word" (John)
  E440, EL520, G395, N74, P454, UM596 (PD), VU500
"Abide with Me" (John)
  C636, CG543, E662, EL629, G836, N99, P543, SA529, SH475,
  UM700 (PD), VU436
"Love the Lord Your God" 1400093 (John)
  G62, S2168
"Healer of Our Every Ill" (John)
  C506, EL612, G795, S2213, SH339, VU619

Additional Contemporary and Modern Suggestions
"Awesome in This Place" 847554 (Acts)
"Doxology" 5465879 (Acts)
"More Precious than Silver" 11335 (Acts)
"We Bring the Sacrifice of Praise" 9990 (Pss)
"Blessed Be Your Name" 3798438 (Pss)
  SH449, WS3002
"Come Just As You Are" 1189479 (Pss)
"Refiner's Fire" 426298 (Pss)
"All Heaven Declares" 120556 (Pss, Easter)
"Holy Spirit, Come to Us" (*"Veni Sancte Spiritus"*) (John)
  EL406, G281, S2118
"Where the Spirit of the Lord Is" 27484 (John)
  C264, S2119
"Live in Charity" (*"Ubi Caritas"*) (John)
  C523, EL642, G205, S2179
"Love the Lord" 4572938 (John)
"Behold, What Manner of Love" 1596 (John)
"Let Your Spirit Rise Within Me" 15355 (John)
"The Power of Your Love" 917491 (John)
"Holy and Anointed One" 164361 (John, Easter)
"Holy Spirit, Rain Down" 2405227 (John)
"Dwell" 4085652 (John)

Vocal Solos
"Wash, O God, Our Sons and Daughters" (1 Pet, Baptism)
  V-5 (1)   p. 64
"Gentle Like Jesus" (John, Easter)
  V-8   p. 42
"This Is My Commandment" (John)
  V-8   p. 284

Anthems
"All Creatures of Our God and King" (Acts)
Arr. Molly Ijames; Beckenhorst BP2143
SATB, piano 4-hands (https://bit.ly/BP2143)

"If You Love Me, Keep My Commandments" (John)
Tallis/arr. Hopson; MorningStar MSM-50-5550
2-part mixed, keyboard (https://bit.ly/MSM-50-5550)

Other Suggestions
Visuals:
  O   Preaching, globe, Acts 17:28a, risen Christ
  P   Feet, refine silver, fire/water, offering, prayer
  E   Hearts, readiness, briefcase, accounting, Christ,
            crucifix, prisoners, resurrection
  G   Advocate (briefcase), Spirit, open Bible, child
Introit: C263, UM328. "Surely the Presence of the Lord" 7909
  (Acts, John)
Litany: C189. Love One Another (John)
Sung Benediction: N249. "Peace I Leave with You" (John)
Blessing: WSL40. "May the Spirit of God" (John)
Theme Ideas: Baptism, God: Faithfulness, Holy Spirit, Love

Acts 1:1-11

[1]In the first book, Theophilus, I wrote about all that Jesus did and taught from the beginning [2]until the day when he was taken up to heaven, after giving instructions through the Holy Spirit to the apostles whom he had chosen. [3]After his suffering he presented himself alive to them by many convincing proofs, appearing to them during forty days and speaking about the kingdom of God. [4]While staying with them, he ordered them not to leave Jerusalem, but to wait there for the promise of the Father. "This," he said, "is what you have heard from me; [5]for John baptized with water, but you will be baptized with the Holy Spirit not many days from now."

[6]So when they had come together, they asked him, "Lord, is this the time when you will restore the kingdom to Israel?" [7]He replied, "It is not for you to know the times or periods that the Father has set by his own authority. [8]But you will receive power when the Holy Spirit has come upon you; and you will be my witnesses in Jerusalem, in all Judea and Samaria, and to the ends of the earth." [9]When he had said this, as they were watching, he was lifted up, and a cloud took him out of their sight. [10]While he was going and they were gazing up toward heaven, suddenly two men in white robes stood by them. [11]They said, "Men of Galilee, why do you stand looking up toward heaven? This Jesus, who has been taken up from you into heaven, will come in the same way as you saw him go into heaven."

Psalm 47 (G261, N653, P194, UM781)

[1]Clap your hands, all you peoples;
    shout to God with loud songs of joy.
[2]For the LORD, the Most High, is awesome,
    a great king over all the earth.
[3]He subdued peoples under us,
    and nations under our feet.
[4]He chose our heritage for us,
    the pride of Jacob whom he loves.   *[Selah]*
[5]God has gone up with a shout,
    the LORD with the sound of a trumpet.
[6]Sing praises to God, sing praises;
    sing praises to our King, sing praises.
[7]For God is the king of all the earth;
    sing praises with a psalm.
[8]God is king over the nations;
    God sits on his holy throne.
[9]The princes of the peoples gather
    as the people of the God of Abraham.
For the shields of the earth belong to God;
    he is highly exalted.

Ephesians 1:15-23

[15]I have heard of your faith in the Lord Jesus and your love toward all the saints, and for this reason [16]I do not cease to give thanks for you as I remember you in my prayers. [17]I pray that the God of our Lord Jesus Christ, the Father of glory, may give you a spirit of wisdom and revelation as you come to know him, [18]so that, with the eyes of your heart enlightened, you may know what is the hope to which he has called you, what are the riches of his glorious inheritance among the saints, [19]and what is the immeasurable greatness of his power for us who believe, according to the working of his great power. [20]God put this power to work in Christ when he raised him from the dead and seated him at his right hand in the heavenly places, [21]far above all rule and authority and power and dominion, and above every name that is named, not only in this age but also in the age to come. [22]And he has put all things under his feet and has made him the head over all things for the church, [23]which is his body, the fullness of him who fills all in all.

Luke 24:44-53

[44]Then he said to them, "These are my words that I spoke to you while I was still with you—that everything written about me in the law of Moses, the prophets, and the psalms must be fulfilled." [45]Then he opened their minds to understand the scriptures, [46]and he said to them, "Thus it is written, that the Messiah is to suffer and to rise from the dead on the third day, [47]and that repentance and forgiveness of sins is to be proclaimed in his name to all nations, beginning from Jerusalem. [48]You are witnesses of these things. [49]And see, I am sending upon you what my Father promised; so stay here in the city until you have been clothed with power from on high."

[50]Then he led them out as far as Bethany, and, lifting up his hands, he blessed them. [51]While he was blessing them, he withdrew from them and was carried up into heaven. [52]And they worshiped him, and returned to Jerusalem with great joy; [53]and they were continually in the temple blessing God.

Primary Hymns and Songs for the Day

"Hail the Day That Sees Him Rise" (Acts, Luke) (O)
　　CG219, E214, N260, SA221, SH203, UM312, VU189
　　　　H-3　　Hbl-72; Chr-50; Desc-69; Org-78
　　　　S-1　　#213-214. Transposition with desc.
　　　　S-1　　#213. Desc.
"Crown Him with Many Crowns" (Acts, Luke)
　　C234, CG223. E494, EL855, G268, N301, P151, SA358,
　　SH208, UM327 (PD), VU211
　　　　H-3　　Hbl-55; Chr-60; Desc-30; Org-27
　　　　S-1　　#86-88. Various treatments
"He Is Exalted" 17827 (Acts, Pss, Luke, Ascension) (C)
　　AH4082, CG342, S2070, SH423
"Thine Be the Glory" (Acts, Pss, Luke) (C)
　　C218, CG222, EL376, G238, N253, P122, SA276, SH192,
　　UM308, VU173 (Fr.)

Additional Hymn Suggestions

"A Hymn of Glory Let Us Sing" (Acts)
　　E218, G258, N259, P141
"Jesus Shall Reign" (Acts)
　　C95, CG158, E544, EL434, G265, N300, P423, SA258, SH209,
　　UM157 (PD), VU330
"I Love to Tell the Story" (Acts)
　　C480, CG581, EL661, G462, N522, SA846, SH569, UM156,
　　VU343
"Loving Spirit" (Acts)
　　C244, EL397, G293, P323, S2123, VU387
"Wonder of Wonders" (Acts, Baptism)
　　C378, G489, N328, P499, S2247
"Christ, Whose Glory Fills the Skies" (Acts, Luke)
　　EL553, G662, P462/463, SA249, UM173, VU336
"Christ the Lord Is Risen Today" (Acts, Luke)
　　C216, CG194, EL373, G245, N233, P113, SA218, SH181,
　　UM302 (PD), VU155/157
"Come, Ye Faithful, Raise the Strain" (Acts, Luke)
　　C215, CG218, E199, EL363, G234, N230, P115, UM315 (PD),
　　VU165
"Christ Jesus Lay in Death's Strong Bands" (Acts, Luke)
　　E186, EL370, G237, P110, UM319 (PD)
"Hail Thee, Festival Day" (Acts, Luke, Ascension)
　　E175, EL394, G277, N262, UM324, VU163
"Blessed Jesus, At Thy Word" (Acts, Luke)
　　E440, EL520, G395, N74, P454, UM596 (PD), VU500
"The Trees of the Field" 20546 (Pss)
　　G80, S2279, VU884
"Holy God, We Praise Thy Name" (Eph)
　　CG9, E366, EL414 (PD), G4, N276, P460, SH431, UM79,
　　VU894 (Fr.)
"Praise to the Lord, the Almighty" (Eph)
　　C25, CG319, E390, EL858 (PD) and 859, G35, N22, P482,
　　SA56, SH453, UM139, VU220 (Fr.) and VU221
"All Hail the Power of Jesus' Name" (Eph)
　　C91/C92, CG339/340, E450/451, EL634, G263, N304,
　　P142/143, SA73, SH207, UM154/155, VU334
"At the Name of Jesus" (Eph)
　　CG424, E435, EL416, G264, P148, SA74, SH657, UM168,
　　VU335
"My Hope Is Built" (Eph)
　　AH4105, C537, CG590, EL596/597, G353, N403, P379,
　　SA662, SH324, UM368 (PD)
"Come, Share the Lord" (Eph, Comm.)
　　C408, CG459, G510, S2269, VU469
"Give Me Jesus" (Eph)
　　CG546, EL770, N409, SH306, WS3140
"Alleluia! Sing to Jesus!" (Luke)
　　C233, CG217, E460/E461, EL392, G260, N257, P144 (PD),
　　SH204

"Christ the Lord Is Risen Today" (Luke Ascension)
　　C216, CG194, EL373, G245, N233, P113, SA218, SH181,
　　UM302 (PD), VU155/157
"Sent Out in Jesus' Name" (*"Enviado Soy de Dios"*) 6290823
(Luke)
　　EL538, G747, S2184, SH718
"The Spirit Sends Us Forth to Serve" (Luke)
　　CG520, EL551, S2241

Additional Contemporary and Modern Suggestions

"Holy Spirit, Come to Us" (*"Veni Sancte Spiritus"*) (Acts)
　　EL406, G281, S2118
"Come, Holy Spirit" 3383953 (Acts)
　　WS3092 (See also SH223, WS3091)
"Jesus, We Are Here" (*"Yesu Tawa Pano"*) (Acts, Luke)
　　EL529, G392, S2273, SH611
"Holy Spirit, Rain Down" 2405227 (Acts, Eph)
"Clap Your Hands" 806674 (Pss)
"Shout to the Lord" 1406918 (Pss)
　　CG348, EL821, S2074, SA264, SH426
"Lord, I Lift Your Name on High" 117947 (Pss, Ascension)
　　AH4071, CG606, EL857, S2088, SA379, SH205
"Forever" 3148428 (Pss)
　　CG53, SA363, WS3023
"Awesome Is the Lord Most High" 4674159 (Pss, Ascension)
"Open the Eyes of My Heart" 2298355 (Eph)
　　G452, SA270, SH378, WS3008
"Above All" 2672885 (Eph, Ascension)
"Once Again" 1564362 (Ascension)

Vocal Solos

"Give Me Jesus" (Eph)
　　V-3 (1)　　p. 53
　　V-8　　　　p. 256
"Rise Again" (Ascenson, Easter)
　　V-8　　　　p. 31

Anthems

"All Hail the Power of Jesus' Name" (Eph)
Arr. Michael Burkhardt; MorningStar MSM-50-4040
SATB, organ, opt. brass quintet, timp. (https://bit.ly/50-4040)

"He Is Exalted" (Luke)
arr. Lloyd Larson; Hope C5233
SATB, keyboard (https://bit.ly/C-5233)

Other Suggestions

These ideas may be used on May 24 as Ascension Sunday.
Visuals:
　　O　　Risen Christ, baptism, seven flames, ascension, angels
　　P　　Clapping, singing, shouting, crown/throne, shields
　　E　　Open Bible, Christ, right hand, feet, Church
　　G　　Open Bible, crucifix, Christ, lifted hands
Introit: N742. "Gathered Here" (Acts, Luke)
Introit: C220, CG212, E203, EL386/E387, G235/255, N244,
　　P116 (PD), SH190, UM317, VU170, stanza 1. "O Sons and
　　Daughters, Let Us Sing" (Luke)
Greeting: Acts 1:8. Receive power from the Holy Spirit.
Affirmation of Faith: WSL76. "We believe" (Eph)
Song of Preparation: WS3047, stanza 3. "God Almighty, We Are
　　Waiting" (Luke)
Offering Prayer: WSL119. "Alleluia! Christ is risen!" (Easter)
Theme Ideas: Call of God, Discipleship / Following God, Faith,
　　Holy Spirit, Praise, Resurrection

Acts 1:6-14

⁶So when they had come together, they asked him, "Lord, is this the time when you will restore the kingdom to Israel?" ⁷He replied, "It is not for you to know the times or periods that the Father has set by his own authority. ⁸But you will receive power when the Holy Spirit has come upon you; and you will be my witnesses in Jerusalem, in all Judea and Samaria, and to the ends of the earth." ⁹When he had said this, as they were watching, he was lifted up, and a cloud took him out of their sight. ¹⁰While he was going and they were gazing up toward heaven, suddenly two men in white robes stood by them. ¹¹They said, "Men of Galilee, why do you stand looking up toward heaven? This Jesus, who has been taken up from you into heaven, will come in the same way as you saw him go into heaven."

¹²Then they returned to Jerusalem from the mount called Olivet, which is near Jerusalem, a sabbath day's journey away. ¹³When they had entered the city, they went to the room upstairs where they were staying, Peter, and John, and James, and Andrew, Philip and Thomas, Bartholomew and Matthew, James son of Alphaeus, and Simon the Zealot, and Judas son of James. ¹⁴All these were constantly devoting themselves to prayer, together with certain women, including Mary the mother of Jesus, as well as his brothers.

Psalm 68:1-10, 32-35 (G55, N664, UM792)

¹Let God rise up, let his enemies be scattered;
    let those who hate him flee before him.
²As smoke is driven away, so drive them away;
    as wax melts before the fire,
    let the wicked perish before God.
³But let the righteous be joyful;
    let them exult before God;
    let them be jubilant with joy.
⁴Sing to God, sing praises to his name;
    lift up a song to him who rides upon the clouds—
his name is the LORD—
    be exultant before him.
⁵Father of orphans and protector of widows
    is God in his holy habitation.
⁶God gives the desolate a home to live in;
    he leads out the prisoners to prosperity,
    but the rebellious live in a parched land.
⁷O God, when you went out before your people,
    when you marched through the wilderness,   *[Selah]*
⁸the earth quaked, the heavens poured down rain
    at the presence of God, the God of Sinai,
    at the presence of God, the God of Israel.
⁹Rain in abundance, O God, you showered abroad;
    you restored your heritage when it languished;
¹⁰your flock found a dwelling in it;
    in your goodness, O God, you provided for the needy.
. . . .
³²Sing to God, O kingdoms of the earth;
    sing praises to the Lord,   *[Selah]*
³³O rider in the heavens, the ancient heavens;
    listen, he sends out his voice, his mighty voice.
³⁴Ascribe power to God,
    whose majesty is over Israel;
    and whose power is in the skies.
³⁵Awesome is God in his sanctuary,
    the God of Israel;
    he gives power and strength to his people.
Blessed be God!

1 Peter 4:12-14; 5:6-11

¹²Beloved, do not be surprised at the fiery ordeal that is taking place among you to test you, as though something strange were happening to you. ¹³But rejoice in so far as you are sharing Christ's sufferings, so that you may also be glad and shout for joy when his glory is revealed. ¹⁴If you are reviled for the name of Christ, you are blessed, because the spirit of glory, which is the Spirit of God, is resting on you. . . .

5 . . . ⁶Humble yourselves therefore under the mighty hand of God, so that he may exalt you in due time. ⁷Cast all your anxiety on him, because he cares for you. ⁸Discipline yourselves; keep alert. Like a roaring lion your adversary the devil prowls around, looking for someone to devour. ⁹Resist him, steadfast in your faith, for you know that your brothers and sisters throughout the world are undergoing the same kinds of suffering. ¹⁰And after you have suffered for a little while, the God of all grace, who has called you to his eternal glory in Christ, will himself restore, support, strengthen, and establish you. ¹¹To him be the power for ever and ever. Amen.

John 17:1-11

¹After Jesus had spoken these words, he looked up to heaven and said, "Father, the hour has come; glorify your Son so that the Son may glorify you, ²since you have given him authority over all people, to give eternal life to all whom you have given him. ³And this is eternal life, that they may know you, the only true God, and Jesus Christ whom you have sent. ⁴I glorified you on earth by finishing the work that you gave me to do. ⁵So now, Father, glorify me in your own presence with the glory that I had in your presence before the world existed.

⁶"I have made your name known to those whom you gave me from the world. They were yours, and you gave them to me, and they have kept your word. ⁷Now they know that everything you have given me is from you; ⁸for the words that you gave to me I have given to them, and they have received them and know in truth that I came from you; and they have believed that you sent me. ⁹I am asking on their behalf; I am not asking on behalf of the world, but on behalf of those whom you gave me, because they are yours. ¹⁰All mine are yours, and yours are mine; and I have been glorified in them. ¹¹And now I am no longer in the world, but they are in the world, and I am coming to you. Holy Father, protect them in your name that you have given me, so that they may be one, as we are one."

Primary Hymns and Songs for the Day

"Hail the Day That Sees Him Rise" (Acts) (O)
    CG219, E214, N260, SA221, SH203, UM312, VU189
        H-3   Hbl-72; Chr-50; Desc-69; Org-78
        S-1   #213-214. Transposition with desc.
        S-1   #213. Desc.
"Alleluia! Sing to Jesus!" (Heb) (O)
    C233, CG217, E460/E461, EL392, G260, N257, P144 (PD),
    SH204
        H-3   Hbl-46; Chr-26, 134; Desc-53; Org-56
        S-1   #168-171. Various treatments
"Come, Ye Faithful, Raise the Strain" (Acts)
    C215, CG218, E199, EL363, G234, N230, P115, UM315 (PD),
    VU165
"He Is Exalted" 17827 (Acts)
    AH4082, CG342, S2070, SH423
"How Firm a Foundation" (Acts, Pss, 1 Pet) (C)
    C618, CG425, E636/637, EL796, G463, N407, P361, SA804,
    SH291, UM529 (PD), VU660
        H-3   Hbl-27, 69; Chr-102; Desc-41; Org-41
        S-1   #133. Harm.
                #134. Performance note

Additional Hymn Suggestions

"Lo, He Comes with Clouds Descending" (Acts)
    CG100, E57/58, EL435, G348, P6, SA260, UM718, VU25
"Loving Spirit" (Acts)
    C244, EL397, G293, P323, S2123, VU387
"Wonder of Wonders" (Acts, Baptism)
    C378, G489, N328, P499, S2247
"I'll Fly Away" (Acts)
    N595, S2282
"Christ the Lord Is Risen Today" (Acts)
    C216, CG194, EL373, G245, N233, P113, SA218, SH181,
    UM302 (PD), VU155/157
"Immortal, Invisible, God Only Wise" (Acts, John)
    C66, CG58, E423, EL834, G12, N1, P263, SA37, UM103 (PD),
    VU264
"Christ, Whose Glory Fills the Skies" (Acts, John)
    EL553, G662, P462/463, SA249, UM173, VU336
"A Hymn of Glory Let Us Sing" (Acts)
    E218, G258, N259, P141
"Spirit Divine, Attend Our Prayers" (Acts)
    E509, G407, P325, SA210, VU385
"Joyful, Joyful, We Adore Thee" (Pss, John)
    C2, CG310, E376, EL836, G611, N4, P464, SA39, SH390,
    UM89 (PD), VU232
"Lift Every Voice and Sing" (Pss, 1 Pet)
    AH4055, C631, CG638, E599, EL841, G339, N593, P563,
    SH36, UM519
"Christ Is Alive" (1 Pet)
    CG205, E182, EL389, G246, P108, SA217, UM318, VU158
"Blessed Assurance" (1 Pet)
    AH4083, C543, CG619, EL638, G839, N473, P341, SA455,
    SH320, UM369 (PD), VU337
"We Cannot Measure How You Heal" (1 Pet)
    CG540, G797, SH341, VU613, WS3139
"Lead Me, Guide Me" (1 Pet)
    C583, CG403, EL768, G740, S2214, SH582
"Fight the Good Fight" (1 Pet)
    E552, G846, P307 (PD), SA952, VU674
"By Gracious Powers" (1 Pet, John)
    E695/696, EL626, G818, N413, P342, UM517
"O Jesus, I Have Promised" (John)
    C612, E655, EL810, G724/725, N493, P388/389, SA613,
    SH623, UM396 (PD), VU120
"We All Are One in Mission" (John)
    CG269, EL576, G733, P435, S2243

Additional Contemporary and Modern Suggestions

"Holy Spirit, Come to Us" ("*Veni Sancte Spiritus*") (Acts)
    EL406, G281, S2118
"Come, Holy Spirit" 3383953 (Acts)
    WS3092 (See also SH223, WS3091)
"Waiting Here for You" 5925663 (Acts)
"Holy Spirit, Rain Down" 2405227 (Acts, Pss)
"Foundation" 706151 (Acts, Pss, 1 Pet)
"Lord, I Lift Your Name on High" 117947 (Pss)
    AH4071, CG606, EL857, S2088, SA379, SH205
"Shout to the Lord" 1406918 (Pss)
    CG348, EL821, S2074, SA264, SH426
"God Is Good All the Time" 1729073 (1 Pet)
"God Is So Good" 4956994 (1 Pet)
    G658, S2056, SH461
"Humble Thyself in the Sight of the Lord" 26564 (1 Pet)
"Cares Chorus" 25974 (1 Pet, John)
"Today Is the Day" 5200924 (1 Pet)
"I Will Boast" 4662350 (1 Pet)
"Freedom in the Spirit" 7127886 (1 Pet, John)
"Praise You" 863806 (John)
"Lord, Be Glorified" 26368 (John)
    EL744, G468, S2150, SA593, SH420
"Be Glorified" 429226 (John)
"Be Glorified" 2732646 (John)

Vocal Solos

"My Heart Is Steadfast" (1 Pet, John)
    V-5 (2)   p. 40
"Rejoice Now, My Spirit" (Acts, John, Ascension, Easter)
    V-9   p. 30

Anthems

"A Firm Foundation" (Acts, Pss, 1 Pet) (C)
Arr. John Leavitt; Brookfield Press HL-00265056
SATB, piano, opt instruments (https://bit.ly/HL65056)

"Fly Away Home" (Acts)
Pepper Choplin; Lorenz 10/4691L
SATB, piano (https://bit.ly/10-4691L)

Other Suggestions

Today may also be celebrated as Ascension Sunday using the ideas for
    May 25.
Visuals:
    Acts   Cloud, ascension, Jesus ascending, angels, prayer
    P   Melting candle, music notes, clouds, broken chains,
             abundant rain
    E   Fire, trials, testing, suffering, relief from suffering
    G   Jesus ascending, sun, lifted hands
Introit: EL529, G392, S2273, SH611. "Jesus, We Are Here" ("*Yesu*
    Tawa Pano") (Acts)
Call to Worship: WSL35. "Let us gather" (Acts)
Opening Prayer: N827 or N831 (Acts, Pentecost)
Confession and Assurance: N837 and N841 (Acts)
Prayer: WSL34, WSL42, or WSL67 (Acts)
Offertory: S2262, SH644. "Let Us Offer to the Father"
    ("*Te Ofrecemos Padre Nuestro*") (1 Pet)
Introit and Sung Benediction: EL412, WS3017, verses 1 and 3.
    "Come, Join the Dance of Trinity" (Luke)
Theme Ideas: Assurance, Discipleship / Following God, God:
    Providence / God our Help, Holy Spirit, Waiting

Acts 2:1-21

¹When the day of Pentecost had come, they were all together in one place. ²And suddenly from heaven there came a sound like the rush of a violent wind, and it filled the entire house where they were sitting. ³Divided tongues, as of fire, appeared among them, and a tongue rested on each of them. ⁴All of them were filled with the Holy Spirit and began to speak in other languages, as the Spirit gave them ability.

⁵Now there were devout Jews from every nation under heaven living in Jerusalem. ⁶And at this sound the crowd gathered and was bewildered, because each one heard them speaking in the native language of each. ⁷Amazed and astonished, they asked, "Are not all these who are speaking Galileans? ⁸And how is it that we hear, each of us, in our own native language? ⁹Parthians, Medes, Elamites, and residents of Mesopotamia, Judea and Cappadocia, Pontus and Asia, ¹⁰Phrygia and Pamphylia, Egypt and the parts of Libya belonging to Cyrene, and visitors from Rome, both Jews and proselytes, ¹¹Cretans and Arabs—in our own languages we hear them speaking about God's deeds of power." ¹²All were amazed and perplexed, saying to one another, "What does this mean?" ¹³But others sneered and said, "They are filled with new wine."

¹⁴But Peter, standing with the eleven, raised his voice and addressed them, "Men of Judea and all who live in Jerusalem, let this be known to you, and listen to what I say. ¹⁵Indeed, these are not drunk, as you suppose, for it is only nine o'clock in the morning. ¹⁶No, this is what was spoken through the prophet Joel:

¹⁷'In the last days it will be, God declares,
that I will pour out my Spirit upon all flesh,
and your sons and your daughters shall prophesy,
and your young men shall see visions,
and your old men shall dream dreams.
¹⁸ Even upon my slaves, both men and women,
in those days I will pour out my Spirit; and they shall prophesy.
¹⁹ And I will show portents in the heaven above
and signs on the earth below,
blood, and fire, and smoky mist.
²⁰ The sun shall be turned to darkness
and the moon to blood,
before the coming of the Lord's great and glorious day.
²¹ Then everyone who calls on the name of the Lord shall be saved.'"

Psalm 104:24-34, 35b (G34, N689, P224, SH219, UM826)

²⁴O LORD, how manifold are your works!
In wisdom you have made them all;
the earth is full of your creatures.
²⁵Yonder is the sea, great and wide,
creeping things innumerable are there,
living things both small and great.
²⁶There go the ships,
and Leviathan that you formed to sport in it.
²⁷These all look to you
to give them their food in due season;
²⁸when you give to them, they gather it up;
when you open your hand, they are filled with good things.
²⁹When you hide your face, they are dismayed;
when you take away their breath, they die
and return to their dust.
³⁰When you send forth your spirit, they are created;
and you renew the face of the ground.
³¹May the glory of the LORD endure forever;
may the LORD rejoice in his works—
³²who looks on the earth and it trembles,
who touches the mountains and they smoke.
³³I will sing to the LORD as long as I live;
I will sing praise to my God while I have being.
³⁴May my meditation be pleasing to him,
for I rejoice in the LORD.
. . . .
³⁵ᵇBless the LORD, O my soul.
Praise the LORD!

1 Corinthians 12:3b-13

³ᵇ[N]o one can say "Jesus is Lord" except by the Holy Spirit. ⁴Now there are varieties of gifts, but the same Spirit; ⁵and there are varieties of services, but the same Lord; ⁶and there are varieties of activities, but it is the same God who activates all of them in everyone. ⁷To each is given the manifestation of the Spirit for the common good. ⁸To one is given through the Spirit the utterance of wisdom, and to another the utterance of knowledge according to the same Spirit, ⁹to another faith by the same Spirit, to another gifts of healing by the one Spirit, ¹⁰to another the working of miracles, to another prophecy, to another the discernment of spirits, to another various kinds of tongues, to another the interpretation of tongues. ¹¹All these are activated by one and the same Spirit, who allots to each one individually just as the Spirit chooses.

¹²For just as the body is one and has many members, and all the members of the body, though many, are one body, so it is with Christ. ¹³For in the one Spirit we were all baptized into one body—Jews or Greeks, slaves or free—and we were all made to drink of one Spirit.

John 7:37-39

³⁷On the last day of the festival, the great day, while Jesus was standing there, he cried out, "Let anyone who is thirsty come to me, ³⁸and let the one who believes in me drink. As the scripture has said, 'Out of the believer's heart shall flow rivers of living water.'" ³⁹Now he said this about the Spirit, which believers in him were to receive; for as yet there was no Spirit, because Jesus was not yet glorified.

Primary Hymns and Songs for the Day

"On Pentecost They Gathered" (Acts) (O)
    C237, CG225, G289, N272, P128, VU195
        H-3   Hbl-86; Chr-153; Org-95
        S-1   #243. Harmonization
"Every Time I Feel the Spirit" (Acts)
    C592, G66, N282, P315, UM404
"Holy Ground" 21198 (Acts)
    C112, G406, S2272, SA400
"Spirit of the Living God" 23488 (Acts, Pentecost)
    C259, CG233, G288, N283, P322, SA312/313, SH555,
    UM393, VU376
        S-1   #212 Vocal desc. idea
"We Are One in Christ Jesus" ("*Somos Uno en Cristo*") 6368975
    (1 Cor)
    C493, EL643, G322, S2229, SH227
"Forward through the Ages" (1 Cor) (C)
    N377, UM555 (PD)
        H-3   Hbl-59; Chr-156; Org-140
"Breathe on Me, Breath of God" (Acts) (C)
    C254, CG235, E508, G286, N292, P316, SA294, SH224/273,
    UM420 (PD), VU382 (Fr.)
        H-3   Hbl-49; Chr-45; Desc-101; Org-166

Additional Hymn Suggestions

"What Is this Place" (Acts)
    C289, EL524, G404
"Holy Spirit, Truth Divine" (Acts)
    C241, EL398, N63, P321, SA285, UM465, VU368
"Wind Who Makes All Winds That Blow" (Acts)
    C236, CG226, N271, P131, UM538, VU196
"I Love Thy Kingdom, Lord" (Acts)
    C274, CG262, E524, G310, N312, P441, UM540
"Here, O Lord, Your Servants Gather" (Acts)
    C278, EL530, G311, N72, P465, UM552, VU362
"Spirit, Spirit of Gentleness" (Acts, Pentecost)
    C249, EL396, G291, N286, P319, S2120, VU375 (Fr.)
"Loving Spirit" (Acts, Pentecost)
    C244, EL397, G293, P323, S2123, VU387
"In the Midst of New Dimensions" (Acts, Pentecost)
    G315, N391, S2238
"Deep in the Shadows of the Past" (Acts, Pentecost)
    G50, N320, P330, S2246
"Praise God for This Holy Ground" (Acts, Pentecost)
    G405, WS3009
"I Come with Joy" (Acts, Comm.)
    C420, CG456, E304, EL482, G515, N349, P507, SH682,
    UM617, VU477
"One Bread, One Body" (Acts, Comm.)
    C393, EL496, G530, SH678, UM620, VU467
"Come, Share the Lord" (Acts, Comm.)
    C408, CG459, G510, S2269, VU469
"Like the Murmur of the Dove's Song" (Acts, 1 Cor)
    C245, CG233, E513, EL403, G285, N270, P314, SH407,
    UM544, VU205
"Come, O Spirit, Dwell Among Us" (Acts, 1 Cor)
    G280, N267, P129, VU198
"One Bread, One Body" (1 Cor, Comm.)
    C393, EL496, G530, SH678, UM620, VU467
"We All Are One in Mission" (1 Cor)
    CG269, EL576, G733, P435, S2243
"Holy Spirit, Come, Confirm Us" (John, Pentecost)
    N264, UM331
"Make Me a Channel of Your Peace" (John)
    G753, S2171, SA608, SH616 VU684

Additional Contemporary and Modern Suggestions

"Surely the Presence of the Lord" 7909 (Acts, Pentecost)
    C263, UM328; S-2 #200. Stanzas for soloist
"Sweet, Sweet Spirit" (Acts, Pentecost)
    C261, CG241, G408, N293, P398, SH410, UM334
"Spirit Song" 27824 (Acts, Pentecost)
    C352, SH409, UM347
"Holy, Holy" 18792 (Acts, Pentecost)
    P140, S2039
"God Is Here Today" ("*Dios Está Aquí*") 3170575 (Acts)
    G411, S2049, SH382
"Open Our Eyes, Lord" 1572 (Acts)
    CG392, S2086, SA386, SH562
"Where the Spirit of the Lord Is" 27484 (Acts, Pentecost)
    C264, S2119
"Open the Eyes of My Heart" 2298355 (Acts)
    G452, SA270, SH378, WS3008
"Come, Holy Spirit" 3383953 (Acts)
"Holy Spirit, Rain Down" 2405227 (Acts)
"Let It Rise" 2240585 (Acts)
"God of Wonders" 3118757 (Pss)
"I'm Goin'a Sing When the Spirit Says Sing" (1 Cor, Pentecost)
    AH4073, UM333
"We Are the Body of Christ" 2220206 (1 Cor)
"You Who Are Thirsty" 814453 (John)
"The River Is Here" 1475231 (John, Pentecost)
"Who Can Satisfy My Soul Like You?" 208492 (John)
"All Who Are Thirsty" 2489542 (John)
"Dwell" 4085652 (Pentecost)

Vocal Solos

"Spirit of God" (Acts)
    V-8   p. 170
"I Feel the Spirit Moving" (Acts, 1 Cor)
    V-3 (1)   p.22
"One Bread, One Body" (1 Cor)
    V-3 (2)   p. 40
"Ho! Everyone Who Is Thirsty" (John)
    V-8   p. 244

Anthems

"Ev'ry Time I Feel the Spirit" (Acts)
Moses Hogan; Hal Leonard HL-08740285
SATB *a cappella* (https://bit.ly/HL-40285)

"For Everyone Born" (Acts, 1 Cor)
Arr. Tom Trenney; MorningStar MSM-50-5011
SATB, piano, opt. cello (https://bit.ly/MSM-50-5011)

Other Suggestions

Visuals:
    O   Wind, tongues of fire, praise, all races
    P   Sea/ships, whales, dove, volcano, quake, Ps 104:35b
    E   Pile of gifts, seven flames, clasped hands, circle,
          baptism, drinking glasses
    G   Water/pitcher/glasses, river fountain
Introit: G283, S2124/2125, VU383, SH223, WS3091/2092.
    "Come, Holy Spirit" (Acts)
Call to Worship: WSL39. "Spirit of the living God" (Acts,
    Pentecost)
Call to Prayer: EL406, G281, S2118. "Holy Spirit, Come to Us"
    (Acts, 1 Cor)
Prayer: UM329 or UM542 (Acts, Pentecost)
Prayers: WSL37/38, N826/857, UM542/574, C52/243
    (Pentecost)
Response: WS3183. "As We Go" (Pentecost)
Theme Ideas: God: Glory of God, God: Hunger / Thirst for
    God, Holy Spirit, Spiritual Gifts, Unity

Genesis 1:1–2:4a

[1]In the beginning when God created the heavens and the earth, [2]the earth was a formless void and darkness covered the face of the deep, while a wind from God swept over the face of the waters.

[3]Then God said, "Let there be light"; and there was light. [4]And God saw that the light was good; and God separated the light from the darkness. [5]God called the light Day, and the darkness he called Night. And there was evening and there was morning, the first day.

[6]And God said, "Let there be a dome in the midst of the waters, and let it separate the waters from the waters." [7]So God made the dome and separated the waters that were under the dome from the waters that were above the dome. And it was so. [8]God called the dome Sky. And there was evening and there was morning, the second day.

[9]And God said, "Let the waters under the sky be gathered together into one place, and let the dry land appear." And it was so. [10]God called the dry land Earth, and the waters that were gathered together he called Seas. And God saw that it was good. [11]Then God said, "Let the earth put forth vegetation: plants yielding seed, and fruit trees of every kind on earth that bear fruit with the seed in it." And it was so. [12]The earth brought forth vegetation: plants yielding seed of every kind, and trees of every kind bearing fruit with the seed in it. And God saw that it was good. [13]And there was evening and there was morning, the third day.

[14]And God said, "Let there be lights in the dome of the sky to separate the day from the night; and let them be for signs and for seasons and for days and years, [15]and let them be lights in the dome of the sky to give light upon the earth." And it was so. [16]God made the two great lights—the greater light to rule the day and the lesser light to rule the night—and the stars. [17]God set them in the dome of the sky to give light upon the earth, [18]to rule over the day and over the night, and to separate the light from the darkness. And God saw that it was good. [19]And there was evening and there was morning, the fourth day.

[20]And God said, "Let the waters bring forth swarms of living creatures, and let birds fly above the earth across the dome of the sky." [21]So God created the great sea monsters and every living creature that moves, of every kind, with which the waters swarm, and every winged bird of every kind. And God saw that it was good. [22]God blessed them, saying, "Be fruitful and multiply and fill the waters in the seas, and let birds multiply on the earth." [23]And there was evening and there was morning, the fifth day.

[24]And God said, "Let the earth bring forth living creatures of every kind: cattle and creeping things and wild animals of the earth of every kind." And it was so. [25]God made the wild animals of the earth of every kind, and the cattle of every kind, and everything that creeps upon the ground of every kind. And God saw that it was good.

[26]Then God said, "Let us make humankind in our image, according to our likeness; and let them have dominion over the fish of the sea, and over the birds of the air, and over the cattle, and over all the wild animals of the earth, and over every creeping thing that creeps upon the earth." [27]So God created humankind in his image, in the image of God he created them; male and female he created them. [28]God blessed them, and God said to them, "Be fruitful and multiply, and fill the earth and subdue it; and have dominion over the fish of the sea and over the birds of the air and over every living thing that moves upon the earth."

[29]God said, "See, I have given you every plant yielding seed that is upon the face of all the earth, and every tree with seed in its fruit; you shall have them for food. [30]And to every beast of the earth, and to every bird of the air, and to everything that creeps on the earth, everything that has the breath of life, I have given every green plant for food." And it was so.

[31]God saw everything that he had made, and indeed, it was very good. And there was evening and there was morning, the sixth day.

2 Thus the heavens and the earth were finished, and all their multitude. [2]And on the seventh day God finished the work that he had done, and he rested on the seventh day from all the work that he had done. [3]So God blessed the seventh day and hallowed it, because on it God rested from all the work that he had done in creation.

[4a]These are the generations of the heavens and the earth when they were created.

Psalm 8 (G25, N624, P162/163, SH6, UM743)

[1]O LORD, our Sovereign,
   how majestic is your name in all the earth!
You have set your glory above the heavens.
[2]   Out of the mouths of babes and infants
you have founded a bulwark because of your foes,
   to silence the enemy and the avenger.
[3]When I look at your heavens, the work of your fingers,
   the moon and the stars that you have established;
[4]what are human beings that you are mindful of them,
   mortals that you care for them?
[5]Yet you have made them a little lower than God,
   and crowned them with glory and honor.
[6]You have given them dominion over the works of your hands;
   you have put all things under their feet,
[7]all sheep and oxen,
   and also the beasts of the field,
[8]the birds of the air, and the fish of the sea,
   whatever passes along the paths of the seas.
[9]O LORD, our Sovereign,
   how majestic is your name in all the earth!

2 Corinthians 13:11-13

[11]Finally, brothers and sisters, farewell. Put things in order, listen to my appeal, agree with one another, live in peace; and the God of love and peace will be with you. [12]Greet one another with a holy kiss. All the saints greet you.

[13]The grace of the Lord Jesus Christ, the love of God, and the communion of the Holy Spirit be with all of you.

Matthew 28:16-20

[16]Now the eleven disciples went to Galilee, to the mountain to which Jesus had directed them. [17]When they saw him, they worshiped him; but some doubted. [18]And Jesus came and said to them, "All authority in heaven and on earth has been given to me. [19]Go therefore and make disciples of all nations, baptizing them in the name of the Father and of the Son and of the Holy Spirit, [20]and teaching them to obey everything that I have commanded you. And remember, I am with you always, to the end of the age."

Primary Hymns and Songs for the Day
"All Creatures of Our God and King" (Gen, Pss, Trinity) (O)
 C22, CG307, E400, EL835, G15, N17, P455, SA2, SH16,
 UM62, VU217 (Fr.)
  H-3 Hbl-44; Chr-21; Desc-66; Org-73
  S-1 #198-204. Various treatments
"Doxology" 5465879 (Gen, Pss, Trinity)
"Lord, You Give the Great Commission" (2 Cor, Matt) (O) (C)
 C459, CG651, S2176, EL579, G298, P429, UM584, VU512
  H-3 Hbl-61; Chr-132; Org-2
  S-1 #4-5. Instrumental and vocal desc.
"We Shall Overcome" (2 Cor)
 AH4047/4048, C630, G379, N570, UM533
"Sent Out in Jesus' Name" (*"Enviado Soy de Dios"*) 6290823
(Matt) (C)
 EL538, G747, S2184, SH718

Additional Hymn Suggestions
"Crashing Waters at Creation" (Gen)
 EL455, G476, N326, VU449
"Out of Deep, Unordered Water" (Gen)
 G484, P494, VU453
"For the Beauty of the Earth" (Gen)
 C56, CG341, E416, EL879, G14, P473, N28, SA14, SH21,
 UM92 (PD), VU226
"Morning Has Broken" (Gen)
 C53, CG27, E8, EL556, G664, P469, SA44, SH465, UM145,
 VU409
"All Things Bright and Beautiful" (Gen)
 C61, CG23, E405, G20, N31, P267, SA3, SH1, UM147 (PD),
 VU291
"God Who Stretched the Spangled Heavens" (Gen)
 C651, CG21, E580, EL771, G24, N556, P268, UM150
"This Is the Day the Lord Hath Made" (Gen)
 G681, P230, UM658
"O God, We Bear the Imprint of Your Face" (Gen)
 C681, G759, N585, P385
"Mothering God, You Gave Me Birth" (Gen, Trinity)
 C83, EL735, G7, N467, S2050, VU320
"God the Sculptor of the Mountains" (Gen)
 EL736, G5, S2060
"From All That Dwell Below the Skies" (Gen, Pss)
 C49, CG330, E380, G327, N27, P229, UM101 (PD)
"I Sing the Almighty Power of God" (Gen, Pss)
 C64, CG19, E398, G32, N12, P288, SA36, SH15, UM152,
 VU231
"Sweet, Sweet Spirit" (2 Cor)
 C261, CG241, G408, N293, P398, SH410, UM334
"How Clear Is Our Vocation, Lord" (2 Cor)
 EL580, G432, P419, VU504
"God, Whose Giving Knows No Ending" (2 Cor, Matt)
 C606, CG671, G716, N565, P422
"Lord, You Give the Great Commission" (2 Cor, Matt)
 C459, CG651, S2176, EL579, G298, P429, UM584, VU512
"The Church of Christ in Every Age" (Matt)
 C475, EL729, G320, N306, P421, UM589, VU601
"Guide My Feet" (Matt)
 CG637, G741, N497, P354, S2208, SH54
"Day of Arising" (Matt, Comm.)
 CG203, G252, EL374, WS3086
"Go to the World" (Matt)
 CG481, G295, SH720, VU420, WS3158
"We Were Baptized in Christ Jesus" (Trinity, Baptism)
 EL451, S2251

Additional Contemporary and Modern Suggestions
"Thou Art Worthy" 14789 (Gen)
 C114, S2041
"Holy Spirit, Come to Us" (*"Veni Sancte Spiritus"*) (Gen)
 EL406, G281, S2118
"Come, Holy Spirit" 26351 (Gen)
 S2125 (See also S2124)
"Come, Holy Spirit" 3383953 (Gen)
 WS3092 (See also SH223, WS3091)
"Ah, Lord God" 17896 (Gen, Trinity)
"For Us" 7119349 (Gen, Trinity)
"How Great Is Our God" 4348399 (Gen, Pss, Trinity)
 CG322, SH458, WS3003
"Sing the Praise of God Our Maker" (Gen, Pss, Trinity)
 WS3013
"Across the Lands" 3709898 (Gen, Pss)
 SH654, WS3032
"God of Wonders" 3118757 (Gen, Pss)
 SH9, WS3034
"Hallelujah" ("Your Love Is Amazing") 3091812 (Pss)
"Majestic" 4573308 (Pss)
"There's a Song" 2041825 (2 Cor)
"Make Me a Channel of Your Peace" (2 Cor)
 G753, S2171, SA608, SH616 VU684
"Make Me a Channel of Your Peace" 6399315 (2 Cor)
"Song of Hope" (*"Canto de Esperanza"*) 5193990 (2 Cor)
 G765, P432, S2186, SH721, VU424
"They'll Know We Are Christians" 26997 (2 Cor, Trinity)
 AH4074, C494, CG272, G300, S2223, SH232
"Rising" 4662460 (Matt)
"A New Hallelujah" 5285860 (Matt)
"Celebrate Jesus" 16859 (Matt)
"Because We Believe" 2133379 (Trinity)
"Holy, Holy" 18792 (Trinity)

Vocal Solos
"This Is My Father's World" (Gen)
 V-6   p. 42
"In the Image of God" (Gen)
 V-8   p. 362
"A Song of Joy" (Pss)
 V-1   p. 2
"Alleluia" (Trinity)
 V-8   p. 358

Anthems
"I Sing the Mighty Power of God" (Gen, Pss)
Arr. Anna Laura Page; Lorenz 10/4397L
SATB, piano/organ duet (https://bit.ly/10-4397L)

"Wings of the Morning" (Trinity)
Arr. Alice Parker; Kjos Music Company 9178
SATB *a cappella* (https://bit.ly/K-9178)

Other Suggestions
Visuals: Symbols of the Trinity, 3-wick candle
 O Wind, light/dark, sky (evening/morning)
 P Majesty, earth, infants, sky/stars, people, sheep/ox
 E Waving, circle (unity), dove/branch, kiss/parting
 G Jesus, eleven men, Christ candle, worship, globe,
    baptism
Introit: C278, EL530, G311, N72, P465, UM552, VU362. "Here,
 O Lord, Your Servants Gather" (2 Cor)
Opening Prayer: N826 (Gen) or N830 (Trinity)
Litany: CG11. "God the Trinity" (Trinity)
Prayer: N864 or WSL69 (Pss)
Theme Ideas: Call of God, Creation, Discipleship / Following
 God, God: Glory of God, Peace, Praise

Genesis 12:1-9

¹Now the Lord said to Abram, "Go from your country and your kindred and your father's house to the land that I will show you. ²I will make of you a great nation, and I will bless you, and make your name great, so that you will be a blessing. ³I will bless those who bless you, and the one who curses you I will curse; and in you all the families of the earth shall be blessed."

⁴So Abram went, as the Lord had told him; and Lot went with him. Abram was seventy-five years old when he departed from Haran. ⁵Abram took his wife Sarai and his brother's son Lot, and all the possessions that they had gathered, and the persons whom they had acquired in Haran; and they set forth to go to the land of Canaan. When they had come to the land of Canaan, ⁶Abram passed through the land to the place at Shechem, to the oak of Moreh. At that time the Canaanites were in the land. ⁷Then the Lord appeared to Abram, and said, "To your offspring I will give this land." So he built there an altar to the Lord, who had appeared to him. ⁸From there he moved on to the hill country on the east of Bethel, and pitched his tent, with Bethel on the west and Ai on the east; and there he built an altar to the Lord and invoked the name of the Lord. ⁹And Abram journeyed on by stages toward the Negeb.

Psalm 33:1-12 (G40, N643, P185, SH4, UM767)

¹Rejoice in the Lord, O you righteous.
    Praise befits the upright.
²Praise the Lord with the lyre;
    make melody to him with the harp of ten strings.
³Sing to him a new song;
    play skillfully on the strings, with loud shouts.
⁴For the word of the Lord is upright,
    and all his work is done in faithfulness.
⁵He loves righteousness and justice;
    the earth is full of the steadfast love of the Lord.
⁶By the word of the Lord the heavens were made,
    and all their host by the breath of his mouth.
⁷He gathered the waters of the sea as in a bottle;
    he put the deeps in storehouses.
⁸Let all the earth fear the Lord;
    let all the inhabitants of the world stand in awe of him.
⁹For he spoke, and it came to be;
    he commanded, and it stood firm.
¹⁰The Lord brings the counsel of the nations to nothing;
    he frustrates the plans of the peoples.
¹¹The counsel of the Lord stands forever,
    the thoughts of his heart to all generations.
¹²Happy is the nation whose God is the Lord,
    the people whom he has chosen as his heritage.

Romans 4:13-25

¹³For the promise that he would inherit the world did not come to Abraham or to his descendants through the law but through the righteousness of faith. ¹⁴If it is the adherents of the law who are to be the heirs, faith is null and the promise is void. ¹⁵For the law brings wrath; but where there is no law, neither is there violation.

¹⁶For this reason it depends on faith, in order that the promise may rest on grace and be guaranteed to all his descendants, not only to the adherents of the law but also to those who share the faith of Abraham (for he is the father of all of us, ¹⁷as it is written, "I have made you the father of many nations")—in the presence of the God in whom he believed, who gives life to the dead and calls into existence the things that do not exist. ¹⁸Hoping against hope, he believed that he would become "the father of many nations," according to what was said, "So numerous shall your descendants be." ¹⁹He did not weaken in faith when he considered his own body, which was already as good as dead (for he was about a hundred years old), or when he considered the barrenness of Sarah's womb. ²⁰No distrust made him waver concerning the promise of God, but he grew strong in his faith as he gave glory to God, ²¹being fully convinced that God was able to do what he had promised. ²²Therefore his faith "was reckoned to him as righteousness." ²³Now the words, "it was reckoned to him," were written not for his sake alone, ²⁴but for ours also. It will be reckoned to us who believe in him who raised Jesus our Lord from the dead, ²⁵who was handed over to death for our trespasses and was raised for our justification.

Matthew 9:9-13, 18-26

⁹As Jesus was walking along, he saw a man called Matthew sitting at the tax booth; and he said to him, "Follow me." And he got up and followed him.

¹⁰And as he sat at dinner in the house, many tax collectors and sinners came and were sitting with him and his disciples. ¹¹When the Pharisees saw this, they said to his disciples, "Why does your teacher eat with tax collectors and sinners?" ¹²But when he heard this, he said, "Those who are well have no need of a physician, but those who are sick. ¹³Go and learn what this means, 'I desire mercy, not sacrifice.' For I have come to call not the righteous but sinners." . . .

¹⁸While he was saying these things to them, suddenly a leader of the synagogue came in and knelt before him, saying, "My daughter has just died; but come and lay your hand on her, and she will live." ¹⁹And Jesus got up and followed him, with his disciples. ²⁰Then suddenly a woman who had been suffering from hemorrhages for twelve years came up behind him and touched the fringe of his cloak, ²¹for she said to herself, "If I only touch his cloak, I will be made well." ²²Jesus turned, and seeing her he said, "Take heart, daughter; your faith has made you well." And instantly the woman was made well. ²³When Jesus came to the leader's house and saw the flute players and the crowd making a commotion, ²⁴he said, "Go away; for the girl is not dead but sleeping." And they laughed at him. ²⁵But when the crowd had been put outside, he went in and took her by the hand, and the girl got up. ²⁶And the report of this spread throughout that district.

Primary Hymns and Songs for the Day

"Lift Every Voice and Sing" (Gen, Pss)
    AH4055, C631, CG638, E599, EL841, G339, N593, P563,
    SH36, UM519
          H-3   Chr-128
"Lead Me, Lord" (Gen)
    C593, N774, UM473 (PD), VU662
"Lord of the Dance" 78529 (Matt)
    G157, P302, SA141, UM261, VU352
          H-3   Chr-106; Org-81
"I Come with Joy" (Matt, Comm.)
    C420, CG456, E304, EL482, G515, N349, P507, SH682,
    UM617, VU477
          H-3   Hbl-70; Chr-105; Org-30
          S-2   #52. Choral and keyboard arrangement
"Trust and Obey" (Gen, Matt) (C)
    C556, CG509, SA690, SH636, UM467 (PD)
          H-3   Chr-202
          S-1   #336. Harmonization

Additional Hymn Suggestions

"The God of Abraham Praise" (Gen, Rom) (O)
    C24, CG45, E401, EL831, G49, N24, P488, SH50, UM116
    (PD), VU255
"To Abraham and Sarah" (Gen)
    CG251, G51 (VU634)
"God of the Ages" (Gen)
    C725, CG62, E718, G331, N592, P262, SA19, UM698
"God Made from One Blood" (Gen)
    C500, CG686, N427, S2170, VU554
"Deep in the Shadows of the Past" (Gen)
    G50, N320, P330, S2246
"Rain Down" (Pss)
    CG388, G48
"We Will Go Out with Joy" (Pss)
    G539
"La Palabra Del Señor Es Recta" ("Righteous and Just Is the Word
of the Lord") (Pss)
    G40, UM107, SH4
"Cantemos al Señor" ("Let's Sing unto the Lord") (Pss)
    C60, EL555, G669, N39, SH432, UM149
"Come Sing, O Church, in Joy!" (Rom)
    G305, P430
"Alleluia, Alleluia" 32376 (Rom)
    CG196, E178, G240, P106, SA216, SH189, UM162, VU179
"O Love, How Deep" (Rom, Matt)
    E448/449, EL322, G618, N209, P83, SH115, UM267, VU348
"Standing on the Promises" (Rom)
    AH4057, C552, CG625, G838, SA522, SH45, UM374 (PD)
"Faith of Our Fathers" ("the Martyrs") Rom)
    C635, CG645, EL812/813, N381, UM710 (PD), VU580
"There Are Some Things I May Not Know" (Rom)
    N405, S2147
"We Walk by Faith" (Rom)
    CG634, E209, EL635, G817, N256, P399, S2196, SH660
"In the Singing" (Rom, Comm.)
    EL466, G533, S2255
"O Christ, the Healer" (Rom, Matt)
    C503. EL610, G793, N175, P380, UM265
"Woman in the Night" (Matt)
    C188, G161, UM274
"Draw Us in the Spirit's Tether" (Matt, Comm.)
    C392, EL470, G529, N337, P504, UM632, VU479
"My Hope Is Built" (Pss, Rom) (C)
    AH4105, C537, CG590, EL596/597, G353, N403, P379,
    SA662, SH324, UM368 (PD)

Additional Contemporary and Modern Suggestions

"El-Shaddai" 26856 (Gen, Matt)
          S-2   #54. Verses for Vocal Solo
"Clap Your Hands" 806674 (Pss)
"Awesome God" 41099 (Pss)
    G616, S2040
"As It Is in Heaven" 4669748 (Pss)
"Our God Saves" 4972837 (Pss)
"Someone Asked the Question" 1640279 (Pss, Rom)
    N523, S2144
"Our Love Is Loud" 3560817 (Pss)
"Grace Like Rain" 3689877 (Rom)
"Sing Alleluia to the Lord" NO- SS (Rom, Comm.)
    C32, S2258, SH685
"Here Is Bread, Here Is Wine" 983717 (Rom, Comm.)
    EL483, S2266
"Lord, Have Mercy" (Rom, Matt)
    C299, S2277
"Something Beautiful" 18060 (Matt)
"O Lord, You're Beautiful" 14514 (Matt)
"Cry of My Heart" 844980 (Matt)
"What Does the Lord Require of You" 456859 (Matt)
    C661, CG690, G70, S2174, VU701
"We Will Follow" ("Somlandela") (Matt)
    WS3160
"As We Go" 5043277 (Matt)
"I Will Never Be (the Same Again)" 1874911 (Matt)
"Jesus, Lover of My Soul" 1198817 (Matt)
"From Ashes to Beauty" 5288953 (Matt)
"Freedom in the Spirit" 7127886 (Matt)

Vocal Solos

"Great Is Thy Faithfulness" (Gen, Matt)
    V-8   p. 48
"Amazing Grace" (Rom)
    V-8   p. 56
"Redeeming Grace" (Rom)
    V-4   p. 47

Anthems

"You Shall Have a Song" (Pss)
Harriet Ziegenhals; Hope Publishing A-577
2-part, keyboard, opt. flute (https://bit.ly/A-577)

"Come, Ye Sinners, Poor and Needy" (Matt)
Kathryn Bonner; Lorenz 10/3491L
SATB, keyboard and/or handbells (https://bit.ly/10-3491L)

Other Suggestions

Visuals:
      O   elderly man/woman, altar, tent
      P   harp, scales of justice, creation, water/bottle/
            storehouse, UN, 33:1b,3a,12a
      E   Abraham/old man, risen Christ
      G   tax forms, dinner, medical bag, woman/robe/girl
*A celebration of music ministry may be celebrated on this day in
   relationship to the Psalm.*
Response: C299, EL152, G576, S2275, S2277, WS3133. "Lord,
   Have Mercy" (Matt)
Response: C7, CG309, E420, EL850/851, G641, N561, P264,
   UM68, VU533. "When In Our Music, God is Glorified"
Prayer: UM69. For True Singing
Prayer: UM481. "Lord, Make Me an Instrument"
Alternate Lessons: Hos 5:15-6:6, Ps 50:7-15
Theme Ideas: Call of God, Covenant, Discipleship / Following
   God, Faith, Healing, Praise

Genesis 18:1-15, (21:1-7)

[1]The Lord appeared to Abraham by the oaks of Mamre, as he sat at the entrance of his tent in the heat of the day. [2]He looked up and saw three men standing near him. When he saw them, he ran from the tent entrance to meet them, and bowed down to the ground. [3]He said, "My Lord, if I find favor with you, do not pass by your servant. [4]Let a little water be brought, and wash your feet, and rest yourselves under the tree. [5]Let me bring a little bread, that you may refresh yourselves, and after that you may pass on—since you have come to your servant." So they said, "Do as you have said." [6]And Abraham hastened into the tent to Sarah, and said, "Make ready quickly three measures of choice flour, knead it, and make cakes." [7]Abraham ran to the herd, and took a calf, tender and good, and gave it to the servant, who hastened to prepare it. [8]Then he took curds and milk and the calf that he had prepared, and set it before them; and he stood by them under the tree while they ate.

[9]They said to him, "Where is your wife Sarah?" And he said, "There, in the tent." [10]Then one said, "I will surely return to you in due season, and your wife Sarah shall have a son." And Sarah was listening at the tent entrance behind him. [11]Now Abraham and Sarah were old, advanced in age; it had ceased to be with Sarah after the manner of women. [12]So Sarah laughed to herself, saying, "After I have grown old, and my husband is old, shall I have pleasure?" [13]The Lord said to Abraham, "Why did Sarah laugh, and say, 'Shall I indeed bear a child, now that I am old?' [14]Is anything too wonderful for the Lord? At the set time I will return to you, in due season, and Sarah shall have a son." [15]But Sarah denied, saying, "I did not laugh"; for she was afraid. He said, "Oh yes, you did laugh." . . .

21 The Lord dealt with Sarah as he had said, and the Lord did for Sarah as he had promised. [2]Sarah conceived and bore Abraham a son in his old age, at the time of which God had spoken to him. [3]Abraham gave the name Isaac to his son whom Sarah bore him. [4]And Abraham circumcised his son Isaac when he was eight days old, as God had commanded him. [5]Abraham was a hundred years old when his son Isaac was born to him. [6]Now Sarah said, "God has brought laughter for me; everyone who hears will laugh with me." [7]And she said, "Who would ever have said to Abraham that Sarah would nurse children? Yet I have borne him a son in his old age."

Psalm 116:1-2, 12-19 (G655, N699, P228, SH344, UM837)

[1]I love the Lord, because he has heard
   my voice and my supplications.
[2]Because he inclined his ear to me,
   therefore I will call on him as long as I live.
. . . .
[12]What shall I return to the Lord
   for all his bounty to me?
[13]I will lift up the cup of salvation
   and call on the name of the Lord,
[14]I will pay my vows to the Lord
   in the presence of all his people.
[15]Precious in the sight of the Lord
   is the death of his faithful ones.
[16]O Lord, I am your servant;
   I am your servant, the child of your serving girl.
   You have loosed my bonds.
[17]I will offer to you a thanksgiving sacrifice
   and call on the name of the Lord.
[18]I will pay my vows to the Lord
   in the presence of all his people,
[19]in the courts of the house of the Lord,
   in your midst, O Jerusalem.
Praise the Lord!

Romans 5:1-8

[1]Therefore, since we are justified by faith, we have peace with God through our Lord Jesus Christ, [2]through whom we have obtained access to this grace in which we stand; and we boast in our hope of sharing the glory of God. [3]And not only that, but we also boast in our sufferings, knowing that suffering produces endurance, [4]and endurance produces character, and character produces hope, [5]and hope does not disappoint us, because God's love has been poured into our hearts through the Holy Spirit that has been given to us.

[6]For while we were still weak, at the right time Christ died for the ungodly. [7]Indeed, rarely will anyone die for a righteous person—though perhaps for a good person someone might actually dare to die. [8]But God proves his love for us in that while we still were sinners Christ died for us.

Matthew 9:35–10:8, (9-23)

[35]Then Jesus went about all the cities and villages, teaching in their synagogues, and proclaiming the good news of the kingdom, and curing every disease and every sickness. [36]When he saw the crowds, he had compassion for them, because they were harassed and helpless, like sheep without a shepherd. [37]Then he said to his disciples, "The harvest is plentiful, but the laborers are few; [38]therefore ask the Lord of the harvest to send out laborers into his harvest."

10 Then Jesus summoned his twelve disciples and gave them authority over unclean spirits, to cast them out, and to cure every disease and every sickness. [2]These are the names of the twelve apostles: first, Simon, also known as Peter, and his brother Andrew; James son of Zebedee, and his brother John; [3]Philip and Bartholomew; Thomas and Matthew the tax collector; James son of Alphaeus, and Thaddaeus; [4]Simon the Cananaean, and Judas Iscariot, the one who betrayed him.

[5]These twelve Jesus sent out with the following instructions: "Go nowhere among the Gentiles, and enter no town of the Samaritans, [6]but go rather to the lost sheep of the house of Israel. [7]As you go, proclaim the good news, 'The kingdom of heaven has come near.' [8]Cure the sick, raise the dead, cleanse the lepers, cast out demons. You received without payment; give without payment. [9]Take no gold, or silver, or copper in your belts, [10]no bag for your journey, or two tunics, or sandals, or a staff; for laborers deserve their food. [11]Whatever town or village you enter, find out who in it is worthy, and stay there until you leave. [12]As you enter the house, greet it. [13]If the house is worthy, let your peace come upon it; but if it is not worthy, let your peace return to you. [14]If anyone will not welcome you or listen to your words, shake off the dust from your feet as you leave that house or town. [15]Truly I tell you, it will be more tolerable for the land of Sodom and Gomorrah on the day of judgment than for that town.

[16]"See, I am sending you out like sheep into the midst of wolves; so be wise as serpents and innocent as doves. [17]Beware of them, for they will hand you over to councils and flog you in their synagogues; [18]and you will be dragged before governors and kings because of me, as a testimony to them and the Gentiles. [19]When they hand you over, do not worry about how you are to speak or what you are to say; for what you are to say will be given to you at that time; [20]for it is not you who speak, but the Spirit of your Father speaking through you. [21]Brother will betray brother to death, and a father his child, and children will rise against parents and have them put to death; [22]and you will be hated by all because of my name. But the one who endures to the end will be saved. [23]When they persecute you in one town, flee to the next; for truly I tell you, you will not have gone through all the towns of Israel before the Son of Man comes."

Primary Hymns and Songs for the Day

"The God of Abraham Praise" (Gen, Rom) (O)
    C24, CG45, E401, EL831, G49, N24, P488, SH50, UM116
    (PD), VU255
        H-3   Hbl-62, 95; Chr-59; Org-77
        S-1   #211. Harmonization
"I Love the Lord" 1168957 (Pss)
    CG613, G799, P362, N511, SH343, VU617, WS3142
"O Love That Wilt Not Let Me Go" (Gen, Rom)
    C540, CG631, G833, N485, P384, SA616, SH314, UM480,
    VU658
        H-3   Chr-146; Org-142
"Where Cross the Crowded Ways of Life" (Matt)
    C665, CG657, E609, EL719, G343, N543, UM427, VU681
        H-3   Chr-178, 180; Org-44
        S-1   #141-3 Various treatments
"Go to the World" (Matt) (C)
    CG481, G295, SH720, VU420, WS3158
        H-3   Hbl-58; Chr-65; Org-152
        S-1   #314-318. Various treatments
"The Summons" ("Will You Come and Follow Me") (Matt) (C)
    CG473, EL798, G726, S2130, SA695, SH598, VU567
        H-3   Chr-220

Additional Hymn Suggestions

"Children of the Heavenly Father" (Gen, Father's Day)
    CG69, EL781, N487, SH42, UM141
"Deep in the Shadows of the Past" (Gen)
    G50, N320, P330, S2246
"We Walk by Faith" (Gen, Rom)
    CG634, E209, EL635, G817, N256, P399, S2196, SH660
"My Tribute" 11218 (Pss, Matt)
    AH4080, C39, CG574, N14, SH434, UM99; V-8 p. 5. Solo
"Sent Forth by God's Blessing" (Pss, Matt) (C)
    CG519, EL547, N76, SH715, UM664, VU481
"Come, Holy Spirit, Heavenly Dove" (Rom)
    C248, E510, G279, N281, P126
"In the Cross of Christ I Glory" (Rom)
    C207, CG183, E441, EL324, G213, N193, SA174, UM295
"When I Survey the Wondrous Cross" (Rom)
    C195, CG186, E474, EL803, G223/ 224, N224, P100/101,
    SA208, SH163/164, UM298/299, VU149 (Fr.)
"Blessed Assurance" (Rom)
    AH4083, C543, CG619, EL638, G839, N473, P341, SA455,
    SH320, UM369 (PD), VU337
"Standing on the Promises" (Rom)
    AH4057, C552, CG625, G838, SA522, SH45, UM374 (PD)
"Open My Eyes, That I May See" (Rom)
    C586, CG395, G451, P324, SH583, UM454, VU371
"Spirit of God, Descend upon My Heart" (Rom)
    C265, CG243, EL800, G688, N290, P326, SA290, SH277,
    UM500 (PD), VU378
"By Gracious Powers" (Rom)
    E695/696, EL626, G818, N413, P342, UM517
"O For a Thousand Tongues to Sing" (Rom, Matt)
    C5, CG332, E493, EL886, G610, N42, P466, SA89, SH439,
    UM57 (PD), VU326 (See also WS3001)
"Gather Us In" (Matt) (O)
    C284, EL532, G401, S2236, SH393
"To God Be the Glory" (Matt)
    C72, CG349, G634, P485, SA279, SH545, UM98 (PD)
"Come, Labor On" (Matt)
    E541, G719, N532, P415
"Jesus Shall Reign" (Matt)
    C95, CG158, E544, EL434, G265, N300, P423, SA258, SH209,
    UM157 (PD), VU330
"We All Are One in Mission" (Matt)
    CG269, EL576, G733, P435, S2243

"In Remembrance of Me" 25156 (Matt, Comm.)
    C403, CG462, G521, S2254, SH667
"Lord, You Give the Great Commission" (Matt) (C)
    C459, CG651, S2176, EL579, G298, P429, UM584, VU512
"Sent Out in Jesus' Name" ("Enviado Soy de Dios") 6290823
(Matt) (C)
    EL538, G747, S2184, SH718

Additional Contemporary and Modern Suggestions

"Daughter of God" 4509781 (Gen)
"Hungry" ("Falling on My Knees") 2650364 (Gen, Pss)
"I Will Call upon the Lord" 11263 (Pss)
    G621, S2002
"We Bring the Sacrifice of Praise" 9990 (Pss)
"I Love You, Lord" 25266 (Pss)
    CG362, G627, S2068, SA369, SH417
"Because of Your Love" 4662501 (Pss)
"You Are" 4387343 (Pss)
"I Could Sing of Your Love Forever" 1043199 (Pss, Rom)
"I Stand Amazed" 769450 (Pss, Rom)
"I Will Not Forget You" 2694306 (Pss, Rom, Matt)
"O How He Loves You and Me" 15850 (Rom)
    CG600, S2108, SH535
"Something Beautiful" 18060 (Rom)
"Celebrate Love" 155246 (Rom)
"O Lord, Your Tenderness" 38136 (Rom)
"God Is Good All the Time" 1729073 (Rom)
"I Will Boast" 4662350 (Rom)
"Grace Like Rain" 3689877 (Rom)
"O For a Thousand Tongues to Sing" 4048754 (Rom, Matt)
"The King of Glory Comes" (Matt)
    CG177, S2091, SH206
"I'm Gonna Live So God Can Use Me" (Matt)
    C614, G700, P369, S2153, SH632, VU575
"The Family Prayer Song" 1680466 (Father's Day)

Vocal Solos

"Redeeming Grace" (Rom)
    V-4   p. 47
"Here I Am" (Matt)
    V-1   p. 19

Anthems

"The God of Abraham Praise" (Gen)
arr. David Giardiniere; Augsburg 0-8006-2025-9
SATB, organ (https://bit.ly/A-2025-9)

"When I Survey the Wondrous Cross" (Rom)
Arr. Brian L. Hanson; Choristers Guild CGA1430
SATB, piano (https://bit.ly/CGA1430)

Other Suggestions

Visuals:
    O   Oaks, tent, noon, three men eating, old man/woman/
            laugh
    P   Prayer, raised cup, recent dead, open manacles, praise
    E   Crucifix, suffering, pouring
    G   Jesus, lost/helpless, one sheep, harvest, few working,
            prayer, twelve disciples, Matt 10:7b, 8b
Opening Prayer: N831 (Gen, Matt)
Response: N500, UM418, stanzas 3-4. "We Are Climbing Jacob's
    Ladder" (Rom, Matt)
Benediction: WSL161. "Sisters and brothers" (Matt)
Alternate Lessons: Exod 19:2-8a; Ps 100
Theme Ideas: Call of God, Children / Family of God, Cross,
    Discipleship / Following God, Faith, God: Love of God,
    Grace

Genesis 21:8-21

⁸The child grew, and was weaned; and Abraham made a great feast on the day that Isaac was weaned.

⁹But Sarah saw the son of Hagar the Egyptian, whom she had borne to Abraham, playing with her son Isaac. ¹⁰So she said to Abraham, "Cast out this slave woman with her son; for the son of this slave woman shall not inherit along with my son Isaac."

¹¹The matter was very distressing to Abraham on account of his son. ¹²But God said to Abraham, "Do not be distressed because of the boy and because of your slave woman; whatever Sarah says to you, do as she tells you, for it is through Isaac that offspring shall be named for you. ¹³As for the son of the slave woman, I will make a nation of him also, because he is your offspring."

¹⁴So Abraham rose early in the morning, and took bread and a skin of water, and gave it to Hagar, putting it on her shoulder, along with the child, and sent her away. And she departed, and wandered about in the wilderness of Beer-sheba. ¹⁵When the water in the skin was gone, she cast the child under one of the bushes. ¹⁶Then she went and sat down opposite him a good way off, about the distance of a bowshot; for she said, "Do not let me look on the death of the child." And as she sat opposite him, she lifted up her voice and wept. ¹⁷And God heard the voice of the boy; and the angel of God called to Hagar from heaven, and said to her, "What troubles you, Hagar? Do not be afraid; for God has heard the voice of the boy where he is. ¹⁸Come, lift up the boy and hold him fast with your hand, for I will make a great nation of him." ¹⁹Then God opened her eyes and she saw a well of water. She went, and filled the skin with water, and gave the boy a drink. ²⁰God was with the boy, and he grew up; he lived in the wilderness, and became an expert with the bow. ²¹He lived in the wilderness of Paran; and his mother got a wife for him from the land of Egypt.

Psalm 86:1-10, 16-17 (G844, N677)

¹Incline your ear, O Lord, and answer me,
　　for I am poor and needy.
²Preserve my life, for I am devoted to you;
　　save your servant who trusts in you. You are my God;
³be gracious to me, O Lord,
　　for to you do I cry all day long.
⁴Gladden the soul of your servant,
　　for to you, O Lord, I lift up my soul.
⁵For you, O Lord, are good and forgiving,
　　abounding in steadfast love to all who call on you.
⁶Give ear, O Lord, to my prayer;
　　listen to my cry of supplication.
⁷In the day of my trouble I call on you,
　　for you will answer me.
⁸There is none like you among the gods, O Lord,
　　nor are there any works like yours.
⁹All the nations you have made shall come and bow down before
　　　　you, O Lord,
　　and shall glorify your name.
¹⁰For you are great and do wondrous things;
　　you alone are God.
． ．
¹⁶Turn to me and be gracious to me;
　　give your strength to your servant;
　　save the child of your serving girl.
¹⁷Show me a sign of your favor,
　　so that those who hate me may see it and be put to shame,
　　because you, Lord, have helped me and comforted me.

Romans 6:1b-11

¹ᵇShould we continue in sin in order that grace may abound? ²By no means! How can we who died to sin go on living in it? ³Do you not know that all of us who have been baptized into Christ Jesus were baptized into his death? ⁴Therefore we have been buried with him by baptism into death, so that, just as Christ was raised from the dead by the glory of the Father, so we too might walk in newness of life.

⁵For if we have been united with him in a death like his, we will certainly be united with him in a resurrection like his. ⁶We know that our old self was crucified with him so that the body of sin might be destroyed, and we might no longer be enslaved to sin. ⁷For whoever has died is freed from sin. ⁸But if we have died with Christ, we believe that we will also live with him. ⁹We know that Christ, being raised from the dead, will never die again; death no longer has dominion over him. ¹⁰The death he died, he died to sin, once for all; but the life he lives, he lives to God. ¹¹So you also must consider yourselves dead to sin and alive to God in Christ Jesus.

Matthew 10:24-39

²⁴"A disciple is not above the teacher, nor a slave above the master; ²⁵it is enough for the disciple to be like the teacher, and the slave like the master. If they have called the master of the house Beelzebul, how much more will they malign those of his household!

²⁶"So have no fear of them; for nothing is covered up that will not be uncovered, and nothing secret that will not become known. ²⁷What I say to you in the dark, tell in the light; and what you hear whispered, proclaim from the housetops. ²⁸Do not fear those who kill the body but cannot kill the soul; rather fear him who can destroy both soul and body in hell. ²⁹Are not two sparrows sold for a penny? Yet not one of them will fall to the ground unperceived by your Father. ³⁰And even the hairs of your head are all counted. ³¹So do not be afraid; you are of more value than many sparrows.

³²"Everyone therefore who acknowledges me before others, I also will acknowledge before my Father in heaven; ³³but whoever denies me before others, I also will deny before my Father in heaven.

³⁴"Do not think that I have come to bring peace to the earth; I have not come to bring peace, but a sword.

³⁵　"For I have come to set a man against his father,
　　and a daughter against her mother,
　　and a daughter-in-law against her mother-in-law;
³⁶　and one's foes will be members of one's own household.

³⁷"Whoever loves father or mother more than me is not worthy of me; and whoever loves son or daughter more than me is not worthy of me; ³⁸and whoever does not take up the cross and follow me is not worthy of me. ³⁹Those who find their life will lose it, and those who lose their life for my sake will find it."

Primary Hymns and Songs for the Day

"At the Name of Jesus" (Rom) (O)
  CG424, E435, EL416, G264, P148, SA74, SH657, UM168, VU335

"We Know That Christ Is Raised" (Rom, Baptism) (O)
  E296, EL449, G485, P495, UM610, VU448
      H-3   Hbl-100; Chr-214; Desc-38; Org-37
      S-1   #118-127. Various treatments

"Give to the Winds Thy Fears" (Gen, Matt)
  CG55, G815, N404, P286, SA643, UM129 (PD), VU636
      H-3   Chr-71; Desc-39; Org-39
      S-1   #129. Desc.

"Children of the Heavenly Father" (Gen, Matt)
  CG69, EL781, N487, SH42, UM141
      H-3   Chr-46; Desc-102
      S-2   #180-185. Various treatments.

"Take Up Thy Cross" (Matt) (C)
  E675, EL667, G718, N204, P393, SH605, UM415, VU561

"I Have Decided to Follow Jesus" (Matt) (C)
  C344, CG497, S2129, SH610

Additional Hymn Suggestions

"The God of Abraham Praise" (Gen)
  C24, CG45, E401, EL831, G49, N24, P488, SH50, UM116 (PD), VU255

"Great Is Thy Faithfulness" (Gen)
  AH4011, C86, CG48, EL733, G39, N423, P276, SA26, SH48, UM140, VU288

"Saranam, Saranam" ("Refuge") (Gen)
  G789, UM523

"Deep in the Shadows of the Past" (Gen)
  G50, N320, P330, S2246

"I Need Thee Every Hour" (Gen, Pss)
  C578, CG404, G735, N517, SA707, UM397, VU671

"O Master, Let Me Walk with Thee" (Gen, Pss)
  C602, CG660, E659/E660, EL818, G738, N503, P357, SA667, SH612, UM430 (PD), VU560

"Hear My Prayer, O God" (Gen, Pss)
  G782, WS3131

"His Eye Is on the Sparrow" (Gen, Matt)
  C82, G661, N475, S2146, SH322

"Christ Is Alive" (Rom)
  CG205, E182, EL389, G246, P108, SA217, UM318, VU158

"Amazing Grace" (Rom)
  AH4091, C546, CG587, E671, EL779, G649, N547/548, P280, SA453, SH523, UM378 (PD), VU266 (Fr.)

"Nearer, My God, to Thee" (Rom)
  C577, N606, SA611, UM528 (PD), VU497 (Fr.)

"Baptized in Water" (Rom, Baptism)
  CG449, E294, EL456, G482, P492, S2248, SH666

"Built on a Rock" (Rom)
  C273, CG247, EL652, WS3147

"It Is Well with My Soul" (Rom, Matt)
  C561, CG573, EL785, G840, N438, SA741, SH305, UM377

"Blessed Quietness" (Rom, Matt)
  C267, CG244, N284, S2142

"God Will Take Care of You" (Matt)
  N460, SA5, SH289, UM130 (PD)

"Swiftly Pass the Clouds of Glory" (Matt)
  G190, P73, S2102

"You, Lord, Are Both Lamb and Shepherd" (Matt)
  G274, SH210, VU210. WS3043

Additional Contemporary and Modern Suggestions

"Hungry" ("Falling on My Knees") 2650364 (Gen)
"Daughter of God" 4509781 (Gen)
"Came to My Rescue" 4705190 (Gen, Pss)

"I Will Call upon the Lord" 11263 (Pss)
  G621, S2002

"We Will Glorify" 19038 (Pss)
  CG360, S2087

"Glorify Thy Name" 1383 (Pss)
  CG8, S2016, SA582, SH427

"Lord, Listen to Your Children" 659072 (Pss)
  EL752, S2207

"I Exalt You" 17803 (Pss)

"Grace Alone" 2335524 (Rom)
  CG43, S2162, SA699.

"God Is Good All the Time" (Rom)
  AH4010, WS3026

"God Is Good All the Time" 1729073 (Rom)

"Amazing Grace" ("My Chains Are Gone") 4768151 (Rom)

"We Fall Down" 2437367 (Rom)
  G368, WS3187

"Salvation Is Here" 4451327 (Rom)

"Grace Like Rain" 3689877 (Rom)

"I've Got Peace Like a River" (Rom, Matt)
  C530, G623, N478, P368, S2145, SH276, VU577

"Let It Be Said of Us" 1855882 (Matt)

"Every Move I Make" 1595726 (Matt)

"Everyday" 2798154 (Matt)

"One Way" 4222082 (Matt)

"Take Up Our Cross" 5358955 (Matt)

"We Will Follow" (*"Somlandela"*) (Matt)
  WS3160

Vocal Solos

"Lost in the Night" (Gen, Pss)
  V-5 (1)   p. 18

"His Eye Is on the Sparrow" (Gen, Matt)
  V-8   p. 166

"Waterlife" (Rom, Baptism)
  V-5 (3)   p. 17

"Amazing Grace" (Rom)
  V-8   p. 56

"Lead Me to Calvary" (Matt)
  V-8   p. 226

Anthems

"What Grace Is Mine" (Rom, Matt)
Getty/arr. Lloyd Larson; Hope C6131
SATB, piano (https://bit.ly/Hope-C6131)

"Like a River In My Soul" (Rom, Matt)
Arr. Tim Osiek; Beckenhorst BP2159
SATB, piano (https://bit.ly/BP2159)

Other Suggestions

Visuals:
  O   Toddler/woman, bread/waterbag, wilderness, well
  P   Praying hands, people bowing, Ps 86:9
  E   Baptism, crucifix, open manacles
  G   Cross for each, light, housetop, two sparrows/penny, hair, sword

Litany: WSL49. "For rebirth and resilience" (Gen, Pss, Matt)
Affirmation of Faith: WSL82. "We are children of God" (Rom)
Response: EL814, G698, SH620, WS3119. "Take, O Take Me As I Am" (Rom)
Prayer: UM531 (Gen)
Response: CG399, EL751, G471, S2200, SH311/517. "O Lord, Hear My Prayer" (Pss)
Alternate Lessons: Jer 20:7-13; Ps 69:7-10 (11-15), 16-18
Theme Ideas: Baptism, Discipleship / Following God, God: Providence / God our Help, Grace

Genesis 22:1-14

[1]After these things God tested Abraham. He said to him, "Abraham!" And he said, "Here I am." [2]He said, "Take your son, your only son Isaac, whom you love, and go to the land of Moriah, and offer him there as a burnt offering on one of the mountains that I shall show you." [3]So Abraham rose early in the morning, saddled his donkey, and took two of his young men with him, and his son Isaac; he cut the wood for the burnt offering, and set out and went to the place in the distance that God had shown him. [4]On the third day Abraham looked up and saw the place far away. [5]Then Abraham said to his young men, "Stay here with the donkey; the boy and I will go over there; we will worship, and then we will come back to you." [6]Abraham took the wood of the burnt offering and laid it on his son Isaac, and he himself carried the fire and the knife. So the two of them walked on together. [7]Isaac said to his father Abraham, "Father!" And he said, "Here I am, my son." He said, "The fire and the wood are here, but where is the lamb for a burnt offering?" [8]Abraham said, "God himself will provide the lamb for a burnt offering, my son." So the two of them walked on together.

[9]When they came to the place that God had shown him, Abraham built an altar there and laid the wood in order. He bound his son Isaac, and laid him on the altar, on top of the wood. [10]Then Abraham reached out his hand and took the knife to kill his son. [11]But the angel of the LORD called to him from heaven, and said, "Abraham, Abraham!" And he said, "Here I am." [12]He said, "Do not lay your hand on the boy or do anything to him; for now I know that you fear God, since you have not withheld your son, your only son, from me." [13]And Abraham looked up and saw a ram, caught in a thicket by its horns. Abraham went and took the ram and offered it up as a burnt offering instead of his son. [14]So Abraham called that place "The LORD will provide"; as it is said to this day, "On the mount of the LORD it shall be provided."

Psalm 13 (G777, N626, SH518, UM746)

[1]How long, O LORD? Will you forget me forever?
  How long will you hide your face from me?
[2]How long must I bear pain in my soul,
  and have sorrow in my heart all day long?
How long shall my enemy be exalted over me?
[3]Consider and answer me, O LORD my God!
  Give light to my eyes, or I will sleep the sleep of death,
[4]and my enemy will say, "I have prevailed";
  my foes will rejoice because I am shaken.
[5]But I trusted in your steadfast love;
  my heart shall rejoice in your salvation.
[6]I will sing to the LORD,
  because he has dealt bountifully with me.

Romans 6:12-23

[12]Therefore, do not let sin exercise dominion in your mortal bodies, to make you obey their passions. [13]No longer present your members to sin as instruments of wickedness, but present yourselves to God as those who have been brought from death to life, and present your members to God as instruments of righteousness. [14]For sin will have no dominion over you, since you are not under law but under grace.

[15]What then? Should we sin because we are not under law but under grace? By no means! [16]Do you not know that if you present yourselves to anyone as obedient slaves, you are slaves of the one whom you obey, either of sin, which leads to death, or of obedience, which leads to righteousness? [17]But thanks be to God that you, having once been slaves of sin, have become obedient from the heart to the form of teaching to which you were entrusted, [18]and that you, having been set free from sin, have become slaves of righteousness. [19]I am speaking in human terms because of your natural limitations. For just as you once presented your members as slaves to impurity and to greater and greater iniquity, so now present your members as slaves to righteousness for sanctification.

[20]When you were slaves of sin, you were free in regard to righteousness. [21]So what advantage did you then get from the things of which you now are ashamed? The end of those things is death. [22]But now that you have been freed from sin and enslaved to God, the advantage you get is sanctification. The end is eternal life. [23]For the wages of sin is death, but the free gift of God is eternal life in Christ Jesus our Lord.

Matthew 10:40-42

[40]"Whoever welcomes you welcomes me, and whoever welcomes me welcomes the one who sent me. [41]Whoever welcomes a prophet in the name of a prophet will receive a prophet's reward; and whoever welcomes a righteous person in the name of a righteous person will receive the reward of the righteous; [42]and whoever gives even a cup of cold water to one of these little ones in the name of a disciple—truly I tell you, none of these will lose their reward."

Primary Hymns and Songs for the Day

"The God of Abraham Praise" (Gen) (O)
    C24, CG45, E401, EL831, G49, N24, P488, SH50, UM116
    (PD), VU255

"El-Shaddai" 26856 (Gen)
        S-2   #54 Verses for Vocal Solo

"Breathe on Me, Breath of God" (Rom)
    C254, CG235, E508, G286, N292, P316, SA294, SH224/273,
    UM420 (PD), VU382 (Fr.)
        H-3   Hbl-49; Chr-45; Desc-101; Org-166

"Living for Jesus" (Rom, Matt)
    C610, S21

"Baptized in Water" (Rom, Baptism)
    CG449, E294, EL456, G482, P492, S2248, SH666

"Let Us Build a House Where Love Can Dwell" (Matt)
    EL641, G301, SH228 (See also WS3152)

"The Spirit Sends Us Forth to Serve" (Matt) (C)
    CG520, EL551, S2241
        H-3   Hbl-129; Chr-106; Desc-65; Org-72
        S-2   #105. Flute/violin desc.
               #106. Harm.

Additional Hymn Suggestions

"God of Our Life" (Gen)
    C713, G686, N366, P275

"Here I Am, Lord" (Gen)
    C452, CG482, EL574, G69, P525, SA1002, SH608, UM593,
    VU509

"Faith of Our Fathers" (Gen)
    C635, CG645, EL812/813, N381, UM710 (PD), VU580

"We Walk by Faith" (Gen)
    CG634, E209, EL635, G817, N256, P399, S2196, SH660

"Why Stand So Far Away, My God?" (Gen, Pss)
    C671, G786, S2180

"By Gracious Powers" (Gen, Pss)
    E695/696, EL626, G818, N413, P342, UM517

"Rock of Ages, Cleft for Me" (Gen, Rom)
    C214, E685, EL623, G438, N596, SA671, SH301, UM361
    (PD)

"Ye Servants of God" (Rom)
    C110, CG420, E535, EL825 (PD), G299, N305, P477, SA97,
    UM181 (PD), VU342

"Amazing Grace" (Rom)
    AH4091, C546, CG587, E671, EL779, G649, N547/548, P280,
    SA453, SH523, UM378 (PD), VU266 (Fr.)

"O Jesus, I Have Promised" (Rom)
    C612, E655, EL810, G724/725, N493, P388/389, SA613,
    SH623, UM396 (PD), VU120

"Take My Life, and Let It Be" (Rom)
    C609, CG490, E707, EL583/EL685, G697, P391, N448,
    SA623, SH627/628, UM399 (PD), VU506

"I Am Thine, O Lord" (Rom)
    AH4087, C601, CG504, N455, SA586, UM419 (PD)

"Where Cross the Crowded Ways of Life" (Rom, Matt)
    C665, CG657, E609, EL719, G343, N543, P408, UM427 (PD),
    VU681

"Jesu, Jesu" 3049039 (Rom, Matt)
    C600, CG656, E602, EL708, G203, N498, P367, SH155,
    UM432, VU593, S-1 #63. Vocal part

"There's a Spirit in the Air" (Matt)
    C257, P433, N294, UM192, VU582

"O Master, Let Me Walk with Thee" (Matt)
    C602, CG660, E659/E660, EL818, G738, N503, P357, SA667,
    SH612, UM430 (PD), VU560

"Cuando el Pobre" ("When the Poor Ones") (Matt)
    C662, EL725, G762, P407, SH240, UM434, VU702

"You Satisfy the Hungry Heart" (Matt, Comm.)
    C429, CG468, EL484, G523, P521, SH672, UM629, VU478

"God Made from One Blood" (Matt)
    C500, CG686, N427, S2170, VU554

"Together We Serve" (Matt)
    G767, S2175

"In Remembrance of Me" 25156 (Matt, Comm.)
    C403, CG462, G521, S2254, SH667

"As We Gather at Your Table" (Matt, Comm.)
    EL522, N332, S2268, SH411, VU457

"This Is My Song" (Independence Day)
    C722, CG697, EL887, G340, N591, UM437

Additional Contemporary and Modern Suggestions

"We Fall Down" 2437367 (Gen, Rom)
    G368, WS3187

"Hungry" ("Falling on My Knees") 2650364 (Gen, Pss)

"Your Love, Oh Lord" 1894255 (Gen, Pss)

"I Will Call upon the Lord" 11263 (Pss)
    G621, S2002

"Someone Asked the Question" 1640279 (Pss)
    N523, S2144

"Forever" 3148428 (Pss)
    CG53, SA363, WS3023

"How Great Are You, Lord" 2888576 (Pss, Rom)

"There's a Song" 2041825 (Rom)

"Grace Alone" 2335524 (Rom)
    CG43, S2162, SA699.

"In the Lord I'll Be Ever Thankful" (Rom)
    G654, S2195, SH316

"I Am Crucified with Christ" 2652874 (Rom)

"Amazing Grace" ("My Chains Are Gone") 4768151 (Rom)

"Grace Like Rain" 3689877 (Rom)

"Make Me a Servant" 33131 (Matt)
    CG651, S2176

"People Need the Lord" 18084 (Matt)
    S2244, SA418

Vocal Solos

"Here I Am" (Gen, Rom)
    V-1   p. 19

"Take My Life" ("Consecration") (Rom)
    V-8   p. 262

"Reach Out to Your Neighbor" (Matt)
    V-8   p. 372

Anthems

"By Gracious Powers" (Gen, Pss)
John Ferguson; Augsburg 9780800675493
SATB, organ, opt. flute, congregation (https://bit.ly/A-75493)

"Whoever Welcome You Welcomes Me" (Matt)
Larry E. Schultz; Choristers Guild CGA1067
Unison/2-part, piano, opt. flute (https://bit.ly/CGA1067)

Other Suggestions

Visuals:
    O   Gen 22:1c, mountain, dawn, donkey, man/boy,
            wood/knife, altar, angel. ram
    P   Praying hands, eyes/sleep, joy, singing
    E   Baptism, manacles, Rom 6:23
    G   Welcome, cup of water offered

Greeting: N819 (Gen, Pss) or N816 (Matt) or N824 (Rom)

Response: CG399, EL751, G471, S2200, SH311/517. "O Lord,
    Hear My Prayer" (Pss)

Prayer: WSL203. "God of all nations" (Independence Day)

Alternate Lessons: Jer 28:5-9, Ps 89:1-4, 15-18

Theme Ideas: Covenant, Faith, Grace, Inclusion, Lament, Sin
    and Forgiveness, Welcome

Genesis 24:34-38, 42-49, 58-67

³⁴So he said, "I am Abraham's servant. ³⁵The Lord has greatly blessed my master, and he has become wealthy; he has given him flocks and herds, silver and gold, male and female slaves, camels and donkeys. ³⁶And Sarah my master's wife bore a son to my master when she was old; and he has given him all that he has. ³⁷My master made me swear, saying, 'You shall not take a wife for my son from the daughters of the Canaanites, in whose land I live; ³⁸but you shall go to my father's house, to my kindred, and get a wife for my son.' . . .

⁴²"I came today to the spring, and said, 'O Lord, the God of my master Abraham, if now you will only make successful the way I am going! ⁴³I am standing here by the spring of water; let the young woman who comes out to draw, to whom I shall say, "Please give me a little water from your jar to drink," ⁴⁴and who will say to me, "Drink, and I will draw for your camels also"—let her be the woman whom the Lord has appointed for my master's son.' ⁴⁵ "Before I had finished speaking in my heart, there was Rebekah coming out with her water jar on her shoulder; and she went down to the spring, and drew. I said to her, 'Please let me drink.' ⁴⁶She quickly let down her jar from her shoulder, and said, 'Drink, and I will also water your camels.' So I drank, and she also watered the camels. ⁴⁷Then I asked her, 'Whose daughter are you?' She said, 'The daughter of Bethuel, Nahor's son, whom Milcah bore to him.' So I put the ring on her nose, and the bracelets on her arms. ⁴⁸Then I bowed my head and worshiped the Lord, and blessed the Lord, the God of my master Abraham, who had led me by the right way to obtain the daughter of my master's kinsman for his son. ⁴⁹Now then, if you will deal loyally and truly with my master, tell me; and if not, tell me, so that I may turn either to the right hand or to the left." . . .

⁵⁸And they called Rebekah, and said to her, "Will you go with this man?" She said, "I will." ⁵⁹So they sent away their sister Rebekah and her nurse along with Abraham's servant and his men. ⁶⁰And they blessed Rebekah and said to her,

"May you, our sister, become
  thousands of myriads;
may your offspring gain possession
  of the gates of their foes."

⁶¹Then Rebekah and her maids rose up, mounted the camels, and followed the man; thus the servant took Rebekah, and went his way.

⁶²Now Isaac had come from Beer-lahai-roi, and was settled in the Negeb. ⁶³Isaac went out in the evening to walk in the field; and looking up, he saw camels coming. ⁶⁴And Rebekah looked up, and when she saw Isaac, she slipped quickly from the camel, ⁶⁵and said to the servant, "Who is the man over there, walking in the field to meet us?" The servant said, "It is my master." So she took her veil and covered herself. ⁶⁶And the servant told Isaac all the things that he had done. ⁶⁷Then Isaac brought her into his mother Sarah's tent. He took Rebekah, and she became his wife; and he loved her. So Isaac was comforted after his mother's death.

Psalm 45:10-17 (G333, N650)

¹⁰Hear, O daughter, consider and incline your ear;
  forget your people and your father's house,
¹¹ and the king will desire your beauty.
Since he is your lord, bow to him;
¹² the people of Tyre will seek your favor with gifts,
  the richest of the people ¹³with all kinds of wealth.
The princess is decked in her chamber with gold-woven robes;
¹⁴ in many-colored robes she is led to the king;
  behind her the virgins, her companions, follow.
¹⁵With joy and gladness they are led along
  as they enter the palace of the king.
¹⁶In the place of ancestors you, O king, shall have sons;
  you will make them princes in all the earth.
¹⁷I will cause your name to be celebrated in all generations;
  therefore the peoples will praise you forever and ever.

Romans 7:15-25a

¹⁵I do not understand my own actions. For I do not do what I want, but I do the very thing I hate. ¹⁶Now if I do what I do not want, I agree that the law is good. ¹⁷But in fact it is no longer I that do it, but sin that dwells within me. ¹⁸For I know that nothing good dwells within me, that is, in my flesh. I can will what is right, but I cannot do it. ¹⁹For I do not do the good I want, but the evil I do not want is what I do. ²⁰Now if I do what I do not want, it is no longer I that do it, but sin that dwells within me.

²¹So I find it to be a law that when I want to do what is good, evil lies close at hand. ²²For I delight in the law of God in my inmost self, ²³but I see in my members another law at war with the law of my mind, making me captive to the law of sin that dwells in my members. ²⁴Wretched man that I am! Who will rescue me from this body of death? ²⁵ᵃThanks be to God through Jesus Christ our Lord!

Matthew 11:16-19, 25-30

¹⁶"But to what will I compare this generation? It is like children sitting in the marketplaces and calling to one another,

¹⁷'We played the flute for you, and you did not dance;
  we wailed, and you did not mourn.'

¹⁸For John came neither eating nor drinking, and they say, 'He has a demon'; ¹⁹the Son of Man came eating and drinking, and they say, 'Look, a glutton and a drunkard, a friend of tax collectors and sinners!' Yet wisdom is vindicated by her deeds." . . .

²⁵At that time Jesus said, "I thank you, Father, Lord of heaven and earth, because you have hidden these things from the wise and the intelligent and have revealed them to infants; ²⁶yes, Father, for such was your gracious will. ²⁷All things have been handed over to me by my Father; and no one knows the Son except the Father, and no one knows the Father except the Son and anyone to whom the Son chooses to reveal him.

²⁸"Come to me, all you that are weary and are carrying heavy burdens, and I will give you rest. ²⁹Take my yoke upon you, and learn from me; for I am gentle and humble in heart, and you will find rest for your souls. ³⁰For my yoke is easy, and my burden is light."

Primary Hymns and Songs for the Day

"Love Divine, All Loves Excelling" (Rom) (O)
C517, CG281, E657, EL631, G366, N43, P376, SA262,
SH353/354, UM384 (PD), VU333
>> H-3   Chr-134; Desc-18; Org-13
>> S-1   #41-42. Desc. and harm.

"Lord, I Want to Be a Christian" (Rom)
C589, CG507, G729, N454, P372 (PD), SH621, UM402
>> H-3   Chr-130

"Come, Thou Fount of Every Blessing" (Rom, Matt, Comm.)
AH4086, C16, CG295/559, E686, EL807, G475, N459, P356,
SA830, SH394, UM400 (PD), VU559
>> H-3   Chr-57; Desc-79; Org-96
>> S-1   #244. Desc.

"Just a Closer Walk with Thee" (Rom, Matt)
C557, EL697, G835, S2158, SH584

"How Firm a Foundation" (Rom, Matt) (C)
C618, CG425, E636/637, EL796, G463, N407, P361, SA804,
SH291, UM529 (PD), VU660
>> H-3   Hbl-27, 69; Chr-102; Desc-41; Org-41
>> S-1   #133. Harm.
>>   #134. Performance note

Additional Hymn Suggestions

"O God, in a Mysterious Way" (Gen)
CG39, E677, G30, N412, P270, SA17, SH47

"When Love Is Found" (Gen, Pss, Comm.)
C499, CG524, N362, SH279, UM643, VU489

"Your Love, O God, Has Called Us Here" (Gen, Pss, Rom)
E353, N361, UM647

"To God Be the Glory" (Rom)
C72, CG349, G634, P485, SA279, SH545, UM98 (PD)

"Jesu, Thy Boundless Love to Me" (Rom)
G703, P366, UM183, VU631

"Spirit of God, Descend upon My Heart" (Rom)
C265, CG243, EL800, G688, N290, P326, SA290, SH277,
UM500 (PD), VU378

"Blessed Jesus, At Thy Word" (Rom)
E440, EL520, G395, N74, P454, UM596 (PD), VU500

"Before I Take the Body of My Lord" (Rom)
C391, G428, VU462

"If Thou But Suffer God to Guide Thee" (Rom, Matt)
C565, CG76, E635, EL769, G816, N410, P282, SA40, SH326,
UM142 (PD), VU285 (Fr.) and VU286

"O Love, How Deep" (Rom, Matt)
E448/449, EL322, G618, N209, SH115, UM267, VU348

"Jesus Loves Me" (Matt)
C113, CG603, EL595 (PD), G188, N327, P304, SA807,
SH570, UM191, VU365

"I Heard the Voice of Jesus Say" (Matt)
CG577, E692, EL611, G182, N489, SA424, SH127, VU626

"Softly and Tenderly, Jesus Is Calling" (Matt)
C340, CG474, EL608, G418, N449, SA435, SH601, UM348

"Be Thou My Vision" (Matt)
C595, CG71, E488, EL793, G450, N451, P339, SA573, SH640,
UM451, VU642

"Near to the Heart of God" (Matt)
C581, CG383, G824, P527, UM472 (PD)

"O Love That Wilt Not Let Me Go" (Matt)
C540, CG631, G833, N485, P384, SA616, SH314, UM480,
VU658

"What a Friend We Have in Jesus" (Matt)
C585, CG409, EL742, G465, N506, P403, SH585/586,
UM526 (PD), VU661

"Feed Us, Lord" 4636207 (Matt, Comm.)
G501, WS3167

Additional Contemporary and Modern Suggestions

"Daughter of God" 4509781 (Gen)

"I Could Sing of Your Love Forever" 1043199 (Pss, Matt)

"I Will Celebrate" 21239 (Pss)

"I Love You, Lord" 25266 (Pss)
CG362, G627, S2068, SA369, SH417

"In the Lord I'll Be Ever Thankful" (Rom)
G654, S2195, SH316

"Come! Come! Everybody Worship" 1327592 (Rom)

"My Tribute" 11218 (Rom)
AH4080, C39, CG574, N14, SH434, UM99; V-8 p. 5. Vocal
Solo

"Thy Word Is a Lamp" 14301 (Rom)
C326, CG38, G458, UM601

"Counting on God" 5064366 (Rom)

"Foundation" 706151 (Rom, Matt)

"Give Thanks" 20285 (Rom, Matt)
C528, CG373, G647, S2036, SA364, SH489

"You Who Are Thirsty" 814453 (Matt)

"Cares Chorus" 25974 (Matt)

"Fill My Cup, Lord" 15946 (Matt, Comm.)
C351, UM641 (refrain only), WS3093

"Still" 3940963 (Matt)

"Come to the Table of Grace" 7034746 (Matt, Comm.)
G507, WS3168

"Holy and Anointed One" 164361 (Matt)

"Jesus I Trust in You" 4510828 (Matt)

"My Redeemer Lives" 2397964 (Matt)

Vocal Solos

"A Song of Joy" (Pss, Matt)
>> V-1   p. 2

"Just a Closer Walk with Thee" (Rom, Matt)
>> V-5 (2)   p. 31
>> V-8   p. 323

"He Shall Feed His Flock" from Messiah (Matt)
>> V-2
>> V-8   p. 334

"A Song of Trust" (Matt)
>> V-4   p. 20

Anthems

"How Firm a Foundation" (Rom, Matt)
Arr. Tom Trenney; MorningStar MSM-50-5180
SATB, organ, opt. congregation (https://bit.ly/50-5180)

"I Will Arise and Go to Jesus" (Rom, Matt)
arr. Robert W. Lehman; Paraclete Press PPM01220
SATB a cappella (https://bit.ly/PPM-01220)

Other Suggestions

Visuals:

O	Spring, water jar, nose ring, bracelets, ring
P	Many-colored/gold robes, joy, bride/maids
E	Open Bible, manacles (closed/open), Christ
G	Children playing, marketplace, flute, John, Jesus, eating/drinking, infants, burdens, yoke

Celebrate marriage covenant renewal (Gen)
Call to Worship: WSL65. "Jesus said Come unto me" (Matt)
Canticle: UM646. "Canticle of Love" (Gen, Pss)
Call to Prayer: WS3094. "Come to Me" (Matt)
Sung Confession: WS3138. "Confession" (Rom)
Response: WS3110, verses 4-5 "By Grace We Have Been Saved"
(Rom)
Prayer: UM423. Finding Rest in God (Matt)
Alternate Lessons: Zech 9:9-12, Ps 145:8-14
Theme Ideas: Assurance, Children / Family of God, Comfort,
Covenant, Love, Sin and Forgiveness

Genesis 25:19-34

¹⁹These are the descendants of Isaac, Abraham's son: Abraham was the father of Isaac, ²⁰and Isaac was forty years old when he married Rebekah, daughter of Bethuel the Aramean of Paddan-aram, sister of Laban the Aramean. ²¹Isaac prayed to the LORD for his wife, because she was barren; and the LORD granted his prayer, and his wife Rebekah conceived. ²²The children struggled together within her; and she said, 'If it is to be this way, why do I live?' So she went to inquire of the LORD. ²³And the LORD said to her,

> "Two nations are in your womb,
>   and two peoples born of you shall be divided;
> the one shall be stronger than the other,
>   the elder shall serve the younger."

²⁴When her time to give birth was at hand, there were twins in her womb. ²⁵The first came out red, all his body like a hairy mantle; so they named him Esau. ²⁶Afterwards his brother came out, with his hand gripping Esau's heel; so he was named Jacob. Isaac was sixty years old when she bore them.

²⁷When the boys grew up, Esau was a skillful hunter, a man of the field, while Jacob was a quiet man, living in tents. ²⁸Isaac loved Esau, because he was fond of game; but Rebekah loved Jacob.

²⁹Once when Jacob was cooking a stew, Esau came in from the field, and he was famished. ³⁰Esau said to Jacob, 'Let me eat some of that red stuff, for I am famished!' (Therefore he was called Edom.) ³¹Jacob said, 'First sell me your birthright.' ³²Esau said, 'I am about to die; of what use is a birthright to me?' ³³Jacob said, 'Swear to me first.' So he swore to him, and sold his birthright to Jacob. ³⁴Then Jacob gave Esau bread and lentil stew, and he ate and drank, and rose and went his way. Thus Esau despised his birthright.

Psalm 119:105-112 (G64, N701, UM840)

¹⁰⁵Your word is a lamp to my feet
    and a light to my path.
¹⁰⁶I have sworn an oath and confirmed it,
    to observe your righteous ordinances.
¹⁰⁷I am severely afflicted;
    give me life, O LORD, according to your word.
¹⁰⁸Accept my offerings of praise, O LORD,
    and teach me your ordinances.
¹⁰⁹I hold my life in my hand continually,
    but I do not forget your law.
¹¹⁰The wicked have laid a snare for me,
    but I do not stray from your precepts.
¹¹¹Your decrees are my heritage forever;
    they are the joy of my heart.
¹¹²I incline my heart to perform your statutes
    forever, to the end.

Romans 8:1-11

¹There is therefore now no condemnation for those who are in Christ Jesus. ²For the law of the Spirit of life in Christ Jesus has set you free from the law of sin and of death. ³For God has done what the law, weakened by the flesh, could not do: by sending his own Son in the likeness of sinful flesh, and to deal with sin, he condemned sin in the flesh, ⁴so that the just requirement of the law might be fulfilled in us, who walk not according to the flesh but according to the Spirit. ⁵For those who live according to the flesh set their minds on the things of the flesh, but those who live according to the Spirit set their minds on the things of the Spirit. ⁶To set the mind on the flesh is death, but to set the mind on the Spirit is life and peace. ⁷For this reason the mind that is set on the flesh is hostile to God; it does not submit to God's law—indeed it cannot, ⁸and those who are in the flesh cannot please God.

⁹But you are not in the flesh; you are in the Spirit, since the Spirit of God dwells in you. Anyone who does not have the Spirit of Christ does not belong to him. ¹⁰But if Christ is in you, though the body is dead because of sin, the Spirit is life because of righteousness. ¹¹If the Spirit of him who raised Jesus from the dead dwells in you, he who raised Christ from the dead will give life to your mortal bodies also through his Spirit that dwells in you.

Matthew 13:1-9, 18-23

¹That same day Jesus went out of the house and sat beside the sea. ²Such great crowds gathered around him that he got into a boat and sat there, while the whole crowd stood on the beach. ³And he told them many things in parables, saying: "Listen! A sower went out to sow. ⁴And as he sowed, some seeds fell on the path, and the birds came and ate them up. ⁵Other seeds fell on rocky ground, where they did not have much soil, and they sprang up quickly, since they had no depth of soil. ⁶But when the sun rose, they were scorched; and since they had no root, they withered away. ⁷Other seeds fell among thorns, and the thorns grew up and choked them. ⁸Other seeds fell on good soil and brought forth grain, some a hundredfold, some sixty, some thirty. ⁹Let anyone with ears listen!" . . .

¹⁸"Hear then the parable of the sower. ¹⁹When anyone hears the word of the kingdom and does not understand it, the evil one comes and snatches away what is sown in the heart; this is what was sown on the path. ²⁰As for what was sown on rocky ground, this is the one who hears the word and immediately receives it with joy; ²¹yet such a person has no root, but endures only for a while, and when trouble or persecution arises on account of the word, that person immediately falls away. ²²As for what was sown among thorns, this is the one who hears the word, but the cares of the world and the lure of wealth choke the word, and it yields nothing. ²³But as for what was sown on good soil, this is the one who hears the word and understands it, who indeed bears fruit and yields, in one case a hundredfold, in another sixty, and in another thirty."

Primary Hymns and Songs for the Day
"O Spirit of the Living God" (Rom) (O)
    N263, SH222, UM539
        H-3   Hbl-44; Chr-21; Desc-40; Org-40
        S-1   #131-132. Intro. and desc.
"Spirit of the Living God" 23488 (Rom)
        S-1   #212 Vocal desc. idea
    C259, CG233, G288, N283, P322, SA312/313, SH555,
    UM393, VU376
"Thy Word Is a Lamp" 14301 (Pss, Matt)
    C326, CG38, G458, UM601
"Sois la Semilla" ("You Are the Seed") (Matt)
    C478, N528, UM583
"O Blessed Spring" (Matt)
    EL447, S2076, VU632
        H-3   Chr-200; Org-45
"Hymn of Promise" (Matt) (C)
    C638, CG545, G250, N433, UM707, VU703
        H-3   Chr-112; Org-117
        S-1   #270. Desc.

Additional Hymn Suggestions
"The God of Abraham Praise" (Gen)
    C24, CG45, E401, EL831, G49, N24, P488, SH50, UM116
    (PD), VU255
"Where Cross the Crowded Ways of Life" (Gen)
    C665, CG657, E609, EL719, G343, N543, P408, UM427 (PD),
    VU681
"For the Healing of the Nations" (Gen)
    C668, CG698, G346, N576, SA1000, UM428, VU678
"Let There Be Peace on Earth" (Gen)
    C677, UM431
"Come Down, O Love Divine" (Gen, Rom)
    C582, E516, EL804, G282, N289, SA295, UM475, VU367
"Out of the Depths" (Gen)
    C510, N554, S2136, VU611
"God Made from One Blood" (Gen)
    C500, CG686, N427, S2170, VU554
"Blessed Jesus, at Thy Word" (Pss, Matt)
    E440, EL520, G395, N74, P454, UM596 (PD), VU500
"O Word of God Incarnate" (Pss, Matt)
    C322, E632, EL514, G459, N315, P327, UM598 (PD), VU499
"Wonderful Words of Life" (Pss, Matt)
    C323, CG163, N319, SA434, SH549, UM600 (PD)
"Be Thou My Vision" (Pss, Rom)
    C595, CG71, E488, EL793, G450, N451, P339, SA573, SH640,
    UM451, VU642
"Just a Closer Walk with Thee" (Pss, Rom)
    C557, EL697, G835, S2158, SH584
"Lead Me, Guide Me" (Pss, Rom)
    C583, CG403, EL768, G740, S2214, SH582
"Spirit Divine, Attend Our Prayers" (Rom)
    E509, G407, P325, SA210, VU385
"O For a Thousand Tongues to Sing" (Rom)
    C5, CG332, E493, EL886, G610, N42, P466, SA89, SH439,
    UM57 (PD), VU326 (See also WS3001)
"To God Be the Glory" (Rom)
    C72, CG349, G634, P485, SA279, SH545, UM98 (PD)
"Alas! and Did My Savior Bleed" (Rom)
    AH4067, C204, CG182/595, EL337, G212, N199/200, P78,
    SA159, UM294/359, SH172/173
"Every Time I Feel the Spirit" (Rom)
    C592, G66, N282, P315, UM404
"Breathe on Me, Breath of God" (Rom, Matt)
    C254, CG235, E508, G286, N292, P316, SA294, SH224/273,
    UM420 (PD), VU382 (Fr.)
"Holy Spirit, Truth Divine" (Rom, Matt)
    C241, EL398, N63, P321, SA285, UM465, VU368

"Creating God, Your Fingers Trace" (Matt)
    C335, E394/394, EL684, N462, P134, UM109, VU265
"Lord, Dismiss Us with Thy Blessing" (Matt)
    C439, E344, EL545, G546, N77, P538, UM671 (PD), VU425
"Come, Ye Thankful People, Come" (Matt)
    C718, CG372, E290, EL693, G367, N422, P551, SA9, SH355,
    UM694 (PD), VU516
"Come, We That Love the Lord" (Matt) (O)
    CG549, E392, N379, SA831, UM732, VU715
"Marching to Zion" (Matt) (O)
    C707, CG550, EL625, N382, SA831, UM733, VU714
"Mothering God, You Gave Me Birth" (Matt, Comm.)
    C83, EL735, G7, N467, S2050, VU320
"Bring Forth the Kingdom" (Matt)
    N181, S2190, SH130

Additional Contemporary and Modern Suggestions
"The Family Prayer Song" 1680466 (Gen)
"A Wilderness Wandering People" 7068566 (Gen)
"Daughter of God" 4509781 (Gen)
"My Life Is in You, Lord" 17315 (Pss)
"Cry of My Heart" 844980 (Pss)
"God Is the Strength of My Heart" 80919 (Pss)
"Holy and Anointed One" 164361 (Pss)
"Show Me Your Ways" 1675024 (Pss)
"Ancient Words" 2986399 (Pss)
"Jesus, the Light of the World" 6363190 (Pss)
    WS3056 (See also AH4038, CG129, G127, N160, SH103)
"Breathe" 1874117 (Pss, Rom)
"More Precious than Silver" 11335 (Pss, Rom)
"To Know You More" 1767420 (Pss, Rom)
"O For a Thousand Tongues to Sing" 4048754 (Rom)
"My Tribute" 11218 (Rom)
    AH4080, C39, CG574, N14, SH434, UM99; V-8 p. 5. Solo
"Step by Step" 696994 (Matt)
    CG495, G743, WS3004

Vocal Solos
"Just a Closer Walk with Thee" (Pss, Rom, Matt)
    V-5 (2)   p. 31
    V-8   p. 323
"Keep A-Inchin' Along" (Rom, Matt)
    V-7   p. 32

Anthems
"O Blessed Spring" (Matt)
David Cherwien, Augsburg 9781451420753
SATB, keyboard, opt. flute (https://bit.ly/A-20753)

"The Best of Rooms" (Matt)
Wood / arr. Wagner; H.W. Gray GCMRM05002
SATB, organ (https://bit.ly/J-5002)

Other Suggestions
Visuals:
    O   Wedding, prayer, newborn twins, birth certificate
    P   Open Bible, lamp, path, open hand, snare, Ps 119:11
    E   Open manacles, Spirit symbols, open/closed Bibles
    G   Boat/sea, sower/seed, birds/sun/thorns, soil/grain
Matthew as drama can be enacted by one sower or a dozen persons, acting as sower, seeds, birds, and thorns.
Sung Blessing: WS3159. "Let Our Earth Be Peaceful" (Matt)
Alternate Lessons: Isa 55:10-13, Ps 65: (1-8), 9-13
Theme Ideas: Children / Family of God, Conflict, God: Kingdom of God, God: Word of God, Growth, Holy Spirit, Jesus: Mind of Christ

Genesis 28:10-19a

[10]Jacob left Beer-sheba and went toward Haran. [11]He came to a certain place and stayed there for the night, because the sun had set. Taking one of the stones of the place, he put it under his head and lay down in that place. [12]And he dreamed that there was a ladder set up on the earth, the top of it reaching to heaven; and the angels of God were ascending and descending on it. [13]And the LORD stood beside him and said, "I am the LORD, the God of Abraham your father and the God of Isaac; the land on which you lie I will give to you and to your offspring; [14]and your offspring shall be like the dust of the earth, and you shall spread abroad to the west and to the east and to the north and to the south; and all the families of the earth shall be blessed in you and in your offspring. [15]Know that I am with you and will keep you wherever you go, and will bring you back to this land; for I will not leave you until I have done what I have promised you." [16]Then Jacob woke from his sleep and said, "Surely the LORD is in this place—and I did not know it!" [17]And he was afraid, and said, "How awesome is this place! This is none other than the house of God, and this is the gate of heaven."

[18]So Jacob rose early in the morning, and he took the stone that he had put under his head and set it up for a pillar and poured oil on the top of it. [19a]He called that place Bethel.

Psalm 139:1-12, 23-24 (G28/29/426, N715, P248, UM854)

[1]O LORD, you have searched me and known me.
[2]You know when I sit down and when I rise up;
 you discern my thoughts from far away.
[3]You search out my path and my lying down,
 and are acquainted with all my ways.
[4]Even before a word is on my tongue,
 O LORD, you know it completely.
[5]You hem me in, behind and before,
 and lay your hand upon me.
[6]Such knowledge is too wonderful for me;
 it is so high that I cannot attain it.
[7]Where can I go from your spirit?
 Or where can I flee from your presence?
[8]If I ascend to heaven, you are there;
 if I make my bed in Sheol, you are there.
[9]If I take the wings of the morning
 and settle at the farthest limits of the sea,
[10]even there your hand shall lead me,
 and your right hand shall hold me fast.
[11]If I say, "Surely the darkness shall cover me,
 and the light around me become night,"
[12]even the darkness is not dark to you;
 the night is as bright as the day,
 for darkness is as light to you.
. . . .
[23]Search me, O God, and know my heart;
 test me and know my thoughts.
[24]See if there is any wicked way in me,
 and lead me in the way everlasting.

Romans 8:12-25

[12]So then, brothers and sisters, we are debtors, not to the flesh, to live according to the flesh—[13]for if you live according to the flesh, you will die; but if by the Spirit you put to death the deeds of the body, you will live. [14]For all who are led by the Spirit of God are children of God. [15]For you did not receive a spirit of slavery to fall back into fear, but you have received a spirit of adoption. When we cry, "Abba! Father!" [16]it is that very Spirit bearing witness with our spirit that we are children of God, [17]and if children, then heirs, heirs of God and joint heirs with Christ—if, in fact, we suffer with him so that we may also be glorified with him.

[18]I consider that the sufferings of this present time are not worth comparing with the glory about to be revealed to us. [19]For the creation waits with eager longing for the revealing of the children of God; [20]for the creation was subjected to futility, not of its own will but by the will of the one who subjected it, in hope [21]that the creation itself will be set free from its bondage to decay and will obtain the freedom of the glory of the children of God. [22]We know that the whole creation has been groaning in labor pains until now; [23]and not only the creation, but we ourselves, who have the first fruits of the Spirit, groan inwardly while we wait for adoption, the redemption of our bodies. [24]For in hope we were saved. Now hope that is seen is not hope. For who hopes for what is seen? [25]But if we hope for what we do not see, we wait for it with patience.

Matthew 13:24-30, 36-43

[24]He put before them another parable: "The kingdom of heaven may be compared to someone who sowed good seed in his field; [25]but while everybody was asleep, an enemy came and sowed weeds among the wheat, and then went away. [26]So when the plants came up and bore grain, then the weeds appeared as well. [27]And the slaves of the householder came and said to him, 'Master, did you not sow good seed in your field? Where, then, did these weeds come from?' [28]He answered, 'An enemy has done this.' The slaves said to him, 'Then do you want us to go and gather them?' [29]But he replied, 'No; for in gathering the weeds you would uproot the wheat along with them. [30]Let both of them grow together until the harvest; and at harvest time I will tell the reapers, Collect the weeds first and bind them in bundles to be burned, but gather the wheat into my barn.'" . . .

[36]Then he left the crowds and went into the house. And his disciples approached him, saying, "Explain to us the parable of the weeds of the field." [37]He answered, "The one who sows the good seed is the Son of Man; [38]the field is the world, and the good seed are the children of the kingdom; the weeds are the children of the evil one, [39]and the enemy who sowed them is the devil; the harvest is the end of the age, and the reapers are angels. [40]Just as the weeds are collected and burned up with fire, so will it be at the end of the age. [41]The Son of Man will send his angels, and they will collect out of his kingdom all causes of sin and all evildoers, [42]and they will throw them into the furnace of fire, where there will be weeping and gnashing of teeth. [43]Then the righteous will shine like the sun in the kingdom of their Father. Let anyone with ears listen!"

Primary Hymns and Songs for the Day

"Come, Ye Thankful People, Come" (Matt) (O)
    C718, CG372, F.290, EL693, G367, N422, P551, SA9, SH355,
    UM694 (PD), VU516
        H-3   Hbl-54; Chr-58; Desc-94; Org-137
        S-1   #302-303. Harm. with desc.
"We Are Climbing Jacob's Ladder" (Gen)
    N500, UM418
        H-3   Chr-205
        S-1   #187. Choral arr.
"Nearer, My God, to Thee" (Gen)
    C577, N606, SA611, UM528 (PD), VU497 (Fr.)
"Bring Forth the Kingdom" (Matt)
    N181, S2190, SH130
"Love Divine, All Loves Excelling" (Rom) (C)
    C517, CG281, E657, EL631, G366, N43, P376, SA262,
    SH353/354, UM384 (PD), VU333

Additional Hymn Suggestions

"Guide Me, O Thou Great Jehovah" (Gen)
    C622, CG33, E690, EL618, G65, N18/19, P281, SA27, SH51,
    UM127 (PD), VU651 (Fr.)
"Touch the Earth Lightly" (Gen)
    C693, EL739, G713, N569, VU307, WS3129
"Feed Us, Lord" 4636207 (Gen, Comm.)
    G501, WS3167
"Guide My Feet" (Gen, Pss)
    CG637, G741, N497, P354, S2208, SH54
"Lead Me, Guide Me" (Gen, Pss)
    C583, CG403, EL768, G740, S2214, SH582
"Womb of Life" (Pss, Rom, Comm.)
    C14, G3, N274, S2046
"Mothering God, You Gave Me Birth" (Pss, Rom)
    C83, EL735, G7, N467, S2050, VU320
"Loving Spirit" (Pss, Rom)
    C244, EL397, G293, P323, S2123, VU387
"Gather Us In" (Pss, Matt)
    C284, EL532, G401, S2236, SH393
"Hope of the World" (Rom)
    C538, E472, G734, N46, P360, UM178, VU215
"Every Time I Feel the Spirit" (Rom)
    C592, G66, N282, P315, UM404
"For the Healing of the Nations" (Rom, Matt)
    C668, CG698, G346, N576, SA1000, UM428, VU678
"We Shall Overcome" (Rom)
    AH4047/4048, C630, G379, N570, UM533
"The Church's One Foundation" (Rom)
    C272, CG246, E525, EL654, G321, N386, P442, SH233,
    UM545/546, VU332 (Fr.)
"Holy" ("*Santo*") (Rom)
    EL762, G594, SH39, S2019
"O Holy Spirit, Root of Life" (Rom)
    C251, EL399, N57, S2121, VU379
"Baptized in Water" (Rom, Baptism)
    CG449, E294, EL456, G482, P492, S2248, SH666
"Live Into Hope" (Rom)
    G772, P332, VU699
"*Sois la Semilla*" ("You Are the Seed") (Matt)
    C478, N528, UM583
"God the Sculptor of the Mountains" (Matt)
    EL736, G5, S2060
"Come to Tend God's Garden" (Matt)
    N586
"Christ will Come Again" (Matt)
    N608

Additional Contemporary and Modern Suggestions

"Surely the Presence of the Lord" 7909 (Gen)
    C263, UM328; S-2 #200. Stanzas for soloist
"He Who Began a Good Work in You" 15238 (Gen)
"Holy Ground" 21198 (Gen)
    C112, G406, S2272, SA400
"Shout to the North" 1562261 (Gen)
    G319, SA1009, WS3042
"In God Alone" (Gen)
    G814, WS3135
"How Great Is Our God" 4348399 (Gen, Pss)
    CG322, SH458, WS3003
"Ah, Lord God" 17896 (Gen, Pss)
"God Will Make a Way" 458620 (Gen, Pss)
    SA492, SH57
"In the Secret" 1810119 (Gen, Pss)
"Lead Me, Lord" 1609045 (Gen, Pss)
"He Knows My Name" 2151368 (Gen, Pss)
"God of Wonders" 3118757 (Pss)
    SH9, WS3034
"The Potter's Hand" 2449771 (Pss)
"These Hands" 3251827 (Pss)
"Song of Hope" ("Heaven Come Down") 5111477 (Rom)
"Spirit of the Living God" 23488 (Rom)
    C259, CG233, G288, N283, P322, SA312/313, SH555,
    UM393, VU376
"Holy" ("*Santo*") (Rom)
    EL762, G594, SH39, S2019
"Holy, Holy" 18792 (Rom)
"Come, Holy Spirit" 3383953 (Rom)
    WS3092 (See also SH223, WS3091)
"On Eagle's Wings" (Matt)
    C77, CG51, EL787, G43, N775, SH318, UM143, VU807/808;
    S-2 #143. Stanzas for soloist

Vocal Solos

"When I Lay My Burden Down" (Gen)
    V-7   p. 76
"I Am His, and He Is Mine" (Gen, Rom)
    V-8   p. 348
"Then Shall the Righteous Shine Forth" (Matt 13:43)
    V-8   p. 274

Anthems

"The Gate of Heaven" (Gen)
Craig Courtney; Beckenhorst BP1979
SATB, piano, cello or violin (https://bit.ly/BP1979)

"O Lord, You Know Me Completely" (Pss)
Hal H. Hopson; Choristers Guild CGA-833
Unison/2-part, keyboard (https://bit.ly/CGA-833)

Other Suggestions

Visuals:
    O   Night, stone, ladder, angels, dust, gate, oil
    P   Sit/stand, path, bed, hand, wings, sea, light/dark
    E   Children, fear, adoption papers, will, fruit, labor
    G   Seed, bundle of weeds/wheat, scythe, harvest/field,
           angels, fire, Matt 13: 43, sun
Call to Worship: N774 (Pss)
Opening Prayer: N828 or N831 (Rom, Matt)
Confession and Assurance: N835 and N841 (Matt, Rom)
Canticle: UM205. "Canticle of Light and Darkness" (Pss)
Sung Prayer: WS3115. "Covenant Prayer" (Rom)
*Alternate Lessons: Wisdom of Sol 12:13, 16-19 or Isa 44:6-8,
    Ps 86:11-17*
Theme Ideas: Children / Family of God, God: Faithfulness, God:
    Kingdom of God, God: Presence, Growth, Holy Spirit, Hope

Genesis 29:15-28

¹⁵Then Laban said to Jacob, "Because you are my kinsman, should you therefore serve me for nothing? Tell me, what shall your wages be?" ¹⁶Now Laban had two daughters; the name of the elder was Leah, and the name of the younger was Rachel. ¹⁷Leah's eyes were lovely, and Rachel was graceful and beautiful. ¹⁸Jacob loved Rachel; so he said, "I will serve you seven years for your younger daughter Rachel." ¹⁹Laban said, "It is better that I give her to you than that I should give her to any other man; stay with me." ²⁰So Jacob served seven years for Rachel, and they seemed to him but a few days because of the love he had for her. ²¹Then Jacob said to Laban, "Give me my wife that I may go in to her, for my time is completed." ²²So Laban gathered together all the people of the place, and made a feast. ²³But in the evening he took his daughter Leah and brought her to Jacob; and he went in to her. ²⁴(Laban gave his maid Zilpah to his daughter Leah to be her maid.) ²⁵When morning came, it was Leah! And Jacob said to Laban, "What is this you have done to me? Did I not serve with you for Rachel? Why then have you deceived me?" ²⁶Laban said, "This is not done in our country—giving the younger before the firstborn. ²⁷Complete the week of this one, and we will give you the other also in return for serving me another seven years." ²⁸Jacob did so, and completed her week; then Laban gave him his daughter Rachel as a wife.

Psalm 105:1-11, 45b (G59, N691, UM828)

¹O give thanks to the LORD, call on his name,
  make known his deeds among the peoples.
²Sing to him, sing praises to him;
  tell of all his wonderful works.
³Glory in his holy name;
  let the hearts of those who seek the LORD rejoice.
⁴Seek the LORD and his strength;
  seek his presence continually.
⁵Remember the wonderful works he has done,
  his miracles, and the judgments he uttered,
⁶O offspring of his servant Abraham,
  children of Jacob, his chosen ones.
⁷He is the LORD our God;
  his judgments are in all the earth.
⁸He is mindful of his covenant forever,
  of the word that he commanded, for a thousand generations,
⁹the covenant that he made with Abraham,
  his sworn promise to Isaac,
¹⁰which he confirmed to Jacob as a statute,
  to Israel as an everlasting covenant,
¹¹saying, "To you I will give the land of Canaan
  as your portion for an inheritance."
. . . .
⁴⁵ᵇPraise the LORD!

Romans 8:26-39

²⁶Likewise the Spirit helps us in our weakness; for we do not know how to pray as we ought, but that very Spirit intercedes with sighs too deep for words. ²⁷And God, who searches the heart, knows what is the mind of the Spirit, because the Spirit intercedes for the saints according to the will of God. ²⁸We know that all things work together for good for those who love God, who are called according to his purpose. ²⁹For those whom he foreknew he also predestined to be conformed to the image of his Son, in order that he might be the firstborn within a large family. ³⁰And those whom he predestined he also called; and those whom he called he also justified; and those whom he justified he also glorified. ³¹What then are we to say about these things? If God is for us, who is against us? ³²He who did not withhold his own Son, but gave him up for all of us, will he not with him also give us everything else? ³³Who will bring any charge against God's elect? It is God who justifies. ³⁴Who is to condemn? It is Christ Jesus, who died, yes, who was raised, who is at the right hand of God, who indeed intercedes for us. ³⁵Who will separate us from the love of Christ? Will hardship, or distress, or persecution, or famine, or nakedness, or peril, or sword? ³⁶As it is written,
  "For your sake we are being killed all day long;
    we are accounted as sheep to be slaughtered."
³⁷No, in all these things we are more than conquerors through him who loved us. ³⁸For I am convinced that neither death, nor life, nor angels, nor rulers, nor things present, nor things to come, nor powers, ³⁹nor height, nor depth, nor anything else in all creation, will be able to separate us from the love of God in Christ Jesus our Lord.

Matthew 13:31-33, 44-52

³¹He put before them another parable: "The kingdom of heaven is like a mustard seed that someone took and sowed in his field; ³²it is the smallest of all the seeds, but when it has grown it is the greatest of shrubs and becomes a tree, so that the birds of the air come and make nests in its branches." ³³He told them another parable: "The kingdom of heaven is like yeast that a woman took and mixed in with three measures of flour until all of it was leavened." . . .
⁴⁴"The kingdom of heaven is like treasure hidden in a field, which someone found and hid; then in his joy he goes and sells all that he has and buys that field.
⁴⁵"Again, the kingdom of heaven is like a merchant in search of fine pearls; ⁴⁶on finding one pearl of great value, he went and sold all that he had and bought it.
⁴⁷"Again, the kingdom of heaven is like a net that was thrown into the sea and caught fish of every kind; ⁴⁸when it was full, they drew it ashore, sat down, and put the good into baskets but threw out the bad. ⁴⁹So it will be at the end of the age. The angels will come out and separate the evil from the righteous ⁵⁰and throw them into the furnace of fire, where there will be weeping and gnashing of teeth.
⁵¹"Have you understood all this?" They answered, "Yes." ⁵²And he said to them, "Therefore every scribe who has been trained for the kingdom of heaven is like the master of a household who brings out of his treasure what is new and what is old."

Primary Hymns and Songs for the Day

"I Love Thy Kingdom, Lord" (Matt) (O)
  C274, CG262, E524, G310, N312, P441, UM540
    H-3   Hbl-53; Chr-167; Desc-97; Org-147
    S-1   #311. Desc. and harm.
"Bring Forth the Kingdom" (Matt)
  N181, S2190, SH130
"Seek Ye First" 1352 (Matt)
  C354, CG436, E711, G175, P333, SA675, SH126, UM405,
  VU356
"O Day of God, Draw Nigh" (Matt, Pss) (C)
  C700, E601, N611, P452, UM730 (PD), VU688/689 (Fr.)
    H-3   Hbl-79; Chr-141; Desc-95; Org-143
    S-1   #306-308. Various treatments

Additional Hymn Suggestions

"Where Cross the Crowded Ways of Life" (Gen)
  C665, CG657, E609, EL719, G343, N543, P408, UM427 (PD),
  VU681
"When Love Is Found" (Gen)
  C499, CG524, N362, SH279, UM643, VU489
"O God, in a Mysterious Way" (Gen, Rom)
  CG39, E677, G30, N412, P270, SA17, SH47
"God Made from One Blood" (Gen)
  C500, CG686, N427, S2170, VU554
"We Sing to You, O God" (Pss)
  EL791, N9, S2001
"Praise Our God Above" (Pss, Matt)
  N424, P480, S2061
"Holy God, We Praise Thy Name" (Rom)
  CG9, E366, EL414 (PD), G4, N276, P460, SH431, UM79,
  VU894 (Fr.)
"Children of the Heavenly Father" (Rom)
  CG69, EL781, N487, SH42, UM141
"Hope of the World" (Rom)
  C538, E472, G734, N46, P360, UM178, VU215
"I am Thine, O Lord" (Rom)
  AH4087, C601, CG504, N455, SA586, UM419 (PD)
"O Love That Wilt Not Let Me Go" (Rom)
  C540, CG631, G833, N485, P384, SA616, SH314, UM480, VU658
"Prayer Is the Soul's Sincere Desire" (Rom)
  CG391, N508, SA784, UM492
"By Gracious Powers" (Rom)
  E695/696, EL626, G818, N413, P342, UM517
"Like the Murmur of the Dove's Song" (Rom)
  C245, CG233, E513, EL403, G285, N270, P314, SH407,
  UM544, VU205
"O Holy Spirit, Root of Life" (Rom)
  C251, EL399, N57, S2121, VU379
"Fight the Good Fight" (Rom)
  E552, G846, P307 (PD), SA952, VU674
"Jesus, Priceless Treasure" (Matt)
  E701, EL775, G830, N480 P365, UM532 (PD), VU667 and
  VU668 (Fr.)
"Sois la Semilla" ("You Are the Seed") (Matt)
  C478, N528, UM583
"Come, Ye Thankful People, Come" (Matt) (O)
  C718, CG372, E290, EL693, G367, N422, P551, SA9, SH355,
  UM694 (PD), VU516
"Bring Forth the Kingdom" (Matt)
  N181, S2190, SH130
"We All Are One in Mission" (Matt)
  CG269, EL576, G733, P435, S2243
"Enter in the Realm of God" (Matt)
  N615

Additional Contemporary and Modern Suggestions

"Your Love, Oh Lord" 1894255 (Gen, Pss)
"You Never Let Go" 4674166 (Gen, Rom)
"How Great Is Our God" 4348399 (Pss)
  CG322, SH458, WS3003
"You Are Good" 3383788 (Pss)
  AH4018, SH455, WS3014
"Forever" 3148428 (Pss)
  CG53, SA363, WS3023
"In the Lord I'll Be Ever Thankful" (Pss)
  G654, S2195, SH316
"Celebrate Love" 155246 (Rom)
"There's a Song" 2041825 (Rom)
"Change My Heart, O God" 1565 (Rom)
  EL801, G695, S2152, SA409, SH507
"Cry of My Heart" 844980 (Rom)
"In His Time" 25981 (Rom)
"Hallelujah" ("Your Love Is Amazing") 3091812 (Rom)
"Come, Holy Spirit" 3383953 (Rom)
  WS3092 (See also SH223, WS3091)
"Your Grace Is Enough" 4477026 (Rom)
"Love Moves You" ("Love Alone") 5775514 (Rom)
"Think about His Love" 16299 (Rom)
"No Greater Love" 930887 (Rom)
"The Power of Your Love" 917491 (Rom)
"I Could Sing of Your Love Forever" 1043199 (Rom)
"Show Me Your Ways" 1675024 (Rom)
"Good to Me" 313480 (Rom)
"The Happy Song" 1043209 (Rom)
"You Are My All in All" 825356 (Rom, Matt)
  CG571, G519, SH335, WS3040
"More Precious than Silver" 11335 (Matt)
"Fill My Cup, Lord" 15946 (Matt) (Stanzas 2-3)
  C351, UM641 (refrain only), WS3093
"When It's All Been Said and Done" 2788353 (Matt)
"Forever Reign" 5639997 (Matt)

Vocal Solos

"A Song of Joy" (Pss)
  V-1   p. 2
"If God Be For Us" (Rom)
  V-2
"Who Shall Separate Us?" (Rom)
  V-8   p. 265

Anthems

"If God Be for Us" (Rom)
Joseph M. Martin; Shawnee Press HL35031837
SATB, keyboard (https://bit.ly/HL31837)

"He Is Mine (*Ni Wangu*)" (Rom)
arr. Hal H. Hopson; Hope C5193
SAB, keyboard, opt. percussion (https://bit.ly/C-5193)

Other Suggestions

Visuals:
  O   Young lovers, "7," feast, engagement
  P   Singing, hearts, covenant, praise
  E   Prayer, Spirit, heart, Rom 8:28, 31, 38, Jesus, newborn,
         cross, disaster, love
  G   Mustard seed/shrub, birds/nest, yeast/flour, treasure,
         pearl, net/fish/baskets, fire, new/old
Call to Prayer: N521. "In Solitude" (Rom)
Call to Prayer: SH223, WS3091. "Come, Holy Spirit" (Rom)
Affirmation of Faith: UM887 or WSL76 or WSL77 (Rom)
Theme Ideas: Children / Family of God, Conflict, Discipleship
  / Following God, God: Kingdom of God, God: Love of God,
  God: Providence / God our Help, Growth, Holy Spirit, Love

Genesis 32:22-31

[22]The same night he got up and took his two wives, his two maids, and his eleven children, and crossed the ford of the Jabbok. [23]He took them and sent them across the stream, and likewise everything that he had. [24]Jacob was left alone; and a man wrestled with him until daybreak. [25]When the man saw that he did not prevail against Jacob, he struck him on the hip socket; and Jacob's hip was put out of joint as he wrestled with him. [26]Then he said, "Let me go, for the day is breaking." But Jacob said, "I will not let you go, unless you bless me." [27]So he said to him, "What is your name?" And he said, "Jacob." [28]Then the man said, "You shall no longer be called Jacob, but Israel, for you have striven with God and with humans, and have prevailed." [29]Then Jacob asked him, "Please tell me your name." But he said, "Why is it that you ask my name?" And there he blessed him. [30]So Jacob called the place Peniel, saying, "For I have seen God face to face, and yet my life is preserved." [31]The sun rose upon him as he passed Penuel, limping because of his hip.

Psalm 17:1-7, 15 (G211, N629, UM749)

[1]Hear a just cause, O LORD; attend to my cry;
  give ear to my prayer from lips free of deceit.
[2]From you let my vindication come;
  let your eyes see the right.
[3]If you try my heart, if you visit me by night,
  if you test me, you will find no wickedness in me;
  my mouth does not transgress.
[4]As for what others do, by the word of your lips
  I have avoided the ways of the violent.
[5]My steps have held fast to your paths;
  my feet have not slipped.
[6]I call upon you, for you will answer me, O God;
  incline your ear to me, hear my words.
[7]Wondrously show your steadfast love,
  O savior of those who seek refuge
  from their adversaries at your right hand.
. . . .
[15]As for me, I shall behold your face in righteousness;
  when I awake I shall be satisfied, beholding your likeness.

Romans 9:1-5

[1]I am speaking the truth in Christ—I am not lying; my conscience confirms it by the Holy Spirit—[2]I have great sorrow and unceasing anguish in my heart. [3]For I could wish that I myself were accursed and cut off from Christ for the sake of my own people, my kindred according to the flesh. [4]They are Israelites, and to them belong the adoption, the glory, the covenants, the giving of the law, the worship, and the promises; [5]to them belong the patriarchs, and from them, according to the flesh, comes the Messiah, who is over all, God blessed forever. Amen.

Matthew 14:13-21

[13]Now when Jesus heard this, he withdrew from there in a boat to a deserted place by himself. But when the crowds heard it, they followed him on foot from the towns. [14]When he went ashore, he saw a great crowd; and he had compassion for them and cured their sick. [15]When it was evening, the disciples came to him and said, "This is a deserted place, and the hour is now late; send the crowds away so that they may go into the villages and buy food for themselves." [16]Jesus said to them, "They need not go away; you give them something to eat." [17]They replied, "We have nothing here but five loaves and two fish." [18]And he said, "Bring them here to me." [19]Then he ordered the crowds to sit down on the grass. Taking the five loaves and the two fish, he looked up to heaven, and blessed and broke the loaves, and gave them to the disciples, and the disciples gave them to the crowds. [20]And all ate and were filled; and they took up what was left over of the broken pieces, twelve baskets full. [21]And those who ate were about five thousand men, besides women and children.

Primary Hymns and Songs for the Day

"Holy God, We Praise Thy Name" (Rom) (O)
  CG9, E366, EL414 (PD), G4, N276, P460, SH431, UM79,
  VU894 (Fr.)
    H-3   Chr-78, 98; Desc-48; Org-48
    S-1   #151-153. Harmonization and descants
"O Love That Wilt Not Let Me Go" (Gen)
  C540, CG631, G833, N485, P384, SA616, SH314, UM480,
  VU658
    H-3   Chr-146; Org-142
"Break Thou the Bread of Life" (Matt, Comm.)
  C321, CG35, EL515, G460, N321, P329, SA802, SH552,
  UM599 (PD), VU501
    H-3   Chr-44; Org-15
"Where Cross the Crowded Ways of Life" (Matt) (C)
  C665, CG657, E609, EL719, G343, N543, P408, UM427 (PD),
  VU681
    H-3   Chr-178, 180; Org-44
    S-1   #141-3 Various treatments

Additional Hymn Suggestions

"The God of Abraham Praise" (Gen)
  C24, CG45, E401, EL831, G49, N24, P488, SH50, UM116
  (PD), VU255
"When Morning Gilds the Skies" (Gen)
  C100, CG345, E427, EL853 (PD), G667, N86, P487, SA403,
  SH466, UM185, VU339 (Fr.)
"Be Thou My Vision" (Gen) (O)
  C595, CG71, E488, EL793, G450, N451, P339, SA573, SH640,
  UM451, VU642
"Here, O My Lord, I See Thee" (Gen, Comm.)
  C416, CG460, E318, G517, N336, P520, UM623, VU459
"We Walk By Faith" (Gen)
  CG634, E209, EL635, G817, N256, P399, S2196, SH660
"Jesus, Lover of My Soul" (Gen, Pss)
  C542, CG406, E699, G440, N546, P303, SA257, SH542/543,
  UM479, VU669
"Sweet Hour of Prayer" (Gen, Matt)
  C570, CG412, N505, SA787, SH578, UM496 (PD)
"God Be With You Till We Meet Again" (Gen, Matt)
  C434, CG523, EL536, G541/542, N81, P540, SA1027,
  UM672/673, VU422/423
"Open Your Ears" (Jer)
  E536, EL519, G453, VU272
"If Thou But Suffer God to Guide Thee" (Rom)
  C565, CG76, E635, EL769, G816, N410, P282, SA40, SH326,
  UM142 (PD), VU285 (Fr.) and VU286
"Standing on the Promises" (Rom)
  AH4057, C552, CG625, G838, SA522, SH45, UM374 (PD)
"Holy Spirit, Truth Divine" (Rom)
  C241, EL398, N63, P321, SA285, UM465, VU368
Tú Has Venido a la Orilla ("Lord, You Have Come to the
Lakeshore") (Matt)
  C342, EL817, G721, N173, P377, SH599, UM344, VU563
"Softly and Tenderly, Jesus Is Calling" (Matt)
  C340, CG474, EL608, G418, N449, SA435, SH601, UM348
"Dear Lord and Father of Mankind" (Matt)
  (Alternate Text—"Parent of Us All")
  C594, CG413, E652/563, G169, N502, P345, SA456, UM358
  (PD), VU608
"For the Bread Which You Have Broken" (Matt, Comm.)
  C411, E340/E341, EL494, G516, P508/P509, UM614/
  UM615, VU470
"Let Us Break Bread Together" (Matt, Comm.)
  AH4140, C425, CG461, EL471 (PD), G525, N330, P513,
  SH674, UM618, VU480

"Bread of the World" (Matt, Comm.)
  C387, E301, G499, N346, P502, UM624, VU461
"All Who Hunger" (Matt)
  C419, CG303, EL461, G509, S2126, VU460
"Come, Share the Lord" (Matt, Comm.)
  C408, CG459, G510, S2269, VU469

Additional Contemporary and Modern Suggestions

"Surely the Presence of the Lord" 7909 (Gen)
  C263, UM328; S-2 #200. Stanzas for soloist
"Spirit of the Living God" 23488 (Gen)
  C259, CG233, G288, N283, P322, SA312/313, SH555,
  UM393, VU376
"Seek Ye First" 1352 (Gen)
  C354, CG436, E711, G175, P333, SA675, SH126, UM405,
  VU356
"He Who Began a Good Work in You" 15238 (Gen)
"Holy Ground" 21198 (Gen)
  C112, G406, S2272, SA400
"How Great Is Our God" 4348399 (Gen, Pss)
  CG322, SH458, WS3003
"Just Let Me Say" 1406413 (Gen)
"He Knows My Name" 2151368 (Gen, Pss)
"The Steadfast Love of the Lord" 21590 (Gen, Pss)
"Your Love, Oh Lord" 1894255 (Gen, Pss)
"Jesus, Name above All Names" 21291 (Rom)
  S2071, SA82
"Spirit Song" 27824 (Matt, Comm.)
  C352, SH409, UM347
"Jesus, We Are Here" (*"Yesu Tawa Pano"*) (Matt)
  EL529, G392, S2273, SH611
"You Who Are Thirsty" 814453 (Matt, Comm.)
"Across the Lands" 3709898 (Matt)
  SH654, WS3032
"There Will Be Bread" 4512352 (Matt)
"You Are" 4387343 (Matt)

Vocal Solos

"Come, O Thou Traveler Unknown" (Gen)
  V-9   p. 44
"A Contrite Heart" (Pss)
  V-4   p. 10
"Softly and Tenderly" (Matt)
  V-5 (3)   p. 52
"Let Us Break Bread Together" (Matt, Comm.)
  V-6   p. 38

Anthems

"O Love" (Gen)
Elaine Hagenberg: Beckenhorst Press BP2097
SATB, piano (https://bit.ly/BP-2097)

"At the Table of the Lord" (Matt, Comm.)
Jay Althouse; Hope C5336
SAB, piano (SATB C5180) (https://bit.ly/C-5336)

Other Suggestions

Visuals:
  O   River ford, wrestling, hip, cane, Gen 32:26b, name
  P   Prayer, heart, night, feet/path, listening
  E   Broken heart, salvation history, Christ
  G   Boat, healing, loaves, two fish, twelve baskets, 5,000
Opening Prayer: N818 or UM477 (Gen)
Poem: UM387. Come, O Thou Traveler Unknown (Gen)
Benediction: WSL167. "Go! Never stop going out" (Matt)
Alternate Lessons: Isa 55:1-5, Ps 145:8-9, 14-21
Theme Ideas: Bread of Life, Communion, God: Hunger / Thirst
  for God, God: Love of God, God: Presence

Genesis 37:1-4, 12-28

¹Jacob settled in the land where his father had lived as an alien, the land of Canaan. ²This is the story of the family of Jacob. Joseph, being seventeen years old, was shepherding the flock with his brothers; he was a helper to the sons of Bilhah and Zilpah, his father's wives; and Joseph brought a bad report of them to their father.

³Now Israel loved Joseph more than any other of his children, because he was the son of his old age; and he had made him a long robe with sleeves. ⁴But when his brothers saw that their father loved him more than all his brothers, they hated him, and could not speak peaceably to him. . . .

¹²Now his brothers went to pasture their father's flock near Shechem. ¹³And Israel said to Joseph, "Are not your brothers pasturing the flock at Shechem? Come, I will send you to them." He answered, "Here I am." ¹⁴So he said to him, "Go now, see if it is well with your brothers and with the flock; and bring word back to me." So he sent him from the valley of Hebron.

He came to Shechem, ¹⁵and a man found him wandering in the fields; the man asked him, "What are you seeking?" ¹⁶"I am seeking my brothers," he said; "tell me, please, where they are pasturing the flock." ¹⁷The man said, "They have gone away, for I heard them say, 'Let us go to Dothan.'" So Joseph went after his brothers, and found them at Dothan. ¹⁸They saw him from a distance, and before he came near to them, they conspired to kill him. ¹⁹They said to one another, "Here comes this dreamer. ²⁰Come now, let us kill him and throw him into one of the pits; then we shall say that a wild animal has devoured him, and we shall see what will become of his dreams." ²¹But when Reuben heard it, he delivered him out of their hands, saying, "Let us not take his life." ²²Reuben said to them, "Shed no blood; throw him into this pit here in the wilderness, but lay no hand on him" —that he might rescue him out of their hand and restore him to his father. ²³So when Joseph came to his brothers, they stripped him of his robe, the long robe with sleeves that he wore; ²⁴and they took him and threw him into a pit. The pit was empty; there was no water in it.

²⁵Then they sat down to eat; and looking up they saw a caravan of Ishmaelites coming from Gilead, with their camels carrying gum, balm, and resin, on their way to carry it down to Egypt. ²⁶Then Judah said to his brothers, "What profit is it if we kill our brother and conceal his blood? ²⁷Come, let us sell him to the Ishmaelites, and not lay our hands on him, for he is our brother, our own flesh." And his brothers agreed. ²⁸When some Midianite traders passed by, they drew Joseph up, lifting him out of the pit, and sold him to the Ishmaelites for twenty pieces of silver. And they took Joseph to Egypt.

Psalm 105:1-6, 16-22, 45b (G59, N691, UM828)

¹O give thanks to the LORD, call on his name,
    make known his deeds among the peoples.
²Sing to him, sing praises to him;
    tell of all his wonderful works.
³Glory in his holy name;
    let the hearts of those who seek the LORD rejoice.
⁴Seek the LORD and his strength;
    seek his presence continually.
⁵Remember the wonderful works he has done,
    his miracles, and the judgments he uttered,
⁶O offspring of his servant Abraham,
    children of Jacob, his chosen ones.
. . . .
¹⁶When he summoned famine against the land,
    and broke every staff of bread,
¹⁷he had sent a man ahead of them,
    Joseph, who was sold as a slave.
¹⁸His feet were hurt with fetters,
    his neck was put in a collar of iron;

¹⁹until what he had said came to pass,
    the word of the LORD kept testing him.
²⁰The king sent and released him;
    the ruler of the peoples set him free.
²¹He made him lord of his house,
    and ruler of all his possessions,
²²to instruct his officials at his pleasure,
    and to teach his elders wisdom.
. . . .
⁴⁵ᵇPraise the LORD!

Romans 10:5-15

⁵Moses writes concerning the righteousness that comes from the law, that "the person who does these things will live by them." ⁶But the righteousness that comes from faith says, "Do not say in your heart, 'Who will ascend into heaven?'" (that is, to bring Christ down) ⁷or 'Who will descend into the abyss?'" (that is, to bring Christ up from the dead). ⁸But what does it say?
    "The word is near you,
        on your lips and in your heart"
(that is, the word of faith that we proclaim); ⁹because if you confess with your lips that Jesus is Lord and believe in your heart that God raised him from the dead, you will be saved. ¹⁰For one believes with the heart and so is justified, and one confesses with the mouth and so is saved. ¹¹The scripture says, "No one who believes in him will be put to shame." ¹²For there is no distinction between Jew and Greek; the same Lord is Lord of all and is generous to all who call on him. ¹³For, "Everyone who calls on the name of the Lord shall be saved."

¹⁴But how are they to call on one in whom they have not believed? And how are they to believe in one of whom they have never heard? And how are they to hear without someone to proclaim him? ¹⁵And how are they to proclaim him unless they are sent? As it is written, "How beautiful are the feet of those who bring good news!"

Matthew 14:22-33

²²Immediately he made the disciples get into the boat and go on ahead to the other side, while he dismissed the crowds. ²³And after he had dismissed the crowds, he went up the mountain by himself to pray. When evening came, he was there alone, ²⁴but by this time the boat, battered by the waves, was far from the land, for the wind was against them. ²⁵And early in the morning he came walking toward them on the sea. ²⁶But when the disciples saw him walking on the sea, they were terrified, saying, "It is a ghost!" And they cried out in fear. ²⁷But immediately Jesus spoke to them and said, "Take heart, it is I; do not be afraid."

²⁸Peter answered him, "Lord, if it is you, command me to come to you on the water." ²⁹He said, "Come." So Peter got out of the boat, started walking on the water, and came toward Jesus. ³⁰But when he noticed the strong wind, he became frightened, and beginning to sink, he cried out, "Lord, save me!" ³¹Jesus immediately reached out his hand and caught him, saying to him, "You of little faith, why did you doubt?" ³²When they got into the boat, the wind ceased. ³³And those in the boat worshiped him, saying, "Truly you are the Son of God."

Primary Hymns and Songs for the Day

"How Firm a Foundation" (Rom, Matt) (O)
  C618, CG425, E636/637, EL796, G463, N407, P361, SA804,
  SH291, UM529 (PD), VU660
    H-3　Hbl-14, 19, 27; Chr-102; Desc-41; Org-41
    S-1　#133. Harmonization
    　　　#134. Performance note
"Children of the Heavenly Father" (Gen, Pss)
  CG69, EL781, N487, SH42, UM141
    H-3　Chr-46; Desc-102
    S-2　#180-185. Various treatments
"Holy" ("*Santo*") (Rom)
  EL762, G594, SH39, S2019
"Here I Am, Lord" (Gen, Matt, Rom) (C)
  C452, CG482, EL574, G69, P525, SA1002, SH608, UM593,
  VU509
    H-3　Chr-97; Org-54

Additional Hymn Suggestions

"Guide Me, O Thou Great Jehovah" (Gen) (O)
  C622, CG33, E690, EL618, G65, N18/19, P281, SA27, SH51,
  UM127 (PD), VU651 (Fr.)
"We Shall Overcome" (Gen)
  AH4047/4048, C630, G379, N570, UM533
"Praise to the Lord, the Almighty" (Gen, Pss)
  C25, CG319, E390, EL858 (PD) and 859, G35, N22, P482,
  SA56, SH453, UM139, VU220 (Fr.) and VU221
"To God Be the Glory" (Rom)
  C72, CG349, G634, P485, SA279, SH545, UM98 (PD)
"I Love to Tell the Story" (Rom)
  C480, CG581, EL661, G462, N522, SA846, SH569, UM156,
  VU343
"At the Name of Jesus" (Rom)
  CG424, E435, EL416, G264, P148, SA74, SH657, UM168,
  VU335
"Here, O Lord, Your Servants Gather" (Rom, Comm.)
  C278, EL530, G311, N72, P465, UM552, VU362
"Just As I Am" (Rom)
  C339, CG500, E693, EL592, G442, N207, P370, SA503,
  SH500, UM357 (PD), VU508
"In Christ There Is No East or West" (Rom)
  C687, CG273, E529, EL650 (PD), G317/318, N394/395,
  P439/440, SA1006, SH226, UM548, VU606
"A Place at the Table" (Rom, Comm.)
  G769, WS3149
"We Walk by Faith" (Rom, Matt)
  CG634, E209, EL635, G817, N256, P399, S2196, SH660
"Take, O Take Me as I Am" 4562041 (Rom, Matt)
  EL814, G698, SH620, WS3119
"Give to the Winds Thy Fears" (Matt)
  CG55, G815, N404, P286, SA643, UM129 (PD), VU636
"I Sing the Almighty Power of God" (Matt)
  C64, CG19, E398, G32, N12, P288, SA36, SH15, UM152,
  VU231
"O Sing a Song of Bethlehem" (Matt)
  CG164, G159, N51, P308, UM179 (PD)
"My Hope Is Built" (Matt)
  AH4105, C537, CG590, EL596/597, G353, N403, P379,
  SA662, SH324, UM368 (PD)
"Precious Lord, Take My Hand" (Matt)
  C628, CG400, EL773, G834, N472, P404, SH336, UM474,
  VU670
"Jesus, Lover of My Soul" (Matt)
  C542, CG406, E699, G440, N546, P303, SA257, SH542/543,
  UM479, VU669
"Jesus, Savior, Pilot Me" (Matt)
  EL755, N441, SA655, UM509 (PD), VU637

"Wade in the Water" (Matt)
  AH4046, C371, EL459 (PD), S2107
"I'm So Glad Jesus Lifted Me" (Matt)
  C529, EL860 (PD), N474, S2151
"Eternal Father, Strong to Save" (Matt)
  C85, CG14, E608, EL756, G8, P562 (PD), S2191, SA11,
  VU659
"My Life Flows On" (Matt)
  C619, CG592, EL763, G821, N476, S2212, SA663, VU716

Additional Contemporary and Modern Suggestions

"Give Thanks" 20285 (Pss)
  C528, CG373, G647, S2036, SA364, SH489
"In the Lord I'll Be Ever Thankful" (Pss)
  G654, S2195, SH316
"How Great Is Our God" 4348399 (Pss)
  CG322, SH458, WS3003
"Step by Step" 696994 (Pss, Matt)
  CG495, G743, WS3004
"How Can I Keep from Singing" 4822372 (Pss, Matt)
"Came to My Rescue" 4705190 (Pss, Matt)
"He Is Lord" 1515225 (Rom)
  C117, CG208, SA222, SH657, UM177
"One Bread, One Body" (Rom, Comm.)
  C393, EL496, G530, SH678, UM620, VU467
"God Is So Good" 4956994 (Rom)
  G658, S2056, SH461
"Please Enter My Heart, Hosanna" 2485371 (Rom)
"God Is Good All the Time" 1729073 (Rom)
"The Heavens Shall Declare" 904033 (Rom)
"We Will Dance" 1034438 (Rom)
"I Will Call upon the Lord" 11263 (Rom, Matt)
  G621, S2002
"Cares Chorus" 25974 (Matt)
"You Never Let Go" 4674166 (Matt)
"Foundation" 706151 (Matt)
"Freedom in the Spirit" 7127886 (Matt)

Vocal Solos

"Here I Am" (Gen)
  V-1　　　p. 19
"Wade in the Water" (Matt, Baptism)
  V-5 (2)　p. 46

Anthems

"I Sought the Lord" (Matt)
Karen Marrolli; MorningStar MSM-50-3094
SATB, piano (https://bit.ly/MSM-50-3094)

"O Lord, Increase My Faith" (Matt)
Orlando Gibbons; E.C. Schirmer 375
SATB *a cappella* (https://bit.ly/ECS375)

Other Suggestions

Visuals:
  O　Staff, colorful robe, pit, caravan, twenty coins, Egypt
  P　Singing, hearts, famine, open manacles, iron collar
  E　Christ, heart, speaking, Rom 10:8b, 13, 15b, feet
  G　Boat, mountain, prayer, storm/sea
Greeting: N822 (Pss)
Opening Prayer: N828 (Matt)
Medley: "Take This Moment, Sign, and Space" (WS3118) and
  "Take, O Take Me As I Am" (EL814, G698, SH620, WS3119)
  (John)
Blessing: N876 (Matt)
Alternate Lessons: 1 Kgs 19:9-18, Ps 85:8-13
Theme Ideas: Children / Family of God, Conflict, Doubt, Faith,
  God: Providence / God our Help, Inclusion

Genesis 45:1-15

[1]Then Joseph could no longer control himself before all those who stood by him, and he cried out, "Send everyone away from me." So no one stayed with him when Joseph made himself known to his brothers. [2]And he wept so loudly that the Egyptians heard it, and the household of Pharaoh heard it. [3]Joseph said to his brothers, "I am Joseph. Is my father still alive?" But his brothers could not answer him, so dismayed were they at his presence.

[4]Then Joseph said to his brothers, "Come closer to me." And they came closer. He said, "I am your brother, Joseph, whom you sold into Egypt. [5]And now do not be distressed, or angry with yourselves, because you sold me here; for God sent me before you to preserve life. [6]For the famine has been in the land these two years; and there are five more years in which there will be neither plowing nor harvest. [7]God sent me before you to preserve for you a remnant on earth, and to keep alive for you many survivors. [8]So it was not you who sent me here, but God; he has made me a father to Pharaoh, and lord of all his house and ruler over all the land of Egypt. [9]Hurry and go up to my father and say to him, 'Thus says your son Joseph, God has made me lord of all Egypt; come down to me, do not delay. [10]You shall settle in the land of Goshen, and you shall be near me, you and your children and your children's children, as well as your flocks, your herds, and all that you have. [11]I will provide for you there—since there are five more years of famine to come—so that you and your household, and all that you have, will not come to poverty.' [12]And now your eyes and the eyes of my brother Benjamin see that it is my own mouth that speaks to you. [13]You must tell my father how greatly I am honored in Egypt, and all that you have seen. Hurry and bring my father down here." [14]Then he fell upon his brother Benjamin's neck and wept, while Benjamin wept upon his neck. [15]And he kissed all his brothers and wept upon them; and after that his brothers talked with him.

Psalm 133 (G397/398, N712, P241, UM850)

[1]How very good and pleasant it is
　when kindred live together in unity!
[2]It is like the precious oil on the head,
　running down upon the beard,
on the beard of Aaron,
　running down over the collar of his robes.
[3]It is like the dew of Hermon,
　which falls on the mountains of Zion.
For there the LORD ordained his blessing,
　life forevermore.

Romans 11:1-2a, 29-32

[1]I ask, then, has God rejected his people? By no means! I myself am an Israelite, a descendant of Abraham, a member of the tribe of Benjamin. [2a]God has not rejected his people whom he foreknew. . . .

[29]for the gifts and the calling of God are irrevocable. [30]Just as you were once disobedient to God but have now received mercy because of their disobedience, [31]so they have now been disobedient in order that, by the mercy shown to you, they too may now receive mercy. [32]For God has imprisoned all in disobedience so that he may be merciful to all.

Matthew 15:(10-20), 21-28

[10]Then he called the crowd to him and said to them, "Listen and understand: [11]it is not what goes into the mouth that defiles a person, but it is what comes out of the mouth that defiles." [12]Then the disciples approached and said to him, "Do you know that the Pharisees took offense when they heard what you said?" [13]He answered, "Every plant that my heavenly Father has not planted will be uprooted. [14]Let them alone; they are blind guides of the blind. And if one blind person guides another, both will fall into a pit." [15]But Peter said to him, "Explain this parable to us." [16]Then he said, "Are you also still without understanding? [17]Do you not see that whatever goes into the mouth enters the stomach, and goes out into the sewer? [18]But what comes out of the mouth proceeds from the heart, and this is what defiles. [19]For out of the heart come evil intentions, murder, adultery, fornication, theft, false witness, slander. [20]These are what defile a person, but to eat with unwashed hands does not defile."

[21]Jesus left that place and went away to the district of Tyre and Sidon. [22]Just then a Canaanite woman from that region came out and started shouting, "Have mercy on me, Lord, Son of David; my daughter is tormented by a demon." [23]But he did not answer her at all. And his disciples came and urged him, saying, "Send her away, for she keeps shouting after us." [24]He answered, "I was sent only to the lost sheep of the house of Israel." [25]But she came and knelt before him, saying, "Lord, help me." [26]He answered, "It is not fair to take the children's food and throw it to the dogs." [27]She said, "Yes, Lord, yet even the dogs eat the crumbs that fall from their masters' table." [28]Then Jesus answered her, "Woman, great is your faith! Let it be done for you as you wish." And her daughter was healed instantly.

Primary Hymns and Songs for the Day
"My Faith Looks Up to Thee" (Matt) (O)
    C576, CG407, E691, EL759, G829, P383, SA726, UM452,
    VU663
        H-3   Hbl-77; Chr-138; Org-108
        S-2   #142. Flute/violin desc.
"Where Charity and Love Prevail" (Gen, Pss)
    CG264, EL359, G316, N396, SH271
        H-3   Hbl-71, 104; Chr-111-112, 219; Desc-95; Org-143
        S-2   #162. Harmonization
    E581, UM549
"This Is a Day of New Beginnings" (Gen, Matt) (C)
    C518, N417, UM383
        H-3   Chr-196
"In Christ There Is No East or West" (Pss, Rom) (C)
    C687, G318, N395, P439, SA1006
        H-3   Hbl-71, 104; Chr-111; Desc-95; Org-143
        S-2   #162. Harmonization
    CG273, E529, EL650 (PD), G317, N394, P440, UM548,
    VU606
        H-3   Chr-111; Desc-74; Org-88
        S-1   #231-233. Various treatments
    SH226

Additional Hymn Suggestions
"Great Is Thy Faithfulness" (Gen) (O)
    AH4011, C86, CG48, EL733, G39, N423, P276, SA26, SH48,
    UM140, VU288
"Forgive Our Sins as We Forgive" (Gen)
    CG694 E674, EL605, G444, P347, SH504, UM390, VU364
"Forgive Us, Lord" ("Perdón, Señor") 3409466 (Gen)
    G431, S2134, SH505
"God, How Can We Forgive" (Gen)
    G445, S2169
"Come, Share the Lord" (Gen, Comm.)
    C408, CG459, G510, S2269, VU469
"Help Us Accept Each Other" (Gen, Pss)
    C487, G754, N388, P358, UM560
"Draw Us in the Spirit's Tether" (Gen, Pss, Comm.)
    C392, EL470, G529, N337, P504, UM632, VU479
"God Made from One Blood" (Gen, Pss)
    C500, CG686, N427, S2170, VU554
"Rock of Ages, Cleft for Me" (Gen, Matt) (C)
    C214, E685, EL623, G438, N596, SA671, SH301, UM361
"How Clear Is Our Vocation, Lord" (Rom)
    EL580, G432, P419, VU504
"I Greet Thee, Who My Sure Redeemer Art" (Rom)
    G624, N251, P457, VU393
"There's a Wideness in God's Mercy" (Rom, Matt)
    C73, CG41, E470, EL587/88G435, N23, P298, SH526,
    UM121, VU271
"O Christ, the Healer" (Rom, Matt)
    C503. EL610, G793, N175, P380, UM265
"Standing on the Promises" (Rom, Matt)
    AH4057, C552, CG625, G838, SA522, SH45, UM374 (PD)
"O Spirit of the Living God" (Rom, Matt)
    N263, SH222, UM539
"O For a Thousand Tongues to Sing" (Matt)
    C5, CG332, E493, EL886, G610, N42, P466, SA89, SH439,
    UM57 (PD), VU326 (See also WS3001)
"I'll Praise My Maker While I've Breath" (Matt)
    C20, CG336, E429 (PD), G806, P253, UM60, VU867
"All Hail the Power of Jesus' Name" (Matt)
    C91/C92, CG339/340, E450/451, EL634, G263, N304,
    P142/143, SA73, SH207, UM154/155, VU334
"Jesus Shall Reign" (Rom, Matt)
    C95, CG158, E544, EL434, G265, N300, P423, SA258, SH209,
    UM157 (PD), VU330

"My Hope Is Built" (Matt)
    AH4105, C537, CG590, EL596/597, G353, N403, P379,
    SA662, SH324, UM368 (PD)
"Lord, I Want to Be a Christian" (Matt)
    C589, CG507, G729, N454, P372 (PD), SH621, UM402
"We Walk by Faith" (Matt)
    CG634, E209, EL635, G817, N256, P399, S2196, SH660
"Healer of Our Every Ill" (Matt)
    C506, EL612, G795, S2213, SH339, VU619

Additional Contemporary and Modern Suggestions
"Something Beautiful" 18060 (Gen)
"Make Me a Channel of Your Peace" (Gen)
    G753, S2171, SA608, SH616 VU684
"Make Me a Channel of Your Peace" 6399315 (Gen)
"Make Us One" 695737 (Gen, Pss)
    AH4142, S2224
"Let It Be Said of Us" 1855882 (Gen, Pss)
"People Need the Lord" 18084 (Gen, Matt)
    S2244, SA418
"Mighty to Save" 4591782 (Gen, Matt)
"Your Grace Is Enough" 4477026 (Gen, Matt)
"Live in Charity" ("Ubi Caritas") (Pss)
    C523, EL642, G205, S2179
"O Look and Wonder" ("¡Miren Qué Bueno!") (Pss, Rom)
    C292, EL649, G397, S2231, SH230, VU856
"I'm So Glad Jesus Lifted Me" (Matt)
    C529, EL860 (PD), N474, S2151
"Lord, Listen to Your Children Praying" 22829 (Matt)
    C305, CG389, G469, S2193, SH577, VU400
"O For a Thousand Tongues to Sing" 4048754 (Matt)
"Come, Emmanuel" 3999938 (Matt)
"You Hear" 6005063 (Matt)

Vocal Solos
"Make Me a Channel of Your Peace" (Gen)
    V-3 (2)   p. 25
    V-3 (3)   p. 28
"Help Us Accept Each Other" (Gen, Pss)
    V-8   p. 343
"I Heard About a Man" (Matt)
    V-8   p. 72

Anthems
"Christ Has Broken Down the Wall" (Gen, Matt)
Mark Miller, Choristers Guild CGA-1224
SATB, piano (https://bit.ly/CGA-1224)

"Hine Mah Tov" (Pss)
Simon Sargon; Transcontinental Music 00191235
SATB, keyboard, flute (https://bit.ly/S-91235)

Other Suggestions
Visuals:
    O   Weeping, remnant, famine, Gen 45:5c, 8, men
         hugging
    P   Unity, Ps. 133:1, oil, robe, dew, mountain
    E   No/yes, Rom 11:29, 32, gifts, calling, prison/manacles
    G   Woman shouting, Jesus, dogs/crumbs, girl healed
Greeting: N824 (Pss)
Call to Prayer: CG576, SA466, SH537, UM371, stanza 1. "I Stand
    Amazed" (Matt)
Response: WS3133. "Kyrie" (Gen, Matt)
Prayer: C483. For a Renewed Sense of Compassion (Gen)
Alternate Lessons: Isa 56:1, 6-8, Ps. 67
Theme Ideas: Children / Family of God, Conflict, Grace,
    Healing, Reconciliation, Sin and Forgiveness, Unity

Exodus 1:8–2:10

⁸Now a new king arose over Egypt, who did not know Joseph. ⁹He said to his people, "Look, the Israelite people are more numerous and more powerful than we. ¹⁰Come, let us deal shrewdly with them, or they will increase and, in the event of war, join our enemies and fight against us and escape from the land." ¹¹Therefore they set taskmasters over them to oppress them with forced labor. They built supply cities, Pithom and Rameses, for Pharaoh. ¹²But the more they were oppressed, the more they multiplied and spread, so that the Egyptians came to dread the Israelites. ¹³The Egyptians became ruthless in imposing tasks on the Israelites, ¹⁴and made their lives bitter with hard service in mortar and brick and in every kind of field labor. They were ruthless in all the tasks that they imposed on them.

¹⁵The king of Egypt said to the Hebrew midwives, one of whom was named Shiphrah and the other Puah, ¹⁶"When you act as midwives to the Hebrew women, and see them on the birthstool, if it is a boy, kill him; but if it is a girl, she shall live." ¹⁷But the midwives feared God; they did not do as the king of Egypt commanded them, but they let the boys live. ¹⁸So the king of Egypt summoned the midwives and said to them, "Why have you done this, and allowed the boys to live?" ¹⁹The midwives said to Pharaoh, "Because the Hebrew women are not like the Egyptian women; for they are vigorous and give birth before the midwife comes to them." ²⁰So God dealt well with the midwives; and the people multiplied and became very strong. ²¹And because the midwives feared God, he gave them families. ²²Then Pharaoh commanded all his people, "Every boy that is born to the Hebrews you shall throw into the Nile, but you shall let every girl live."

2 Now a man from the house of Levi went and married a Levite woman. ²The woman conceived and bore a son; and when she saw that he was a fine baby, she hid him three months. ³When she could hide him no longer she got a papyrus basket for him, and plastered it with bitumen and pitch; she put the child in it and placed it among the reeds on the bank of the river. ⁴His sister stood at a distance, to see what would happen to him.

⁵The daughter of Pharaoh came down to bathe at the river, while her attendants walked beside the river. She saw the basket among the reeds and sent her maid to bring it. ⁶When she opened it, she saw the child. He was crying, and she took pity on him, "This must be one of the Hebrews' children," she said. ⁷Then his sister said to Pharaoh's daughter, "Shall I go and get you a nurse from the Hebrew women to nurse the child for you?" ⁸Pharaoh's daughter said to her, "Yes." So the girl went and called the child's mother. ⁹Pharaoh's daughter said to her, "Take this child and nurse it for me, and I will give you your wages." So the woman took the child and nursed it. ¹⁰When the child grew up, she brought him to Pharaoh's daughter, and she took him as her son. She named him Moses, "because," she said, "I drew him out of the water."

Psalm 124 (G330, N706, P236, UM846)

¹If it had not been the Lord who was on our side
  —let Israel now say—
²if it had not been the Lord who was on our side,
  when our enemies attacked us,
³then they would have swallowed us up alive,
  when their anger was kindled against us;
⁴then the flood would have swept us away,
  the torrent would have gone over us;
⁵then over us would have gone
  the raging waters.
⁶Blessed be the Lord,
  who has not given us
  as prey to their teeth.
⁷We have escaped like a bird
  from the snare of the fowlers;
the snare is broken,
  and we have escaped.
⁸Our help is in the name of the Lord,
  who made heaven and earth.

Romans 12:1-8

¹I appeal to you therefore, brothers and sisters, by the mercies of God, to present your bodies as a living sacrifice, holy and acceptable to God, which is your spiritual worship. ²Do not be conformed to this world, but be transformed by the renewing of your minds, so that you may discern what is the will of God—what is good and acceptable and perfect.

³For by the grace given to me I say to everyone among you not to think of yourself more highly than you ought to think, but to think with sober judgment, each according to the measure of faith that God has assigned. ⁴For as in one body we have many members, and not all the members have the same function, ⁵so we, who are many, are one body in Christ, and individually we are members one of another. ⁶We have gifts that differ according to the grace given to us: prophecy, in proportion to faith; ⁷ministry, in ministering; the teacher, in teaching; ⁸the exhorter, in exhortation; the giver, in generosity; the leader, in diligence; the compassionate, in cheerfulness.

Matthew 16:13-20

¹³Now when Jesus came into the district of Caesarea Philippi, he asked his disciples, "Who do people say that the Son of Man is?" ¹⁴And they said, "Some say John the Baptist, but others Elijah, and still others Jeremiah or one of the prophets." ¹⁵He said to them, "But who do you say that I am?" ¹⁶Simon Peter answered, "You are the Messiah, the Son of the living God." ¹⁷And Jesus answered him, "Blessed are you, Simon son of Jonah! For flesh and blood has not revealed this to you, but my Father in heaven. ¹⁸And I tell you, you are Peter, and on this rock I will build my church, and the gates of Hades will not prevail against it. ¹⁹I will give you the keys of the kingdom of heaven, and whatever you bind on earth will be bound in heaven, and whatever you loose on earth will be loosed in heaven." ²⁰Then he sternly ordered the disciples not to tell anyone that he was the Messiah.

Primary Hymns and Songs for the Day

"Guide Me, O Thou Great Jehovah" (Exod) (O)
C622, CG33, E690, EL618, G65, N18/19, P281, SA27, SH51, UM127 (PD), VU651 (Fr.)
H-3　Hbl-25, 51, 58; Chr-89; Desc-26; Org-23
S-1　#76-77. Desc. and harm.
"Forward through the Ages" (Matt) (O)
N377, UM555 (PD)
H-3　Hbl-59; Chr-156; Org-140
"Glorious Things of Thee Are Spoken" (Exod, Pss, Matt)
C709, CG282, E522/523, EL647, G81, N307, P446, SA535, UM731 (PD)
"I'm Gonna Live So God Can Use Me" (Rom)
C614, G700, P369, S2153, SH632, VU575
"Take My Life, and Let It Be" (Rom) (C)
C609, CG490, E707, EL583/EL685, G697, P391, N448, SA623, SH627/628, UM399 (PD), VU506

Additional Hymn Suggestions

"O God Our Help in Ages Past" (Exod)
C67, CG566, E680, EL632, G687, N25, P210, SA47, SH41, UM117 (PD), VU806
"God Will Take Care of You" (Exod)
N460, SA5, SH289, UM130 (PD)
"Amazing Grace" (Exod)
AH4091, C546, CG587, E671, EL779, G649, N547/548, P280, SA453, SH523, UM378 (PD), VU266 (Fr.)
"Jesus, Lover of My Soul" (Exod)
C542, CG406, E699, G440, N546, P303, SA257, SH542/543, UM479, VU669
"Spirit, Spirit of Gentleness" (Exod)
C249, EL396, G291, N286, P319, S2120, VU375 (Fr.)
"Why Stand So Far Away, My God?" (Exod)
C671, G786, S2180
"Deep in the Shadows of the Past" (Exod, Pss)
G50, N320, P330, S2246
"Come, Thou Fount of Every Blessing" (Exod, Rom)
AH4086, C16, CG295/559, E686, EL807, G475, N459, P356, SA830, SH394, UM400 (PD), VU559
"Rock of Ages, Cleft for Me" (Pss, Matt)
C214, E685, EL623, G438, N596, SA671, SH301, UM361
"I Am Thine, O Lord" (Rom)
AH4087, C601, CG504, N455, SA586, UM419 (PD)
"I Love Thy Kingdom, Lord" (Rom)
C274, CG262, E524, G310, N312, P441, UM540
"Like the Murmur of the Dove's Song" (Rom)
C245, CG233, E513, EL403, G285, N270, P314, SH407, UM544, VU205
"I Come with Joy" (Rom, Comm.)
C420, CG456, E304, EL482, G515, N349, P507, SH682, UM617, VU477
"Draw Us in the Spirit's Tether" (Rom, Comm.)
C392, EL470, G529, N337, P504, UM632, VU479
"Una Espiga" ("Sheaves of Summer") (Rom, Comm.)
C396, G532, N338, UM637
"We Are the Body of Christ" 2220206 (Rom)
G768, SH229, S2227
"The Church's One Foundation" (Rom, Matt)
C272, CG246, E525, EL654, G321, N386, P442, SH233, UM545/546, VU332 (Fr.)
"Christ Is Made the Sure Foundation" (Rom, Matt)
C275, CG248, E518, EL645, G394, N400, P416/417, SA246, SH225, UM559 (PD), VU325
"The Church of Christ, in Every Age" (Rom, Matt)
C475, EL729, G320, N306, P421, UM589, VU601
"Here I Am, Lord" (Rom, Matt)
C452, CG482, EL574, G69, P525, SA1002, SH608, UM593, VU509

"We Would Be Building" (Rom, Matt)
N607
"Jesus, the Very Thought of Thee" (Matt)
C102, CG386, E642, EL754, G629, N507, P310, SA85, UM175 (PD)
"My Hope Is Built" (Matt)
AH4105, C537, CG590, EL596/597, G353, N403, P379, SA662, SH324, UM368 (PD)
"I'm So Glad Jesus Lifted Me" (Matt)
C529, EL860 (PD), N474, S2151

Additional Contemporary and Modern Suggestions

"Freedom Is Coming" 4194244 (Exod)
G359, S2192, SA29
"Daughter of God" 4509781 (Exod)
"Grace Like Rain" 3689877 (Exod)
"One Bread, One Body" (Rom, Comm.)
C393, EL496, G530, SH678, UM620, VU467
"Take Our Bread" (Rom, Comm.)
C413, UM640
"We Bring the Sacrifice of Praise" 9990 (Rom)
"Grace Alone" 2335524 (Rom)
CG43, S2162, SA699.
"Sanctuary" 24140 (Rom)
G701, S2164, SH265
"Bind Us Together" 1228 (Rom)
"All of Me" 6290160 (Rom)
"These Hands" 3251827 (Rom)
"I Will Not Forget You" 2694306 (Rom)
"There Will Be Bread" 4512352 (Rom, Comm.)
"Foundation" 706151 (Rom, Matt)
"Amazing Grace" ("My Chains Are Gone") 4768151 (Matt)

Vocal Solos

"Oh, Freedom" (Exod)
V-7　p. 10
"I Will Lift Up Mine Eyes" (Pss)
V-1　p. 27
"Take My Life" ("Consecration") (Rom)
V-8　p. 262
"A Covenant Prayer" (Rom)
V-1　p. 6

Anthems

"Take My Life and Let It Be" (Rom)
Kevin A. Memley; Hal Leonard 08301943
SATB, piano (https://bit.ly/HL-01943)

"Greater" (Rom)
Arr. David Angerman; Hal Leonard 00151402
SATB *a cappella*, opt. fiddle, cajon (https://bit.ly/HL-51402)

Other Suggestions

Visuals:
O　Bricks/mortar, birthstool, newborn, basket/reeds/river
P　Enemies, flood/torrent/water, bird/broken snare, Ps 124:8
E　Transformer, dance, offering plate, seven gifts
G　Jesus teaching, Peter, large rock/keys, Matt 16:15, 16
Greeting: WSL192. "All your gifts are welcome" (Rom)
Prayer: UM607. A Covenant Prayer (Rom)
Reading: N574. "In Egypt Under Pharaoh" (Exod)
Offering Prayer: N844 (Rom)
Alternate Lessons: Isa 51:1-6, Ps 138
Theme Ideas: Discipleship / Following God, God: Faithfulness, God: Providence / God our Help, Humility, Jesus: Body of Christ, Spiritual Gifts, Unity

THEME INDEX

SCRIPTURE INDEX

SCRIPTURE INDEX

New Testament

WORSHIP PLANNING SHEET 1

Date: _____ Color:_____

Preacher: _____

Liturgist: _____

Selected Scripture: _____

Selected Hymns	No.	Placement

Psalter #_____

Keyboard Selections

Title	Composer	Placement

Anthems

Title	Choir	Composer	Placement

Vocal Solos

Title	Singer	Composer	Placement

Other Ideas:

Acolytes: _____

Head Usher: _____

Altar Guild Contact: _____

Other Participants: _____

_____

WORSHIP PLANNING SHEET 2

Date: _____ Sunday: _____ Color: _____

Preacher: _____

Liturgist: _____

Opening Voluntary   Composer

_____

_____

Hymn   Tune Name   No.

_____

Opening Prayer: _____

Prayer for Illumination: _____

First Lesson: _____

Psalter: _____

Second Lesson: _____

Gospel Lesson: _____

Hymn   Tune Name   No.

_____

Response to the Word: _____

Prayers of the People: _____

Offertory   Composer

_____

Communion Setting: _____

Communion Hymns   Tune Name   No.

_____

_____

Closing Hymn   Tune Name   No.

_____

Benediction: _____

Closing Voluntary   Composer

_____

CONTEMPORARY WORSHIP PLANNING SHEET

Because of the diversity in orders of worship, you will want to adjust this planning sheet to meet the needs of your worship planning team. A common order used would consist of three to four opening praise choruses and lively hymns, a time of informal prayers of the congregation along with songs of prayer, reading of the primary scripture for the day, a drama or video to illustrate the day's theme, a message from the preacher, a testimony on the theme for the day (if a drama or video was not presented earlier), followed by closing songs appropriate to the mood of the service and the message. Any offering would usually be taken early in the service, and Holy Communion would normally take place following the message. Special music (solos, duets, instrumental music) can be used wherever it best expresses the theme of the service.

Date: _____ Sunday: _____

Thematic Emphasis or Topic: _____

Color: _____ Visual Focus: _____

Opening Songs:

_____

_____

Prayer Songs:

_____

Scripture Selection(s):

_____

Drama or Video:

_____

Message Title:

_____

Testimony: _____

Special Music:

_____

Closing Songs:

_____

Preacher: _____ Music Leader: _____

Worship Facilitator: _____ Prayer Leader: _____

From *Prepare!* Copyright © 2022 by Abingdon Press. Used by permission.

2022–2023 Lectionary Calendar

Lectionary verses and worship suggestions in this edition of *Prepare!* relate to the unshaded dates in the calendar below. Lectionary Year C: September 4, 2022–November 24, 2022; Lectionary Year A: November 27, 2022–August 27, 2023

2022

JANUARY
S	M	T	W	T	F	S
						1
2	3	4	5	6	7	8
9	10	11	12	13	14	15
16	17	18	19	20	21	22
23	24	25	26	27	28	29
30	31					

FEBRUARY
S	M	T	W	T	F	S
		1	2	3	4	5
6	7	8	9	10	11	12
13	14	15	16	17	18	19
20	21	22	23	24	25	26
27	28					

MARCH
S	M	T	W	T	F	S
		1	2	3	4	5
6	7	8	9	10	11	12
13	14	15	16	17	18	19
20	21	22	23	24	25	26
27	28	29	30	31		

APRIL
S	M	T	W	T	F	S
					1	2
3	4	5	6	7	8	9
10	11	12	13	14	15	16
17	18	19	20	21	22	23
24	25	26	27	28	29	30

MAY
S	M	T	W	T	F	S
1	2	3	4	5	6	7
8	9	10	11	12	13	14
15	16	17	18	19	20	21
22	23	24	25	26	27	28
29	30	31				

JUNE
S	M	T	W	T	F	S
			1	2	3	4
5	6	7	8	9	10	11
12	13	14	15	16	17	18
19	20	21	22	23	24	25
26	27	28	29	30		

JULY
S	M	T	W	T	F	S
					1	2
3	4	5	6	7	8	9
10	11	12	13	14	15	16
17	18	19	20	21	22	23
24	25	26	27	28	29	30
31						

AUGUST
S	M	T	W	T	F	S
	1	2	3	4	5	6
7	8	9	10	11	12	13
14	15	16	17	18	19	20
21	22	23	24	25	26	27
28	29	30	31			

SEPTEMBER
S	M	T	W	T	F	S
				1	2	3
4	5	6	7	8	9	10
11	12	13	14	15	16	17
18	19	20	21	22	23	24
25	26	27	28	29	30	

OCTOBER
S	M	T	W	T	F	S
						1
2	3	4	5	6	7	8
9	10	11	12	13	14	15
16	17	18	19	20	21	22
23	24	25	26	27	28	29
30	31					

NOVEMBER
S	M	T	W	T	F	S
		1	2	3	4	5
6	7	8	9	10	11	12
13	14	15	16	17	18	19
20	21	22	23	24	25	26
27	28	29	30			

DECEMBER
S	M	T	W	T	F	S
				1	2	3
4	5	6	7	8	9	10
11	12	13	14	15	16	17
18	19	20	21	22	23	24
25	26	27	28	29	30	31

2023

JANUARY
S	M	T	W	T	F	S
1	2	3	4	5	6	7
8	9	10	11	12	13	14
15	16	17	18	19	20	21
22	23	24	25	26	27	28
29	30	31				

FEBRUARY
S	M	T	W	T	F	S
			1	2	3	4
5	6	7	8	9	10	11
12	13	14	15	16	17	18
19	20	21	22	23	24	25
26	27	28				

MARCH
S	M	T	W	T	F	S
			1	2	3	4
5	6	7	8	9	10	11
12	13	14	15	16	17	18
19	20	21	22	23	24	25
26	27	28	29	30	31	

APRIL
S	M	T	W	T	F	S
						1
2	3	4	5	6	7	8
9	10	11	12	13	14	15
16	17	18	19	20	21	22
23	24	25	26	27	28	29
30						

MAY
S	M	T	W	T	F	S
	1	2	3	4	5	6
7	8	9	10	11	12	13
14	15	16	17	18	19	20
21	22	23	24	25	26	27
28	29	30	31			

JUNE
S	M	T	W	T	F	S
				1	2	3
4	5	6	7	8	9	10
11	12	13	14	15	16	17
18	19	20	21	22	23	24
25	26	27	28	29	30	

JULY
S	M	T	W	T	F	S
						1
2	3	4	5	6	7	8
9	10	11	12	13	14	15
16	17	18	19	20	21	22
23	24	25	26	27	28	29
30	31					

AUGUST
S	M	T	W	T	F	S
		1	2	3	4	5
6	7	8	9	10	11	12
13	14	15	16	17	18	19
20	21	22	23	24	25	26
27	28	29	30	31		

SEPTEMBER
S	M	T	W	T	F	S
					1	2
3	4	5	6	7	8	9
10	11	12	13	14	15	16
17	18	19	20	21	22	23
24	25	26	27	28	29	30

OCTOBER
S	M	T	W	T	F	S
1	2	3	4	5	6	7
8	9	10	11	12	13	14
15	16	17	18	19	20	21
22	23	24	25	26	27	28
29	30	31				

NOVEMBER
S	M	T	W	T	F	S
			1	2	3	4
5	6	7	8	9	10	11
12	13	14	15	16	17	18
19	20	21	22	23	24	25
26	27	28	29	30		

DECEMBER
S	M	T	W	T	F	S
					1	2
3	4	5	6	7	8	9
10	11	12	13	14	15	16
17	18	19	20	21	22	23
24	25	26	27	28	29	30
31						